# PUBLIC SPACE ACUPUNCTURE

casanova+hernandez architects

I0803307

# Urban Form, Another Principal Actor: Mending and Acupuncture

Oriol Bohigas

Urban compactness as opposed to territorial dispersion. Building on what has already been built is better than expansion and urban enlargement. Recovering the testimonies of the historical and functional dialectic. Flexibility and the capacity for transformation. Restoration, reconstruction, reuse, rehabilitation, renovation. DIY, recycling, provisionality, sustainability. Against zoning and in favor of multi-functionality. Architecture for compactness and urban continuity.

The above words, phrases and references, complemented by their accompanying rhetorical discourses, now appear on all the plans and urban designs for European cities, reinforcing the tendency to move beyond the tired old frameworks laid out by the rationalist avant-garde. Many cultural and social premises in urban planning have emerged since the Athens Charter. For example, with a redundancy that encompasses both justifications and consequences, one tendency that has been gaining importance involves boasting, with a certain amount of frivolity, about "humanizing urban planning", in contrast to the revolutionary – dehumanized? – geometric abstraction that was upheld in foundational rallies with the intent of social transformation. Yet, this presumed humanization is based almost entirely on one single step: curtailing the radicality of political proposals and opening up the field for consensus to less radical and possibly more ambiguous stances. "Humanization" – like tolerance, pact-making, religion and mutual aid – nearly always implies diluting the revolutionary purposes that were expressed in the synopses that are still heroically dehumanized. It is the mute in the trumpets of the revolution.

However, diminishing radical political foundations also has positive consequences in the planning process and in urban design. The relative flexibility of the political arena – and the loss of programmatic dogmatism – has allowed for more freedom with respect to the formal models for urban organization. As a result, certain traditional layouts have been recovered that were eliminated as one of the starting points for architecture and urban planning in the Modern Movement and the absence of which in the large-scale experiences of European reconstruction led to irreparable errors and deficiencies. The street, the city block, the square, expressive intensity, collective spaces as formal guidelines, continuity, overlapping functions, legibility have been confirmed as new tools for urban planning as the result of a reduction in revolutionary radicality and the acceptance of approximation and prompt evolution. Thus, urban morphology has once again taken on an important role in urban planning decisions since it provides justifications and because, in addition to forms, it carries consequential content that is easy to convey, such as history, culture, economy, anthropology, aesthetics.

This new prominence of form – or of its conceptual value – leads to changes in the descriptive methods and the professionalism of urban planners. Whereas Strategic Plans and their derivatives were once responsible for expressing operations, which they did above all using percentages that referred to pre-established quantitative methods, now a set of Urban Designs – developed according to a methodology that is more like a preliminary design in architecture – is responsible for defining the character and the script. Urban Design instead of Strategic Planning. This new situation also proposes the type of professional who is most suited to taking on the authorship of urban planning. It is only logical that architects, as specialists in urban form, should take back the authorship and the responsibility for the conceptual and operative unit, city-architecture. For the same reasons, it seems ineffective to entrust all of the fundamental content and comprehensive proposals to other types of professionals who have offered sector-specific techniques; not even the so-called town planners, who tend to have their capacity for global thought hampered by their predominantly administrative duties.

Considerations concerning the formal content of urban structures have offshoots on a wider territorial and methodological scale: for example, the requirements of compactness and continuity so often demanded today, especially when it comes to refurbishing historic city centers and rearranging the outskirts of cities and the suburbs, spaces where social and physical aging, attempts at modernization or the misguided rhythms of speculative building have left behind barren and unproductive sectors that interrupt the artificial coherence of the city. These two requirements are tied in with the intensity of cohabitation and the expression of an obvious social unity, two fundamental and indispensable qualities in the great models of urban civilization. Therefore, the question cannot be reduced to arguing over the percentages of occupation, the distribution of services, or circulation patterns. The goal is to produce a suitable urban space across the entire scope of the settlement, which is truly a city, is read as a city, and maintains the urban social tension in the intentional artificiality of all of its sectors.

It should be acknowledged that compactness and continuity were not very clear issues in the emergence of the Modern Movement. Even in certain formulations of the functional city –the most theoretical and radical ones– these two issues were used and accentuated to promote admittedly anti-urban, and therefore anti-modern, lifestyles. Communist anti-urbanization and the bourgeois references of social democracy characterized reconstruction efforts in Europe after the First World War, with a dubious reference to rural life as an antidote to the social and political ills plaguing new cities that were undergoing constant abusive growth. An apparently rural life based precisely on programmed dispersion and discontinuity, almost as a sign of populism. More or less the same thing happened in the wake of World War II, with one difference: the traditional developers and builders adopted the architectural forms of dogmatic modernity, although it was only insofar as it suited their own interests – i.e., in the ease of construction and the economy of identical, repetitive blocks simplified by industrial serialization – and they were therefore not all too interested in urban transformation. That led to housing blocks, towers, supermarkets in drab industrial zones, with no communal space but the leftover roadsides, with no identifiable overall design for the urban expression.

In recent years, compactness and continuity have been introduced as basic themes in the new resources for urban planning, and other operative strategies have appeared with them. The most frequent of them can be grouped into two chapters that we tend to refer to using two separate metaphors, one from sewing and the other from the clinical sphere. "Mending" is often the easiest way to achieve a nearly natural continuity, in an apparent uniformity, thanks to the mender's talent, and the help of methods of adaptation that work to conceal the patch. But it doesn't actually need to be concealed: the patch could also suggest another compositional structure made famous by other figurative adventures, like the "trencadís" or patchwork, for example. There is also the path of the clinical metaphor, "acupuncture", which acts on a point chosen specifically for its strategic value, for its significance and, overall, for its suitable system of relationships and its ability to use that system to autonomously direct the cure for a more general and widespread illness, often with the support of private activity seduced and contaminated by nearby examples. Mending and acupuncture are now common methods used in the rising "humanization" and reduction of the programmatic radicalism characteristic of the Modern Movement and, naturally, they have been reinforced by ideas that opt for chance over permanence, and creativity over regulations. Or, in other words, as someone commented years ago in a critical analysis of the church of Santa Maria de la Pace in Rome, "the repair over the model".

The special tendency toward the aesthetics of "repair" and anormality has also had an influence on this reduction in canonical contents. We need only look at the indiscriminate defense of what has been restored and rebuilt compared with modern aesthetics and organization, which began as a gesture of social continuity or historical testimony and which ended up as a model for the aesthetic ignorance of the new sub-bourgeoisie. Or the appetite for the picturesque, or local culture. Or the flirtation with insalubrious self-built neighborhoods, which have a vitality that is interesting as a non-conformist counterproject. Or cultural support for waste materials and the dramatized expression of poverty.

This interpretation of certain methods used in urban planning in recent years is only a simplified, rough approximation that requires more documented verification. But, I think that it points out an obvious fact. One of the initial goals of modern urban planning was to put certain political principles with a socialist underpinning into effect, which were supposed to contribute to a radical change in urban society. Those principles never managed to encompass the practice of urban planning as a whole, probably because their quasi-utopian radicality was beyond the reach of society's real possibilities. Thus began a process aimed at curtailing radicality, which we have called, with excessive semantic delapidation, "humanization", as though humanity were the sublimation of frustrations. This alignment utopia–real capabilities led to an action plan that was more evolution than revolution and, with it, factors that were more directly morphological came to the forefront. Many new and positive factors were also introduced into urban planning, which have come to constitute stance that is less ideological, yet closer to actual forms of social coexistence and organization.

However, in this relatively ambiguous situation, it is wise to remember that these corrective factors and their positive results are all a consequence of the failure to achieve a new, more balanced society with respect to the communal use of land and services, equitable yields, and socialized hierarchies. None of the characteristics we have mentioned can be viable without first recovering the revolutionary principles.

# Public Space Acupuncture

Jesús Hernández

Throughout history, cities have often been compared with living organisms. The analogy between the city and the human body has been explored in depth by figures as varied as Plato, Vitruvius or Leonardo DaVinci. Urban tissue, a city's heart, arteries and lungs are some of the terms that comprise the extensive urban planning vocabulary that has been created by comparing fragments of the city with organs or elements of the human anatomy. While the human body has served as a recurring metaphor to describe the complex functioning of cities, sickness has often been the allegory used to illustrate urban dysfunction. Above and beyond anthropomorphic conceptions of the city, statements like "Paris is sick", proclaimed by Le Corbusier[1] in 1929, or Frank Lloyd Wright's comparison, from 1958, between the cross-section of any city plan and the section of a fibrous tumor,[2] highlight the city's metaphorical capacity to fall ill. "Sickness", in this context, is not understood as intrinsic to the natural functioning of any organism, but rather as an evil that must be combated.

Le Corbusier, Frank Lloyd Wright, and many other architects and urban planners at the time, compared traditional cities with sick organisms in order to justify the need for undertaking large-scale urban interventions in keeping with the historic moment they were living through, thus promoting the functionalist utopia of the modern city. In many cases, an incomplete diagnosis of urban pathologies was used to argue the need to apply drastic therapies, which consisted in amputating affected tissues and substituting them for entirely new ones. The striking image of Le Corbusier's Plan Voisin for the center of Paris perfectly summarized how a new "artificial organ" was implanted onto an amputated fragment of the ailing city. At the time, this image became a provocative icon that represented part of the Modern Movement's approach, which had a broad influence on numerous projects for urban renewal across Europe and America.

## Acupuncture

In the 1970s and 1980s, serious questions emerged concerning the Modern movement's model for urban planning and large-scale urban renewal in particular. The shocking image of the demolition of the enormous Pruitt-Igoe housing project, which was an icon of modern urban planning for the city of St. Louis, on March 16, 1972, became a powerful symbol, comparable with the image of Le Corbusier's Plan Voisin from 1925. It represented the end of an era and a changing sensitivity toward how our cities should be regenerated. Charles Jencks referred to its demolition as "the day Modern architecture died,"[3] and at the end of the 70s and the beginning of the 80s a new way of understanding cities emerged, along with a new way of diagnosing their pathologies and implementing the proper therapy.

This new way of understanding urban regeneration catalyzed in Barcelona in the 1980s under the name Urban Acupuncture. Just as Le Corbusier's famous black-and-white image of the Plan Voisin transmitted, in a precise yet closed-off manner, one way of understanding planning in the Modern movement, the term "urban acupuncture" became a powerful abstract metaphor to evoke numerous images and mental associations representing an alternative way of understanding urban planning. The term was coined and spread by a series of urban planners, architects and politicians who participated in Barcelona's urban renewal in the 1980s, such as Oriol Bohigas, Manuel de Solà-Morales and Joan Busquets, among others, and was later used by many other professionals, including the Brazilian urban planner and mayor of Curitiba, Jaime Lerner, author of the book *Acupuntura Urbana*, published in 2003.[4]

From that point on, the term Urban Acupuncture has been incorporated into the urban planning vocabulary to describe strategies based on a series of independent interventions applied in the urban fabric that have a direct impact on their immediate surroundings, but since they are coordinated they also produce a larger-scale effect. Manuel de Solà-Morales highlighted the "strategic, systematic and interdependent" character of the term Urban Acupuncture, and emphasized that its field of action is what he called "the urban skin" or the "epidermis", understood "as a rich, complex, and enormously influential membrane" that constitutes a system in itself.[5]

Public space is part of this "urban skin", where most of the urban acupuncture strategies were developed in Barcelona, which focused on reinforcing the role of small squares, boulevards and parks as elements that articulate public life. In his book *Barcelona: The Urban Evolution of a Compact City*, Joan Busquets points to Oriol Bohigas as the originator of this strategy, which led to the creation of hundreds of interventions in the city's public space during the 1980s, classified into four different types: inner-city parks, squares and gardens, parks with facilities, and urban axes.[6] As a result of these strategies and the subsequent urban plans to open the city to the sea for the 1992 Olympic Games, public space in Barcelona acquired international fame, highlighting the political importance of promoting a vibrant public space capable of activating public life, while serving as a symbol of urban quality.

## Public Space

Three decades after the urban phenomenon of Barcelona in the 1980s, public space is again in the spotlight since, according to many sociologists and urban theorists, it is gradually becoming a lifeless space that is also losing its public role. Martin Pawley anticipated this phenomenon in the 1970s in his book *The Private Future*, where he maintained that, in our consumer society, "the decline of public life is both a result and cause of privatization."[7] More recently, the sociologist Richard Sennett described dead public space as the space devoted to the circulation of vehicles and people, claiming that it has lost its character as a place to remain, arguing that "the erasure of alive public space contains an even more perverse idea – that of making space contingent upon motion... the public space is an area to move through, not to be in."[8]

Different factors contribute to the spread of this phenomenon. On the one hand, new commercial tendencies based on the concentration of commercial activities in shopping centers and department stores, combined with the current rise in Internet sales, are causing the gradual disappearance of small shops along our streets and, therefore, the decline of street life. On the other hand, the development of new technologies and the Internet has led to the birth of new media and virtual social networks, as well as new kinds of leisure activities like videogames and in-home cinema, which have changed our social behavior. The direct repercussion has been that numerous group activities that were traditionally held in public space have moved into the private sphere, so that parks and public squares have lost part of their function as meeting places.

One of the consequences of the lack of use of public space is that it can sometimes result in a generalized perception of insecurity among citizens. This, in turn, creates a nocebo effect, making citizens afraid of using public space because they consider it to be dangerous, which in some cases can actually end up coming to pass. In other cases, although public space may still be used, it no longer operates as a collective space for sharing activities, or as a place to connect and meet new people. In short, public space's tendency to lose its public function deactivates part of the city's socializing capability, which is especially important in an era that is characterized by a steady rise in cultural diversity among the inhabitants of our medium-sized and large cities. Public space, as a setting for cohabitation, contributes to teaching citizens to be tolerant with the unknown. On the contrary, the loss of its public facet can erode social cohesion and urban cohabitation.

Although the pragmatic vision of certain theorists and professionals defends that this change in the role of public space is part of the inevitable natural evolution of our contemporary society, many others have warned about the negative consequences that these changes can generate in our cities. The sociologist Zygmunt Bauman defends the fundamental role played by public space as a regulator of social relations with the phrase: "Public places are the very spots where the future of urban life (and given that the growing majority of the planetary population is made up of urban dwellers, also the future of planetary cohabitation) is being at this very moment decided".[9]

With more than half of humanity living in cities and growth predictions for a worldwide urban population of 70% by 2050, Bauman directs our attention toward the importance of the role of public places, among them public space, for urban cohabitation and alerts us to the transcendence of our present moment. But, what role can public space really play today in reviving urban life? How can public space effectively contribute to improving cohabitation among citizens? And lastly, what kind of mechanisms or tools can be used to achieve these aims in the present?

## Acupuncture + Public Space = Public Space Acupuncture

The growing awareness of the importance of public space as a regulator of urban cohabitation has led some cities to look for new ways of understanding its creation, design and management according to what might be called public space acupuncture strategies, born from applying *urban acupuncture* strategies exclusively to the sphere of *public space*.

*Public space acupuncture* is defined as a set of urban strategies applied exclusively to public space based on independent and catalytic interventions that can be realized in a relatively short period of time. These interventions are not only capable of creating a direct positive impact on their immediate surroundings, but even more importantly, they are also coordinated with the aim of activating the use of public space on a larger scale and of balancing, revitalizing or renewing urban life.

Although, as Milan Kundera said, “metaphors are dangerous”, the simile that compares acupuncture with a strategy applied to public space helps to understand an alternative approach that is based on a greater sensitivity in terms of the analysis of symptoms and the diagnostic methods used. To that end, it is important to take into account all kinds of urban and social symptoms that indicate a deterioration of urban life, such as a lack of use of public space, a large presence of run-down vacant lots, high crime rates, widespread unemployment, social segregation or a socially excluded immigrant population. However, it is also important to detect positive symptoms, weak as they may be, of urban activity, such as the areas in public space that receive the most use and where citizen interaction is greatest, the common ground among different social groups, and the collective or public activities that have the potential to be enhanced.

The metaphor of acupuncture as urban therapy in public space also suggests using solutions that stimulate or complement existing urban activity, avoiding drastic or traumatic changes. The city, like the human body, has its own defense mechanisms, and sickness can be understood as a mere imbalance so that therapy is only an aid to recover the lost equilibrium. This approach leads to minimizing each action, working on the existing foundation and devising new ways of solving problems that do not necessarily need to be based on permanent physical interventions in public space, but that can also consist of temporary interventions, or even actions without any physical component.

As a part of traditional Chinese medicine, acupuncture is also a thousand-year old practice of preventive medicine. Paradoxically, in antiquity, when Chinese doctors applied this practice, they only charged for keeping their patients healthy and received no pay if their patients fell ill, which also represented a serious loss of prestige for the doctor. The term “preventive” is destined to take on greater importance in present-day urban planning, especially in urban contexts where an increase in social instability has already been detected, in neighborhoods with large, socially excluded immigrant populations, in city centers where public life is disappearing from the streets, accompanied by a rise in urban insecurity, or in new urban developments where there is a lack of social cohesion.

Public space acupuncture is an especially useful tool in contexts that have been affected by economic recession in the wake of the global financial crisis. Given that many urban development projects funded with private capital, which could help revitalize our cities, have been halted and that it is also difficult to put through public initiatives because of the austerity measures that are in place in an attempt to reduce the public deficit, numerous city councils have been forced to look for new, low-cost or temporary strategies that have the ability to create a positive impact on the urban habitat.

In parallel, in recent years public space has also become a focal point for municipal authorities in many developing countries. The strong economic growth and rapid industrialization process that have taken place in many countries have given rise to migratory waves as workers have moved from the countryside into the city, leading to dramatic urban growth in a short period of time. These still-expanding cities are now assessing the quality of the recently created public space, as well as studying new strategies for supplementing and enriching it, to be implemented in coming years. The aim is to create a vibrant public space with a rich public life, which also prevents segregation, promotes citizen interaction and helps toward the development of social cohesion. Public space acupuncture strategies can be an effective working tool for this type of rapidly built urban structures because they can offer flexible and quick-effect solutions that can be adapted to any urban and social context.

On the other hand, both in the case of invertebrate cities characterized by a less visible nervous system of public space and in the case of generic cities where the design, program and quality of public space have not been considered a priority in urban planning, public space acupuncture strategies stand out as the ideal tool for helping to improve many aspects of urban life.

In conclusion, different kinds of strategies that could be classified as public space acupuncture have emerged in very different contexts. Despite the fact that, at the moment, these strategies are still in the pioneering stage and they tend to emerge as isolated actions, they share many common factors and could eventually constitute a new tool which municipal management bodies could use systematically. These initiatives might become a specific branch of urban planning in the future that would serve to complement traditional planning approaches, but which would have its own mechanisms for analysis, strategy development and process management.

### Strategies of Public Space Acupuncture

The origin of the term "strategy" can be found in military discipline since its etymology goes back to "stratos", the Greek word for army, and "agein", which means leader or guide. Strategy, then, is defined as a set of actions that are systematically planned over time, which are undertaken to achieve a particular mission.

Based on this definition, it can be deduced that the word strategy implies a purpose. Public space acupuncture strategies don't have an aesthetic purpose, such as beautifying public space, nor do they have a merely functional end, but rather they tend to respond to social needs or to the desire to improve specific aspects of urban life.

Systematic planning over time, which is implicitly associated with public space acupuncture strategies, suggests the possibility of an implementation by phases, as well as close monitoring of how the strategy evolves and the evaluation of the results obtained. This allows for the possibility of correcting the strategy during the process to achieve the desired goals in the end.

Each public space acupuncture strategy is made up of a set of actions or interventions that can be executed independently, but which are coordinated under a series of guidelines that dictate the precise place and the right time for each one to be carried out, so that all of them together can produce a broader effect than if they acted separately.

The term "strategy" suggests that there are generally a limited amount of resources available for achieving the desired objectives. That is why public space acupuncture strategies are sometimes, though not always, based on low-cost interventions that attempt to achieve maximum impact using a minimum of resources.

Different actors tend to intervene in public space acupuncture strategies, including politicians, municipal managers, urban planners, landscape architects, architects, artists, urban sociologists, citizens' groups, residents' associations and independent citizens. The strategies may be initiated by different entities, from municipalities opting for traditional top-down strategies, to citizens' groups promoting bottom-up strategies, as well as all kinds of hybrid combinations between private entities and public bodies. A strategy that is understood as an open creative process provides a broad field for experimenting with a vast number of collaborative models, both in creating and developing the strategy and in its management.

### Interventions

The term "intervention" designates the specific actions that make up the strategies. An intervention may have a temporary or a permanent character and it may be material or even immaterial. An intervention may consist in temporarily installing street furniture elements in existing public space, building a new square, organizing a resident participation day to plant community gardens, developing an artistic action, or even staging an event that invites residents to use public space on a massive scale. Sometimes, material interventions are combined with immaterial actions, and permanent interventions are combined with other temporary ones, generating an ample catalog of hybrid interventions.

In most cases, the interventions act on existing urban and social structures. Material interventions complement the existing public space with new additions that act as overlapping layers. These layers add new uses and meanings to public space, generating places for citizens to meet and interact that did not exist before. When the interventions are immaterial actions, they are applied to existing social relationships in order to reinforce them or to generate new, more complex and profound ties among people.

"Intervention" often implies an action that can be reversible, modifiable, expandable or repositionable. Working with the time factor, the intervention can acquire enormous versatility, becoming a temporary or ephemeral intervention, a test intervention, or even a mutating intervention with the ability to transform over time. This characteristic provides the strategy with immense flexibility, allowing for freer experimentation with the unknown, so that an unsuccessful intervention is not considered a failure if it provides a learning experience that allows for correcting the strategy in order to move forward toward the final objective.

Finally, the interventions can also be conceived as tools for experimenting with a variety of models for citizen participation during different parts of the process: in making decisions, in the design process or even in the tasks of realization and maintenance.

## Public Space Acupuncture, the Publication

The publication *Public Space Acupuncture* analyzes nine case studies realized in eight European cities by different designers in collaboration with different stakeholders. Based on this analysis, nine strategies of public space acupuncture have been defined, which are grouped into three general categories: time-based strategies, citizen participation and re-placemaking. The characteristics of the different strategies and how they work are illustrated using 21 projects or test-cases developed by Casanova+Hernandez in collaboration with a number of municipalities, public and private clients, as well as universities and cultural institutions. In this way, the theoretical investigation is complemented with examples of its implementation in the fields of urban planning and landscape architecture, as well as with the diffusion of the built knowledge through educational activities and thematic lectures held at several universities and cultural institutions worldwide.

The strategies included in the book Public Space Acupuncture experiment with a wide variety of topics, including flexible strategies, bottom-up strategies, temporary interventions, citizen participation, low-cost interventions, self-building, transformable structures and nomadic interventions.

1 Le Corbusier, *The City of To-morrow and Its Planning.* Payson & Clarke Ltd, New York, 1929.
2 Frank Lloyd Wright, *The Living City.* Horizon Press, New York, 1958.
3 Charles Jencks, *The Language of Post-Modern Architecture.* Rizzoli, New York, 1977.
4 Jaime Lerner, *Acupuntura Urbana.* Grupo Editorial Record, Rio de Janeiro, 2003.
5 Manuel de Solà-Morales, *A Matter of Things.* Nai Publishers, Rotterdam, 2008.
6 Joan Busquets, *Barcelona: The Urban Evolution of a Compact City.* Nicolodi editore, Rovereto, 2005.
7 Martin Pawley, *The Private Future.* Thames & Hudson, London, 1974.
8 Richard Sennett, *The Fall of Public Man.* Knopf, New York, 1977.
9 Zygmunt Bauman, *Liquid Life.* Polity Press, Cambridge, 2005.

# 1

# Time-Based Strategies

# Time-Based Strategies

The analogy between cities and living organisms reflects the fact that cities can be born, be transformed, and even die, with the time factor playing an important role. The city is a constantly changing social structure. New businesses are founded daily in the city, while many others fail. Every day, hundreds of people arrive looking for new opportunities and others move away. In a city like New York, 665 children are born each day and 315 people die. Hundreds of employees lose their jobs and many other jobless people find work. This dynamism is the motor behind what the economist Edgard Glaeser refers to as the "Triumph of the City",1 which has led more than half of the world's population to live in cities, meaning that our future depends more and more on how they are developed. But, this state of continuous transformation also creates all kinds of social imbalances; though they are sometimes only temporary and are compensated naturally, other times they become endemic, resulting in a deterioration of urban life in certain areas of the city.

Sometimes cities suffer from serious economic crises that produce effects such as a large rise in unemployment, an increase in social inequality, displacement of the most disadvantaged citizens toward marginal neighborhoods, population loss in some city centers, physical deterioration of the urban habitat and an increase in public insecurity. The time factor plays an important role in this process of deterioration of urban life, since some of these situations might be alleviated through rapid or temporary interventions, however many municipal bodies are not equipped with the necessary mechanisms to respond effectively to urban decay. Traditionally, urban and social deterioration in certain areas of the city has been counteracted through regenerative urban planning operations that have involved demolishing part of the consolidated urban structure to build new buildings and facilities. These interventions were viable in a context characterized by a strong economic activity that mobilized the investment of private capital, or where they were supported by good financial health among municipal bodies that could promote public interventions. But what happens when the private sector becomes paralyzed due to an economic crisis, and the public sector can no longer promote urban regeneration because it has been immobilized by austerity measures and spending cuts intended to reduce the public deficit? Which tools do municipalities have at their disposal to bolster public life and social cohesion?

Other times, the rapid economic growth that occurs in certain cities, which drives large-scale migratory movements and the rapid development of residential neighborhoods, can generate different kinds of social imbalances. That is why public space has also become a focal point recently in cities in developing countries that are undergoing a rapid industrialization process, such as China, Brazil or India. Shenzhen, for example, is one of the fastest-growing cities in the world since its population has swelled to 400 times larger than it was thirty years ago, reaching 13 million inhabitants in 2011. After a period during which authorities focused on mass construction of housing intended for the new residents arriving to the city from the countryside, more attention has been directed toward the role of public space as a key element in improving the quality of urban life and promoting social cohesion. During this second stage, how public space is used and how citizens interact are evaluated. Just as an old design tradition studies “desire paths” or trails left by people walking across the grass to lay out the final paths through the park, now is the time to examine the use and the nature of public space in these rapidly growing cities in order to redefine them and supplement them with new interventions.

In all of these cases, characterized by an urban habitat undergoing a profound transformation, the time factor becomes an essential aspect to take into account when planning effective strategies aimed at regenerating life in public space. Sometimes temporary strategies that experiment with emergency interventions are necessary to handle unforeseen urban problems, or test interventions can be used to try out unusual solutions to urban conflicts. On other occasions, it is advisable to implement strategies that evolve over time through mutating interventions, or even long-term strategies based on independent temporary interventions. In all of these cases, controlling the time factor during the planning, development and execution of the strategy or the interventions becomes a decisive element linked to the success of the operation.

1. Edward Glaeser, *Triumph of the City*. Penguin Press, New York, 2011.

# Short-Term Strategies

"Speed" is a term that has gained great significance in recent times. The opportunities for faster movement and communication provided by current technology help us, but they also force us to be more efficient. Time is a precious commodity in contemporary society and a quick response has become synonymous with success. Efficiency and rapid reaction are factors that characterize postmodern society and they are reflected in the rise of inventions such as fast food, SMS, digital news and virtual social networks.

In many situations involving the deterioration of urban life, both classic urban planning following the Haussmannian tradition and modern urban planning react with complex and often traumatic urban renovation operations. This planning model based on the binomial action-reaction provides a dragged-out response to the dizzying rhythm of the social and physical transformation of the city, out of step like slow-motion music accompanying a fast-motion image. As a result, sometimes entire neighborhoods suffer abandonment and begin to decay as they await the execution of slow plans for urban renewal instead of being subject to alternative strategies or quick-response parallel actions.

On the contrary, short-term strategies of public space acupuncture aim for rapid responses by fragmenting the action into numerous coordinated interventions that are temporary in nature. In this way, these strategies offer increased flexibility in terms of implementation both with respect to time, because they can be applied in phases, and with respect to space, because they can be applied independently in sensitive areas of public space.

Although all short-term strategies share their temporary nature, at the same time they can have very different objectives, working as solutions that respond to temporary urban conflicts or acting as test interventions in order to pave the way for the development of more permanent interventions that serve as the basis for analysis.

An exemplary case of a test intervention is the strategy developed by the New York City Transit Authority in Times Square. For a period of a few weeks, the Transit Authority prohibited vehicle traffic in one of the most congested areas of the city and transformed the traffic lanes into a pedestrian area equipped with 376 lawn chairs. The test intervention carried out during the summer of 2009 was not only intended to record traffic patterns around the square and the sub-

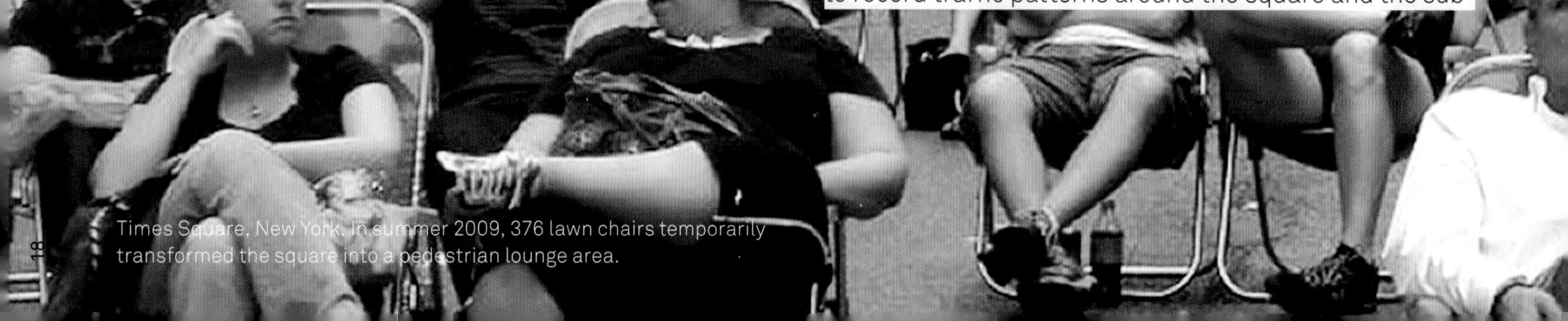

Times Square, New York. In summer 2009, 376 lawn chairs temporarily transformed the square into a pedestrian lounge area.

sequent transformation of urban life in that part of the city, but also aimed to find out what the reaction would be among citizens and in public opinion under these circumstances, as a gauge of the future consequences of a potential long-term intervention.

Other times, temporary interventions are planned by citizens, artists or designers in order to respond to a specific problem with the use of public space or to create a side effect by attracting the attention of public opinion to ultimately influence municipal decisions concerning public space. One interesting example of the consequences that these short-term interventions can have is the Park(ing) project, led by the Rebar group in San Francisco in 2005. Park(ing) began as a guerilla art project meant to draw attention to the lack of green areas in certain San Francisco neighborhoods, questioning the municipality's "commercialization" of public space through the installation of metered parking places. By paying the official fee, a citizen can "rent" a portion of the street and transform it into a small-scale urban park. The intervention-action, which takes place during one day in September each year, has spread to over 30 countries since its beginnings and during recent Park(ing) Days more than 1,000 ephemeral parks have been created by anonymous citizens.

Recently, this type of temporary interventions in public space have also begun to be channeled by municipalities in the form of coordinated strategies or festivals in which different artists, landscape architects and designers are invited all at the same time to create independent interventions that are coordinated to give response to a global problem affecting the city. In addition to the direct effect created by the temporary transformation of a fragment of public space during the festival, another effect is that the city is transformed into an experimental laboratory for trying out innovative proposals that could potentially be applied in the future.

The duration of short-term strategies can vary from just a few months to one or two years, and they are based on the use of temporary or ephemeral interventions. A temporary intervention, which implies a very particular way of understanding public space design, experiments with very different aspects such as quick low-cost construction, working with existing elements, recycling, immaterial artistic actions or prefabrication. In response to the sometimes slow pace of traditional municipal planning, direct and rapid action is promoted and in the face of rigid administrative bureaucracy, flexible strategies and calculated improvisation are proposed.

# LAUSANNE JARDINS
## LAUSANNE, SWITZERLAND

STRATEGY: **Association Jardin Urbain**
INTERVENTIONS: **Multiple designers**
**2009**

Lausanne Jardins is a major festival for temporary interventions involving landscape architecture and urban gardening in public space. For each edition, the organizers decide on a specific theme related to the city's needs. They also determine the festival's area of influence along with the number of interventions, their character and their locations, creating a complete short-term strategy of public space acupuncture.

Lausanne Jardins has taken place in 1997, 2000, 2004 and 2009. In 2009, the festival theme focused on the impact of the construction of the M2 metro line on the public space above it. This new north-south connection between the higher areas of Lausanne and the lake had a profound effect on people's understanding of the city and physically transformed daily urban life.

"Lausanne Jardins 2009" included 34 interventions located at different points along the new M2 metro line. Most of the interventions were located in outdoor public spaces, but some of them were installed underground, inside the new metro stations, working together as part of a complete strategy that affected multiple points of the public domain. The interventions, designed by different professionals, were selected via an international competition. The jury remarked that the varied proposals, while adopting subtle design strategies, deeply questioned the uses of the public space in the city.

Some of the interventions maintained an ephemeral character, playing a temporary role in introducing a new relationship between the citizens and the new infrastructure. Other interventions were given a more stable character and remained in place after the end of the festival, becoming a permanent part of the urban landscape.

The strategy involves a long, carefully planned development process to set up a network of temporary interventions over a period of five months, from June to October. It is

New M2 metro line

**Transformation of Lausanne during the construction of the new M2 metro line**

precisely this concentration of a large number of interventions in a number of points in the city over a short period of time, which produces such a large impact on the citizens' perception of public space.

The official inauguration of the Lausanne M2 metro line was celebrated in September 2008 and in October the service was in full operation. However, the construction work that affected some areas of public space, such as the entrances to the new metro stations and some city squares continued until 2009. In June 2009, the interventions included in Lausanne Jardins were opened to the public, coinciding with the end of the construction in public space.

In a short-term strategy like this one, time is a very important factor that can determine its success. This success can be achieved not only by coordinating the life span of the strategy with the number of interventions, their character and the distance among them, but also by linking the timing of the strategy with a relevant event in the daily lives of inhabitants, such as the end date for construction of infrastructure in the city.

Entresol by Kobler & Kobler and Jean Marie Lausaque

Green Tower by ex.studio

L'Ère du Futur by A. Nasri's team

## Site Plan Interventions in the City Center

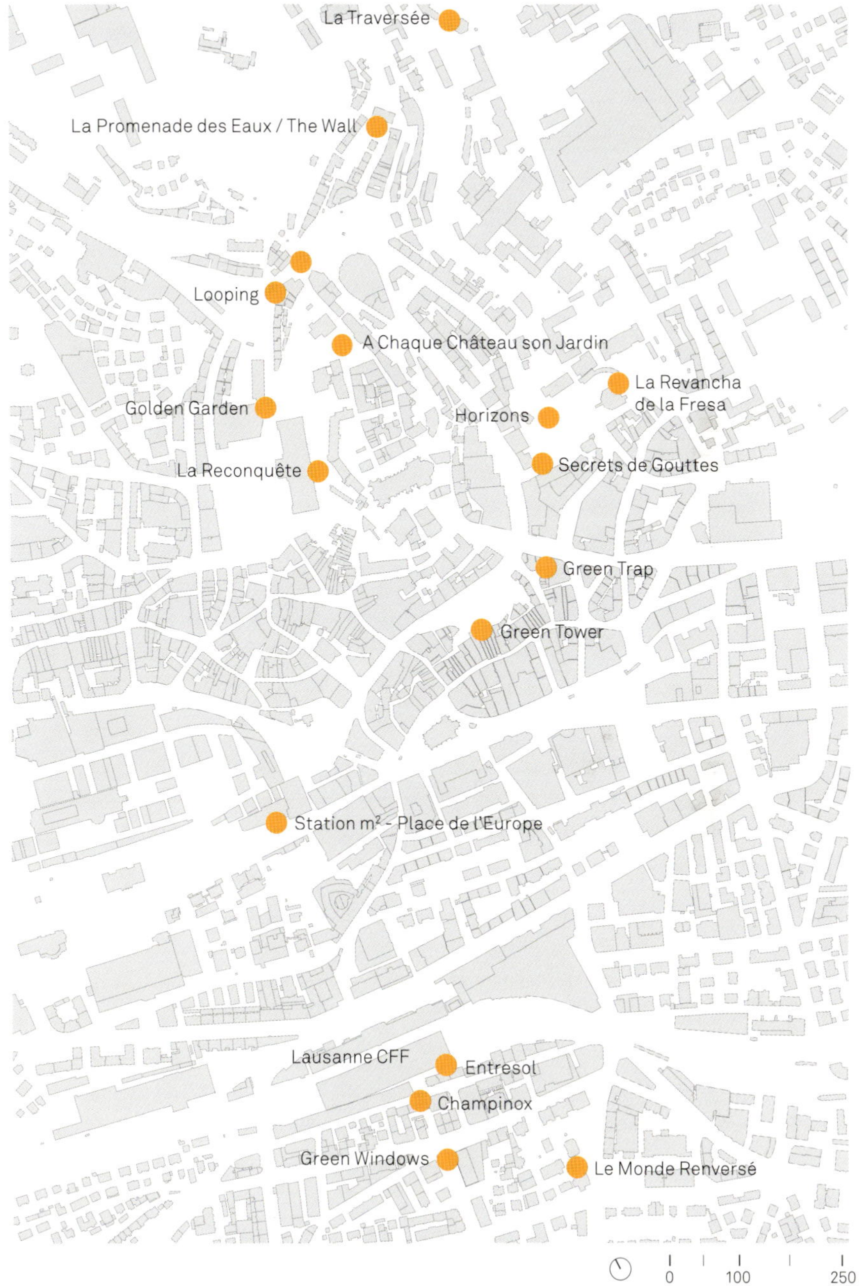

**Urban analysis** The historic center of Lausanne presents a balanced mix of very different activities in public space, which is frequented by different kinds of users: local residents, office workers and tourists.

Urban life has been heavily influenced by the construction of the new M2 metro line, which opened in October of 2008. It stretches 6 kilometers from its highest point in the north of the city down towards the level of the lake in the south, with a height difference of 350 meters and a maximum slope of 12%. This new metro line is a major step in the improvement of Lausanne's public transportation system, serving nearly 25 million passengers each year. The construction of new infrastructures and the modernization of old ones, like the historical Lausanne-Ouchy funicular line built in 1877, has caused a significant impact on the city.

## Aerial View

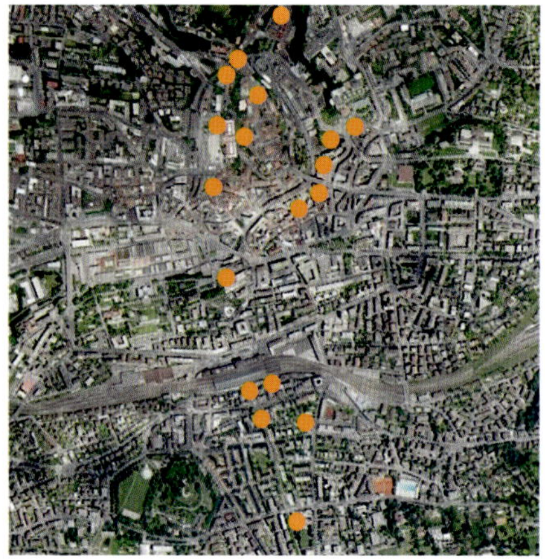

## Users

City Residents

Office workers

Tourists

Neighborhood Residents

## Relation to the City

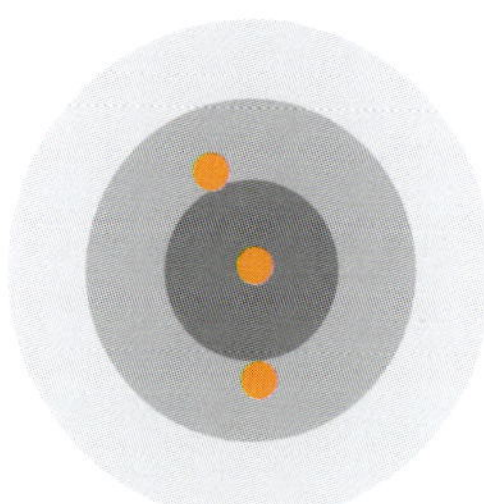

(Old) City center

Suburbs

Initial city expansions

Interventions

## Historic Urban Development

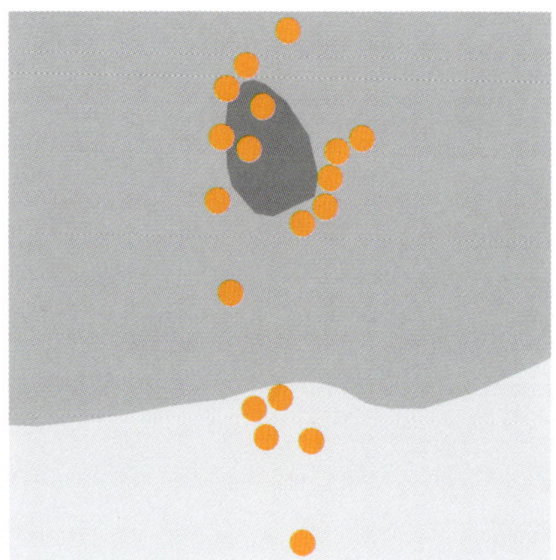

Medieval city

Post-19th century

Pre-18th century

Interventions

## Activities

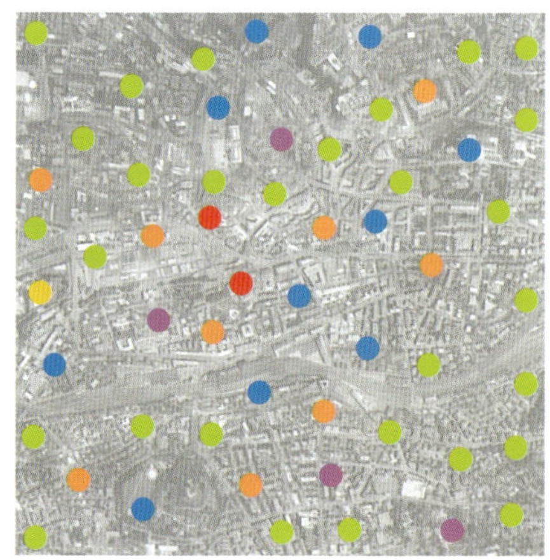

Residential

Industrial

Public buildings

Shops

Offices

Hotel

**Social analysis** In 2011, the municipality of Lausanne had a population of 130,000, 40% of whom were foreigners, almost double the national average of 22% in 2009. Immigrants have strongly contributed to the 10% population growth in Lausanne over the past 10 years. The unemployment rate in 2010 was 8%, double the national average.

More than half of the dwellings are occupied by people living alone, while only a quarter of houses are occupied by families. As a consequence of this situation, the percentage of children and young people under 18 is slightly lower than the average in the country.

## Age Structure

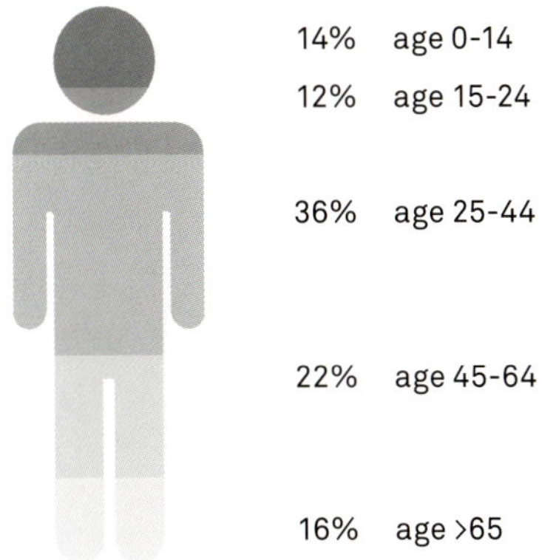


## Household Composition

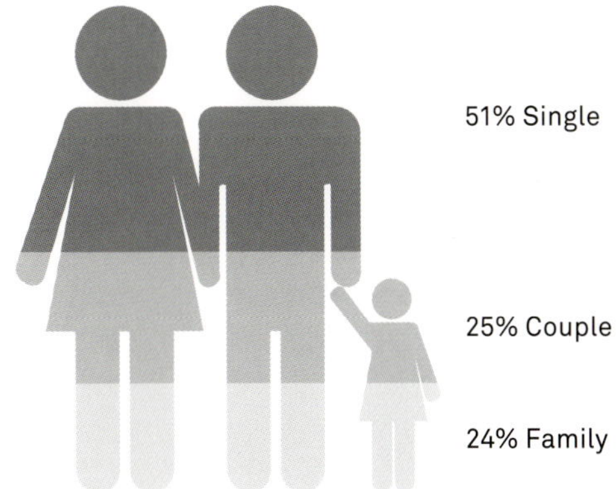

## Immigration

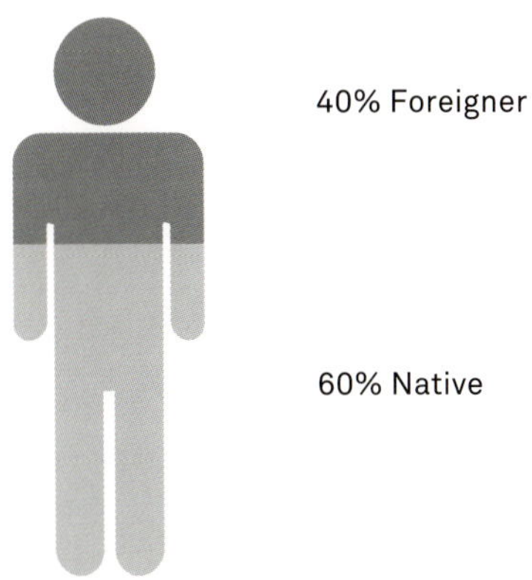


## Unemployment

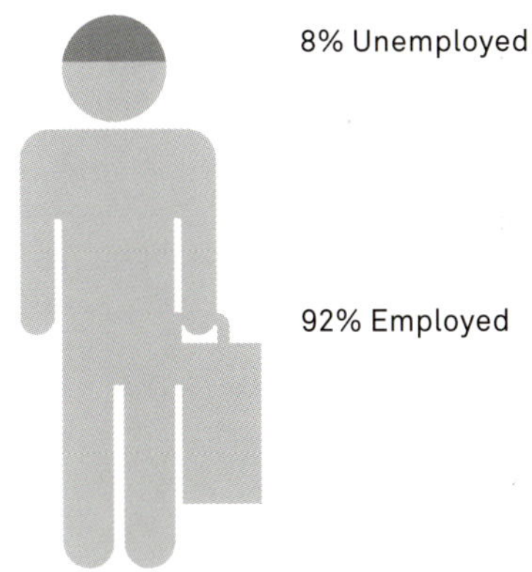


Age structure and Immigration source: STATPOP 2010. Household composition source: Swiss statistics. Unemployment source: Swiss Federal Statistical Office 2010.

**Interventions** The 34 temporary interventions carried out for Lausanne Jardins 2009 were spread along the 6 kilometers of the new M2 line of Lausanne. Five interventions have been chosen for further study. These interventions are concentrated along the southern part of the metro line and affect several important areas of public space in the city center. The selected interventions test the potential of small-scale and subtle temporary projects for transforming citizens' perceptions of the city they live in. They also encourage the use of public space and stimulate citizen interaction in the public domain.

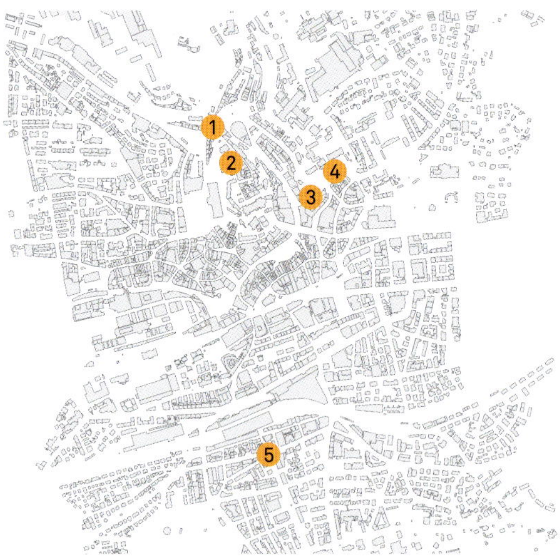


Accesses

Relaxation areas

Sitting areas

Circulation

Vegetation

## 1 Tunnel Dessus-dessous

Author: Jean-Michel Matthey

The intervention is situated above the 56-meter-long Barre Tunnel, designed by the local engineer Adrien Pichard in the 1830s, in an area characterized by heavy vehicular traffic with no special quality for pedestrians. A steel frame serves as the structure for the growth of several plant species. This creates a green vault that protects against the direct sunlight in summer and houses an intimate urban space outfitted with several benches, which is open on two sides and frames splendid views over the city. The intervention works as an outdoor gathering room that transforms a functional infrastructural element designed for vehicles into an accommodating public space for citizens.

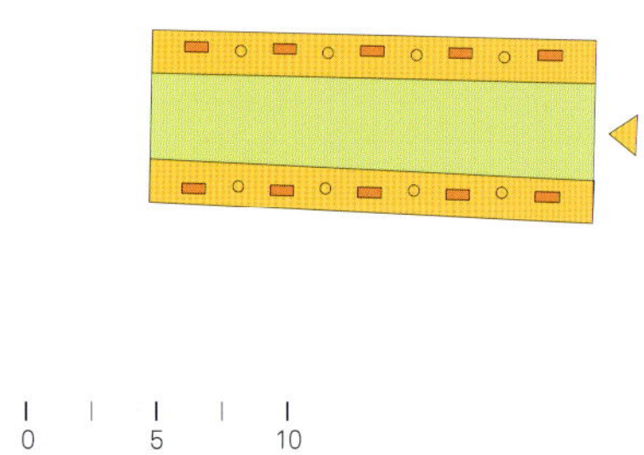


## 2 A Chaque Chateau son Jardin

Authors: Anouk Vogel, Johan Selbing, Francien van Kempen

The temporary intervention was located on the square of the Castle of Lausanne, a historical place of symbolic significance that serves as the venue for numerous institutional ceremonies. The main public space, however, located in front of the building, is normally occupied by parked cars.

The design of the intervention was inspired by the geometrical patterns present in the interior decoration of the Castle of Lausanne, which were subsequently transformed into irregular-shaped planters filled with flowers, changing the character of the square completely.

The intervention questioned the public character of such a symbolic square in the city. For a few months it transformed the current parking function into a space for citizens, thus stimulating discussion about the square's possible future refurbishment.

### 3 Horizons

Author: Collectif vfb

The intervention was located in Solitude Park. The plain grass field was transformed into a rich multicolored garden containing more than 30 different plant species and the standard urban benches were replaced by a large elastic mesh that let users rest while floating a few centimeters above the flowers.

The intervention uses a creative and playful device to challenge the conventional relationship between citizens and their urban habitat. The elastic bed also stimulates people to think about how citizens behave in the public space and opens a door to experimentation that promotes interaction among visitors.

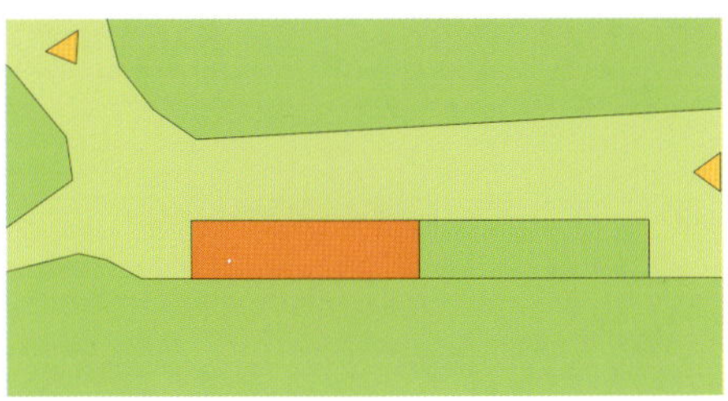

### 4 La Revancha de la Fresa

Author: Julien Rémy

The intervention consisted of the construction of a single small greenhouse for cultivating different species of strawberries. It is open to the public, who can taste, touch and compare eleven different varieties of planted strawberries. The intervention transforms an unused urban area into a "productive" public space where citizens can physically enjoy a sort of urban farming experiment. It is also an educational intervention, since during the month of August visitors are taught how to plant strawberries in pots that can be taken home.

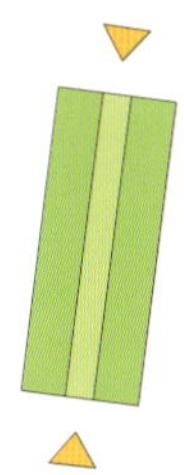

### 5 Green Windows

Author: Casanova+Hernandez

The intervention consisted of a green wall made of ivy, located in between the two elevators that connect the new Grancy metro station, on a lower level, with the public square above.

The green wall works as a visual landmark that attracts the citizens and provides identity to the square. The windows in the green wall establish a relationship between citizens, the views over Lake Geneva and the new infrastructure of the M2 metro line.

The intervention encloses the space of the square, creates a sense of intimacy and virtually reduces its scale, which acquires a more domestic dimension. It promotes a sense of place, generating a popular area for meeting, playing and relaxing.

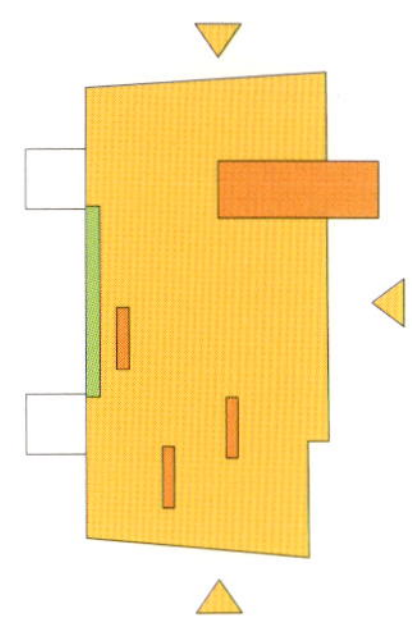

**Process** The festival was initiated in 1996 by the landscape architecture critic and writer Lorette Coen. It was first held in 1997 and is managed by the association Jardin Urbain, which appoints a new curator every two editions.

The main actors involved in the process include the public administration, represented by the municipality of Lausanne, and SPADOM ("Service des parc et domaines de la ville de Lausanne").

Each time the festival is held, a theme is proposed by the curators, who then assemble a multidisciplinary team: architects (to prepare the different documents and gather information for the competition), graphic designers (to create the visual identity and communication), and landscape architects (to supervise and approve the feasibility of the selected projects).

According to the chosen theme, other professionals may be integrated into the team.

## Cost, Financing and Maintenance

The total cost of Lausanne Jardins 2009 was 1,750,000 CHF. The maximum budget allocated for the construction of each intervention is 30,000 CHF. Following a pre-selection of the interventions resulting from an ideas competition, the total budget is distributed in a balanced way to allow for the construction of all the selected interventions.

In 2009, about €800,000 euros went into the realization of the 34 selected interventions. In addition to this budget, funds are reserved for organizing the subsequent festival, including the competition expenses and management costs.

The project is financially supported by the municipality of Lausanne (56%) and the rest by a number of institutional and private sponsors.

Maintenance for all the interventions during the festival is managed by SPANDOM, which gathers all the professionals involved in the maintenance of public space in the city into a single municipal organization. This service also assists designers during the development and construction of their interventions.

## Timing

In a first stage a group of experts in different fields, led by a guest curator, defines the theme for that specific edition.

During the second stage, an international competition is held in two phases. In the first phase, a multidisciplinary international jury selects a limited number of professional teams based on their experience and motivation. In a second phase, the final groups are selected on the basis of the quality of their specific intervention proposal, its feasibility, how it relates to the year's theme, and its compatibility with the other selected interventions.

In April 2008, 34 projects were selected to be carried out. Over the course of one year, the projects were developed and their technical and economical feasibility checked in collaboration with the technical office in Lausanne.

Construction of the interventions began in May. They remained open to the public between June and October, and some of the interventions were later selected to become permanent.

## Use of the Public Space

The festival stimulates curiosity among citizens, who move through different parts of the city following the itinerary traced by the festival and discovering the new interventions installed in public space. Therefore the public space becomes more active during the festival months, awakening the interest of local residents and visiting groups.

Some of the interventions experiment with new ways of using public space, creating new leisure areas and gathering spaces in the city that stimulate the use of its open-air public areas.

Since the character of each edition is marked by its specific theme and coordinated by different curators, the interventions that are realized can be very diverse and are not always focused on activating the use of the public space or on promoting citizen interaction.

28 LAUSANNE

Le M2, futur fil rouge de Lausanne Jardins 2009

BALADES

CROISETTES

CITÉ

## Impact on Citizens

The interventions during the Lausanne Jardins festival are installed in public space and therefore there is no entrance fee. The festival can be visited by day or by night, in part or in their entirety. Since the festival was first held, Lausanne Jardins has become a very popular event that attracts many visitors. The organization estimates that 60,000 people visited the festival specifically in 2009. However, the number of citizens and residents who have visited interventions in their neighborhoods just as passers-by is unknown. The festival also serves as a tourist attraction during the summer months. A survey carried out by the organization shows that 25% of visitors are from Lausanne, 50% are from the rest of the canton and the remaining 25% are from the rest of the country and foreign countries. Among them, 894 people visited the entire festival through guided tours and another 600 people through special tours for VIP groups.

## Media Impact

Lausanne Jardins always enjoys a widespread media impact. It is promoted by the organization "Association Jardin Urbain" in different ways. During the Lausanne Jardins 2009 festival the official website received more than 60,000 visitors between June and October and more than 6,000 copies of the "Carnet de Route", the book that includes information on the interventions and marks the route for visiting the festival, were sold.

Four press conferences were organized to inform journalists about the event. Most of the national and regional newspapers and some of the most important international newspapers, such as El País, Le Soir, Libération and La Repubblica, published articles about Lausanne Jardins. Many websites, television outlets and radio stations promoted the event through special coverage and regular news.

The strategy also caught the attention of many international specialist publications about public space and landscape architecture, creating a considerable impact among professionals in the discipline.

Lausanne Jardins se métisse pour mettre la ville sens dessus dessous

RECONNAISSANCE

LAURÉAT

URBANISME

## TEMPORARY INTERVENTION “GREEN WINDOWS”
LAUSANNE, SWITZERLAND

STRATEGY: **Association Jardin Urbain**
INTERVENTIONS: **Multiple designers**
TEST CASE INTERVENTION “GREEN WINDOWS”:
**Casanova+Hernandez**

“Green Windows” is one of the 34 temporary interventions realized in the public space of Lausanne during the “Lausanne Jardins 2009” festival. “Green Windows” serves as an example for the detailed analysis of how a temporary intervention that is part of a short-term public space acupuncture strategy works, as well as the criteria for its design, production and assembly.

**Strategy** The general strategy outlined by the festival determined many of the parameters for the intervention, such as its duration and approximate location. Since the strategy’s objective centered on improving the relationship between the new infrastructures built for Lausanne’s new M2 metro line and the immediate surroundings, the location for the intervention was limited to the area around the Grancy metro station.

The significance of the location of the intervention was two-fold. First, because of its historic value, since the site marks one of the city’s latest urban transformations, focused on modernizing the old funicular. Built in 1877, it connected the Lausanne train station, at an elevation of 451 meters, with the Ouchy station near Lake Geneva, at an elevation of 373 meters. The historic single track was replaced by a set of parallel tracks after the route was widened, the old funicular carriages were replaced by a modern metro and two new stations were created along the line: Délices and Grancy.

Second, because the intervention marks the exact point where the former open-air route is hidden by the tunnel that connects to the central station, creating a new public square above it. Two towers made of concrete and glass are built on the square to house two elevators that connect the public square with the new Grancy station platforms, situated on the lower level.

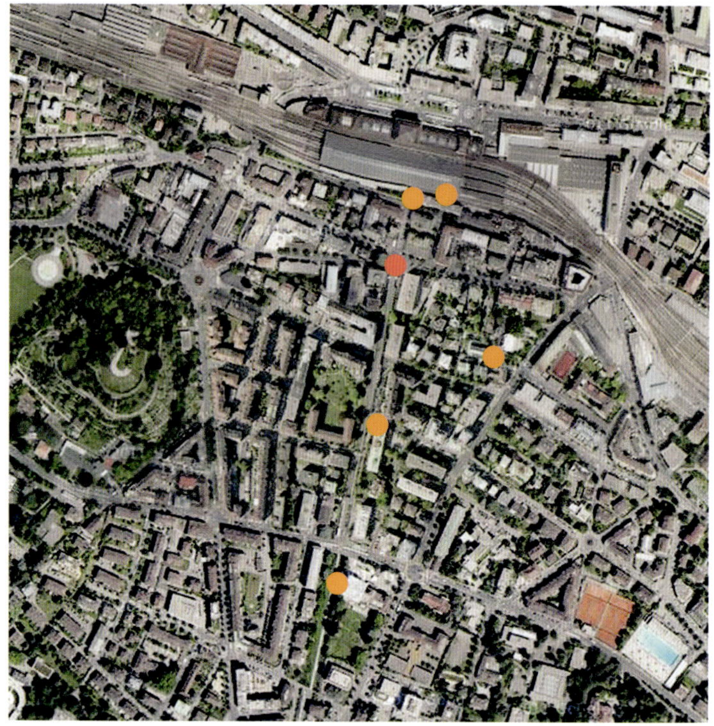

Historic funicular line Lausanne-Ouchy and its transformation into the M2 metro line.

**Intervention** The intervention, situated between the two elevators of the new metro station, consists of a green wall that closes off one side of the open space of the square both visually and spatially. At the same time, it connects the intervention site with the striking views toward Lake Geneva and the mountains in the distance through the use of windows opened into the green wall.

The intervention transforms citizens' perception of this urban square as a space merely for passing through into a space with a domestic scale that transmits a feeling of intimacy, though it remains public space, open to the city. The intentional use of ivy, a plant that is traditionally present in private gardens, and the perforation of the green wall to create windows, reinforces the domestic and welcoming character of this new urban space that is designed on the human scale, and not on an infrastructural one.

Thanks to its position and design, the green wall functions as an intriguing urban element that immediately attracts the attention of passers-by while the windows set at different heights spark visitors' curiosity, encouraging them to pick the right window to look through, according to their height. Standing at the windows, citizens come into contact with Lausanne's natural landscape and contemplate the recent construction of the M2 metro line from a new point of view.

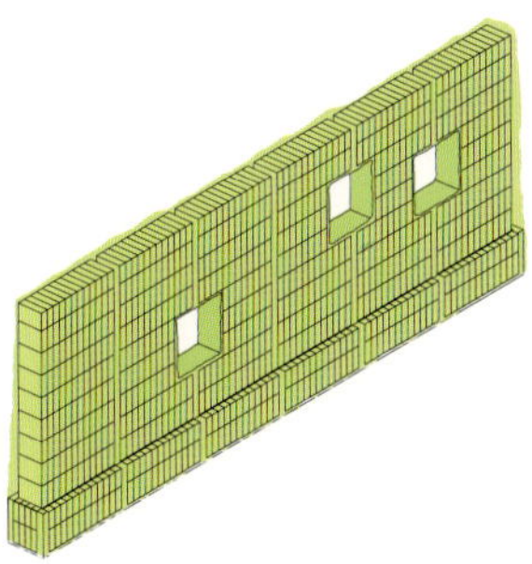

Prefabricated landscape intervention

Cross section

Elevation

01

The intervention experiments with how an anonymous urban space can be transformed, using very few resources, into a domestic space, and how art and landscape architecture can be combined to create more attractive cities for citizens, changing the way they perceive the city they live in.

The intervention promotes reflection on the relationship between nature and artifice in public space, and on the contemporary landscape understood as a local, native product or as an imported, global one. On the one hand, it has a hybrid character conceived as a "prefabricated landscape", a mixture of architecture and landscape, that is materialized through a three-dimensional green wall and the use of windows cut into it. On the other hand, the intervention experiments not only with temporality, but also with the innovative possibility of transporting the landscape. Indeed, it was grown and built in the Netherlands, and later on it was transported to the site in Lausanne, becoming what we could call a "nomad intervention".

## Prefabricated and Nomad Landscape

The intervention is split into two prefabricated modules to make it easier to transport and set up on the site. Each module was built above a stainless steel planter with a layer of thermal isolation inside to prevent the plant roots from freezing. Each planter is fitted with a drain at the bottom to allow for run-off when the intervention is watered, which can be connected to the municipal sewer system. A three-dimensional galvanized steel structure, into which the window openings are sculpted, rises above each planter. The ivy plants, from the species *Hedera helix*, which is especially resistant to changes in temperature, grow up onto the steel structure.

Green Windows is a nomadic intervention. In February of 2008, well before the project was begun, the ivy had already been planted in a greenhouse in De Peel, an area of the Netherlands that is famous for the production of greenhouse plants for exportation. In March of 2009 the three-dimensional steel structure was built and the mature plants were transplanted into the structure where they continued growing during the spring, climbing up the lattice structure and creating a solid green wall. In June, the modules were transported by truck from the Netherlands to Switzerland, and in just a few short hours they were installed on the site. The official opening took place on June 20, just a few days after the installation was completed.

Green Windows was also designed as a recyclable intervention. After the end of the festival it was transported back to Holland and reused in other temporary public space interventions.

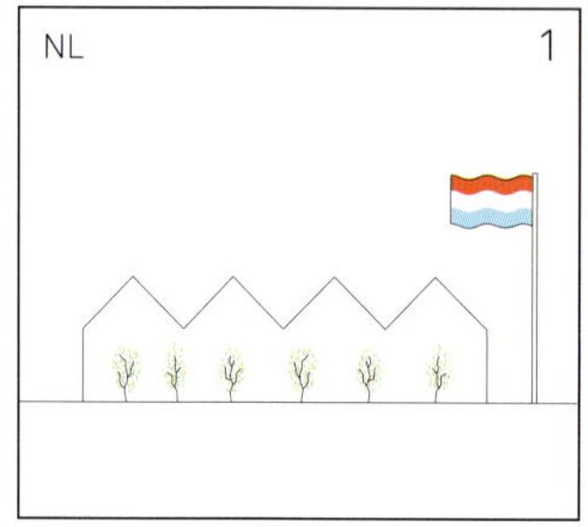


February 2008: plants grow in a greenhouse in the Netherlands

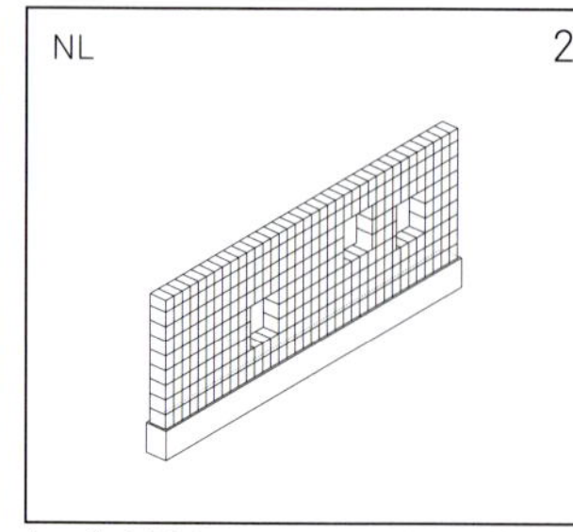


April 2009: construction of a three-dimensional steel structure

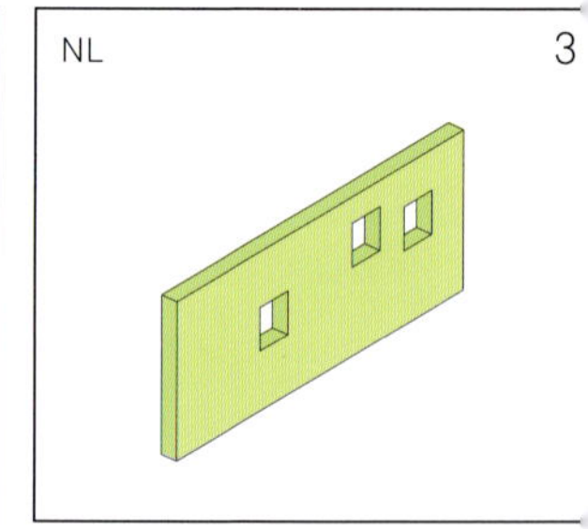


April 2009: plants continue growing on the steel structure

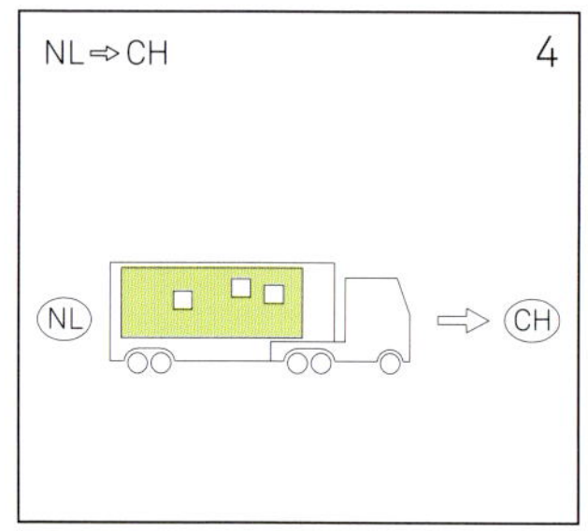


June 209: the prefabricated garden travels to Switzerland

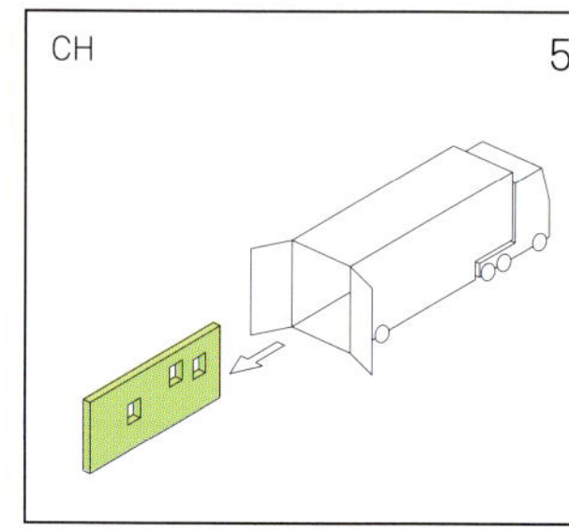


June 2009: placing the Green Windows on site in Lausanne

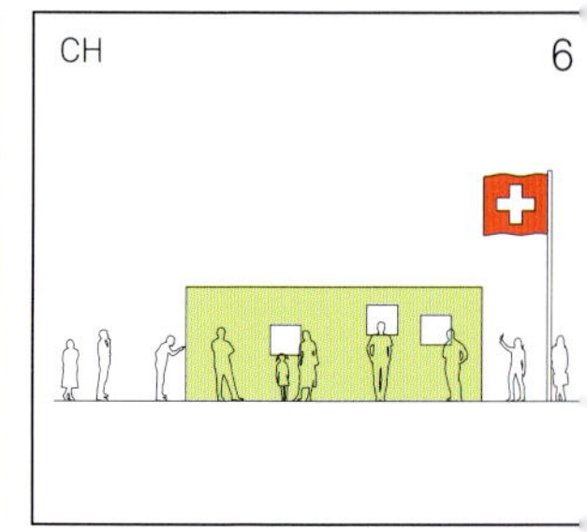


June 20: opening exhibition
October 24: closing exhibition

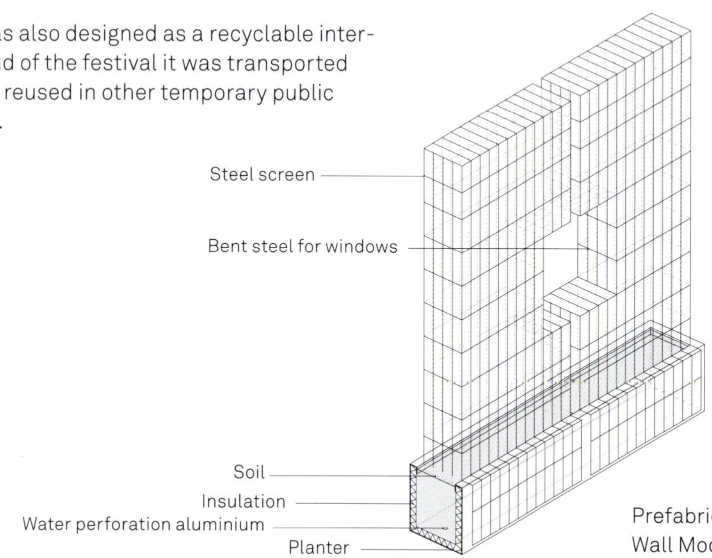


Prefabricated Green Wall Module

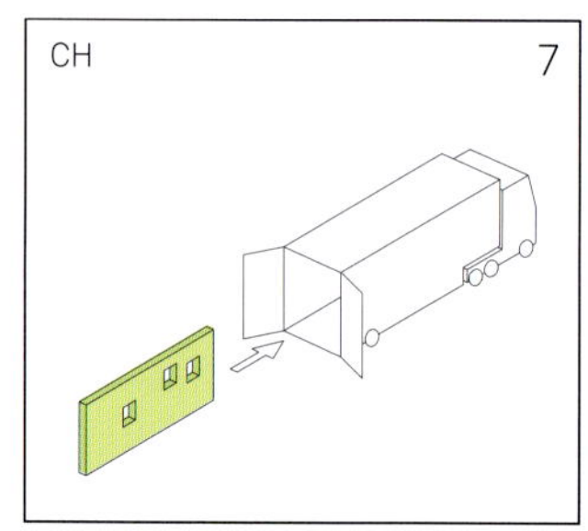


October 2009: dismantling

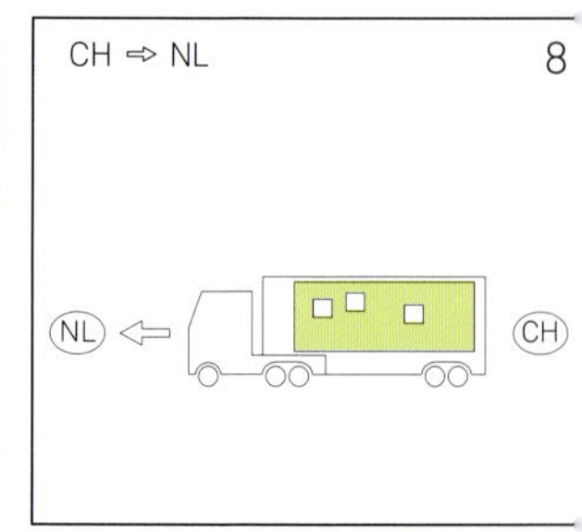


October 2009: back to the Netherlands

TEL. +41 61 716 93 30
FAX +41 61 716 93 34
REINACH - SCHWEIZ
WWW.DONS.CH
DONS
TRANSPORTE
www.dons.ch
PETIT

01

# TEMPORARY INTERVENTION "SENSES COCKTAIL"
## APPELTERN, THE NETHERLANDS

STRATEGY: **De Tuinen van Appeltern**
INTERVENTIONS: **Multiple designers**
TEST CASE INTERVENTION "SENSES COCKTAIL":
**Casanova+Hernandez**

**Strategy** Every year, the small Dutch town of Appeltern holds a Landscape Festival which brings together interventions that experiment with the theme of temporariness. The festival was first held in 2010, gathering ten temporary interventions by different designers, selected via competition. In subsequent years, the number of selected projects has increased to twenty. The temporary interventions are installed in a series of open-air rooms distributed along a pathway through the park. The rooms are square shaped and they all have the same dimensions. Each room is bordered by a hedge a meter and a half high, tall enough to create a certain independence and privacy on the inside, while still allowing visitors to see most of the interventions from the central pedestrian walkway.

Int.#1, Ekkendonk & Bastiaansen

Int.#4, L. Adema & D. de Haas

Int.#2, K. Looman & J. Schaap

Int.#7, Paul Kromhout

Int.#8, Grasveld

Int.#5, Locus Flevum

Visitors experience the park as though they were walking through a series of open-air rooms in a house. Although the spatial conditions of the rooms are similar, they are also all different due to the substantial variation among the interventions they house. This arouses visitor's interest as they walk among the different rooms, seeking out new experiences.

As with all short-term strategies, the interventions must be carefully designed, taking into account not only the limited life-span of the works, but also that they must be installed and dismantled within a short time. There is an added complication when the strategy is based on landscape interventions, since they rely on living natural elements that need time to grow, which stimulates the search for innovative solutions for many of the interventions.

**Intervention** The intervention "Senses Cocktail", designed by Casanova+Hernandez, combines technical investigation centered on temporariness through the design, construction and installation of a short-term intervention with experimentation in transforming a non-place into a room with its own meaning by activating a multisensory perception of the place among visitors. The temporary nature of the intervention leads to experimenting with a hybrid design that combines architecture and nature, landscape and sculpture, an industrial product and natural elements.

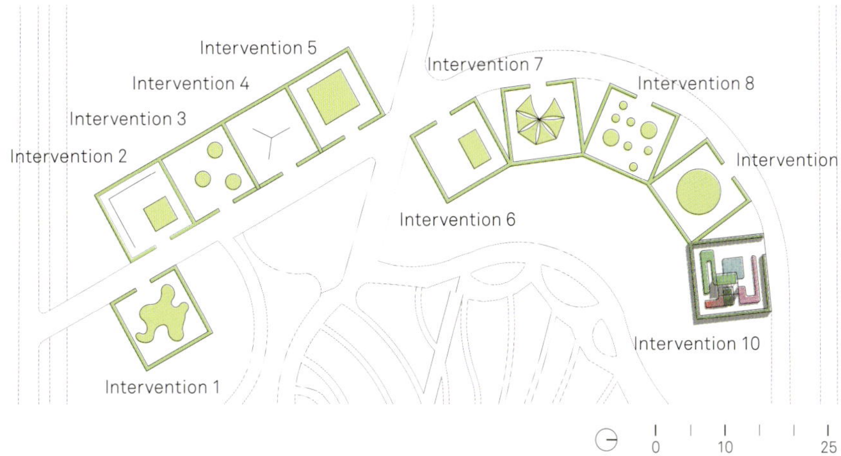

### Multisensory intervention

The intervention "Senses Cocktail" creates a space where visitors are subject to a sensory experience that stimulates all five senses: taste, hearing, smell, touch and sight. In order to achieve this, the design combines five different landscapes. Each one is intended to stimulate a separate sensory experience. The landscape that uses aromatic plants stimulates the sense of smell; the grape vine climbing the trellis, full of fruit, stimulates taste; the bright red geraniums stimulate sight; the sound of falling water created by a water curtain, hearing; and a patch of lawn for relaxing barefoot, the sense of touch. The five landscapes intertwine in a small cubic space placed at the center of the garden, which invites visitors to step inside to enjoy a multisensory experience that stimulates all five senses at the same time.

### Three-dimensional landscape: merging horizontal and vertical gardens

This intervention creates a three-dimensional landscape based on the combination of five gardens where the vegetation, planted horizontally, grows vertically along the walls and the roof of the central cubic structure. Each of the five planted strips uses a different plant species. All together they form a dynamic multi-colored landscape that creates a very different perception of the intervention, depending on the visitor's point of view. As a result, the "Senses Cocktail" intervention becomes a vibrant and surprising space that awakens visitors' curiosity.

### Artistic intervention: a mixture of sculpture and garden

The central cubic structure is a sculptural object, inspired by the spatial studies created by the sculptor Jorge Oteiza in the 1950s, called "empty boxes". In these works the artist shaped the empty space inside the steel boxes and opened their sides partially to reveal their interiors.

The central piece in the intervention uses plants to create a virtual cubic space. Its interior can be seen through gaps in the vegetation, which also allow visitors to step inside the cube. From the inside, visitors not only perceive the five elements that make up the space, but they also see the sky and the outside landscape, framed by the openings.

Cross section and plan

S-N view

S-E view

N-E view

N-W view

Horizontal garden

Vertical garden

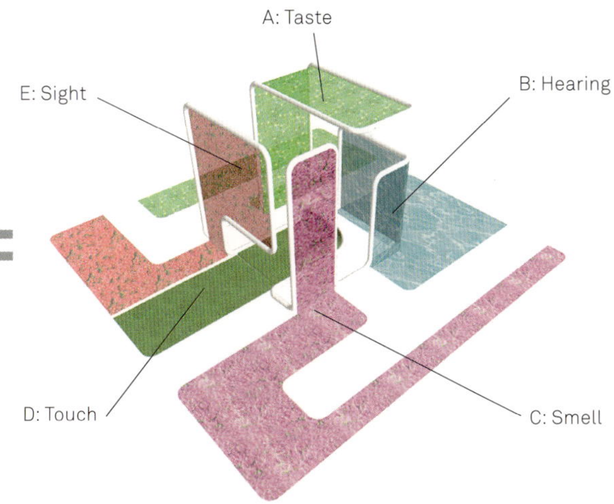


Three-dimensional garden

A: Taste garden

B: Hearing garden

C: Smell garden

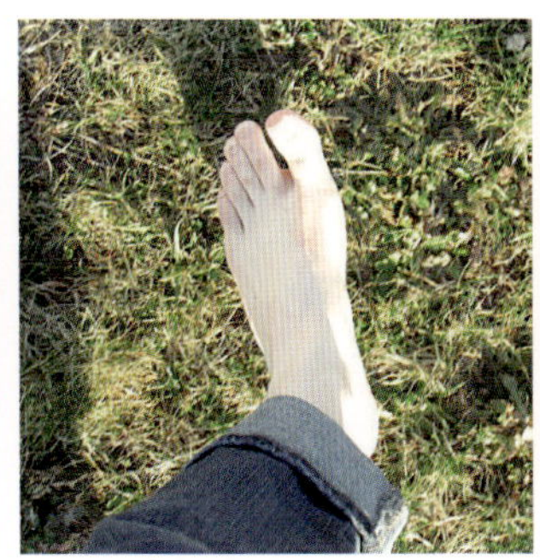

D: Touch garden

E: Sight garden

## Combining Nature and Industry

The intervention explores the collaboration between industrial and natural materials. On the one hand, the structure for the central cubic element, measuring 3x3x3 meters, is designed using a continuous curved tube folded along the three dimensions of space.
On the other hand, the green walls that form the sides of the cubic structure are built with prefabricated elements that are pre-grown in greenhouses to ensure that the intervention can be built and installed within a short period of time.

The structure, built in a factory, and the plants grown in greenhouses were transported by truck to the site for assembly. Throughout the time that the intervention was open to the public, the vegetation kept growing, becoming denser, and therefore causing changes in the appearance of the piece. The time factor was decisive in the conception, design and construction of the intervention, making innovation necessary for the development of specific solutions.

Empty box, Jorge Oteiza, 1958

02

02

# Mutating Strategies

Sometimes we define some public spaces in the city as alive and others as dead. But, what does it really mean for public space to be dead? When Richard Sennett defines the death of public space in his book *The Fall of the Public Man*, he refers to squares and streets where there is a visible absence of pedestrians. This does not mean that the city is lifeless in general or that the nearby buildings are without activity, but rather that this activity is not visually manifest in the street, at least during long periods of time throughout the day. The description of public space as alive or dead is a collective assessment, a subjective term that is commonly associated with the absence of urban activity.

In fact, one of Sennett's criticisms in qualifying public space as dead is directed against the functionalist zoning inherited from the modern movement that fomented the segregation of activities with the aim of achieving a more efficient city, but at the same time it eliminated commercial activity on the ground floor and left large areas of the city unused once working hours ended. Today, urban planning is fighting against this problem by creating more balanced cities that incorporate a functional mix.

On the contrary, alive public space refers to a space that citizens use, full of activity that changes as the day goes by, on different days of the week or throughout the seasons of the year. Certain popular neighborhoods with plenty of businesses on the ground floor, open-air markets and public squares where improvised events are held are considered alive public spaces not only because they attract a large number of citizens with their activities, but also because of their capacity for transformation that projects an image of dynamism. On many occasions an alive public space not only implies that it is full of people, but that a variety of activities takes place there, providing it with a constantly changing appearance.

Small-scale spaces like Paley Park in New York can also be considered alive public spaces. Jerold S. Kayden describes this tiny pocket park, occupying just $390m^2$, as one of the most frequented privately owned public spaces in New York.[1] William H. Whyte analyzes the intense use of this public space in his movie and book *The Social Life of Small Urban Spaces* and he argues that its success is due, in part, to having created an intimate space in the middle of a very crowded area of the city, but also to the flexibility of use offered by its urban furniture.[2] The use of light-weight chairs and moveable tables gives each visitor the possibility of finding the ideal place for sitting in a group enjoying the company, or for having some privacy even if people are very

MuseumsQuartier, Vienna. Mutating strategy designed by PPAG architects.

close to each other, allowing for moving the chairs into sunlit areas in winter and shady places in summer. The continuous movement and spatial reorganization in Paley Park characterizes it as a living and attractive space for citizens, like a mutating space in constant transformation.

This capacity for transformation that certain public spaces adopt in response to citizens' wishes, and the different functional requirements that change over time, can be key to creating alive urban spaces using public space acupuncture strategies. The alternative to the traditional static and mono-functional interventions that form "solid strategies", to paraphrase Zygmunt Bauman, are the mobile, mutating and transformable interventions that constitute what we might call "liquid strategies".[3] In this way, when rigid urban planning makes it difficult to change the distribution of uses and activities within buildings to create a living city, complementary strategies can be designed to give public space this capacity for transformation, increasing and diversifying urban activity at the same time.

Given that mutating strategies consist of a sequence of changing interventions that follow one another over time, it is important to plan them in stages so that public space can acquire different configurations and activities. Just as in a theatrical performance where the script is developed during different scenes and the actors play their roles on a stage with a changing set, a mutating strategy has to be carefully planned taking into account factors like the number and the duration of the scenes, the participating actors and the nature of the physical transformation of public space.

Sometimes the rhythm of transformation of the mutating strategy is adjusted to fit the rhythm of the variation of existing activities in the area, to supplement and enrich them. In other strategies developed in areas with less dynamism, the transformation of public space is articulated according to a new program of independent activities or it responds to the changes in climate that take place throughout the different seasons of the year. In any case, mutating strategies should be based on an exhaustive analysis of the existing urban activity, as well as continuous monitoring and redefinition of the interventions so that they remain effective at any moment.

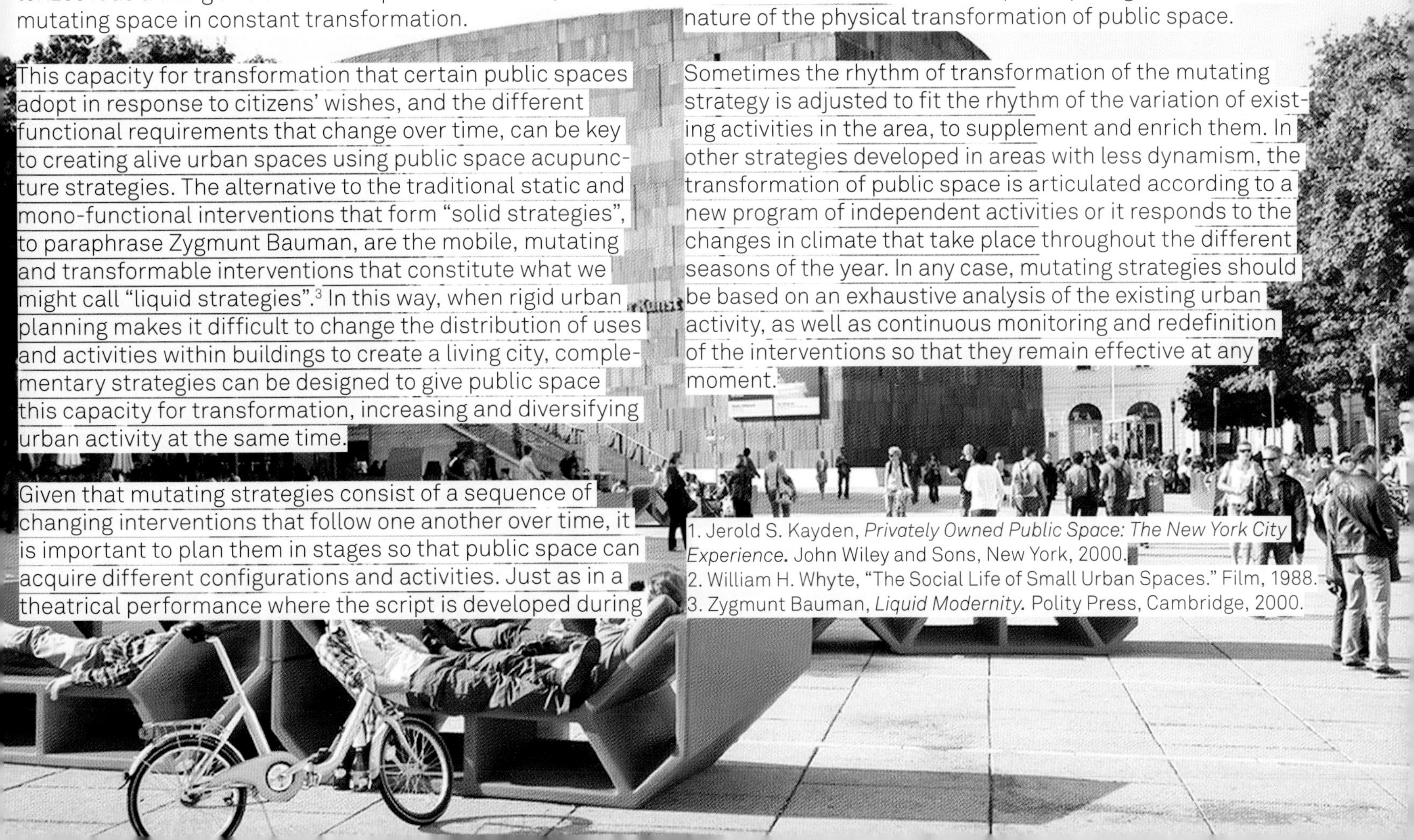

1. Jerold S. Kayden, *Privately Owned Public Space: The New York City Experience*. John Wiley and Sons, New York, 2000.
2. William H. Whyte, "The Social Life of Small Urban Spaces." Film, 1988.
3. Zygmunt Bauman, *Liquid Modernity*. Polity Press, Cambridge, 2000.

# MUSEUMSQUARTIER COURTYARD
## VIENNA, AUSTRIA

STRATEGY: **museumsquartier e+b**
STRATEGY/INTERVENTIONS: **PPAG**

Vienna's MuseumsQuartier was opened in 2001, after years of planning, without a programmed use for the public space located in the courtyards. The elevated cost of the new buildings, combined with problematic handicapped accessibility and a lack of urban life in the associated public space, led to a negative image of the new cultural complex, making it hard to attract visitors and hindering the goal of creating a new activity center for the city and the neighborhood.

To counteract the lifelessness in the public space, the organism responsible for managing the complex announced a competition, open to young architects, for the design of a multipurpose urban furniture system. The PPAG team won the competition with their system called "Enzi" which was presented for the first time in the MuseumsQuartier in the winter of 2002, in the form of igloos.

The strategy implemented in the MuseumsQuartier, intended to promote public life and to transform its empty courtyards into an attractive public space for citizens, is based on the combination of a versatile and attractive urban furniture system with a diverse program of activities, carefully planned for each different season of the year. The 116 modular elements, built from expanded polystyrene (EPS), could be easily moved around the courtyard. They were also designed to allow multiple possible combinations to create different spatial configurations. Soon enough, visitors were enthusiastic about the strategy, using the modular elements for relaxing, making the area a popular meeting place. At the same time, the organizers developed a varied agenda of cultural activities including concerts, dance performances, fashion shows, and winter sports, transforming the MuseumsQuartier into a new vibrant public space in the Viennese cultural scene.

The time factor serves as the axis that articulates the entire strategy, creating something new and exceptional. The strategy is designed, therefore, not as a series of interventions

fixed in different points in space, but as a series of interventions that occur one after the other over time, becoming a mutating strategy that is constantly evolving.

MuseumsQuartier E+B, the organization responsible for the center's cultural programming, coordinates how the strategy evolves over time, in conjunction with PPAG architects, who carry out the specific design for each intervention. Together, they design and program the activities and the different spatial configurations for the modular system, coinciding with the interventions planned throughout the year. They control how activities in the courtyard change, not by reacting rapidly to urban and social conditions, but by creating a basic rhythm for transformation that is flexible enough to eventually introduce new activities or special events that serve to continually revive urban life.

The careful design of the appearance of public space and its programming transforms the city into an urban theatre, where citizens become the actors and the spectators at the same time. This urban theatre highlights the most public aspect of city life, as opposed to other strategies that promote its more domestic or collective aspects.

At the same time, the staging of public life needs the right setting for its performance. The stage is created by the Baroque courtyards of the former Viennese court stables, where the historic identity of the place is mixed with contemporary culture. The courtyard is a space enclosed by the architecture which, like an Italian piazza, is an ideal space for the improvised representation of public life.

First, the meticulous scheduling of the strategy awakens curiosity and attracts citizens because of its novelty. Second, the mutating character of the interventions, combined with a carefully selected program of activities, maintains interest among citizens, generating the habit of using public space. As a result, it becomes an everyday location for many people who use it as an improvised meeting place, for leisure and relaxation, which becomes an integral part of public life in the city.

## Interventions Realized in the Period 2002-2010 (Selection)

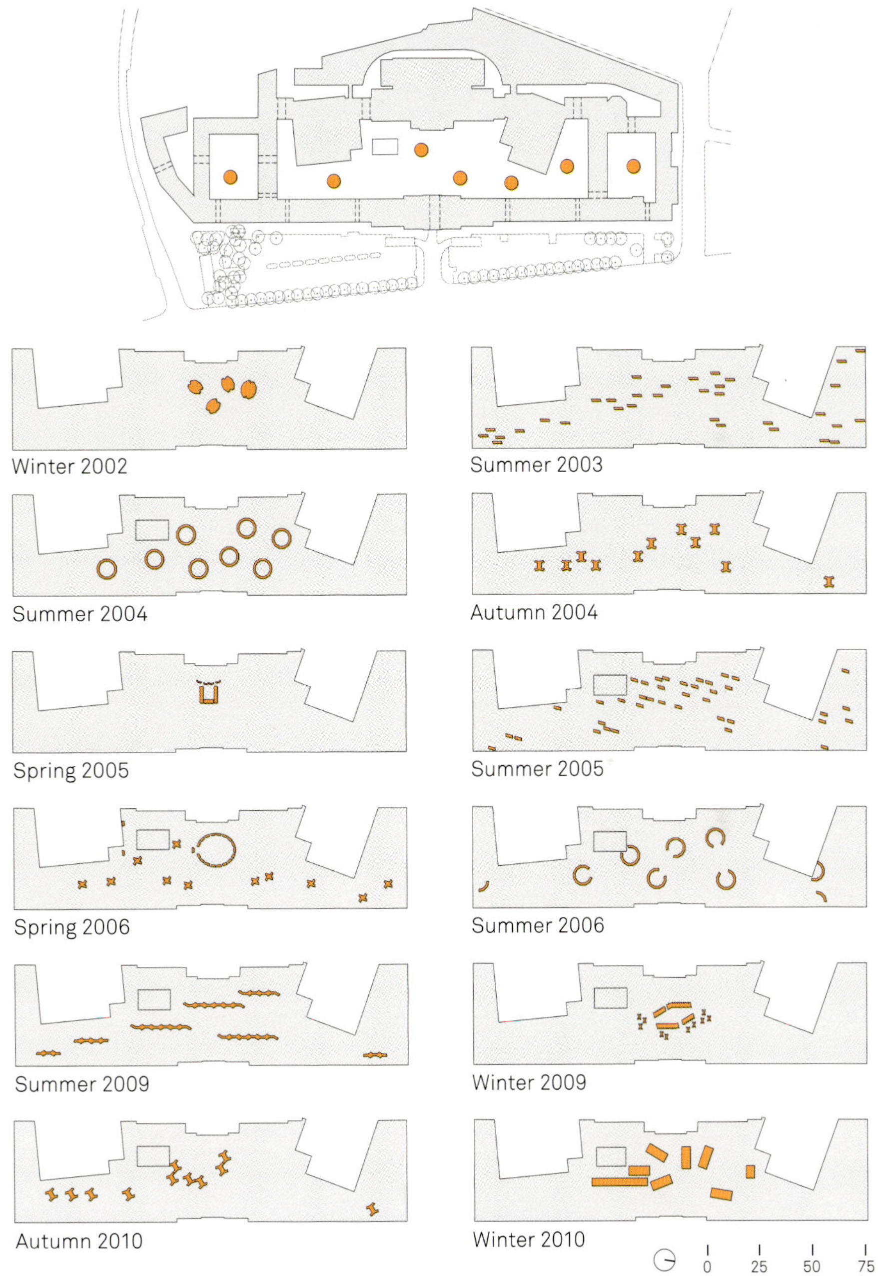

**Urban analysis** MuseumsQuartier (MQ) is a 7 ha cultural complex located in the former Imperial Stalls, which were transformed in several phases and opened to the public in 2001. It belongs to Vienna's seventh district, limiting the old city on the east. The complex is located near the medieval city walls built during the 13th century, which were demolished during the second half of the 19th century in order to create a new monumental boulevard called Ringstraße, where the main public buildings of the city were built.

The population of the seventh district consists of a varied mix of families, many students, creative professionals and a high percentage of foreigners. The central location of the MuseumsQuartier, close to a large number of cultural attractors, means that many tourists and citizens of Vienna visit the area frequently.

## Aerial View

## Users

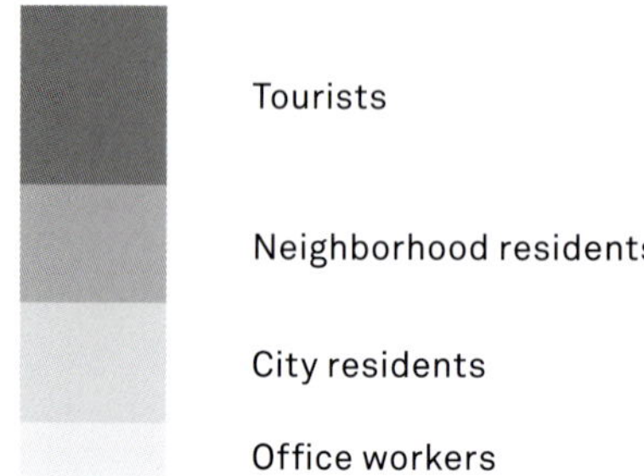


## Relation to the City

(Old) City center
Suburbs
Initial city expansions
Interventions

## Historic Urban Development

Medieval city
Late 19th century
Early 19th century
Interventions

## Activities

Residential
Industrial
Public buildings
Shops
Offices
Hotels

**Social analysis** Vienna is the economic, cultural and political capital of Austria. It attracts many immigrants looking for jobs. Immigration represents 22% of the population and the unemployment rate in the city was 9% in 2010, slightly higher than the national average. The city's numerous educational facilities attract many students and young people, which is reflected in the household composition. Half of all houses are inhabited by a single person and 21% by couples without children. Families living in Vienna represent less than 30% of the population and children make up just 14% of the population.

## Age Structure

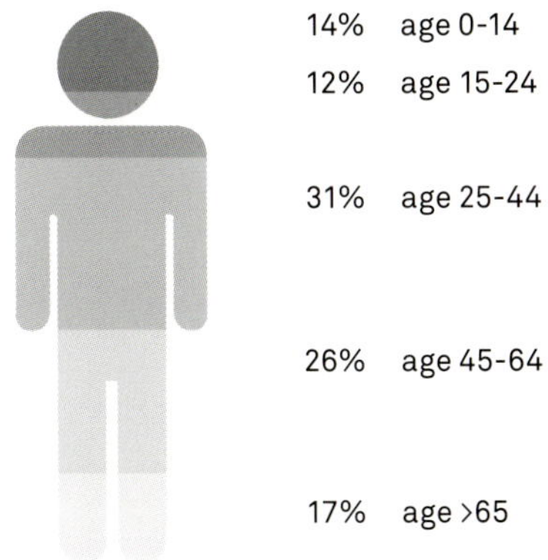


## Household Composition

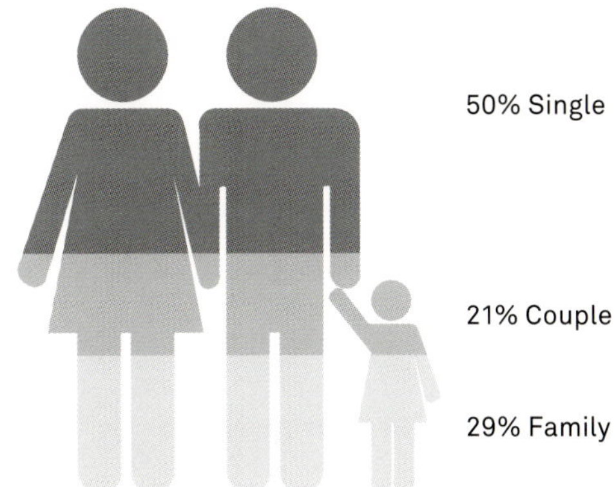

## Immigration

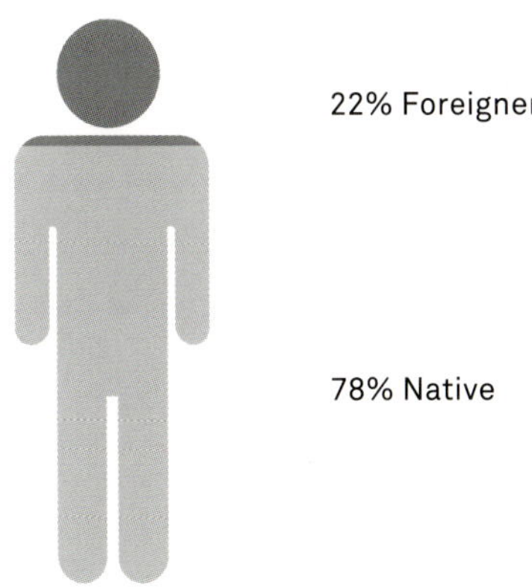


## Unemployment

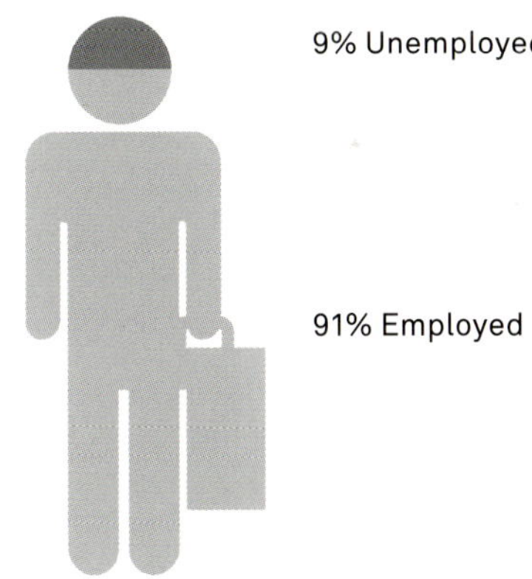


Age structure: Source ST.AT 2008. Household composition: Source Statistik Austria 2010. Immigration: Source Stadt Wien 2011. Unemployment: Source Arbeitsmarkt service 2010.

**Interventions** The main defining factor in the strategy developed for the MuseumsQuartier is time. The interventions that make the strategy possible are not implemented simultaneously, but progressively. Each intervention is planned in advance, using the same modular elements but combining them according to different layouts that depend on the specific function related to the program of activities and the season of the year.

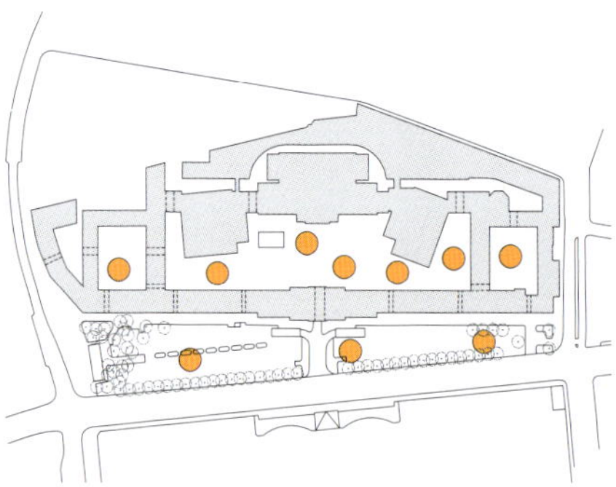

Accesses
Relaxation areas
Sitting areas
Circulation
Vegetation

## 1 Intervention Stars

The Enzi is an element designed with a rectangular base, a length of 200 centimeters and a width of 125 centimeters. The volume is sculpted into 12 planes to create a single piece of furniture based on human dimensions, which can be used comfortably by many people in different ways.

The geometry of the modular element allows for multiple combinations, which in turn enable complex spatial layouts. Some of them consist in combining a number of pieces together to close off a certain area of public space, which acquires a collective character. The layout stimulates visual connections among visitors who become spontaneous spectators and actors on a small urban stage.

Summer 09

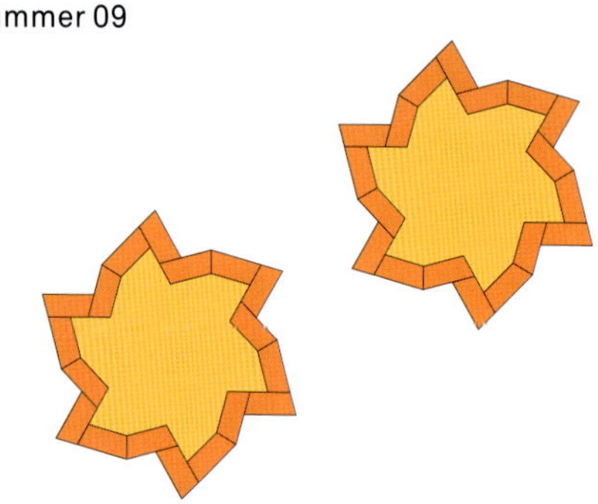

0 5 10

## 2 Intervention Windmill

The intervention, built in spring 2006, enclosed an elliptical space located at the center of the courtyard. It was made using 36 modular elements grouped into 18 double pieces, which were formed by placing two modules one on top of the other. The double pieces created small, personal spaces that were limited on four sides and open on two, providing a feeling of protection and intimacy. At the same time, the extra height of the double pieces enclosed an outdoor space, which acquired a real spatial dimension working as an open room located at the center of the courtyard.

Spring 06

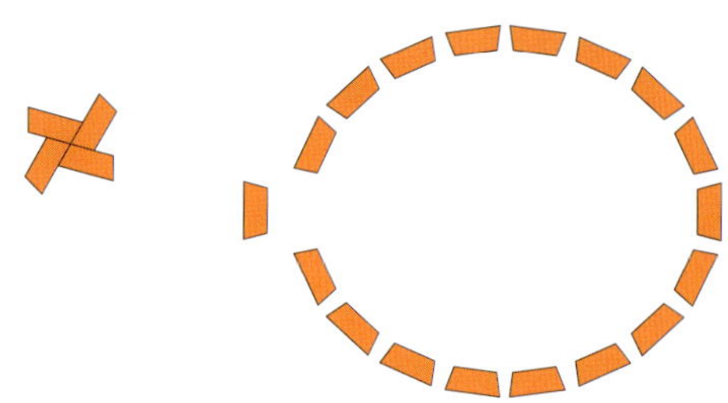

## 3 Intervention Catwalk

One of the programs that stimulates cultural life in the MuseumsQuartier is the MQ Vienna Fashion Week, which has been celebrated every year since 2001. The intervention built in spring 2005 for the Fashion Week was a catwalk set up in the center of the main courtyard. The platform for the models to show the designs was created using 16 modules to form a U shape in plan, which was later covered with a red carpet. A number of modular elements were piled up to build the backstage, where designers and models prepared for the show.

Spring 05

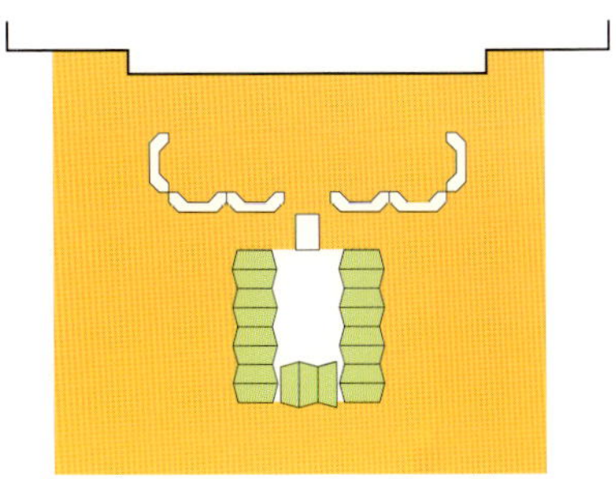

## 4 Intervention Igloos

"Igloos" was the first intervention built using the Enzi modular elements in winter 2002. The modular elements were piled on top of each other to build four small pavilions, each one with an igloo shape. Each pavilion was fitted with a steel door at the entrance. The blue color of the Enzi material reinforced the cold appearance of the igloos, especially by night. The igloo pavilions contained a bar inside where visitors could drink hot punch, making it a very popular place in winter. A curling court and a winter play area for children were placed close to the igloo pavilions.

Winter 02

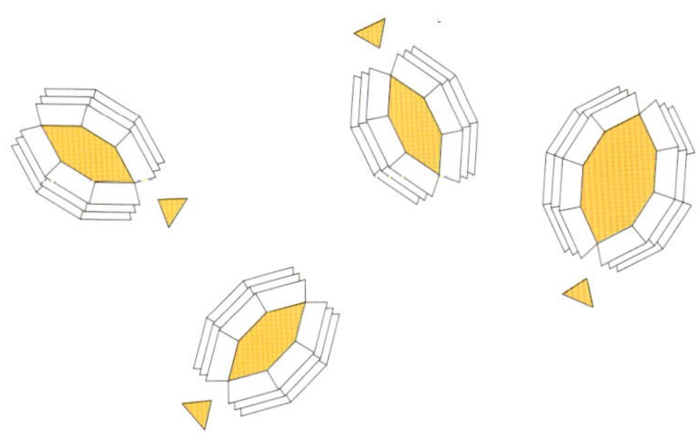

## 5 Intervention Icepalace

The intervention was built in winter 2005. The modular elements were combined to form the high walls of a large pavilion with an irregular footprint, which was known as the "Ice Palace". The pavilion was surrounded by many small seats and some tables, which were created using the same modular elements. DJ's played live music daily and visitors could play on a curling court.

Winter 05

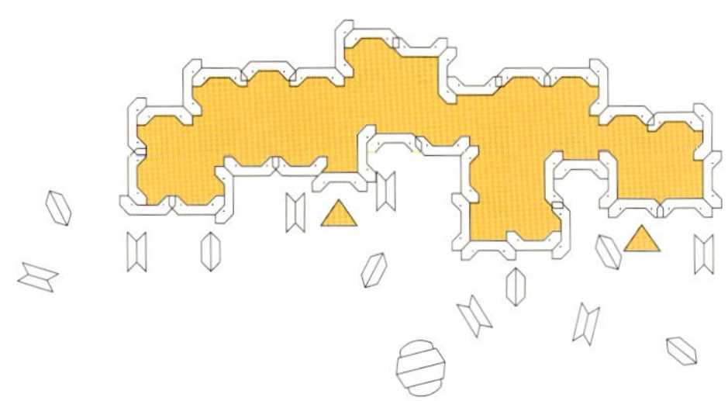

**Process** The Operating Company of the MuseumsQuartier (MuseumsQuartier E+B) initiated the process for developing the outdoor furniture in coordination with the owners of the MQ (the Republic of Austria and the City of Vienna). Wolfgang Waldner, the managing director of the MuseumsQuartier cultural complex, was the commissioner. Several young architecture offices were invited to participate in a competition to select the design to be realized and the team of architects to be in charge of proposing the layouts for the different interventions.

MuseumsQuartier E+B is in charge of programming cultural activities for the outdoor areas in the MuseumsQuartier. This cultural program makes use of the Enzi modular system to create the physical framework, which includes seating elements, small structures and pavilions for the performance of special events.

PPAG architects created the specific design for the modular elements by investigating their versatility based on geometric combinations in order to offer a high degree of variety. The architects, in collaboration with MuseumsQuartier E+B, also designed the layouts for the different interventions that have been built in past years. Some layouts are related to a specific program required by MuseumsQuartier E+B, while others are simply different lounge layouts designed to create a variety of experiences in public space.

## Cost, Financing and Maintenance

The initial total cost in 2002 was €270,000, which included production of the Enzi and the entire recreational program during the year for the MuseumsQuartier courtyard, with a surface of 13,250 m². That works out to a cost of around 20 euros/m². Since then, a yearly budget of approximately €50,000 has been spent on all kinds of interventions, including changes to the layout of the elements in order to create a new set for each season.

The Enzi was the first version of the design of the modular element. It was made of EPS (expanded polystyrene), a very light material that is easy to produce and to transport, though it is also very easy to damage.

The modular elements stayed outside in the MuseumsQuartier courtyards throughout the year. They were also periodically moved to create new configurations. In 2002 and 2003, the elements were used to build igloos which remained in place from November until December. During the winter months from 2005 to 2009 they formed the "Ice Palace." From January to April, the modular elements were arranged in the courtyard in various shapes and configurations. Any damaged elements were periodically restored and new pieces replaced the ones that could no longer be repaired.

In winter 2009, the majority of the elements were destroyed in a fire. In summer 2010 a new batch of furniture was acquired presenting some new features and modifications in the design. The new generation of furniture, called Enzos, are not only different in terms of design (they are hollow, unlike the Enzis) but also in terms of production. They are built from polyethylene, using a rotational molding system. Enzos are stronger, fireproof and more resistant to superficial damage.

## Timing

The temporary character of the interventions is one of the main factors that leads to the success of the strategy. The design can be arranged in different ways, generating a surprise effect each season, which stimulates citizens' curiosity. The public space of the MQ is associated with something dynamic and alive.

The concept of public space in a state of continuous change needs to be supported by a very well-defined strategy and a constant management system. The strategy was defined conceptually by MuseumsQuartier E+B from the beginning and formalized by PPAG with their design of the versatile Enzi elements. Since a strong management system is also required, every year PPAG architects design a new set of layouts and define a new cultural program which they coordinate in conjunction with MuseumsQuartier E+B.

In conventional public space interventions, the time factor is understood as a negative factor which deteriorates the original materialization, resulting in cost outlays for maintenance. In this project, however, it becomes a creative element integrated into the strategy to stimulate the use of public space.

## Use of the Public Space

Without any doubt, the strategy activates urban life in the MuseumsQuartier. The success of the activation of the use of public space is basically related to two main factors. First, the enclosed character of the complex of buildings where the MuseumsQuartier is located makes the spontaneous use of its interior courtyard more difficult when compared to other parts of the city which are easily accessible. A special attraction mechanism is required to stimulate public life in this urban context. The strategy creates a dynamic public space in continuous transformation in conjunction with the many changing cultural programs that take place in the buildings of the MuseumsQuartier, which results in attracting a large number of visitors.

Second, the use of public space during the whole year is stimulated by combining two symbiotic strategies. During the months of the year when citizens can spontaneously participate in outdoor activities because of good weather, the interventions consist of attractive and playful public space layouts based only on creative combinations of the modular elements. During the winter months, a complementary program of activities such as curling, hot punch bars and concerts stimulates the use of public space.

In the first place, the colorful and sculptural character of the interventions visually attracts all kinds of people and, second, it invites people to experience them. The human proportions and the ambiguity of the shape of the modular seating elements tempt different people to use them freely, encouraging citizens to invent their own personal ways of doing so. As a result, a particular relationship is created between each citizen and the objects.

## Impact on Citizens

The strategy developed in the MuseumsQuartier soon became very popular among the citizens of Vienna. Surprisingly, the Enzi elements invaded the Viennese lifestyle. They were reproduced in postcards, in children's coloring books and all kinds of objects. Newspapers and popular magazines published photos of many celebrities and politicians sitting on the Enzis. The Enzis became the symbol of a new creative and playful public space in the city and the interventions became the icon of its new cultural life.

However, the strategy did not just stimulate the use of public areas among visitors to the exhibitions and the cultural events celebrated in the buildings of the MuseumsQuartier. It also attracted many other citizens who did not intend to visit the exhibitions, such as young people and local residents who used the MuseumsQuartier courtyard as a meeting point and a pleasant area to relax. For many citizens, the courtyards became a vibrant part of the city's public space and not just the courtyard associated with a cultural building.

## Media Impact

The strategy for regenerating public life in the MuseumsQuartier had a large media impact. This was partly related to the fact that the opening of the large-scale cultural center initially received negative criticism from public opinion. The media was very sensitive to everything happening in the MuseumsQuartier and the positive reaction of citizens to the new interventions was widely broadcasted by newspapers, radio and television.

The Enzis projected a creative, playful and popular image of the MuseumsQuartier and the media was the vehicle in charge of promoting this image. The MuseumsQuartier's popularity grew fast and the amount of visitors has nearly doubled in ten years, from 2 million people in 2002 to 3.8 million in 2012.

The seasonal programming in the courtyard and its many activities help to maintain media interest. Newspapers and television periodically release news about new activities. The MuseumsQuartier has also become a tourist attraction in Vienna and the activities that take place in its courtyard are an important element of the cultural life in the city.

Test Case 03

## MORPHEUS, 798 ART ZONE
BEIJING, CHINA

STRATEGY / INTERVENTIONS: **Casanova+Hernandez**

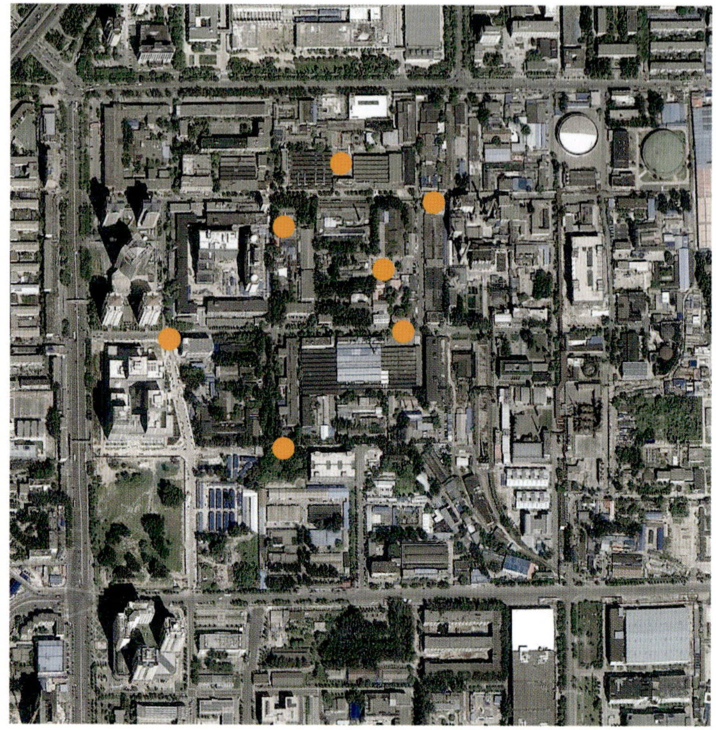

In recent years, 798 Art Zone, also called the Dashanzi Art District, has become the center for artistic activity in the city of Beijing. It is an industrial area that was built in the 1950s as the result of a collaborative program developed by the East German, Soviet and Chinese governments. In the wake of the economic reform carried out by Deng Xiaoping during the 1980s, activity in the area slowed to a halt little by little, leaving behind many abandoned factories.

In the year 2000, the Central Academy of Fine Arts (CAFA) definitively moved into factory 706 and many artists and designers began opening studios in the area, attracted by the big industrial spaces and low rents. A number of art galleries, including many international ones, set up in the area drawn by rapid growth in the Chinese art market. The district soon acquired international fame, which led to the emergence of a number of cultural centers, bookstores, cafes and restaurants. Ultimately, Dashanzi was established as an arts district and branded as 798 Art Zone, taking the name from factory 798, one of the most unique buildings that had been transformed into an artistic space.

In the process of transforming Dashanzi into a new area for culture, leisure and entertainment, public space took on a fundamental role that it did not have before. The streets and small squares, which had previously only been used for industrial transportation, needed to be transformed into places for meeting and relaxing, as well as into open-air exhibition spaces to serve as an extension of the art galleries' interiors. In this particular urban structure, the design of public space had the potential to be organized through a global strategy capable of transforming it into a vibrant space that would be able to change rapidly following the rhythm of the district's evolution.

**Strategy** The strategy is developed based on a series of independent interventions located in certain key points of 798 Art Zone. These points are concentrated near the new cultural and leisure spaces that need areas for relaxing in public space, in the intersections of pedestrian flows where meeting places could be created, or in other key places that could stimulate the spontaneous growth of new public uses around them in the future.

Office cluster

Sport cluster

Drink cluster

Lounge cluster

All the interventions together create a network that guides visitors through the district and provides uniformity to public space in spite of its considerable original spatial differentiation. The interventions are mixed with open-air artwork and cafe and restaurant terraces. Each intervention is designed so that its configuration can be changed coinciding with changes in the programming of the cultural centers in the district or to accompany the presentation of new exhibitions and events. As a result of this constant variation in the different interventions implemented in public space, the strategy is understood as an evolving or mutating strategy.

**Interventions** Each intervention located in a square, street or courtyard is made up of a series of sculptural elements called Morpheus, which all together are perceived as an artistic installation that relates to the outdoor sculptures from nearby galleries, while they also function as areas for relaxing, meeting points, or makeshift seats, providing a particular function and identity to each of the different areas in public space. Each Morpheus piece is designed so that it can be set up in three different positions. Depending on which position is selected, not only the appearance of the pieces changes but also their functions, since they can be used as chairs, chaise longues or stools.

Each mutating intervention is designed so that its configuration can be changed over time, transforming the appearance of public space and how people move through it, as well as how the intervention is used, depending on the position of its pieces. The Morpheus elements can be grouped into clusters of a few pieces in order to create more intimate areas that encourage joint activities. They can also be positioned randomly in space, creating more individualized areas for relaxation, or lined up to create circles or geometric shapes that virtually enclose part of the public space to encourage its use for artistic performances or concerts.

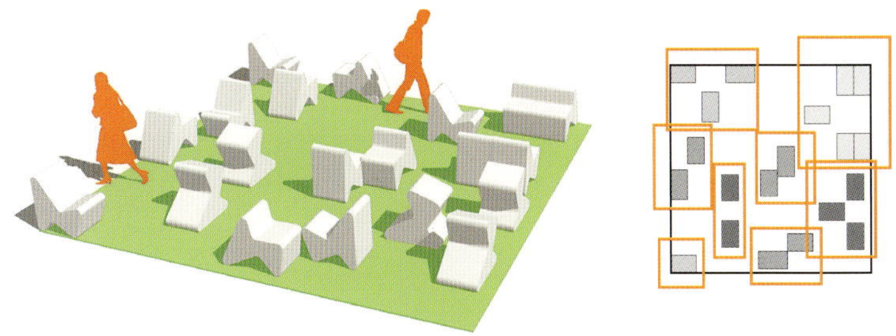

Geometric clusters

Organic clusters

Independent clusters

## Intervention 1: Courtyard

## Intervention 2: Alley

## Intervention 3: Street

## Intervention 4: Square

The rhythm for the transformation of the interventions depends on the conditions determined by each specific location, sometimes in relation to how often the exhibitions change in nearby galleries. Each mutating intervention can have a different rhythm of transformation and can work independently, although the strategy is ultimately conceived as a single whole.

Morpheus pieces can be produced using different materials and colors, such as concrete, steel, polyester, polyethylene, expanded polystyrene or biocomposite. This allows for optimizing the total duration of the strategy and the number of transformations of each intervention, by taking into account the resistance of the material used and the available budget for each intervention.

Although all the interventions are made up of volumetrically identical pieces, each specific intervention can take on a very different appearance through variations in the pieces, from homogeneity created by using Morpheus pieces made with the same material and positioned in the same way, to heterogeneity achieved by using Morpheus pieces in different positions, in different materials and a variety of colors.

## Four Main Positions of the Morpheus Element

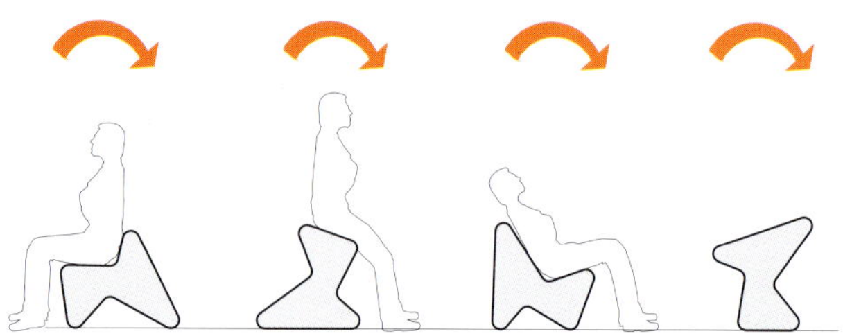

Position 1 chair | Position 2 stool | Position 3 chaise lounge | Position 4 table

## Materialization of the Morpheus Element

## Transformations of Intervention 1 over Time

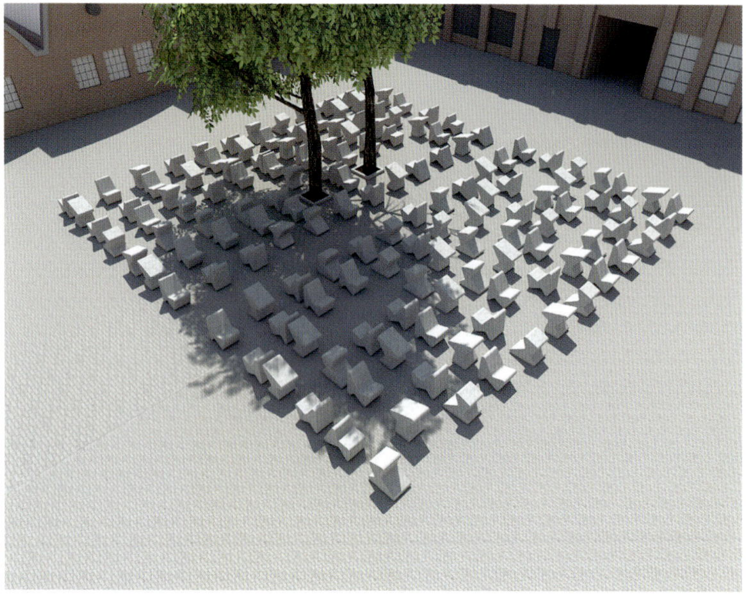

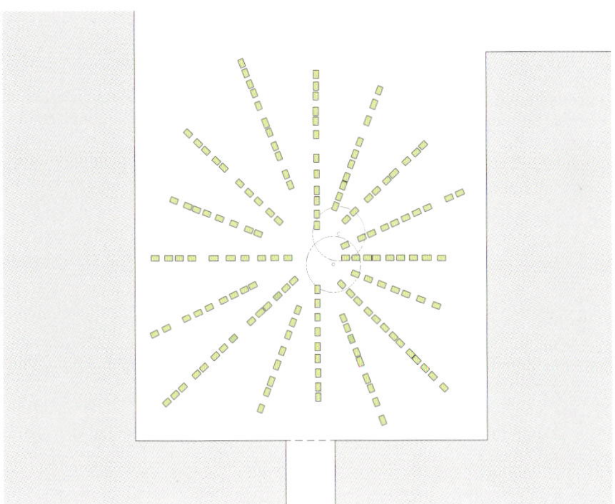

WE
GOTCHA
California since 1978

## GRASSSCAPES
## ANTWERP, BELGIUM

STRATEGY / INTERVENTIONS: **Casanova+Hernandez**

Antwerp Zuid is a neighborhood that is popularly known as "Little Paris" because of its urban layout, inspired by Haussmann's plan for the center of the French capital. Squares and boulevards appear as clear urban voids in a compact and uniform urban fabric, limited by precise geometric shapes such as triangles, squares, rectangles, octagons or circles.

Leopold de Waelplaats is one of the most important squares in Antwerp, where the building that houses the Royal Museum for Fine Arts, built in 1890, is located. The museum is surrounded by gardens, cafés and restaurants that work as an important culture and leisure pole in the area. In 1987, an old grain silo near the port was restored and transformed into the Museum of Modern Art (MuHKA), which extended this cultural pole toward the Schelde River. Later on, in 2004, the Fotomuseum opened in Waalsekaai, creating a cultural triangle formed by the three institutions that has led to the emergence of numerous art galleries, design boutiques, cafés and restaurants in nearby streets. While the opening of these new institutions has partially revitalized commercial activity around the new cultural facilities the program for public space has remained unchanged and has only come to life in certain areas as a result of the outdoor terraces of cafés and restaurants. Antwerp's Zuid district presents all the necessary conditions in terms of space (a large number of squares and boulevards) and program (its considerable cultural program) for carrying out a public space acupuncture strategy to enhance urban life by generating active, attractive and dynamic public space.

**Strategy** The strategy for Antwerp's Zuid district evolves over time, based on a series of interventions located in fixed, strategic points of public space. These points take advantage of the spatial qualities of the city's squares and boulevards to act as open-air urban rooms, each characterized by its own particular identity, though all together they generate a single image of the whole. In this way, the strategy is undertaken based on site-specific interventions that respond to the determining factors for each location (such as sun exposure, commercial activity at ground level, and vehicle and pedestrian traffic flows) and that evolve over time by adapting their morphology and function to the variations in climate conditions throughout the seasons of the year.

The character and function of each intervention is linked to the programming of the nearby cultural institution or group of galleries on a specific street, independently of the other interventions. At the same time, all the interventions are coordinated in order to avoid unnecessary duplications in programming.

**Interventions** Each intervention is intended to enclose an anonymous fragment of public space, providing it with program and meaning. The interventions often function as an extension of the adjacent museums and galleries and also have the ability to transform according to the changes in programming in the exhibition spaces. In this way, the intervention near the Fotomuseum can be used as a lounge area in spring, as an improvised open-air movie theater in summer, or as an outdoor exhibition area in fall.

The interventions are called Grassscapes in reference to their hybrid composition, made of a geometrized artificial landscape with a grass-like appearance that contrasts with the coldness of the hard pavement and the absence of vegetation, which characterizes most of the places where the interventions are located. Each intervention acts as a visual stimulus that attracts citizens' attention and activates the use of public space, creating alluring green oases where people can meet.

Each Grassscape is characterized by a green deck that incorporates seating areas at different heights and is covered by artificial grass. The soft appealing texture of the grass attracts passers-by, inviting them to use the intervention. The reduced dimensions of the Grassscape, similar to the dimensions of a living room, and the softness of its carpet-like floor transform a portion of the city's anonymous public space into a "domestic public space" with a strong identity. The different heights and positions of the green seats invite citizens to use the Grassscape in very different ways. It can become a children's playground, a lounge area, an open-air workspace, a picnic area, an improvised meeting room, an exercise room, a place for playing board games, or the stage for a street theater.

Intervention 1: MuHKA

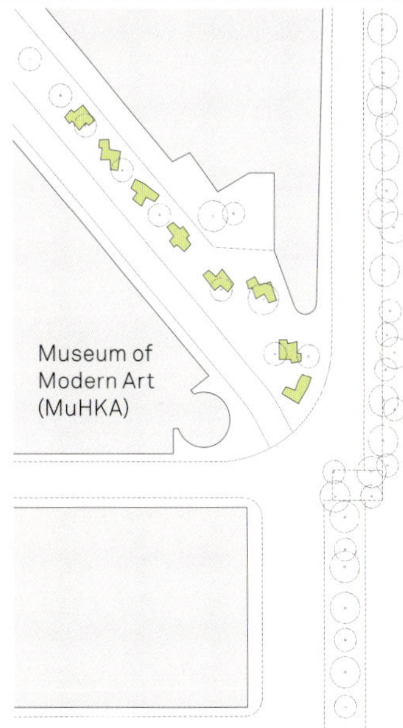


Intervention 2: Art Gallery Axis

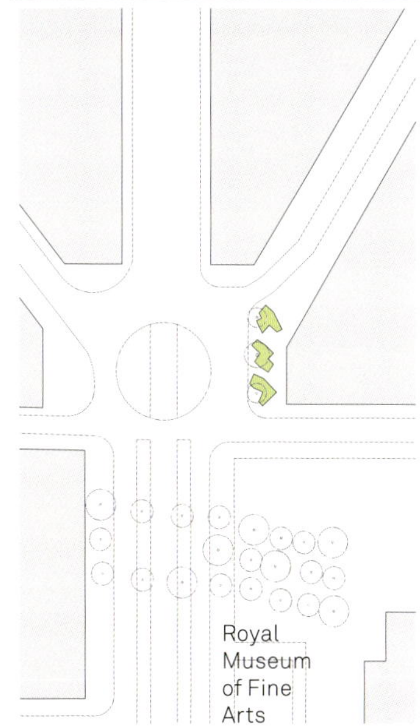


Intervention 3: Photo Museum

Intervention 4: Royal Museum of Fine Arts

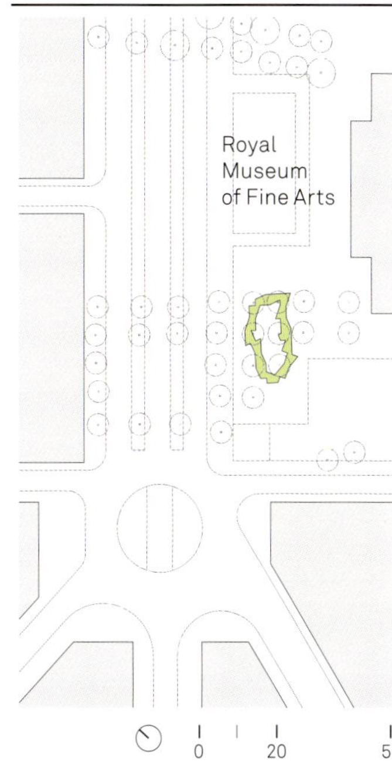

**System** Each Grassscape is made up of a series of modular elements that can be connected to create a wide variety of combinations, putting together an ample catalogue. This variety of elements lends enormous flexibility to the system. As a result, tailor-made interventions can be generated for installation in very different contexts. For instance, four elements can be combined together to create a compact square intervention, they can be placed in public space independently or they can be arranged following an irregular shape, creating an interior space. This space can integrate existing urban lighting or street trees into the intervention and can also create larger spaces, for a children's playground with sand or even an ice skating rink in winter.

Because each intervention is divided into small modular elements, they can be easily transported by truck. The elements can be assembled on site without using any special machinery, creating a single monolithic sculptural piece in just a few hours. The intervention can be easily dismantled in the future and reassembled in another location, thus becoming a nomad landscape. In this case, the mutating intervention is planned as an extremely flexible system that allows for rapid reconfiguration on site through the simple action of disassembling and reassembling the same pieces in a different arrangement.

## Catalog of Grassscapes Combining Four Elements

## Grassscape Layouts as Single Elements or Combined with Other Existing Street Elements

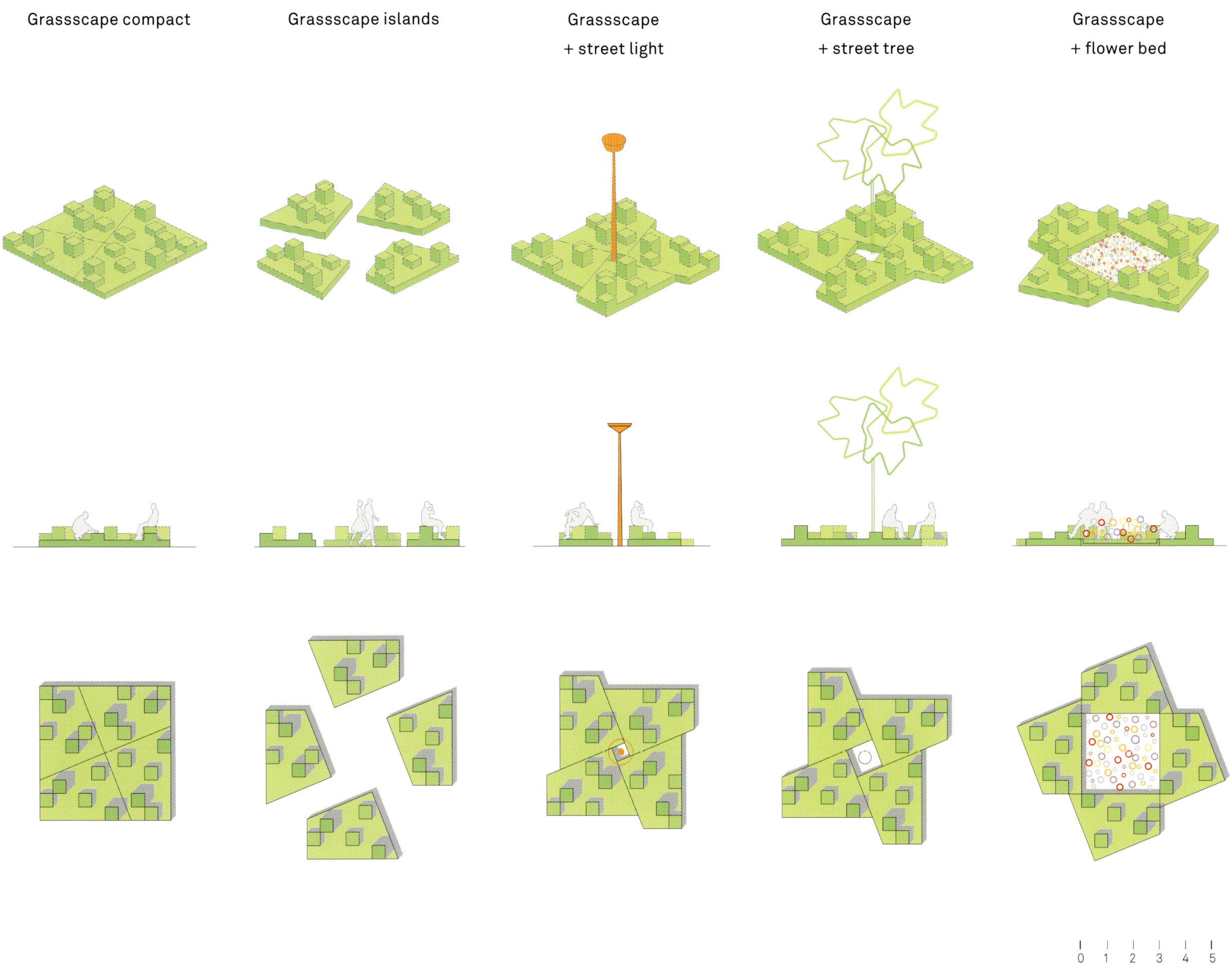

## Mutation of the Intervention at the Royal Museum of Fine Arts

Spring

Summer

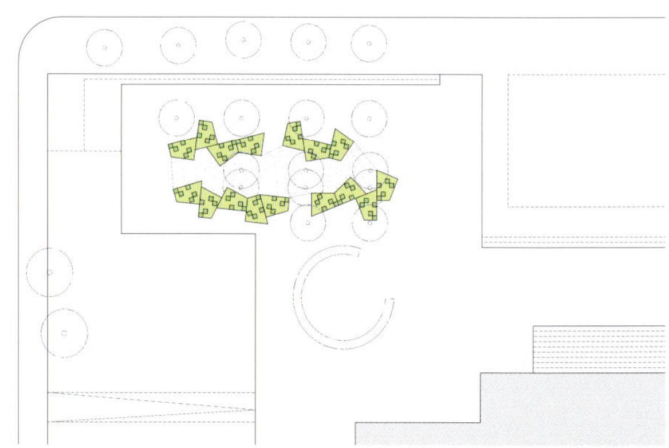

Autumn

Winter

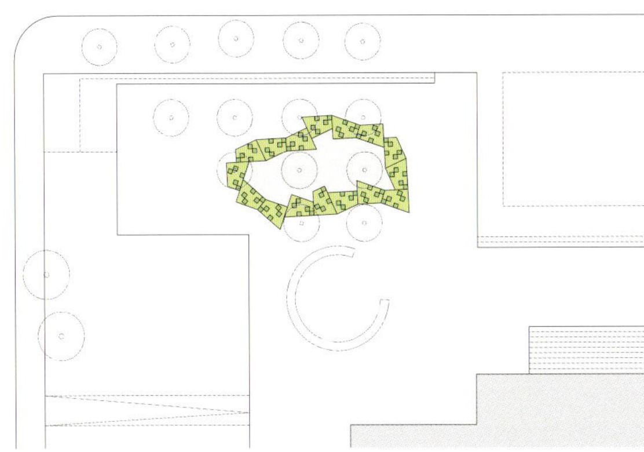

**Grassscape test intervention in Rotterdam** The impact of the Grassscape intervention in its simplest configuration, compact and square, have been tested and analyzed previously in Rotterdam's public space. This first version of the intervention, related to the nomadic intervention The Green Room, was installed in different locations in public space. Very different intensities and types of use were recorded, depending on factors such as pedestrian flow in the area, the type of nearby activities, and the visibility of the installation in public space.

Citizens tend to be more attracted to the intervention when there is a radical contrast between its plant-like aspect and the character of the urban surroundings. This is especially the case with children, who often use it as a place to play, jumping off the different platforms. On the other hand, it has also been observed that, due to its small dimensions, people of different ages, genders and social groups who share the Grassscape often engage in conversation, which might never have occurred otherwise.

## Grassscape Construction

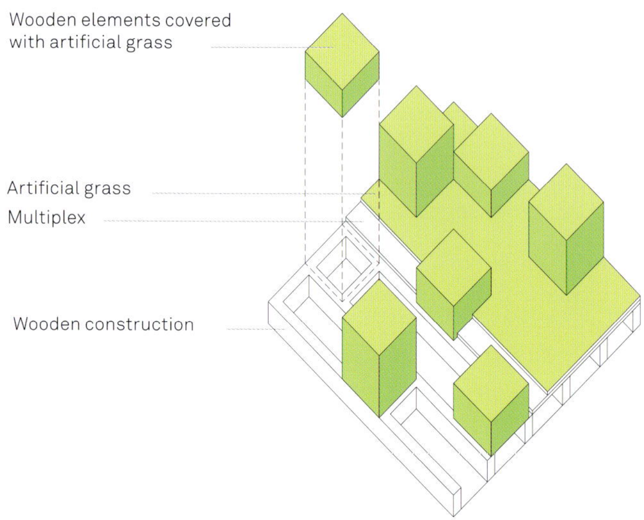

# Long-Term Strategies Based on Temporary Interventions

“You have to change to stay the same” is a well-known quote by the artist Willem De Kooning, which he frequently used to describe the challenge that contemporary artists face in maintaining their art alive over time. Maintaining public space constantly alive also requires the reflexes De Kooning referred to, and it implies a constant questioning of what exists in order to modify it and adapt it to an ever-changing context. This way of understanding public space, not as a unique entity that is static over time, but as a sequence of temporary interventions that are always changing to adapt to the reality in every moment, demands an extra effort that can only be effective and feasible if it is channeled through a calculated strategy.

Conventionally, the design of public space elements such as streets, boulevards and squares has a limited lifespan, since the natural deterioration of the materials used, damages resulting from accidents and acts of vandalism, or a decrease in use due to changes in the surroundings at some point make their partial renovation, and in many cases their complete transformation, a necessity. In light of this fact, new alternative interventions in public space take into account the estimated lifespan of the work to a greater extent, adjusting design and materials to achieve a more efficient and sustainable product. At the same time, the careful synchronization of an adequate program of activities with the lifespan of the intervention helps to promote maximum use of the public space during that period.

The need to maintain and renew public space is not understood in this case as a tedious and costly burden to be combated by creating more durable designs, but rather as an opportunity for keeping public space up to date. If parts of public space have to be subject to continuous renewal, strategies that are based on short-term interventions that overlap over time can be a solution for breathing new energy into urban life. Designing with the idea of temporariness does not just mean designing with flexibility, it can also imply designing with sustainability in the precise choice involving the durability of the materials according to the programmed lifespan of the intervention.

A well-known example of a long-term strategy based on temporary interventions realized in public space was the one developed by Aldo van Eyck between 1947 and 1978 which consisted of creating more than 700 interventions that transformed the many vacant lots and unused small interstitial spaces in Amsterdam’s public space into children’s playgrounds.[1] The strategy provided a response to the growing need for children’s play areas, while also fostering

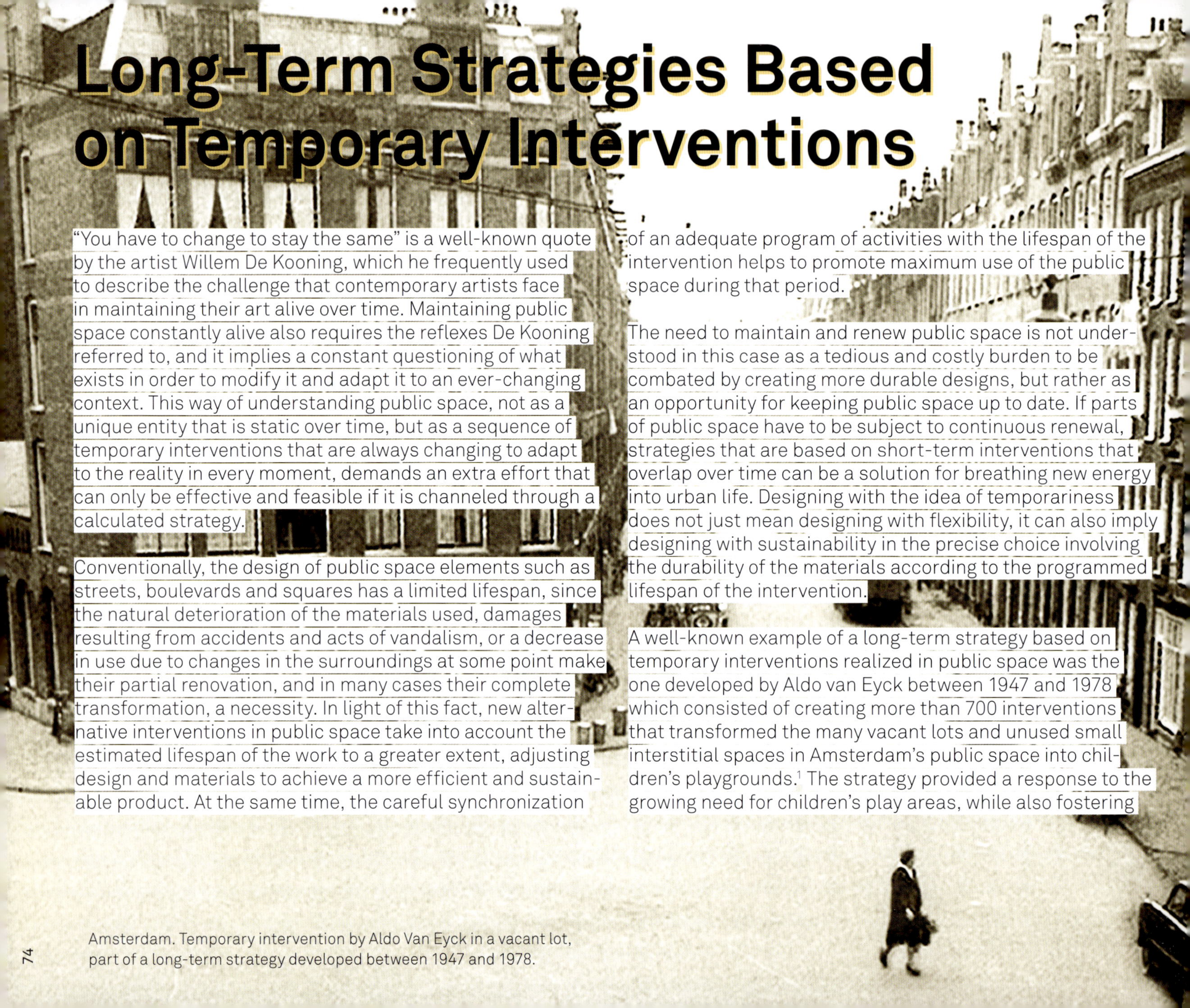

Amsterdam. Temporary intervention by Aldo Van Eyck in a vacant lot, part of a long-term strategy developed between 1947 and 1978.

the use of public space and citizen interaction. For more than thirty years, temporary interventions were created and subsequently demolished as other new interventions were being built in other places. Each intervention took on a more or less temporary nature, while the overall strategy had a long-term duration that spanned several decades.

At present, one of the challenges for contemporary urban design is envisioning a living city over the long term, at a time when society, the economy and citizens' needs are changing very rapidly, especially given the fact that public space has traditionally been managed by public bodies that centralize the decision-making power with respect to its design, maintenance and renewal. This centralization means that in many cases urban public space is understood as a single project directed by municipal specialists who are concerned, above all, with controlling costs and management efficiency. This management efficiency often translates into a tendency to unify the design of public space based on a pre-selected catalog of urban furniture and design solutions that clash head on with the existing urban reality, which tends to be characterized by substantial physical and social diversity, subjected to rapid transformation.

Assuming that it is more effective from the standpoint of municipal management to maintain certain uniformity in the conception of urban public space, there is a growing interest in many cities in developing parallel or complementary strategies that act temporarily on specific points within the network of public space. These urban acupuncture strategies are highly flexible and dynamic and are sometimes coordinated by independent teams or groups working in parallel with municipal experts. These teams tend to have a certain amount of autonomy in generating their own strategies, which are made up of coordinated temporary interventions that can be executed quickly and are easy to dismantle or that may be based on a fleet of mobile interventions that can travel to different points in the city to supplement the fluctuating shortages of facilities in each neighborhood. Like in a city with two speeds, these urban acupuncture strategies need a very dynamic team and management system that allows for constant monitoring of urban activity and certain autonomy to allow for making rapid decisions concerning the interventions.

1. Liane Lefaivre, Ingeborg de Roode, Rudolf Herman Fuchs, *Aldo van Eyck: The Playgrounds and the City*. Stedelijk Museum, Amsterdam, 2002

Case Study C

# "THIS IS NOT A VACANT LOT" PROJECT
## SARAGOSSA, SPAIN

STRATEGY / INTERVENTIONS: **Patrizia Di Monte, technical office Estonoesunsolar, Zaragoza Vivienda**

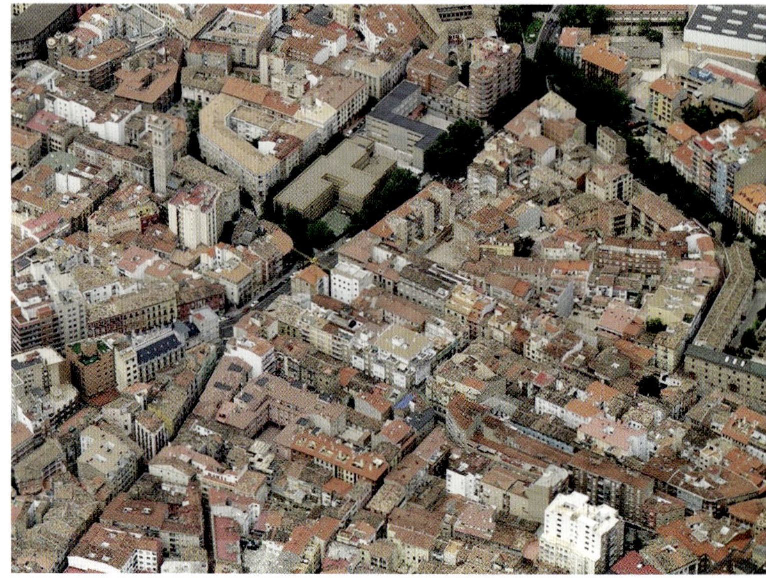

The urban deterioration in certain areas of Saragossa's historic center can be seen in the emergence of a large number of visibly abandoned vacant lots. In parallel to this urban decline, a growing number of immigrants have been moving into disadvantaged areas of the city, coinciding with locals moving out into new residential neighborhoods in the suburbs. These rapid social changes have generated profound transformations in the demographic structure of the historic city center, resulting in the increase of the number of immigrant families and children in the area. Finally, the irruption of the financial crisis in Spain led to an increase in unemployment, which has initially impacted more intensely on the immigrant population living in these areas. All these factors have contributed to an unusual situation brought on by a spiral of events which have caused urban decline and have the potential to create serious social problems in the future, as has been the case in the historic centers of other European cities.

Given this situation, the Saragossa City Council developed a strategy called "Estonoesunsolar" ("This is not a vacant lot"), coordinated by the architect Patrizia di Monte. A technical office was created to provide rapid and effective responses to some of the urban problems mentioned above. The technical office, which depends on the municipal entity Zaragoza Vivienda, combined an employment plan for jobless people in the area with a plan for cleaning up the vacant lots of land that was later transformed into a strategy for enabling public use of those abandoned lots. In this way, the walls and fences around numerous public and private abandoned lots in Saragossa's dense historic center were torn down. The lots were cleaned up and many were transformed into small public squares, children's playgrounds and community gardens integrated into the city's network of urban public spaces.

The time factor played a crucial role in the strategy's development and the quick reaction time combined with the technical office's operational autonomy were some

of the keys to its success. The office was run on a limited budget, most of which was used to pay the salaries of people participating in the employment plan. The remaining money was spent on the materials used in the interventions. In the first year, the office carried out 14 interventions in public space and in the second year, 15. In this way, the process of obtaining the lot owners' permission for each intervention, choosing a specific use for the lot based on citizen participation, designing each intervention and its subsequent construction all took place within an average period of four weeks per intervention. At the same time, the technical office's ability to react quickly in managing and maintaining the completed interventions was essential to guaranteeing the strategy's success and, when necessary, the least successful interventions were modified, serving as a learning experience toward improving future interventions.

The fact that the strategy "This is not a vacant lot" operates on land that will eventually house construction, implies that it can only be based on temporary interventions. Although each intervention will remain in place for a shorter or longer period depending on the lot's availability, the overall strategy has been planned as a long-term strategy that includes the possibility of acquiring a permanent character. Permanency could be achieved by generating a cycle in which, at the same time that temporary interventions are dismantled to build on some lots, new temporary interventions are installed on other abandoned lots so that the number of interventions in use is maintained more or less constant. In this way, "This is not a vacant lot" establishes a long-term public space acupuncture strategy based on temporary interventions.

Espacios

Reocupando el vacío

estonoesunsolar

Strategy published in local and national newspapers such as "La Vanguardia"

**Urban Analysis** Most of the interventions in the program "This is not a vacant lot" are located in the historic center of Saragossa, which includes the former Roman city of Caesaraugusta, founded in 12 B.C., and its subsequent extension until the 19th century. Only a few of the recent interventions are located in new areas of the city developed during the 20th century.

The historic center of Saragossa presents a mix of hybrid residential buildings with commercial spaces on the street level, combined with some working activities. Users of public space in the intervention areas are mostly residents of nearby neighborhoods, eventually mixed with visitors from other parts of the city and office workers.

## Aerial View

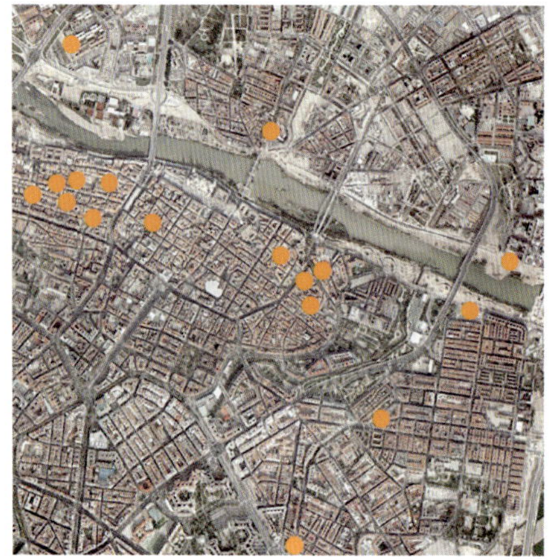

## Users

Neighborhood residents

City residents

Office workers

Tourists

## Relation to the City

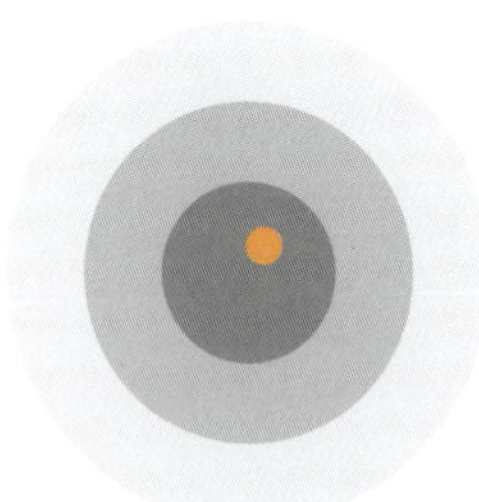

(Old) City center

Initial city expansions

Suburbs

Interventions

## Historic Urban Development

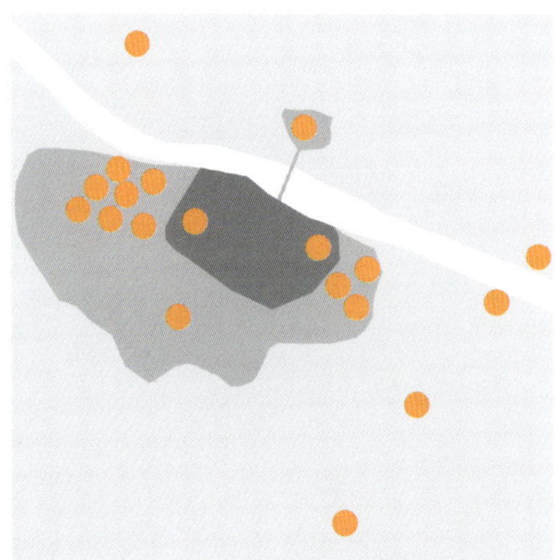

24 b.C.

Pre-18th century

Post-19th century

Interventions

## Activities

Residential

Public buildings

Offices

Industrial

Shops

Hotels

**Social Analysis** The growing population of elderly people living in Saragossa's historic city center has recently been compensated by a growing number of young immigrants. In the study area, immigrants represent 25.5% of the population, whereas the average percentage of immigrants in Saragossa as a whole is just 15.6%. The concentration of immigrant population has led to an increase in young people and families living in the area, but it has also raised the unemployment rate in the neighborhood, 14% in 2011, which is higher than the city's average.

## Age Structure

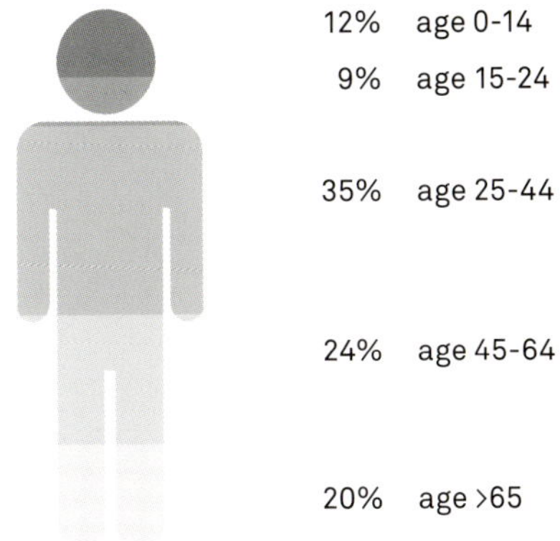


## Household Composition

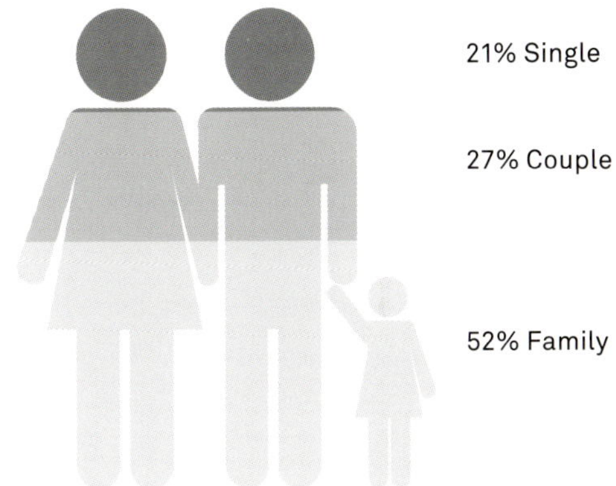

## Immigration

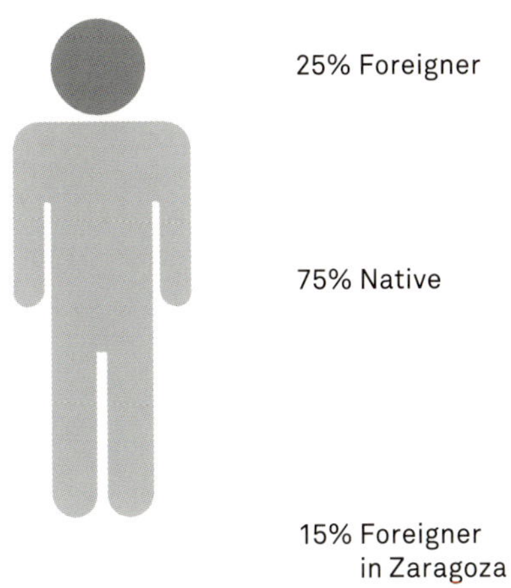


## Unemployment

Age structure and Immigration: Casco Histórico area Source Ayuntamiento de Zaragoza Unidad de Estadística y Gestión Padronal 2011. Household composition: Zaragoza city area Source INE 2001. Unemployment: Zaragoza city area Source FUNDEAR 2011.

**Interventions** The strategy is composed of dozens of interventions, many of them concentrated in the city center, though some have also been built near the river and in other neighborhoods.

Five interventions have been selected to be studied in detail: two are located in San Pablo neighborhood, in the west of the old city center; two are located in La Magdalena neighborhood, in the east; and one is in Las Fuentes neighborhood.

## 1 Intervention San Blas 94

The empty lot, which is limited by the walls of nearby buildings along three sides and opens toward the street on just one side, was opened to the public in 2009.

The space was designed as a thematic garden divided into 4 areas: shrubs, aromatic plants, creepers, and flowers and it is linked to schools and education centers for the promotion of educational and recreational activities. Some benches and an informal bicycle parking area are located in front of the garden. The name "Estonoesunsolar", together with the digit "1" printed in green on one wall of the site, brand the strategy and designate the first intervention in the series.

## 2 Intervention Armas 92

This intervention, located near "San Blas 94", was developed in collaboration with Santo Domingo public school and the children's association Cadeneta in order to transform the lot into an urban garden for recreational and educational purposes. Two containers, painted in the characteristic green color used for branding the entire strategy, serve as storage space and house a winter garden where small plants are grown. The lot is fenced and is used exclusively by people in the neighborhood and the owners of the gardens.

Accesses
Relaxation areas
Sitting areas
Circulation
Vegetation

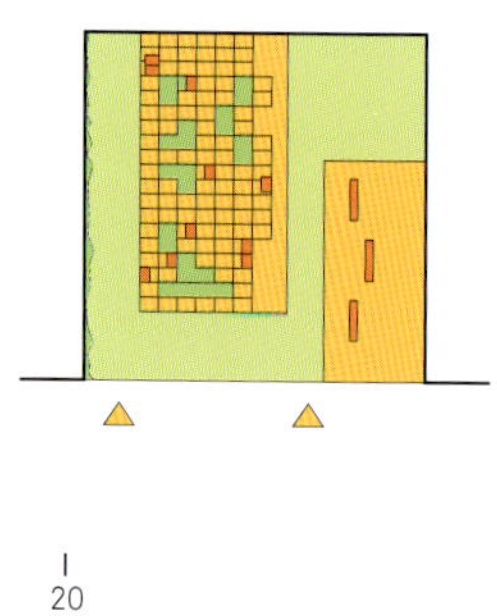


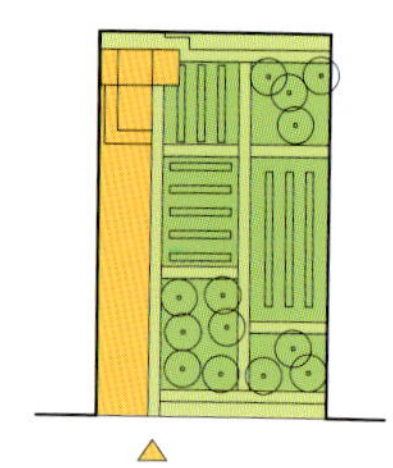

## 3 Intervention Coso 182

This intervention was designed in collaboration with the children from Gusantina primary school, located in the neighborhood. A design atelier and a competition for children between the ages of 5 and 12 resulted in the selection of a winning design, which was subsequently implemented on the site. The involvement of children and parents in the programming and design of the public space was intended to inspire civic pride and raise awareness among neighbors about the urban environment, thus promoting a feeling of belonging. Benches, streetlights and a podium are combined with murals along the lot walls, painted by well-known street artists.

## 4 Intervention San Agustín 25

The pavement on the site was painted in many colors to depict typical children's games, word searches and a small-scale race course. The colorful paintings contrast with the neutral color of the concrete and the whole intervention relies on the use of something immaterial such as paint to transform the lot into a playground. The use of elements that are also present in other interventions, such as the bike racks, the program logo, and a big "5" painted on the wall representing the intervention's number indicate that this intervention is part of a general strategy.

## 5 Intervention San José

The intervention combines a children's playground with facilities for people affected by Alzheimer's disease. Children learning new words come together with adults, many of an advanced age, who need to exercise their memories every day to keep from forgetting the words they already know. Patrizia Di Monte collaborated with a nearby association that takes care of people affected by Alzheimer's disease in order to create a design that integrates special signs to help patients exercise their memories as they walk along the paths through the intervention. A number of tables, sitting areas and prints on the old walls refer to the residential functions that the place once had and lend the intervention a certain domestic character.

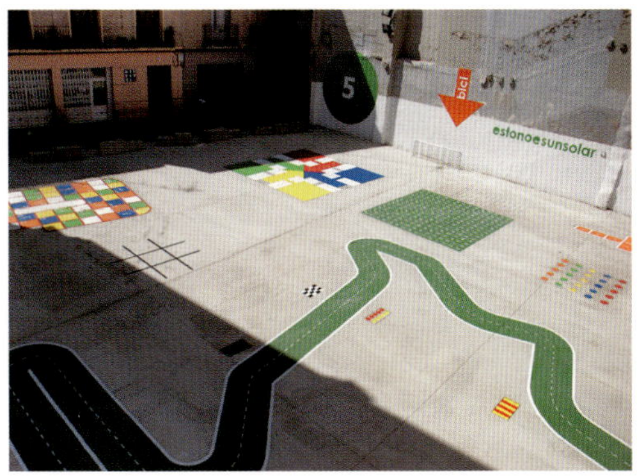

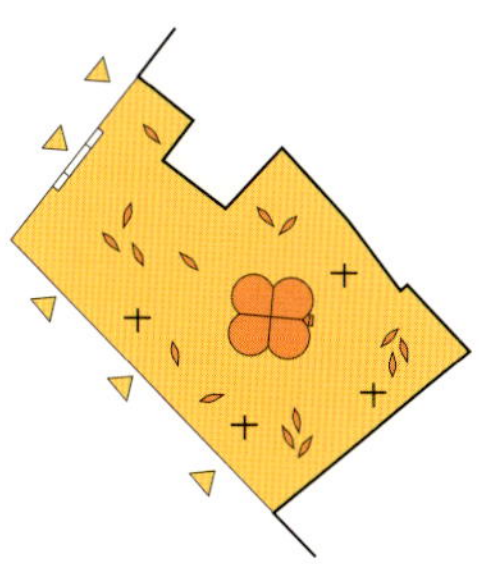

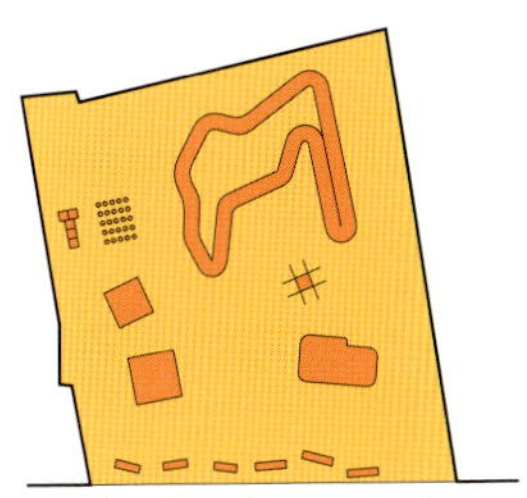

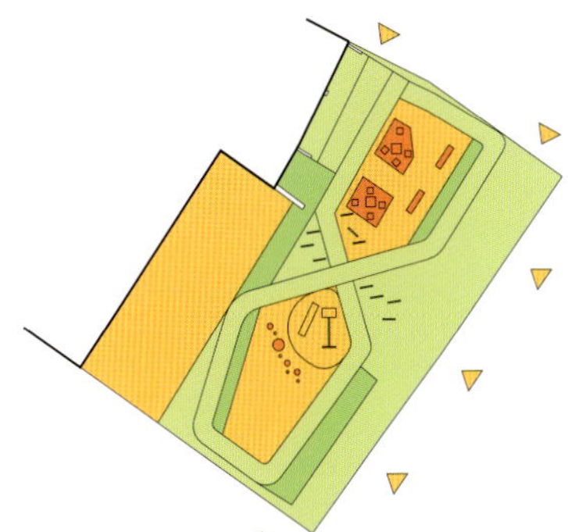

**Process** Zaragoza Vivienda, an organism that depends on the municipality of Saragossa, initiated the strategy in 2009. In 2010, it created the special office called "This is not a vacant lot", the main actor responsible for developing the strategy and dealing with the realization, management and maintenance of all the interventions.

The strategy's initial goal was to combine an employment plan, providing work for long-term unemployed people, with a rehabilitation plan intended to clean up the many vacant lots in Saragossa's city center in order to improve its physical condition. Based on her previous urban studies focused on vacant lots in Saragossa, Patrizia Di Monte, the architect in charge of the "This is not a vacant lot" technical office, proposed demolishing the fences and walls that isolated those lots from public space. By doing this, the empty lots were integrated into the urban network of the city's public space for as long as they remained unbuilt.

The technical office team consists of an architect, who is in charge of the coordination and design of the interventions, a technical architect in charge of the construction, and a manager in charge of controlling the costs. The realization of the interventions was carried out with a group of 40 people participating in the reintegration and unemployment plan. They learned the necessary techniques for building the interventions, assisted by the technical architect.

## Citizen Participation

Citizen participation is widely integrated into the strategy in order to involve local residents in the decision-making process and the design of each intervention. Participation is organized through a series of meetings between the technical office architect and the main local actors: the councils of the affected districts, neighborhood associations, public schools, children's organizations and senior citizens' centers. During those meetings, the neighborhood's needs are discussed and a program is determined. The neighborhood's urban planning commission is also invited to supervise the program and design of the lot, in accordance with city regulations.

Other types of citizen participation have been tested during the strategy. In one of the interventions, the final design was the result of a design competition organized with the participation of children from a nearby school. The children were involved in a workshop, together with their teachers and the technical office architect. The winning design was then developed and carried out by the technical office. The children's participation in the design phase of the intervention played an educational role, but it was also intended to engage parents and residents in the project. It reinforced the relationship between citizens and public space, which translated into increased respect for urban elements, thus reducing vandalism and the need for maintenance.

## Cost, Financing and Maintenance

The available budget for the development of the strategy "This is not a vacant lot" and the construction of the interventions from July to December 2009 was €1 million. Using this budget, 14 vacant lots were opened to the public and transformed into public spaces (12 private vacant lots and 2 public ones). In addition, 44 vacant lots were cleaned and painted fulfilling the program's original objective. This urban renewal encompassed a total surface area of 9,800 m². The €1 million budget was used to pay 40 people's salaries and to cover the expenses for the materials used in the interventions, at a cost of €200,000.

Between June and December 2010, 3 times more public space was transformed than in 2009, reaching a total of 32,000 m², distributed among 15 vacant lots, all of which were publicly owned. The total budget for 2010 was €1.2 million, which was used to pay salaries to 61 people and to cover the costs of the material used to realize the interventions. The low budget made it difficult to use standard urban furniture elements and made it necessary to develop a specific and creative design solution for each intervention. Only the children's playground equipment was purchased separately. The rest of the elements were all built by the working team.

The technical office and the working team were responsible for the management, construction, maintenance and demolition of all the interventions, in keeping with a fixed budget, and working independently from the other municipality services. The interventions enjoy a special status in comparison with the rest of the city's public space. Although they can be considered part of the public domain, many of them are not built on public land, but rather on private property. At any time, the lot owner has the right to build and the technical office is responsible for dismantling the intervention with the help of the working team contracted by Zaragoza Vivienda.

## Timing

The strategy is based on the temporary activation of inactive parts of the city. In periods of economic crisis, the time span during which vacant lots remain inactive is extended. Flexible strategies based on the temporary occupation of empty lots create a rapid positive effect in dense urban environments. However, at the same time they require a flexible management structure that is capable of reacting quickly.

In 2009, the technical office of "This is not a vacant lot" had the priority to develop the vacant lots located in Saragossa's historic center, following a pedestrian route that was designed to link them. Even though most of the lots were privately owned, the strategy was very successful and the number of realized interventions grew at a frenetic pace.

In 2010, the project was already very popular and it was extended to other areas of the city. The interventions were carried out chronologically, based on the order in which requests from the city's different district councils were received. The technical office also proposed a number of public lots to house interventions, which were interesting because of their strategic positions within Saragossa's urban structure such as the river front, or others because they were important for reinforcing the network of interventions.

The interventions' lifespan is variable and depends on the availability of the lots. The long-term scenario foresees a stable strategy based on a variable number of interventions, which change location within the urban structure of the city depending on the gradual construction on vacant lots and the creation of new ones.

## Use of Public Space

The strategy "This is not a vacant lot" has resulted in a general improvement in the use of public space in the city of Saragossa. First, because it created public areas in a dense urban city center and second, because these areas were successfully programmed with activities related to the needs of people who live in those neighborhoods.

However, the overall positive influence of the strategy does not mean that all the interventions were entirely successful. Some of the interventions that experimented with publicly accessible urban gardens experienced maintenance problems and after one year of use they were in such a state of deterioration that they had to be transformed into interventions that were easier to maintain. On the contrary, some urban garden interventions where specific groups or institutions have been responsible for the maintenance are still in good state.

The main criticism of the strategy by some residents has to do with the lack of use of few interventions and their quick deterioration. The temporary and innovative nature of the strategy promotes experimentation with a variety of programs and designs in the lots, in order to test their viability. If the test is successful, the program or design can be implemented in other lots. If not, the management team can quickly transform the intervention, having learned from the experience.

## Impact on Citizens and in the Media

Citizen response to the strategy was very positive. A large number of groups and neighborhood associations were very enthusiastic about the results. The strategy originated such high expectations among citizens that the technical office could not respond to the large number of demands for new interventions.

"This is not a vacant lot" has also had a positive influence on citizens' perception of their own city and the role of the public administration. The transformation of private and unused land into something public and useful bears a strong social message, especially in times of economic crisis. Part of the strategy's success in terms of public opinion was based on breaking with conventional thinking as dictated by the bureaucratic institutional machinery. The fact that the public administration was involved in that kind of transformation, that they were capable of developing an administrative mechanism to make it possible, resulted in strong support from citizens and has opened the door to a new relationship among the city, its citizens and the municipal institutions.

The mass media impact of "This is not a vacant lot" has been enormous. From the beginning of the project, local newspapers supported the strategy with front-page news stories and full-length articles. Later, the most important national newspapers, along with television and radio stations, also gave attention to the project. The first effect of this media attention was an increase in citizens' interest in participating in the project. The second effect was that the municipality increased economic support for the project, programming more interventions and involving more people.

Test Case 05

## TEMPORARY INTERVENTIONS IN VACANT LOTS
## MADRID, SPAIN

STRATEGY: **La Casa Encendida**
STRATEGY / INTERVENTIONS: **Casanova+Hernandez**

Between 1997 and 2007 the Spanish economy underwent rapid growth. This growth was associated with speculation in the real estate market, which brought about the so-called "real estate bubble". As a result, average housing prices tripled over a period of ten years. When the real estate bubble burst in 2008 in the wake of the international financial crisis, the construction industry was suddenly paralyzed. Many housing developers and construction companies went bankrupt and construction projects ground to a halt. Because of this situation, a large number of cities were left with vacant lots because old buildings had been demolished to make way for new ones, but plans had been put on hold due to the economic crisis.

The program Urbanacción put forward a reflection on the temporary use of urban vacant lots in the city of Madrid. The existence of vacant lots is a natural phenomenon associated with urban renovation, where old buildings are demolished so that new ones can be built. Given that the ultimate goal of urban renovation is economic profit, the process tends to be very dynamic and vacant lots tend to remain empty for only a short period of time, since the construction of new buildings usually takes place immediately after demolition is finished. However, this dynamic rhythm slowed down after the real estate bubble burst and an increase in the length of time during which lots remain inactive opens the door to an interesting field for experimentation in public space acupuncture.

Aldo Van Eyck playground on a vacant lot. Dijkstraat, Amsterdam, 1954

**Strategy** The high density of construction concentrated in Madrid's city center and the shortage of public meeting places in certain areas led to the idea of creating temporary public use on the many unused vacant lots. The strategy's duration depends on the availability of enough vacant lots, since construction is likely to coincide with the reactivation of the economy. The project is outlined as a medium-term or long-term strategy made up of independent temporary interventions. As construction takes place on the lots, the interventions will gradually be taken down and new ones will be created in order to maintain a relatively constant number of active interventions at any given time.

The strategy activates inactive areas of the city, transforming private abandoned space into temporary programmatically active public space. The strategy takes into account changes in the location of activated areas as time goes by, depending on the availability of lots, yet it always ensures an adequate balance between uses and distances from one intervention to the next in order to maintain the intensity of action. This control of the time factor characterizes the proposal as a long-term public space acupuncture strategy based on temporary interventions.

Phase 1: A Few Test Interventinos Are Built on Vacant Lots

Next phases: When the Interventions Are Dismantled due to Construction on the Lots, New Ones Are Installed on Other Vacant Lots

Fenced-in vacant lot in Madrid

**Interventions** The temporary interventions are developed following two main steps:

1. Transforming private lots into public space, while codifying them as belonging to a coordinated strategy.
2. Programming the lots with activities related to residents' needs in nearby areas.

Because the historic center of Madrid is dense and compact, the demolition of existing buildings generates interesting urban voids. Depending on their location, on a corner lot or between party walls, they are limited spatially by the horizontal plane of the ground along with one, two or three vertical planes. Each urban void is associated with the color that is used to dye the polyurethane foam, which acts as thermal isolation when it is sprayed onto the party walls, and that also characterizes the vegetation planted on the lot.

Therefore, each intervention is defined by the binomial formed by the mineral pigment used to dye the vertical planes that limit the lot and the species of vegetation planted on the horizontal planes. Some examples of these binomials include: chrome green - *Hedera helix*; cadmium yellow - *Helianthus agnus*; and manganese violet - *Lavandula angustifolia.*

The strategy is based on low-cost interventions in terms of realization and maintenance, since in any case the coloring on the party walls is functionally necessary in order to protect the spray foam from ultra-violet light. Besides that, in certain types of interventions, costs can be minimized by encouraging collaboration from residents in the development and management of the interventions.

The intense coloring of the lot's interior space contrasts with the neutrality of the urban façade. From dead and abandoned urban space, each lot becomes a living place with a certain artistic value. The color code provides each intervention with a distinct particular identity, which distinguishes it from the urban surroundings and from the other interventions. On an urban scale, the set of interventions emphasizes an ever-changing network of urban voids, creating vibrant, dynamic public space recognizable by its intense chromatic variety.

Yellow cadmium

+

Helianthus annuus

Green chrome

Hedera helix

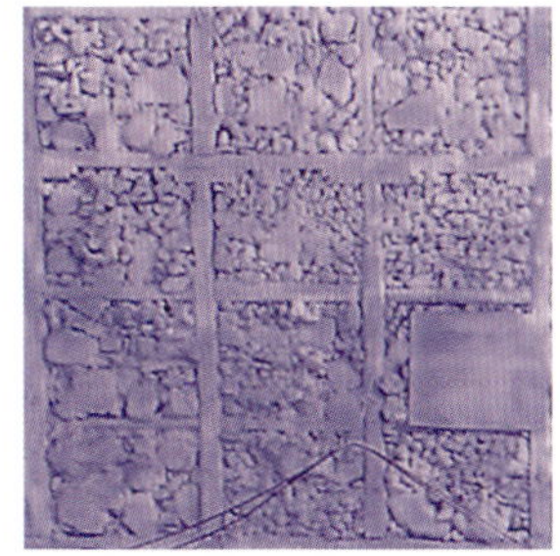

Violet manganese

Lavandula angustifolia

The color code also relates each lot to a specific type of activity. Green is associated with a small urban garden including a lounge area, where the activity level is low. Yellow designates a children's playground and an exercise area for senior citizens. Lastly, violet represents cultural activity, where the lot is equipped with an open-air library provided with free Wi-Fi and classrooms or workshops where residents can exchange knowledge.

There are varying levels of complexity involved in the implementation, maintenance and management of the programs according to the three types of interventions, from low complexity in the green interventions to the highest level in the violet or cultural interventions.

Each type of intervention is characterized by a different level of citizen participation in its programming and function. It can range from no participation at all in the green interventions to active implication in programming, organization and participation in workshops in the case of the violet interventions. This differentiation allows for the interventions to be implemented progressively, adjusting the level of participation for each strategy to its acceptance among residents, while helping to control the costs of the initial investment and maintenance, thus guaranteeing the strategy's sustainability.

The program and the level of citizen participation are distributed throughout the urban fabric depending on residents' needs and the potential of each lot. This generates a coordinated strategy where color, in addition to playing an artistic role, creates a code that helps to structure and differentiate spaces and programs.

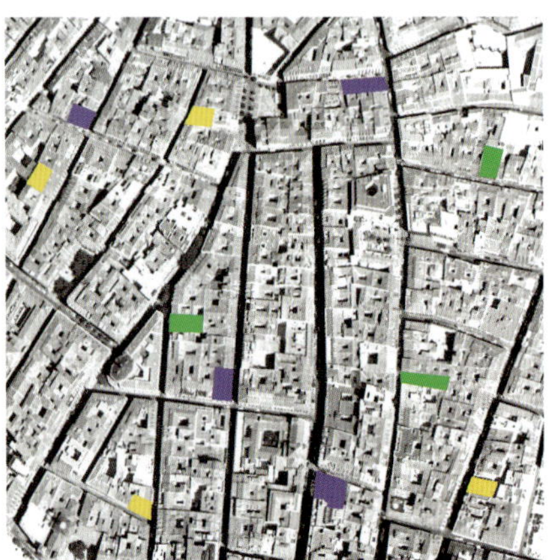

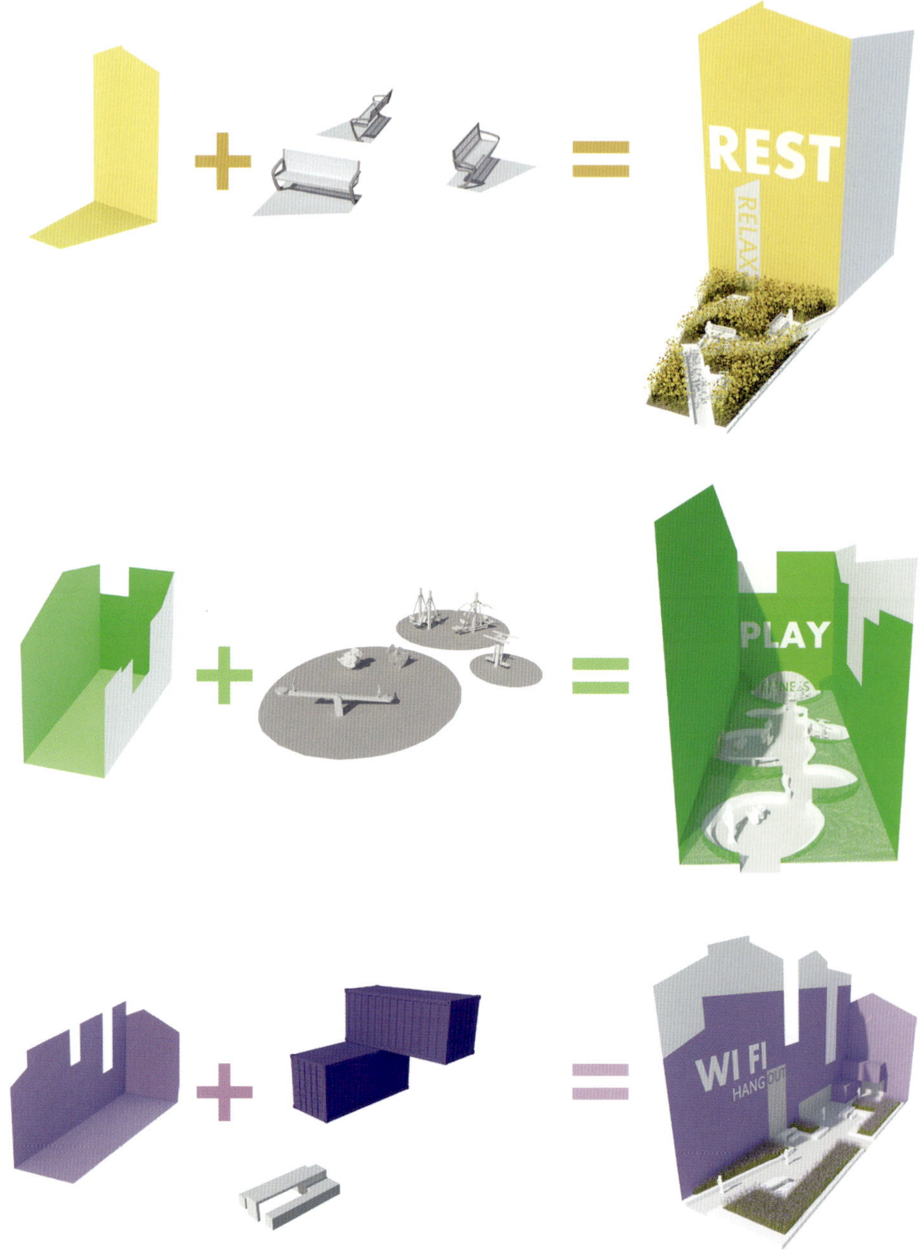

# FLOATING PARKS.
## ROTTERDAM, THE NETHERLANDS

STRATEGY / INTERVENTIONS: **Casanova+Hernandez**

Very often, the constant process of demographic transformation in different districts of the city requires the renovation of many urban facilities in response to new needs among the population. The urban renewal consisting of medium or large scale urban developments changes rapidly the social structure of the neighborhoods, creating a demand for children's facilities to serve the sudden growth in the number of families. At the same time, the population in other neighborhoods gets older and no longer needs that type of facilities.

Usually cities respond to these changes by constantly building, renewing and demolishing facilities. However, there are examples of small-scale urban services that move around the city, stopping in specific places only when they are required. In many countries, open-air markets are active only one or two days per week and the moving shops provide service to several cities during the week. Mobile libraries move books to neighborhoods that do not have their own library. Mobile kiosks change locations throughout the day and the week to serve snacks and refreshments in crowded places, and portable toilets are installed temporarily in public space when a large concentration of crowds is expected for a public event such as a parade, a concert or a sporting event.

These small-scale mobile urban facilities seem to be smart, flexible, efficient and sustainable solutions that raise the question whether mobility might also be applied to medium-scale public space facilities, such as children's playgrounds, sports facilities, parks or swimming pools. Moreover, could a group of nomad facilities create a public space acupuncture strategy that might be capable of satisfying temporary urban needs and/or reactivating the overall use of public space in the city?

The main problem is obviously the difficulty of moving medium- and large-scale elements. There have been many examples of mobile facilities throughout history, such as the portable classrooms, transported by truck, which were used during the post-war baby boom in America to satisfy temporary needs in certain neighborhoods. Others, such as

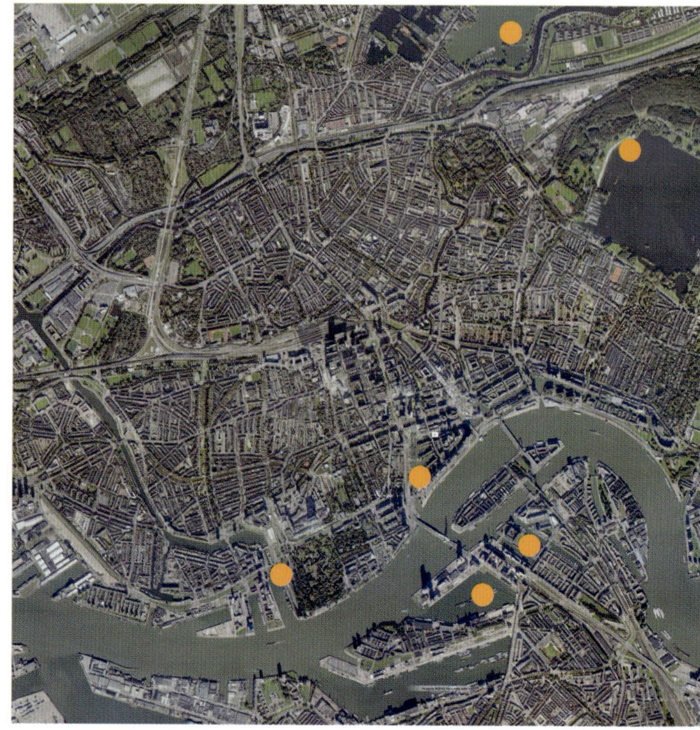

Futuro house. Matti Suuronen

Mullerpier urban development. Rotterdam

the prefabricated Futuro houses designed by the Finnish architect Matti Suuronen in the 1960s, were transported by helicopter.

In the Netherlands in particular, there is a long tradition of floating houses and floating gardens. Part of the territory of the Netherlands was reclaimed from the sea and many Dutch cities are surrounded by water. This fact makes it possible to propose a strategy to try to achieve the utopia of transporting floating public spaces and facilities. Taking advantage of the many rivers, lakes and canals integrated into the urban development of Rotterdam, it is possible to create temporary floating structures that first generate extra land to be used as recreational public space and second, allow for their transportation throughout the connected canals of the city, providing services to different areas when needed.

**Strategy** The strategy "Atoll" is based on building a series of floating public spaces that acquire a number of different functions. This fleet of public spaces sails through the city's network of canals to dock on the shores of neighborhoods that have a temporary need for public facilities, like children's playgrounds, playing fields, or small urban parks. Once the temporary need has disappeared or has been fulfilled by permanent installations on land, the floating public space moves to a new location.

Beyond being an emergency intervention, the plan is conceived as an experimental strategy in the medium- and long-term, based on the use of independent temporary interventions. Unlike fixed urban facilities, these temporary interventions can move to be used again in another place, generating a long-term effect on the scale of the city as a whole. The strategy is extremely sustainable since it pursues the optimization of natural resources, minimizes construction on urban land, avoids earthworks and celebrates recycling as the project's driving force.

At the same time, the strategy also incorporates a powerful psychological component, which promotes the city's public image. The understanding of the river, canals and lakes used by "water-taxis" and "water-buses" as a transportation network, is transformed into a potential meeting place and a setting for recreational activities. At the same time it encourages citizens to acquire a dynamic perception of their city, as a result of constant changes in the structure of public space.

Location of Floating Interventions

Movement Scenario for the Floating Interventions Along Rotterdam's Water Network

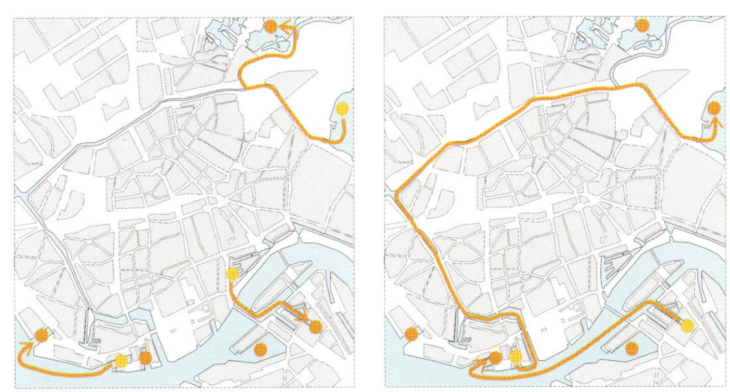

The strategy is extremely versatile and emergency interventions can be combined with test interventions. These interventions can be used as a gauge to determine local needs and the acceptance of certain programs in particular areas of the city.

The strategy is highly flexible not only in temporal terms, given the immediate possibility of installing and dismantling the interventions in a matter of hours, but also in spatial terms. Grouping a number of floating islands together forms archipelagos, which increase the recreational surface area in specific zones and multiply the programmatic diversity, generating interesting multi-functional complexes.

**Interventions** The typological catalog of interventions in the Atoll strategy includes, among others, the park-atoll, the children's playground-atoll, the pool-atoll, the outdoor auditorium-atoll, the water sports-atoll and the beach-atoll.

## Catalog of Floating Interventions

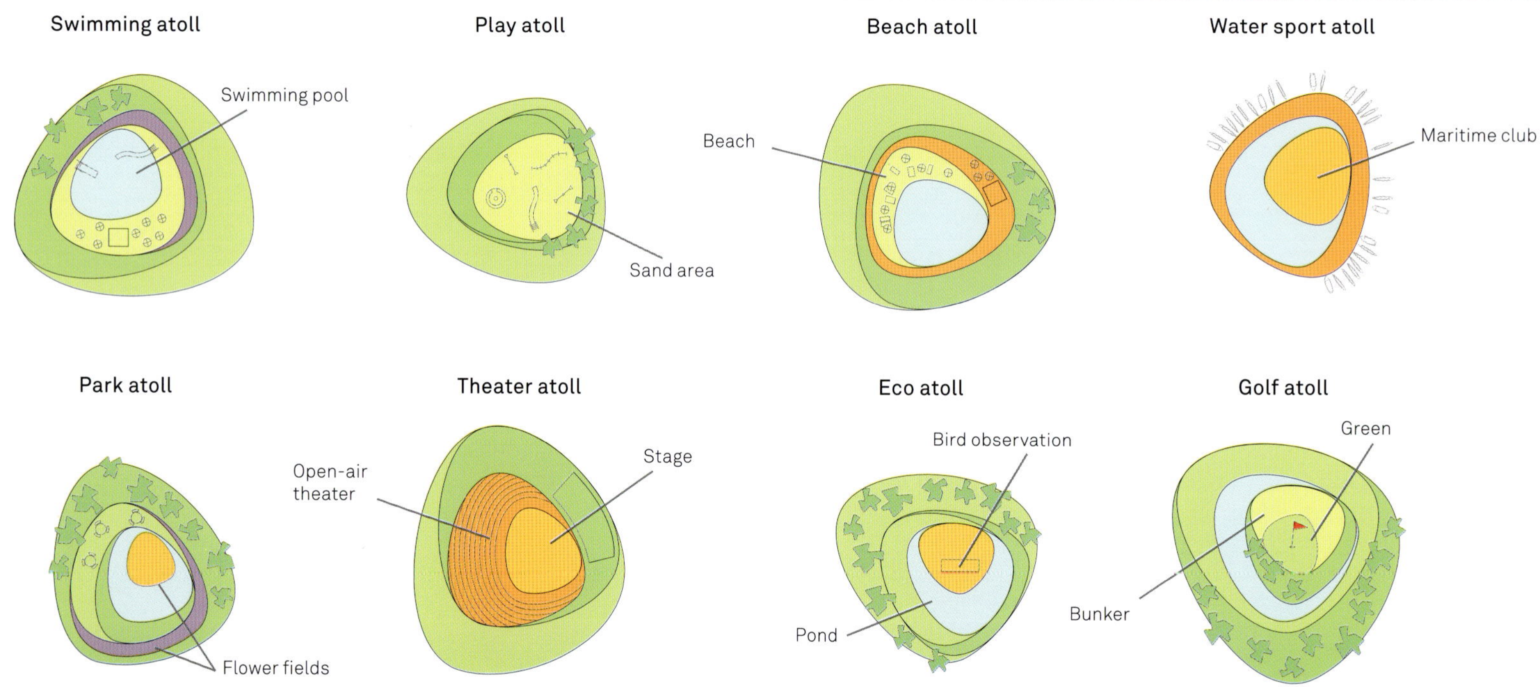

## Different Intervention Contexts

Maas river | Canal | Lake

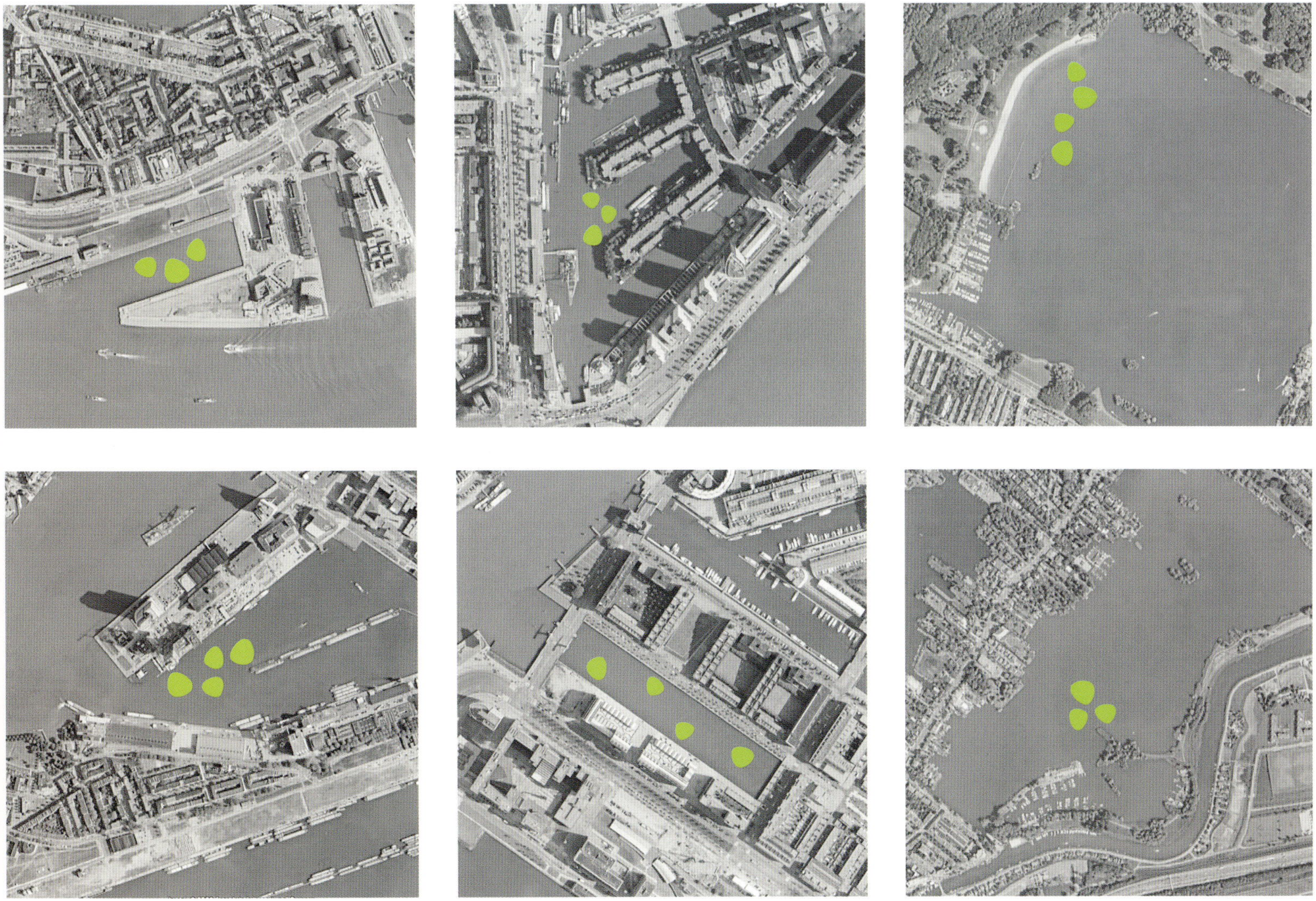

## Aerial View of the Intervention on the Maas River close to Mullerpier Urban Development

0 20 50

The basic atoll structure emerges from the combination of four main layers:

1. A wooden platform in walkable areas.
2. A layer of vegetation based on green roof technology using low-maintenance plants.
3. A floating structure
4. A perimeter of floating plants

## Layers of Floating Intervention

Wooden platform

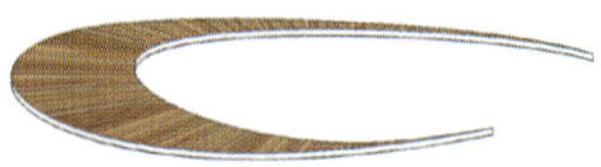

Vegetation

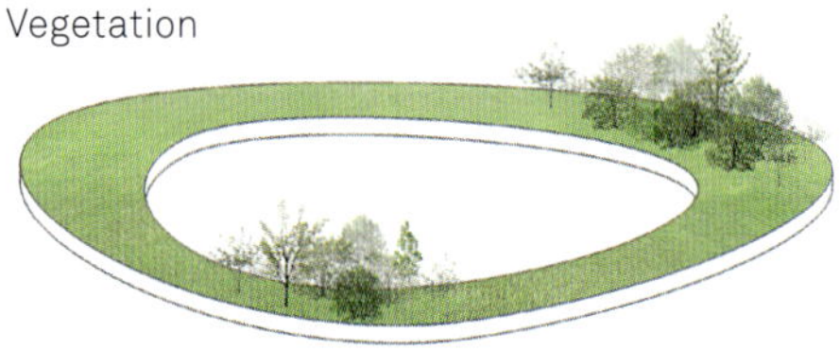

Floating structure

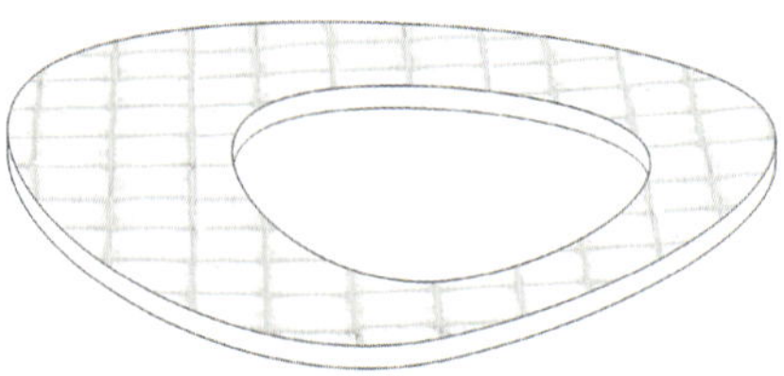

Floating plants

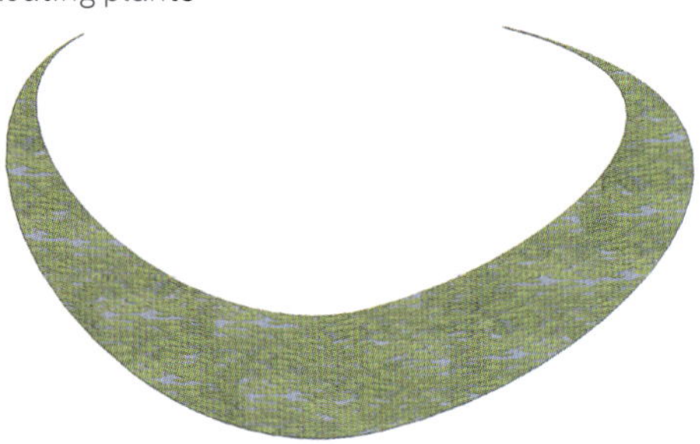

## Beach Atoll

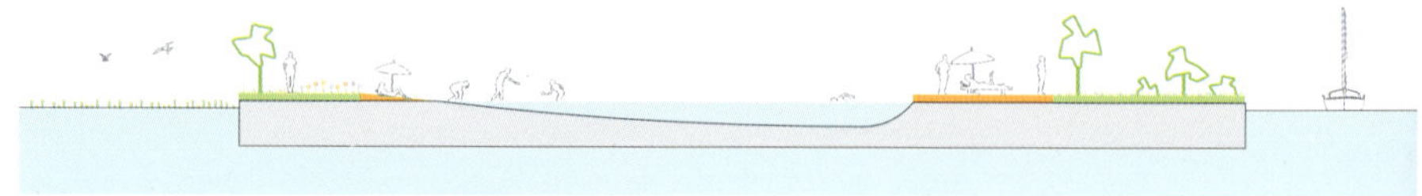

Cross section

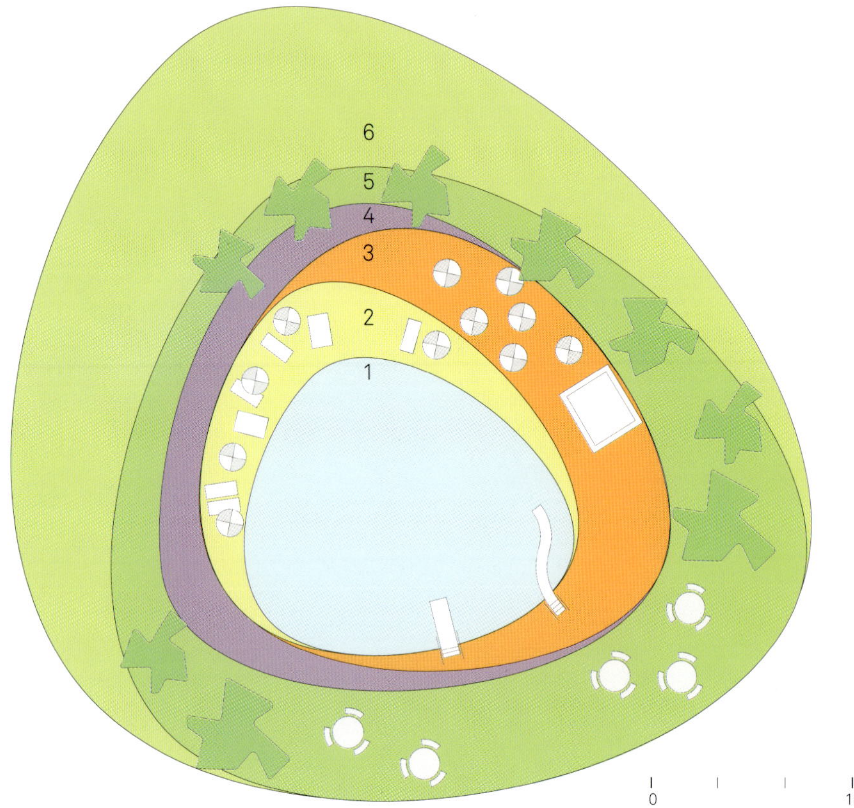


## Materialization

1. Pool

2. Sand

3. Wooden platform

4. Flower bed

5. Grass

6. Floating vegetation

# 2

# Citizen Participation

# Citizen Participation

The term "citizen participation" has taken on renewed meaning in recent years. The possibilities for participation offered by new technologies like opinion forums on the Internet, the emergence of specialized blogs and digital newspaper formats have opened up a new horizon for possibilities in terms of citizen participation in public life. The sociologist Manuel Castells describes this phenomenon as "mass self-communication".[1] Because of the Internet, a single individual can generate a message, edit a video or create a blog that has the potential to reach a global audience, achieving a comparable impact to traditional mass media like television and newspapers. Individual opinions now have a massive distribution channel that did not exist before and that allows for a change in how citizens are positioned with respect to the problems that surround them, shifting from a receptive and passive attitude to a transmissive and critical standpoint.

On the one hand, the Internet's potential for generating influential trends in opinion independently of orthodox channels has led to a change in attitude among many politicians and professionals who are responsible for the conception, design and management of public space, and who have gradually modified their intervention models, in many cases, to incorporate citizens' opinions into the decision-making process in some form. That does not mean that in the past citizens as independent individuals never had a critical attitude with respect to the development of their urban environment, but rather that it was more difficult to make that criticism public and to create a current of opinion capable of influencing political leaders in their decisions about the urban environment.

On the other hand, the Internet has revived citizen participation in many aspects of public life. This has led to a change in attitude among a portion of citizens, especially the youngest, who, in order to respond to the problems around them, have taken on a more active role that can create a direct impact on their surroundings.

The combination of both aspects: greater political interest in listening to public opinion and the participatory tendency in public life generated by new technologies, open up the door to a wide range of possibilities for collaboration between institutions and citizens, which some professionals see as an opportunity to experiment with new models for the creation, design and management of public space.

The way in which individual citizens or groups of citizens as a collective can collaborate in the creation and transformation of their urban environment depends on the sociopolitical context. Frequently, citizens delegate decision making concerning the city to municipal political representatives, which means that if any citizen participation does exist it depends exclusively on the will of the municipal authorities, who are in charge of defining how much influence it is awarded. As a consequence of this dynamic, in practice there are very few instances where citizen groups are in charge of planning and realizing interventions in public space with authorization from the authorities.

Of course, the phenomenon of the so-called citizen participation takes on many different nuances depending on who is promoting the participatory proposals and to what level such participation is achieved. This leads to very different situations that can range from bottom-up strategies created by citizen groups in order to analyze the problems that affect them and come up with solutions either independently or in collaboration with local authorities, to top-down strategies created by municipalities that incorporate some level of citizen participation.

But how can we take advantage of the enormous social capital inherent to the movements that emerge from citizens' collectives? How to create open and efficient strategies that incorporate and even reinforce the energy generated by bottom-up movements? How, and to what extent, can citizens collaborate actively and usefully in top-down strategies aimed not only at improving the use of the urban environment, but also at enhancing social aspects like public life or civil coexistence? The answers to these questions open up a wide range of possibilities for incorporating citizen participation into public space acupuncture strategies, but at the same time they underscore some of the associated problems. First off, it is important to note that all bottom-up initiatives are, by definition, created by citizens' groups in an autonomous way without the intervention of municipal authorities, which is contradictory to the concept of a strategy or plan coordinated by a municipality. Therefore, municipalities obviously cannot generate bottom-up strategies. The most they can do is create sensitive mechanisms to detect such initiatives and help to develop the ones that they believe may create a positive effect on urban life. Second, in top-down strategies promoted by municipalities, we should be especially cautious and critical in determining when citizens are taking on an active and useful role in the participation process and when, on the contrary, citizen participation becomes a populist tool at the service of municipal marketing.

Citizen participation can be incorporated into public space acupuncture strategies in a wide variety of ways, which can be classified into three main groups according to the role that citizens play, whether that involves participation in decision-making about public space, the design of interventions, or the physical construction and maintenance of the realized interventions. In this way, many strategies promote citizen participation by experimenting with new models for collaboration between municipal authorities and citizens through co-management, co-creation, co-production and co-maintenance processes.

1. Manuel Castells, *Communication Power*. Oxford University Press, Oxford, New York, 2009.

# Citizens as Decision Makers: Co-management Strategies

The concept of citizen participation has a clear political dimension. It includes the possibility for independent citizens to gain certain access to some government decisions without being members of a political party or the public administration.

In his book *Politics,* Aristotle defines a human being as a *Zóon politikon* (a social animal or a political animal) referring to humans' natural capacity for social relationships and political organization. According to Aristotle, man, like animals, lives in groups and is thus social by nature, but only man is also political by nature. However, as Hannah Arendt observed in her book *The Human Condition*, the term *Zóon politikon* as defined by Aristotle has a precise connotation associated with the Greek concept of democracy, which was only exercised in the Greek *polis* by those who had the right to be considered citizens.[1] How politics were exercised and the meaning of this term changed with the disappearance of the Greek city-state and the beginning of the Roman Empire and it has continued to evolve through to our times.

Currently, in societies governed by a representative democracy, citizens transfer the decision-making power to specific citizens who are elected via referendum. The only way that citizens can be involved in the construction of public space is through the election of municipal representatives who make decisions in their name concerning the city. Participatory democratic systems include certain complementary mechanisms, through which different citizens' groups can propose initiatives to be approved by the population via plebiscite or referendum. When these participation mechanisms do not exist or are ineffective, citizens organize themselves into groups outside of the system in order to carry out direct actions that can provide an immediate response to pressing problems in their urban environment. The growth of civil society organizations in parallel to the established political model is a sign of the rise of a phenomenon that certain authors like Noam Chomsky have referred to as "the crisis of democracy".[2] Manuel Castells, in a chapter from his trilogy *The Information Age*, called "Informational Politics and the Crisis of Democracy", describes this phenomenon as follows: "While there is a growing crisis of politics-as-usual, there is simultaneously a process of transformation of democracy by offering political avenues to grassroots expression."[3]

A well-known example of this type of response channeled through a bottom-up process of citizen participation is the creation of "Park Fiction". In 1995, the residents of the St. Pauli neighborhood in Hamburg proposed and designed a public park with views over the port on a lot that was property of the municipality and had been sold for the construction of a new urban development. In parallel to the municipal project the residents began a plan to transform the lot into a park, which finally succeeded in halting the construction of the urban development in 1997. "Park Fiction" is a neighborhood initiative in which citizens made urban planning decisions

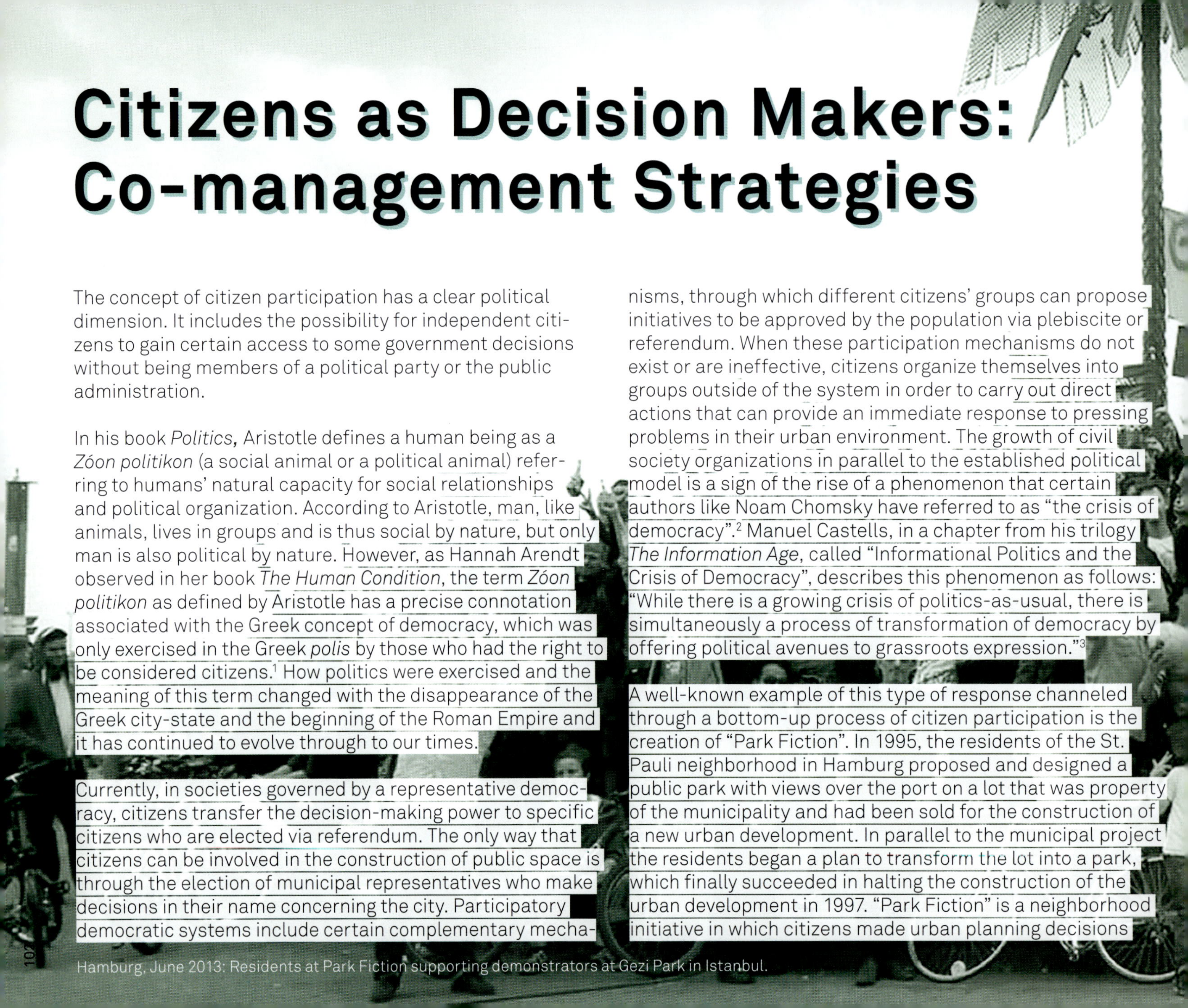

Hamburg, June 2013: Residents at Park Fiction supporting demonstrators at Gezi Park in Istanbul.

concerning public space independently of the municipality and built it, in the end, with their approval. In a similar way, numerous vacant lots in many cities have been transformed through neighborhood initiatives into recreation areas, children's playgrounds or green areas which were lacking in those neighborhoods. In these cases, as in the Park Fiction example, the residents venture into making decisions which, in theory, can only be made by the authorities, so although on the one hand they are transforming lifeless public space into useful areas for the neighborhoods, on the other hand they run the risk of creating conflicts of interest and confrontation if the decisions are not agreed upon among all parties.

Since the 1960s there has been a growing interest among municipal representatives concerning the possibility of including opinions from citizens and communities in urban planning decision making. Municipalities themselves create mechanisms for citizen participation with the aim, on the one hand, of articulating the decision-making process with respect to certain aspects of public space and, on the other hand, to generate a collective consciousness in neighborhoods. Often, what is defined by municipal authorities as citizen participation involves organizing meetings between municipal managers and neighborhood residents to ask for opinions on design options that have already been established. Other times, it consists merely of informative meetings where residents are given a purely passive role. In any case, active citizen participation in real decision making tends to be a goal that is difficult to achieve and complicated to manage for those municipal officials without previous experience in similar processes.

In participatory strategies of public space acupuncture that involve citizens in decision making, the process is just as important as the final goal. A truly constructive process includes informative and educational work and incorporates a discussion of the issues that affect citizens, while seeking to increase their awareness of the urban context in which they live. This awareness implies that when citizens are involved in making decisions about the future of public space, they tend to also take on certain responsibilities with respect to its use and maintenance. By sharing the decision-making power through processes of citizen participation, each citizen is reasserted as ***Zóon politikon*** and the group reinforces its collective feeling.

1. Hannah Arendt, *The Human Condition.* University of Chicago Press, Chicago, 1958.
2. Noam Chomsky, *Language and Politics.* Black Rose Books, Montreal, 1988.
3. Manuel Castells, *The Power of Identity.* John Wiley and Sons Ltd, Oxford, 1997.

## I LOVE TO PLAY! & PAINTING INITIATIVE
## TIRANA, ALBANIA

STRATEGY / INTERVENTIONS: **Municipality of Tirana**

In 1991, after the end of 47 years under a Communist government, Albania changed its political system drastically by adopting a representative democracy and quickly adapting its centrally planned economy into a market economy. In the years that followed, Tirana, as the country's capital and its largest city, underwent a huge transformation, on the one hand, because of the massive migration of population from the countryside to the city and, on the other hand, because of the lack of city planning and urban deregularization. This allowed for chaotic urban development, many illegal constructions and the degradation of public space during years.

In 2000, the former mayor of Tirana, Edi Rama, coordinated several parallel strategies intended to recover the city's public space. He undertook a radical campaign to demolish illegal buildings throughout the city center. Neglected collective areas located between the Communist-built apartment blocks were refurbished. Existing green areas, squares and parks were renovated and many new ones were created. In parallel to this campaign, he developed a global strategy based on small interventions inserted into the existing urban structure, subdivided into different programs that targeted particular aspects of public space.

The program I LOVE TO PLAY! consists of the construction of 100 playgrounds spread throughout the city, making use of the blank walls that are characteristic of Communist residential blocks as well as the small, unused spaces located in between them. The involvement of local residents in the strategy was essential, not only because their collaboration in the process helped in the selection of places close to their homes for creating the children's playgrounds, but also because their participation stimulated debates in the neighborhood about the use of the collective areas, promoting collective awareness about their living environment.

The Painting Initiative was another simultaneous program, initiated by Edi Rama in 2000, aimed at renovating the dete-

riorated grey façades of many Communist-period buildings by painting them with colorful designs, transforming the ruined façades into fascinating paintings. The new vibrant and colorful image of the city became a visual statement that marked the end of a period dictated by Communist urban homogeneity and the start of an era where citizens had a role to play. Many Albanian and international artists have been invited to convert the grey blocks into works of art that transform the city's public space, promote public debate and attract an ever-growing number of visitors and tourists each year.

The strategy experiments with transforming public space using different overlapping layers: in spatial terms, by tearing down kiosks and illegal buildings to create new public space; in visual terms, by transforming the image of the city by painting the façades of existing buildings; in functional terms, by revitalizing inert spaces in the city, creating play areas and spaces for citizen interaction.

In parallel, and perhaps creating an even larger though less visible impact, the strategies are intended to awaken political awareness among individuals, i.e., the inherent human capacity for building social relationships and political organization, by encouraging different levels of citizen participation. After a long period of passivity during which citizens could not take on a political role, first, participatory strategies are intended to generate personal opinions among them, promoting public debate. Second, they attempt to implicate citizens in the transformation of public space and in the decision-making process.

The way this complicity is created consists in inviting citizens to decide where their neighborhoods are in need of new facilities, in addition to collaborating in the process of their realization. In this way, citizens playing the role of experts who know every last corner of their urban habitat better than anyone else, locate inactive areas of the city that have the potential to be transformed into active places. Citizens as decision-makers participate, if only on a small scale, in making decisions about their city, and they have the opportunity to participate in the development of the interventions within the framework of what we might call a co-management strategy.

**Urban analysis** The center of Tirana underwent considerable expansion in the Communist period, from 1944 to 1991, during which massive Communist-style apartment complexes and factories were built.

Then, in the 1990s, Tirana saw enormous urban development intended to absorb the large waves of immigration coming from other parts of the country. Many urban areas that were developed during the Communist period were densified with small constructions, kiosks and apartment buildings that were built on public land, while the spaces in between buildings were also occupied in various forms.

These new urban areas had a largely residential function, combined with commercial activities and working spaces, which are irregularly spread along the main streets. In consequence, from 1991 to 2000, the city's public space was physically reduced to a minimum.

## Aerial View

## Users

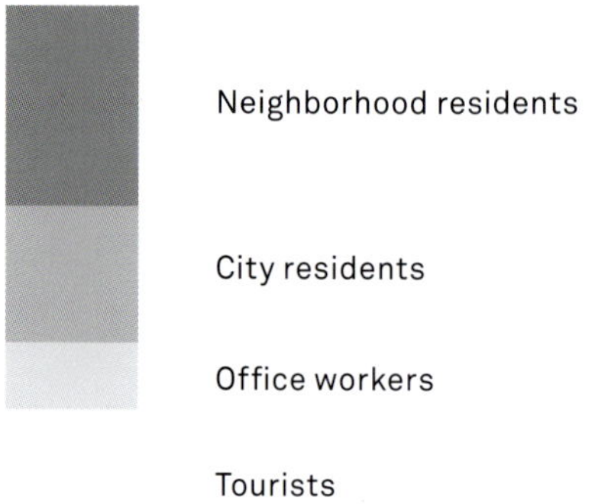


## Relation to the City

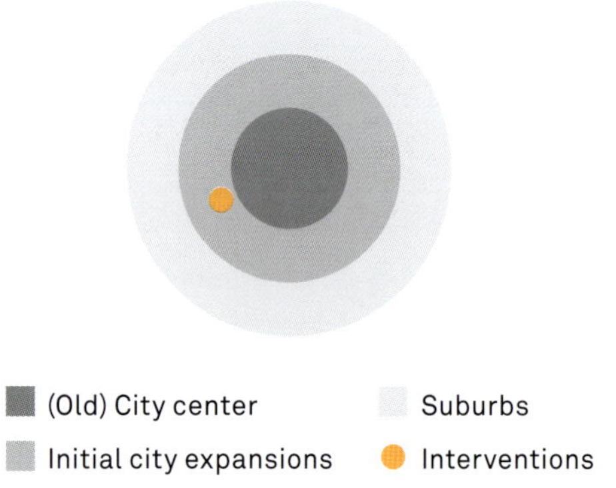


## Historic Urban Development

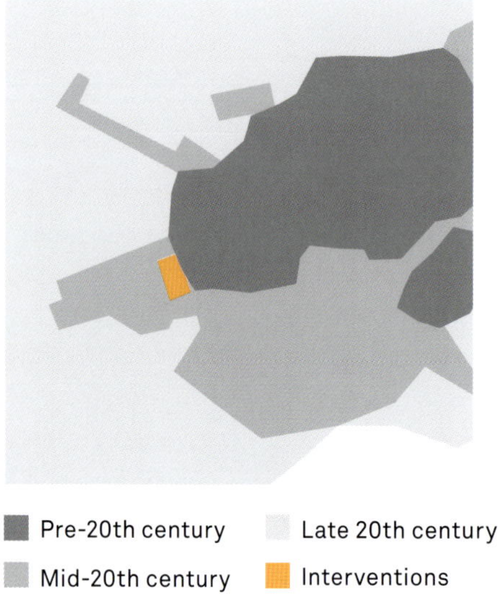


## Activities

**Social analysis** With the end of the Communist period in 1991, Tirana experienced rapid population growth as the result of migration from the country's rural areas to the capital attracted by its growing labor market. Whereas in 1990, Tirana's population was just 250,000, in 2011 the population exploded to 763,000, meaning that the population had tripled in just over 20 years. Officially, in 2011, 421,000 people lived in the city of Tirana proper, and the rest of the population inhabited the suburbs.

Compared to European standards, Tirana's population is relatively young and the average age is around 30. Although Albania has experienced economic growth in recent years, becoming an attractive place for foreign investors and tourists, the country's GDP per capita is still very low, at only 30% of the European average. In 2010, the unemployment rate was quite high, 13.5%.

## Age Structure

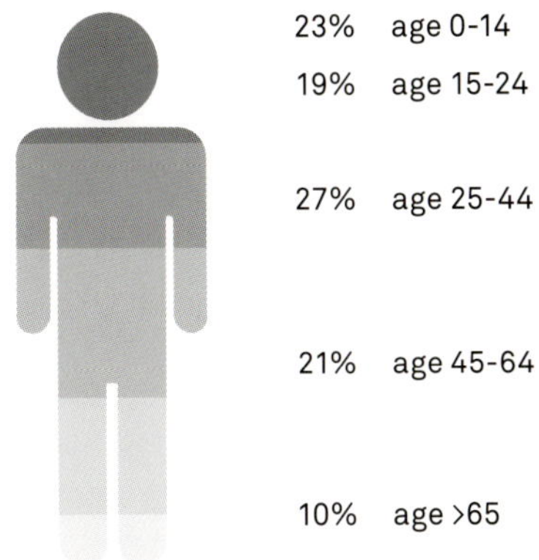


## Household Composition

No data available

## Immigration

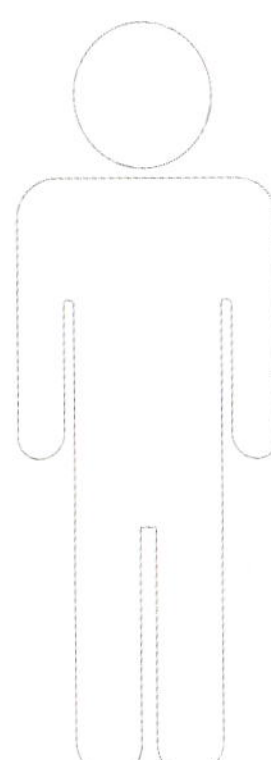

No data available

## Unemployment

Age Structure data for Albania. Source: INSTAT 2009. Unemployment data for Albania. Source: INSTAT 2010.

**Interventions** The strategy "I LOVE TO PLAY!" and the program of painting façades consist of hundreds of small interventions that have been located in many different points throughout the city, creating a dense network.

Five interventions have been selected for analysis in the 21 Dhjetori neighborhood, which is a densely populated area located to the west of the city center.

Two of the interventions, which are located on a popular square and on one of the neighborhood's main streets, consist of colorful façades created thanks to the Painting Initiative. The other interventions, which belong to the program "I LOVE TO PLAY!", are playgrounds located in the small open areas in between urban residential blocks.

Accesses

Relaxation areas

Sitting areas

Circulation

Vegetation

Playing areas

## 1 Painted Façades on Kavaja Street

Kavaja Street is one of the city's main traffic arteries and the façades of some of its buildings are part of the "Painting Initiative" program. The monotonous rhythm of the long urban blocks is broken up visually by painting the front and side façades of the buildings with several colors. Each side of the hanging balconies is also painted in a vibrant color, creating a kind of three-dimensional urban work of art. The fact that the façades corresponding to each apartment are painted in different colors emphasizes the chromatic vibration of the block and, at the same time, redefines the expression of collective housing as the accumulation of the different individual identities of the people who live there.

## 2 Painted Façades on Atatürk Square

During the Communist period, the square was called December 21 to commemorate Stalin's birthday and was later renamed in honor of the Turkish President, Atatürk. The setback of the buildings along the east side of the square produces a small urban space, which was once used as a parking area but has recently been transformed into a pedestrian area, equipped with long benches.

The balconies of the buildings that close off the space of the square have been painted in yellow and green to contrast with the red color of the façades. The painted façades work as a strong chromatic backdrop for a colorful urban stage, where citizens are simultaneously actors and spectators of the urban life performed in it.

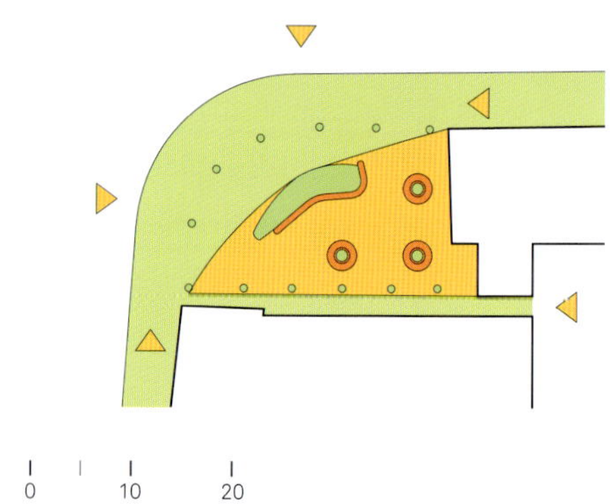

## 3 The Program I Love to Play!

The Intervention is part of the program I LOVE TO PLAY!, which takes advantage of many of the interstitial spaces located in between the characteristic residential buildings built during the Communist period. They are transformed into basketball courts or children's playgrounds. In many cases, the basketball courts are reduced to half of the normal size, with just one basket, or they may adopt unusual proportions, adapted to the small and irregular dimensions of the available lots.

Several concrete seats, painted in a brilliant blue, are situated around the playground, which is fenced with a steel mesh, supported by a metallic structure that is painted in bright red. Again, colors play an important role in identifying the interventions, contrasting with the greyness of the surrounding buildings.

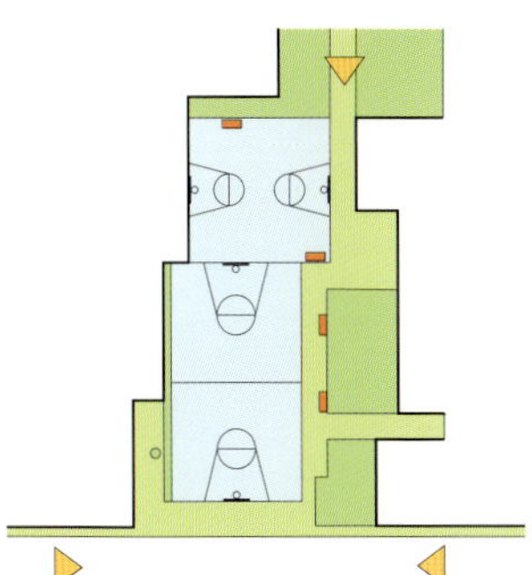

## 4 Playground on Kongresi i Lushnjes Street

The Intervention is located in a rectangular public square surrounded by four housing blocks. In the middle of the square there is a row of concrete seating areas, which are raised a few steps off the ground to separate them from the nearby parking places. A children's playground is located on the east side of the square, equipped with several playground elements painted in bright yellow and orange. A number of concrete benches are placed around these elements. The different faces of the concrete elements in the square are painted in orange, blue and green. The result is a series of polychromatic urban elements that are easy to recognize and are spread throughout the whole neighborhood, providing identity to the entire strategy.

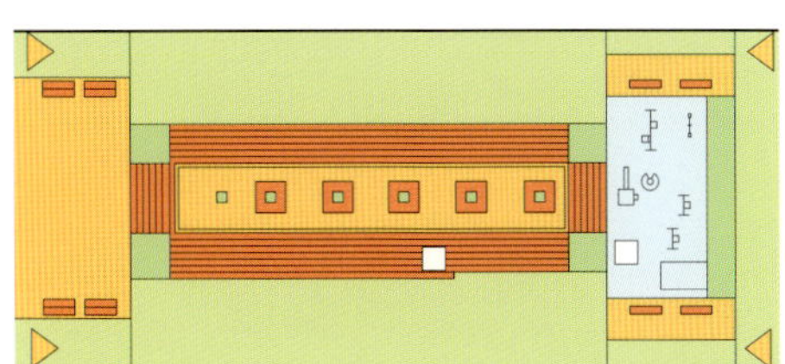

## 5 Picnic Area on Ylbere Bylykbashi Street

The intervention is located in an interstitial empty space between housing blocks that opens toward Ylbere Bylykbashi Street. The pavement of the rectangular lot has been divided into six squares marked by different materials. Prismatic concrete benches and trees are placed in the center of four of the squares, and eight concrete tables with concrete seating elements are set up in the other two. The seating elements and tables are painted in a combination of several colors, similar to what has been done with other new concrete urban elements in the neighborhood. This kind of intervention generates activity in areas that were once used as parking lots or in the empty spaces that are left behind after small illegal constructions in between the housing blocks have been demolished.

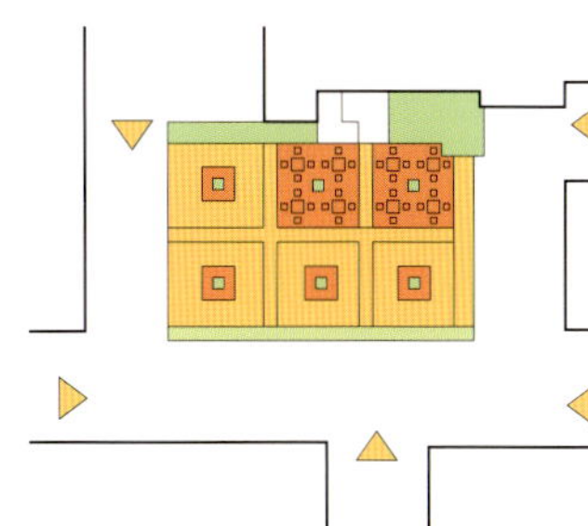

**Process** The process was initiated by Tirana's municipality and it was personally supported by the former mayor, Edi Rama, who was first elected in October 2000. Mr. Rama, who served as Minister of Culture, Youth and Sports from 1998-2000, is an artist, publicist, and a politician and he was voted World Mayor of the Year in December 2004. The fact that the mayor of Tirana was personally involved in the initiation of the process and its further development gives a personal character to the strategy, which was not perceived by the citizens as part of the conventional initiatives of the municipality, but as a personal and alternative proposal. Edi Rama was also personally involved in promoting the strategy and encouraging citizens to participate.

The main actor in the afore-mentioned strategies is the Tirana municipality, which plays the role of promoter and developer for the interventions and is in charge of their maintenance. The citizens, with whom the city council worked closely on the identification of the available spaces to be transformed, are the other important party involved in the strategy.

The process of realizing an intervention starts with detecting the suitable places for its implementation, with the help of residents, in each of Tirana's neighborhoods. In the second step, the technical staff of the city council develops a simple, modest urban project, with the final aim of building a small-scale urban intervention to create sports facilities for the neighborhood's children.

## Citizen Participation

One of the essential objectives of the strategy I LOVE TO PLAY! is to involve local residents in the process of regenerating public life in their neighborhoods. Citizens can participate in the process by selecting the places where interventions will be installed and by co-financing the construction.

The role of citizen participation in the strategy can be perfectly resumed in the words of the mayor of Tirana who said: "I would like to invite all the communities and inhabitants of the capital to be part of this project, by making their demands heard by the staff of the municipality and by making their modest contributions to co-financing this kind of project. The amount is not important, but it has a huge symbolic importance. We want to see these playing fields spring up all over the capital, in full collaboration with the community. We want to cultivate the community spirit day by day, because we believe that it is a need in a city that seeks to involve everyone in the decision-making process, to improve our social life more and more each day."

02

## Cost, Financing and Maintenance

I LOVE TO PLAY! is a low-budget strategy that, using few resources, has a strong impact on neighborhood social life. The modest financial cost of this project was mainly covered by the municipality. Complementary private donations of money, materials and expertise contributed not only to the construction of the interventions themselves, but also to build a sense of community with a symbolic importance.

The management process for the strategy I LOVE TO PLAY! and the painting façades project is coordinated by the Tirana municipality. It consists of a very dynamic mechanism to carry out a continuous search for locations and their subsequent selection, combined with the design and construction of the interventions.

The maintenance of the built interventions also depends mainly on the Tirana municipality. The participative process that engages residents in the construction of the playgrounds also seeks to build up a sense of community, which should translate into a better natural maintenance of the interventions.

## Timing

The strategy I LOVE TO PLAY! is not limited to creating playgrounds between the blank walls of the characteristic Communist-era housing blocks in order to promote exercise and interaction among children. It also seeks to radically transform local residents' perception of their urban context by creating a large network of gathering areas near their houses and by engaging them in the process of transforming their own neighborhoods.

In order to achieve these objectives the promoters of the strategy need to motivate citizens, who are not used to participating in the debate about the city's public space, to get involved for the first time. To that end, the former mayor, Edi Rama, was personally involved in promoting the project via a campaign that used the slogan "I LOVE TO PLAY!" and a logo, and had the clear objective of building 100 playgrounds before 2008. Setting such a difficult objective, to be carried out in a short period of time, was a challenge for citizens and the municipality team alike. But once expectations are created, it is important to take advantage of the inertia to move the strategy forward. To guarantee this, it can be useful to create a versatile mechanism to react very quickly to residents' demands, smoothing out the administrative procedures and realizing the interventions in a very short period of time.

As the number of built interventions grows, more citizens become interested in taking part in the project. A quick reaction time is not only important to establishing a rhythm in the construction of the project, but also serves to transmit the image of a new dynamic administration, capable of collaborating with citizens in the creation of the public space.

## Use of the Public Space

First of all, the strategy I LOVE TO PLAY! creates many playing fields and playground areas for children, away from the city's busy traffic and close to their homes. This works as a very effective initiative to stimulate the use of public space by children and young people. The result is a child-friendly city, where younger people can enjoy the opportunity of meeting each other and exercising, thus promoting their social and physical development.

Second, the use of public space in these specific areas activates the collective life of the neighborhoods and strengthens the sense of community among local residents of different ages.

The painting façades strategy, apart from fulfilling the practical demand of repairing damaged façades that had not been maintained for a long time, has the symbolic effect of transforming the grey and monotonous character of a city that developed during the Communist period into a creative and colorful city that places emphasis on citizens' individual expression.

Although this strategy did not stimulate the use of the public space directly, it led to a huge controversy and a heated public debate among the citizens, which took place in public space, in bars, cafés and workplaces. This public debate about the city, which had only been held at a political level up to that point, reached the level of citizens and was shifted into the public domain, thus contributing to activating the public life of the city.

## Impact on Citizens and in the Media

I LOVE TO PLAY! provoked a positive reaction from the citizens of Tirana. The high demand for playgrounds among many neighborhood groups is an objective indicator of the initiative's popularity.

The painting façades strategy elicited many different reactions from citizens. Some of them were in favor and others were against it. Citizens discussed the artistic value of the interventions, the reasons for undertaking them, their costs, whether someone had the right to realize them, and many other aspects that citizens might never have considered before. Everyone had an opinion and an open public debate began with the public space of the city at its center. The strategy provoked passionate citizens' debates, which generated a collective sense of shared public space and a feeling of collective responsibility.

The controversial nature of some of the strategies produced a large public debate and enjoyed a large echo in local, national and international newspapers, radio and television outlets. At a historical moment, when the country was immersed in a deep political, social and economical transition, the transformation of the city was widely debated in the media, projecting a dynamic image to the public that contrasted with the former image of an immobile city.

Edi Rama acted as the media figure in charge of launching the whole strategy. His creative past as an artist contributed to building up his public image as a visionary politician, a promoter of innovative and polemic initiatives. Far from being perceived as a bureaucratic politician, he played the role of the passionate and instinctive politician, capable of promoting very personal and unorthodox strategies. In 2004, Edi Rama was presented with the World Mayor award by the City Mayors organization in London and in 2005 he was chosen by *Time* magazine as one of the "European Heroes who are changing the world for the better".

# VELLUTERS CITIZENS STRATEGY IN VACANT LOTS
## VALENCIA, SPAIN

STRATEGY: **Agrupació SOSTRE, Agrupació Arquitectes pel Paisatge**
STRATEGY / INTERVENTIONS: **Casanova+Hernandez**

Although until the 1950s Velluters was a bustling neighborhood in Valencia's historic center, full of businesses and movie theaters, it suffered from a speculative spiral during the second half of the 20th century and many of the buildings in the area were abandoned. Over time they deteriorated and were finally demolished, creating numerous empty lots in the urban fabric. Simultaneously, there was a progressive loss of services in the area and many families moved into new apartments with modern amenities on the outskirts of the city. Since 1970, more than 24,000 residents have moved away and the neighborhood has lost 57% of its inhabitants, a fact that, combined with a lack of new tenants moving in, has resulted in an aging population, such that presently one fourth of the neighborhood's residents are over 65 and 36% of the apartments are empty.

As a result of this situation, at the moment Velluters is one of the most deteriorated neighborhoods in Valencia. Compared with the rest of the city, it has five times more crime and double the number of empty homes. According to the results of a survey among residents, in the neighborhood there is a lack of facilities, meeting places, playgrounds and green areas. The problems detected by residents include prostitution, drugs, insecurity, dirty streets and the derelict state of the many empty lots.

**Strategy** Given the problems in the area, several different local associations, in conjunction with Agrupació SOSTRE and Agrupació Arquitectes pel Paisatge, created a platform to promote the neighborhood's rehabilitation and launched an action plan directed at public space and empty lots, called “Imagine Velluters”.

The program called for ideas for the regeneration of the neighborhood by creating temporary interventions in empty lots. The strategy proposed combining landscape interventions or artistic contributions with another series of interventions that would explore citizen participation as the motor for transforming the neighborhood. Citizens would be provided with the opportunity to make decisions about

the use of public space and to participate in collaborative strategies together with public or even private actors.

Despite the physical and economic deterioration in Velluters, which is a sign that its economic activity is low, the social capital in the neighborhood is relatively high. This can be deduced from the results of the surveys, which showed that 58% of its residents think that the neighborhood is active and dynamic and, although only a third of inhabitants are regular participants in neighborhood activities, 92% said they would be willing to participate in the regeneration of the neighborhood.

The willingness for participation among residents, along with the municipal authorities' interest in addressing the neighborhood's problems, join together in a strategy that involves interventions in co-production with the municipality or with private actors. The proposed strategy promotes interventions that are integrated into the urban fabric of the city, based on functional principles, reduced cost and low maintenance, which create a distinct visual impact. In some special cases, the decision-making is shared with residents, who are allowed near total independence in handling the tasks of management.

**Interventions** The possible areas for intervention encompass nearly 30 fenced-in, empty lots. In the future, the strategy could be extended into six empty lots that are currently used for parking purposes and 30 more lots that are occupied by derelict buildings that may be demolished. The strategy identifies, restores and revalues the empty lots in Velluters neighborhood, reactivating their functional, social, ecological and aesthetic potential through different intervention layers that can be applied to each lot independently, depending on their specific location within the neighborhood, their solar orientation, and their potential use.

Fenced-in vacant lots and parking lots (first phase interventions)

Lots occupied by derelict buildings (future interventions)

Each intervention is formed by overlapping layers that are divided into three levels, depending upon whether the interventions are physical interventions that act on the vertical surfaces or the party walls adjacent to the lot (level 1), physical interventions on the surface of the empty lot (level 2), or participatory programs or educational activities organized on the intervention site (level 3).

**Layer 1a – Artistic party walls**
The restoration of the party walls adjacent to the empty lots can be combined with artistic interventions created by guest visual artists or by simply painting the party walls in bright colors.

**Layer 1b – Green party walls**
Party walls in poor condition can be refurbished with green walls, created by using climbing plants or by combining different plant species in colorful compositions.

**Layer 1c – Functional party walls**
Party walls can be reused in a functional way, by transforming them into climbing walls or inventive adventure games for children.

**Layer 2a – Green areas**
According to the surveys, 28% of residents opine that one of the main problems in Velluters neighborhood is the lack of green areas. The strategy proposes creating green areas on vacant lots and opening them to public use, conceiving them simply as gardens, maintained by the municipality or by interested residents.

**Layer 2b – Productive urban farming**
Urban farming promotes the neighborhood's environmental, economic and social sustainability through the production of fresh fruit and vegetables for consumption by residents. At the same time, it provides a leisure activity that encourages interaction among residents.

**Layer 2 – Lounges and leisure areas**
Public space that is designed as an open-air living room for citizens of all ages can be combined with leisure activities such as children's playgrounds, sports fields for teens, or exercise areas for the elderly.

## Configuration System of the Interventions by Superposing Layers

### Layer 1: Interventions on the Walls

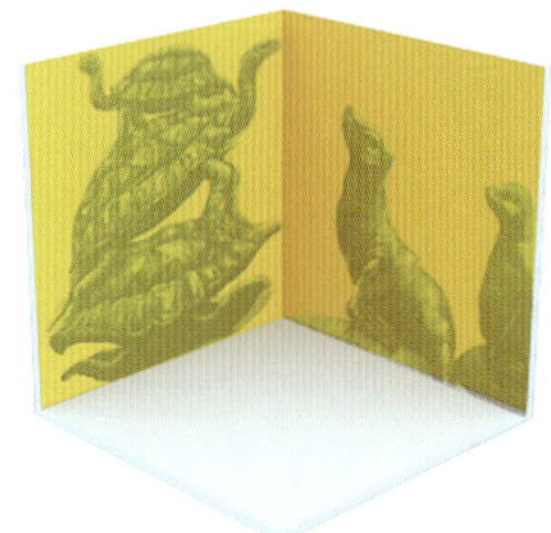

Layer 1a

Layer 1b

Layer 1c

### Layer 2: Interventions on the Ground

Layer 2a

Layer 2b

Layer 2c

### Layer 3: Assignment of a Program

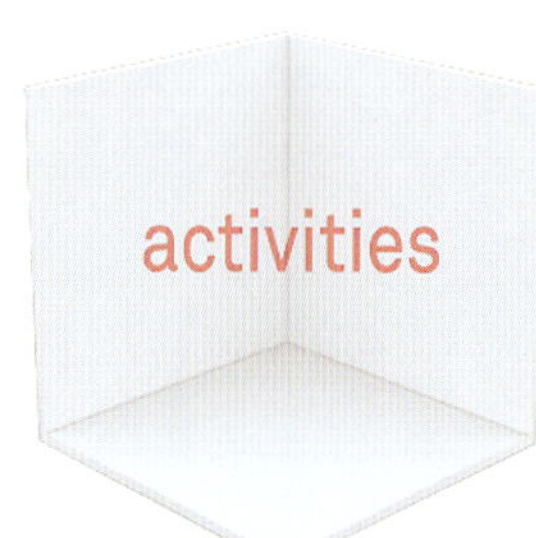


Layer 3a

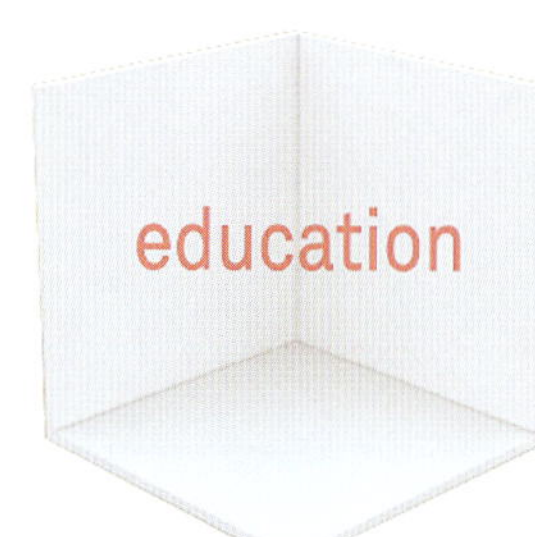


Layer 3b

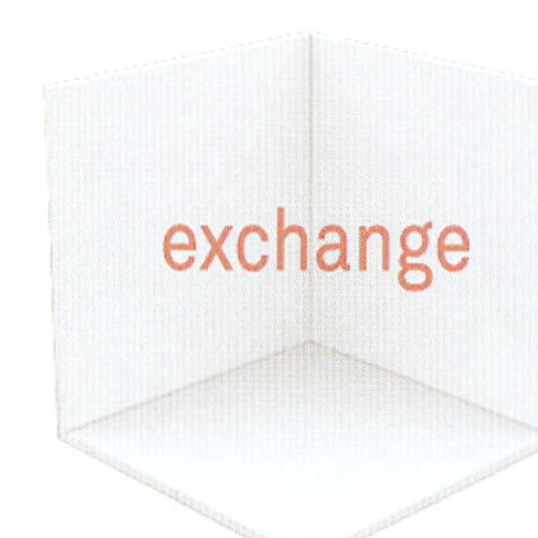


Layer 3c

### Layer 3a – Group Activity Programming

The strategy proposes interventions that strengthen the ties between different social groups and residents of different ages and it is open to promoting neighbors' initiatives and participatory workshops for exchanging experiences and knowledge.

### Layer 3b – Educational Programs

Citizen participation can work as an important educational tool by integrating the participation of primary and secondary schools in the strategy to awaken young people to a constructive engagement with public space and protection of the environment.

### Layer 3c – Exchange Center

The exchange center is managed entirely by residents and works as a flea market, open to everyone, where all kinds of objects and expertise can be exchanged in different spaces provided for that purpose. Second-hand objects, guitar lessons or English classes, can be offered in exchange for cooking lessons or IT expertise. All the neighbors have something to contribute in return for what they need.

The system allows for generating a wide variety of interventions, which can range from the simplest combination of just two or three layers, to the most complex arrangements combining up to nine layers and including participatory programs, as well as a varied agenda of activities, all depending on the specific characteristics of each lot.

The strategy contemplates a balanced distribution of green areas, lounge areas and leisure areas, as well as participatory programs and activities. Each intervention is defined through a citizen participation process, which means that residents in Velluters can be involved in the decision making and in the co-management of some of the proposed interventions.

The citizen participation does not end once the interventions have been realized, but continues with a follow-up and the evaluation of each intervention's performance. The evaluation of results allows for the possible future transformation of interventions in response to new needs and to support new participatory models. The ultimate objective is to achieve an open, sustainable strategy that can be effective in the short, medium and long term.

## Intervention Configurations Created by Overlapping Layers

Combination of layers 1a+2a= green area with lounge zone mixed with street art on walls

| | | |
|---|---|---|
| **1a** | 1b | 1c |
| **2a** | 2b | 2c |
| 3a | 3b | 3c |

Activity level

Citizens management

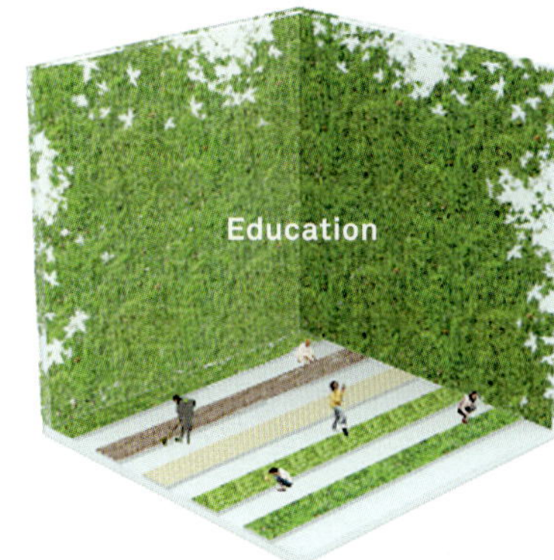


Combination of layers 1b+2b+3b= urban farming mixed with green walls and educational activities

| | | |
|---|---|---|
| 1a | **1b** | 1c |
| 2a | **2b** | 2c |
| 3a | **3b** | 3c |

Activity level

Citizens management

Combination of layers1a+1c+2c+3a= public art with climbing wall combined with resting area and playgrounds

| | | |
|---|---|---|
| **1a** | 1b | **1c** |
| 2a | 2b | **2c** |
| **3a** | 3b | 3c |

Activity level

Citizens management

Combination of layers 1b+1c+2b+2c+3a+3c= urban farming and gathering area combined with climbing walls and green walls for sport and educational activities

| | | |
|---|---|---|
| 1a | **1b** | **1c** |
| 2a | **2b** | **2c** |
| **3a** | 3b | **3c** |

Activity level

Citizens management

## Spatial Distribution of Program, Activities and Citizen Participation Poles with Indication of Programmatic Axis, Activity Circuits and Influence Areas

Velluters street art museum
Loop art promenade

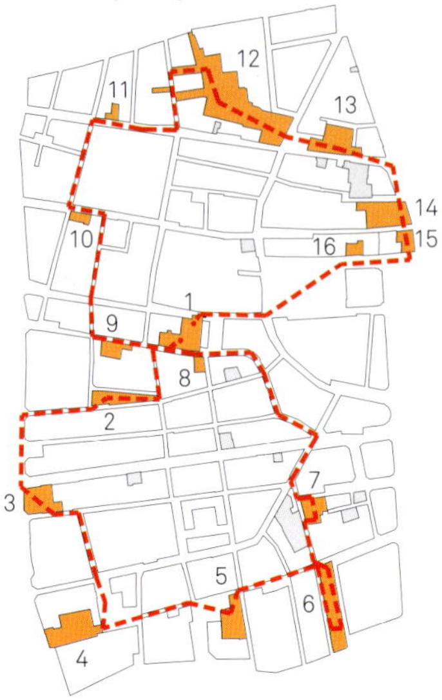


Green, seating and recreational areas

Sports areas
Sports circuit

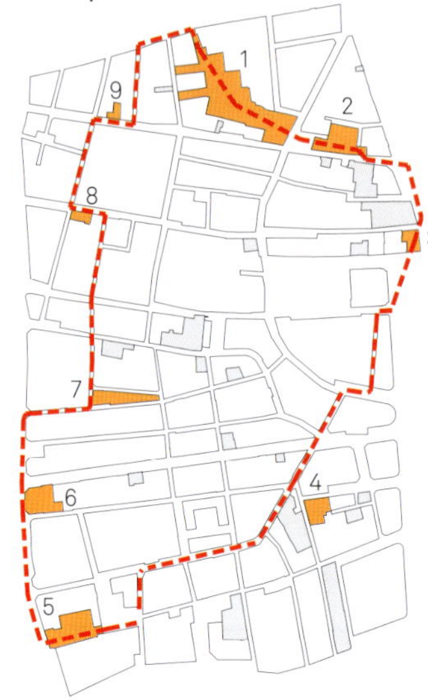


Urban agriculture

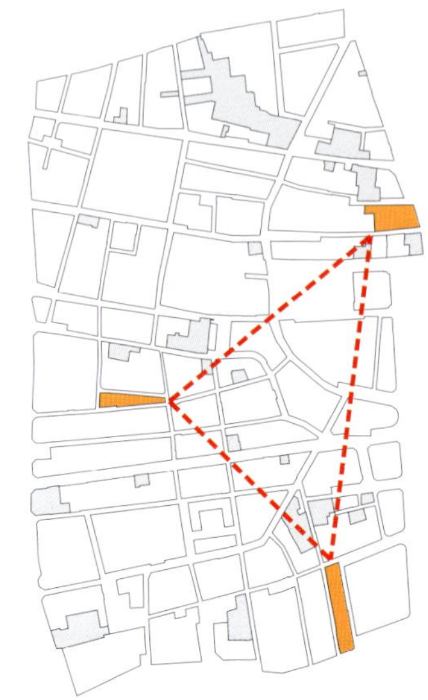

Main citizen participation poles

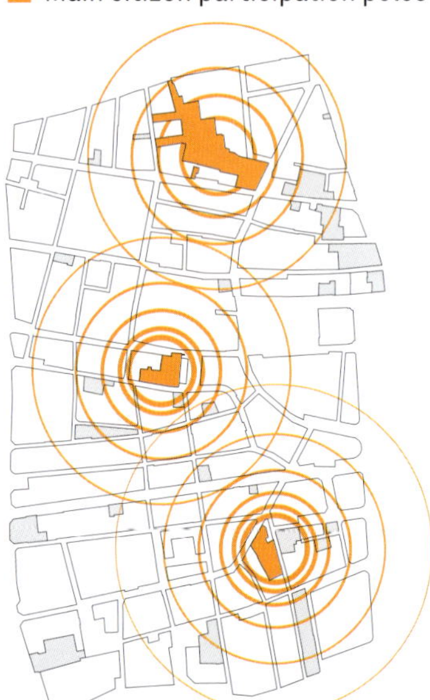

Educational activities

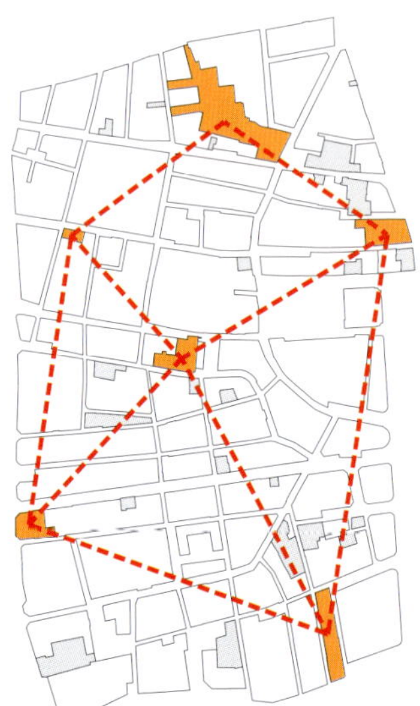

Exchange activities

S.I.P. Self initiative projects

LoveVeg
love food • love cooking •

07

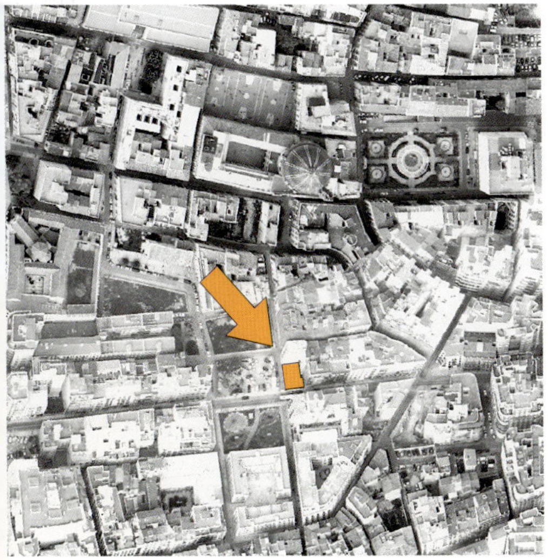

## SANDLEITEN
VIENNA, AUSTRIA

GENERAL STRATEGY/COMMISSIONER: **CULBURB**
"OPEN ROOMS" STRATEGY / FURNITURE INTERVENTIONS: **Casanova+Hernandez**
INTERVENTIONS: **Marcella Pascal, Alexander Felch, Carla Della Beffa, Paul Woodruffe, Walter Klasz**

Sandleiten, built in 1928, and the Karl-Marx-Hof built in 1930, were two milestones in the success of the housing policy in Red Vienna. The policy was created in the 1920s in response to the unsanitary and overcrowded living conditions suffered by Vienna's poor and working class, which became extremely problematic during the period of inflation and high unemployment experienced after World War I.

After the devastation caused by the war, finding solutions to the housing problem became urgent. Following the 1919 municipal elections, the Social Democratic Workers' Party carried out broad social reforms, which included the construction of 380 public housing projects, with more than 64,000 units, between 1923 and 1934. During this period, Vienna became a fertile field for experimentation with large-scale social housing projects. Many projects were generated based on the superblock concept, conceived as an autonomous city within the city with its own infrastructure, services and abundant outdoor areas to improve living conditions for workers.

Although the most internationally well-known projects have been the ones designed as enclosed city blocks built around a large central green area like the Karl Marx-Hof, Sandleiten was the largest social housing experiment of the time, with 1587 apartments. Unlike Karl-Marx-Hof, Sandleiten is designed as a group of meandering linear blocks that are articulated around a series of squares or open spaces, always in contact with the city's public space. The ambiguity of the nature and use of these urban interstitial spaces, which are collective spaces for the residential block but are also part of the public space of the city, marks them as rich and varied urban places, but also as problematic ones.

A century after the creation of Sandleiten, the social conditions in Vienna changed and the social structure of the neighborhood was reorganized due to an aging population, with 80% of residents over 70 in 1990. In parallel, there was a rapid increase in the number of immigrants living

Aerial view of Sandleiten after its construction and Matteottiplatz, Sandleiten

in Sandleiten, attracted by the inexpensive housing, who represent between 7 and 13% of the total population in the neighborhood. In the most damaged buildings, the percentage of immigrants is between 21 and 36%. Therefore, there is currently some concern about the possible ghettoization of the neighborhood, especially when comparing the high percentage of immigrants in the area with the figures in other neighborhoods in Vienna.

As a result of the transformation of the social structure of the area, the sense of community has been degraded, generating mistrust among the elderly local population and young immigrant families who have recently arrived. Urban life in public space reflects the conflicts arising from the cultural and age differences among Sandleiten's population, as well as from youth unemployment, social isolation and insecurity.

**Open Rooms Strategy** The Open Rooms strategy proposed for Sandleiten by Casanova+Hernandez seeks mainly to tackle cohabitation problems, creating meeting places where citizens can interact. To that end, the proposal consists of a hybrid strategy based on a series of independent landscape interventions in public space, which are complemented with a broad program of activities aimed at promoting citizen participation on different levels.

The strategy consists of eight interventions located in eight urban squares, around which dwellings are spatially arranged. Collective life is concentrated in these squares and, therefore, acting on them is an attempt to reinforce their identity, their function as an interaction space and as a generator of social life in the neighborhood.

It is also in these urban squares where the participatory programs take place and each square becomes an open room for citizens that serves as a meeting place.

CIA, (Community in arbeit) intervention by W. Schneider and B. Zobl at Matteottiplatz, 2012

**Furniture Interventions** The proposed interventions are conceived as a piece of furniture, installed in each of the urban squares, that adds a new program to public space. The furniture interventions not only transform the physical appearance and use of each square, they also change the residents' perception of the squares, as they become vibrant and participatory places.

The physical interventions function as small-scale urban icons that characterize each square as an open room with a specific use (play, reading, meeting), helping citizens to visually differentiate the various areas in the neighborhood. All the interventions were designed with a circular shape to react homogeneously to the varying spatial conditions in each square, which establishes a strong formal relationship among them and creates the sense of a whole within a pre-defined strategy.

The circular shape of the interventions also aims to accentuate their participatory character. In some of them, standardized elements of public space such as a basketball court, a ping-pong table, a life-sized game board, or

Circular Maze

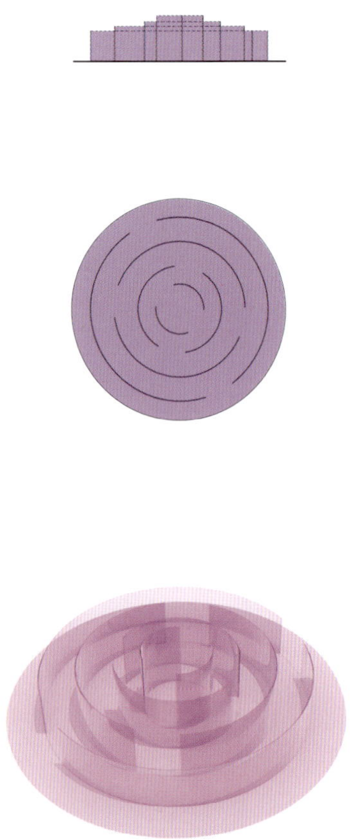

Circular See-Saw

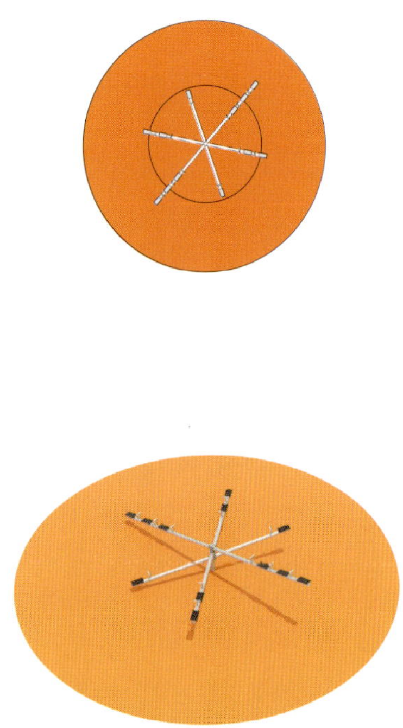

Ping-Pong Table

Circular Basketball Court

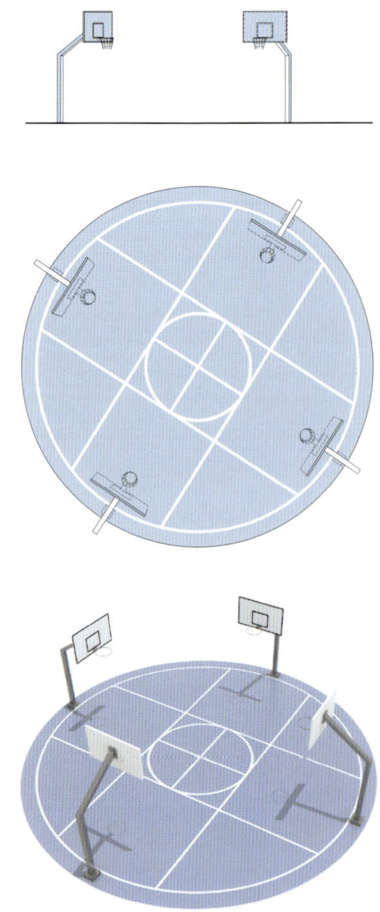

children's swings are redesigned with a circular shape, becoming novel design elements that attract citizens. At the same time, by altering the rules of the game, the interventions spark creativity among citizens who have to reinvent how to use the elements. Other interventions such as the lounge spaces created with artificial grass, the open-air library built around circular tables, or the children's play area experiment with circular forms in their design to promote interaction among users.

Each urban room acquires its own use and identity as it is furnished with a specific intervention, but like all furnishings, these interventions can change position or even be transformed or substituted by new ones according to the residents' wishes. The interventions are only a first step in developing a public space understood as an empty house that is ready to be furnished. A mechanism for citizen participation is then incorporated to furnish this "empty house", which provides the residents with the decision-making power to transform and adapt the furniture intervention to meet their needs.

Open Living Room

Giant Circular Chess Board

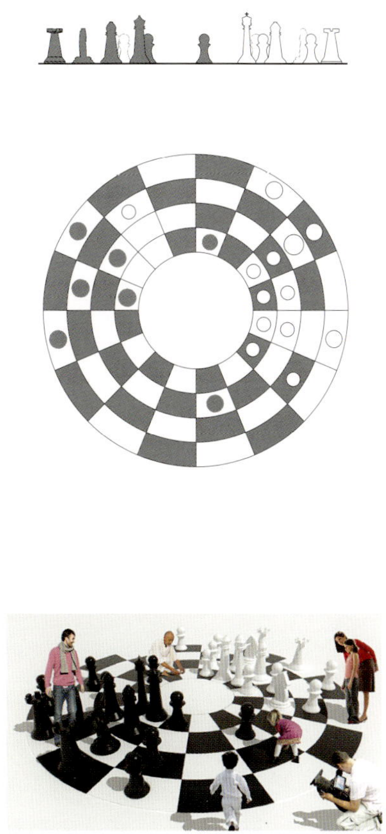

Open Reading Room

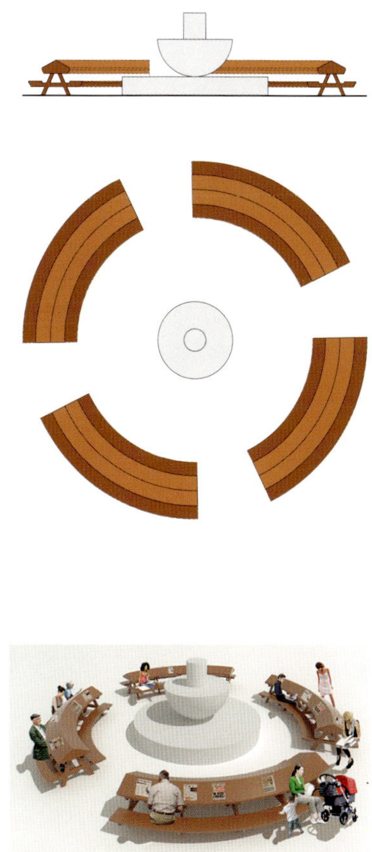

Tube Playground

## Participatory Interventions-Perfomances

The physical interventions in public space are complemented by a series of participatory interventions organized by the platform CULBURB, which aims to activate public space in the suburbs of different central European cities. In many of the interventions initiated by CULBURB, an artist is invited to create a specific program to encourage citizen participation.

One notable CULBURB intervention in the area was Occupy Sandleiten (through movement), realized by Marcella Pascal and Alexander Felch in Matteottiplatz, which invited residents to occupy the square with their movement through the space. The participants were previously inspired by watching participative dance performances and afterward the intervention-action was recorded on video.

The intervention called Love Song Exchange, realized by Carla Della Beffa aimed to bring the inhabitants of Sandleiten together through shared emotions. To that end, 18 participants were invited to take part in a performance in which they sat in a circle of chairs to share and exchange their favorite love songs.

Paul Woodruffe and Walter Klasz proposed the performance Baetsch in the City, where the residents of Sandleiten were invited to collect recyclable material in the neighborhood to build a pavilion together. A local DJ then used the pavilion to broadcast music via www.play.fm.

These artist-directed interventions are an important base for stimulating a feeling of community in the neighborhood and for creating the foundation for the second level of participation, where residents themselves determine their own programming. This is intended to stimulate citizens' interest in their urban environment, inviting them to participate in existing programs, and finally involving them in the decision-making process and even in the management of new programs.

## Occupy Sandleiten Through Movement

Intervention-performance by Marcella Pascal and Alexander Felch at Matteottiplatz

## Love Song Exchange

Intervention-performance by Carla Della Beffa

## Baetsch in the City

Intervention-performance by Paul Woodruffe and Walter Klasz

# Citizens as Designers: Co-creative Strategies

Early in the 2000s, many companies began to use co-creation as a tool to involve clients in the design process for their products. Nike provided online tools so that its customers could design their own sneakers and Converse involved many of its customers in the co-creation of videos to advertise its products. Co-creation became an innovative concept for experimentation, derived from the combination of technological advances in industrial production and new marketing techniques. Co-design helps to blur the line between user and designer, understanding the creative process as a collaborative experience and not just as the individual experience of the designer. This collaboration means that the final product responds more effectively to users' needs and that users feel especially identified with the final result because they have played some role in its creation.

In the case of industrial production, the evolution from the Fordist model, based on the mass manufacture of a single product to make it economically affordable for a large number of consumers, toward the post-Fordist model as a result of the implementation of information technology and the robotization of the industrial process, has allowed for increasing the flexibility of production so that it can be quickly adapted to create a wide variety of different products. Some companies have taken advantage of this increased flexibility to offer customers the possibility of tailoring products to their own particular needs or tastes. But, how can a useful design tool in a collaborative process be distinguished from what is simply part of a sophisticated marketing strategy? Aside from whether the product personalization is real or fictitious, once the functional objective of the design has been satisfied, the added value of co-creation is the user's experience as a co-designer, which creates an emotional link between user and product.

Although the process of designing public space, which has a collective purpose, cannot be compared directly with the design process of a product that only satisfies the specific needs of the user who buys it, it can benefit from the experience associated with co-creative projects developed on another scale. In this case it is not consumers, but citizens, who collaborate in the design process articulated through

Ørestad, Copenhagen. Co-creative strategy based on citizen participation by MUTOPIA for City Park.

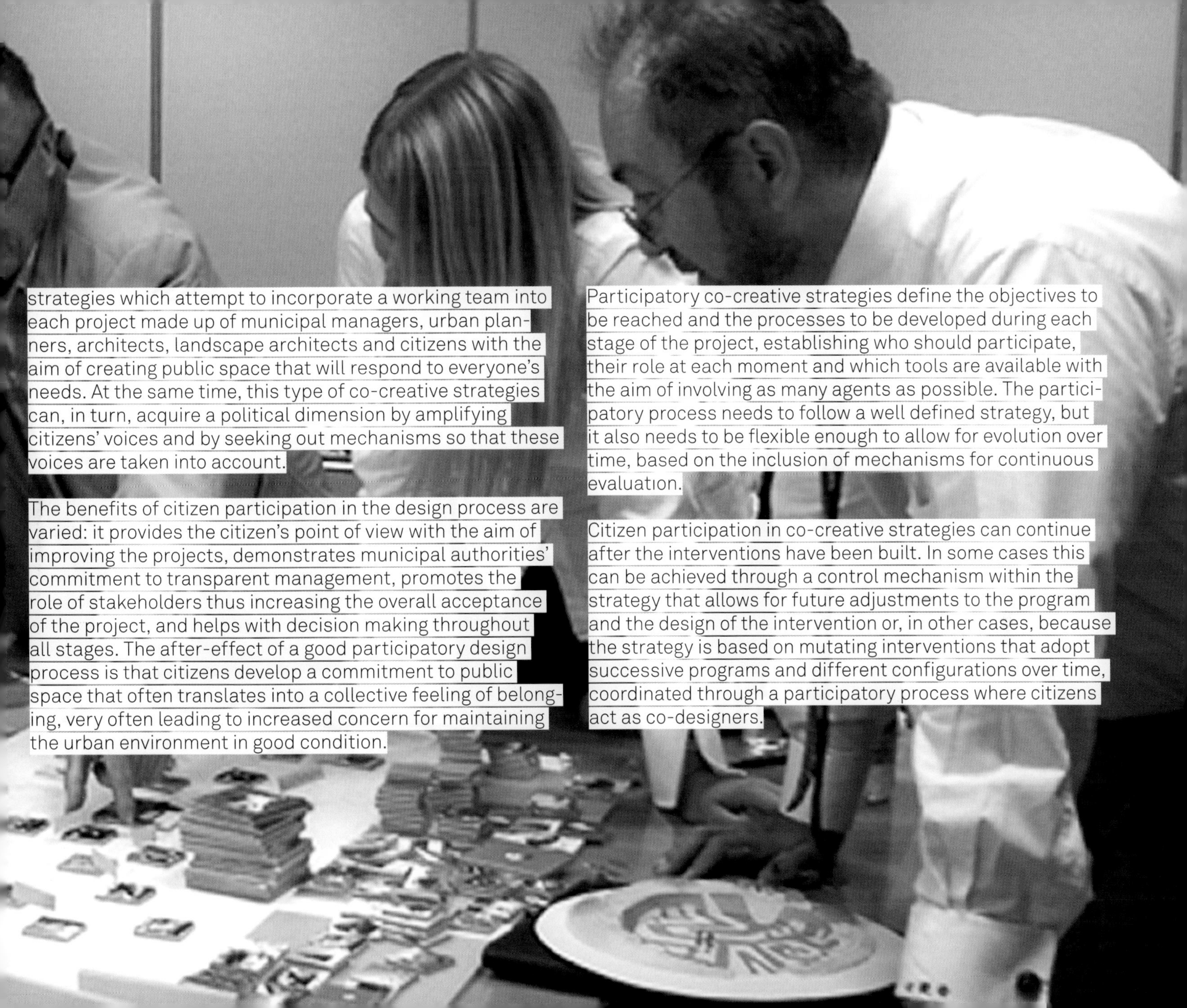

strategies which attempt to incorporate a working team into each project made up of municipal managers, urban planners, architects, landscape architects and citizens with the aim of creating public space that will respond to everyone's needs. At the same time, this type of co-creative strategies can, in turn, acquire a political dimension by amplifying citizens' voices and by seeking out mechanisms so that these voices are taken into account.

The benefits of citizen participation in the design process are varied: it provides the citizen's point of view with the aim of improving the projects, demonstrates municipal authorities' commitment to transparent management, promotes the role of stakeholders thus increasing the overall acceptance of the project, and helps with decision making throughout all stages. The after-effect of a good participatory design process is that citizens develop a commitment to public space that often translates into a collective feeling of belonging, very often leading to increased concern for maintaining the urban environment in good condition.

Participatory co-creative strategies define the objectives to be reached and the processes to be developed during each stage of the project, establishing who should participate, their role at each moment and which tools are available with the aim of involving as many agents as possible. The participatory process needs to follow a well defined strategy, but it also needs to be flexible enough to allow for evolution over time, based on the inclusion of mechanisms for continuous evaluation.

Citizen participation in co-creative strategies can continue after the interventions have been built. In some cases this can be achieved through a control mechanism within the strategy that allows for future adjustments to the program and the design of the intervention or, in other cases, because the strategy is based on mutating interventions that adopt successive programs and different configurations over time, coordinated through a participatory process where citizens act as co-designers.

Case Study E

# CITY PARK ØRESTAD
## COPENHAGEN, DENMARK

STRATEGY / INTERVENTIONS: **MUTOPIA**
STRATEGY: **Ørestadsselskabet**
COMMISSIONER: **Ørestad City**

Ørestad is a large-scale urban development in southern Copenhagen, on the island of Amager, with a capacity for 20,000 inhabitants, 20,000 students and nearly 80,000 workers. It was created from scratch following the new town model and, although it is connected to the center of Copenhagen by metro and train, it is physically isolated from the city. As opposed to the slow and uniform growth of the historic city, Ørestad has been growing in an isolated way over a relatively short period of time. Therefore, the new town hardly establishes any relationship with earlier urban structures, and is home to a population with no previous link to the place, nor do the residents have any prior relationship among them.

Besides the lack of a collective identity, inherent to all recently created new towns, there is the fact that during the first years of the development the neighborhood is not fully operational, since many of the buildings are still under construction and the area does not yet have all the services and facilities that it will have when it is fully occupied.

In this context, the design and programming of activities in public space plays an important role in stimulating spontaneous interaction among citizens and promoting the practice of collective activities that can help to create a feeling of community in the neighborhood. However, if the design and programming of public space is also realized using a co-creative strategy in which citizens are somehow involved, a special link is created between those individuals and public space, which may impact on the increase in its use and reinforce its role as a space for interaction, while promoting a collective consciousness that public space is a space "of" and "for" citizens.

City Park Ørestad was defined in the planning stages as a central park for the district called Ørestad City which, together with the Ørestad Nord, Amager Fælled Kvarteret, and Ørestad Syd districts, form what is known today as Ørestad. It was developed with a low budget thanks to a

flexible participatory strategy based on 28 independent but, at the same time, related interventions called "garden islands", which are located at different points throughout a basic layer of vegetation and between diagonal paths that overlie the park.

Each intervention is unique and has a nickname that defines its identity, its specific program, form, and materialization. At the same time, however, all interventions share a circular perimeter and similar proportions, and they are built with vegetation or warm materials such as wood. All the interventions combined work as a single coordinated strategy that responds to the many different recreational needs of residents, office workers, and students in the new urban development, thereby promoting public space as a meeting place for citizen interaction.

In an urban area that is still under development, the fragmentation of the design into several independent interventions, or garden-islands, works as a flexible strategy that provides the required facilities for the neighborhood's first residents, while offering the possibility of enlarging the project over time with new interventions. It also provides the opportunity to test and, if needed, easily modify the realized interventions to adapt them to the real needs of the residents or future users.

In Ørestad, the fragmentation of the design also simplified the participatory strategy. The design and program of each garden-island was discussed independently with a representative of the users who live or work nearby. During the process, designers and neighbors held several meetings to discuss all aspects related to the program associated with the islands, in what became known as "battles for the park". In these "battles", citizens played the role of designer, coordinated by a group of professional designers, in what could be called a co-creative strategy.

**Urban Analysis** Ørestad is located on the island of Amager, 5 kilometers south of downtown Copenhagen and 4.5 kilometers west of Copenhagen Kastrup Airport. Ørestad is a complete new town developed along a new metro line and the Øresund railway line, which connects Ørestad with Copenhagen Central Station in 7 minutes, with Copenhagen Airport in 6 minutes and with Malmö Central Station in 29 minutes.

In 1993, the Ørestad Development Corporation (Ørestadsselskabet I/S) was founded to manage the urban development of the city district. The first office building was completed in 2001 and the first residential building in 2004. In total, it is expected to take 20 to 30 years to be completely built, and it will provide residential facilities for 20,000 people, educational facilities for 20,000 students and working space for 80,000 people. There is a large diversity of users in public space depending on the time of the day.

## Aerial View

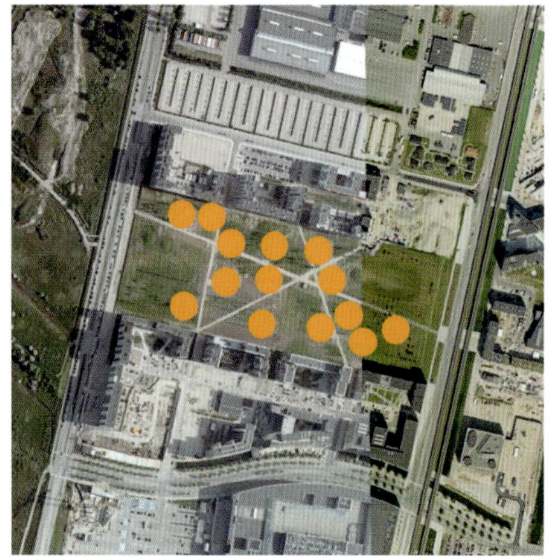

## Users

Neighborhood residents

Office workers

City residents

Tourists

## Relation to the City

(Old) City center | Suburbs

Initial city expansions | Interventions

## Historic Urban Development

Late 19th-early 20th century | 2000-present

Late 20th century | Interventions

## Activities

Residential | Industrial

Public buildings | Shops

Offices | Hotels

**Social Analysis** The social analysis for 2006 revealed that as much as 71% of Ørestad's inhabitants were under 40, a percentage that was much higher than the 48% for the rest of Copenhagen. More than two-thirds of the population had received higher education, whereas the figure was 39% for the rest of the city. There were also more families with young children in Ørestad than in the rest of Copenhagen, and 28% of the interviewees had children who still lived at home. Moreover, under-30s constituted a third of Ørestad's population, a percentage that was considerably higher than the 23% for the rest of Copenhagen.

## Age Structure

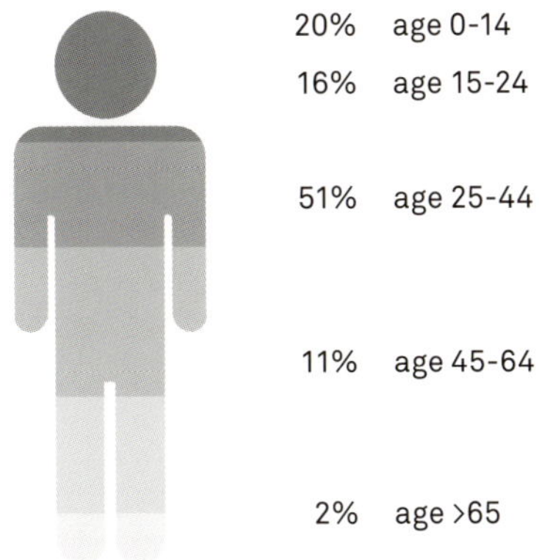


## Household Composition

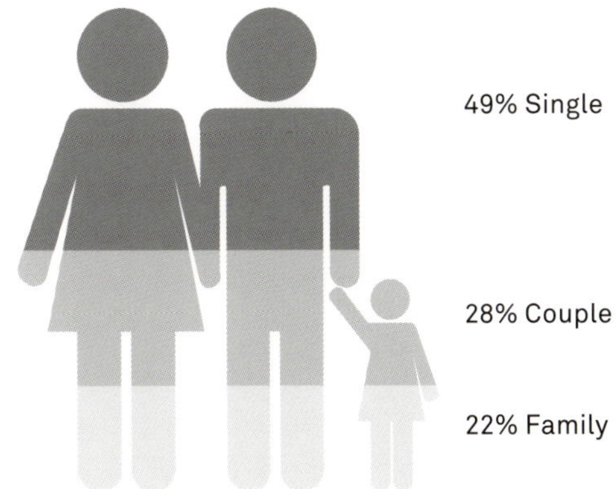

## Immigration

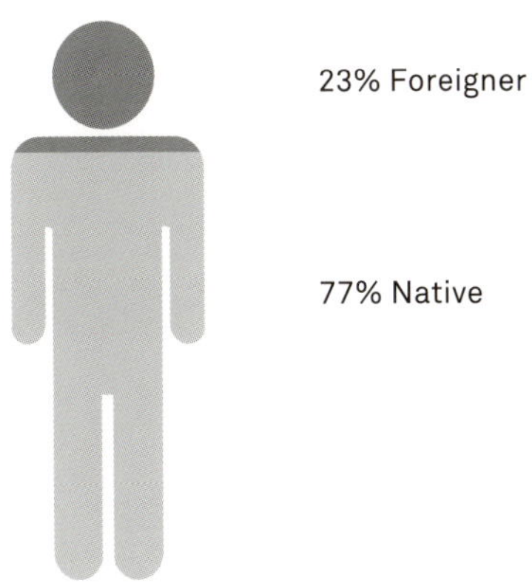


## Unemployment

Age Structure, Immigration, Unemployment data for Ørestad area. Source: Københavns Kommune 2012. Household Composition data for Copenhagen City. Source: Statistics Denmark 2011.

**Interventions** City Park Ørestad can be considered a global strategy, based on 28 independent small-scale interventions. Five of the interventions are just circular mounds that work as landscape elements, fifteen small interventions are dedicated to children's playgrounds and the eight largest islands have specific programs related to specific needs in the neighborhood.

Five of the larger interventions on the site have been selected for analysis. Each one has a different size, function and materialization, but at the same time they present many common elements, which are repeated in the rest of the islands.

## 1 Switchback Island

The island is designed as a children's playground, built around a small artificial hill. Several ramps and stairs allow children to climb to the top of the hill, and they can slide back down on two slides. There are wooden benches at the top, from which to enjoy the views over the whole park and there is also a circular wooden deck that surrounds a sandbox for smaller children. A sculptural playing wheel shelters a slide for small children installed at the edge of the sand area. The green circular façade of the playing wheel works as a visual landmark that identifies the intervention within the park.

## 2 Gilleleje Beach Island

The garden-island combines a beach volleyball area, located at the center of the circle, with a resting area on a wooden deck that provides views over the playground. Light moveable chairs placed on the deck allow for residents to set up their own ideal gathering space. The natural materials used in the wooden deck and the two artificial hills, which protect the area from the wind, provide comfort and intimacy, combining areas for relaxation and for activity to create an attractive urban space. The referee's seat is placed on a small pyramidal tower painted in white and green stripes.

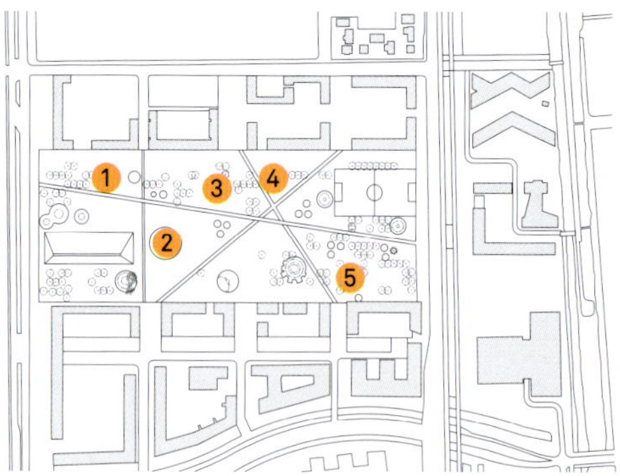

Accesses
Relaxation areas
Sitting areas
Circulation
Vegetation
Playing areas

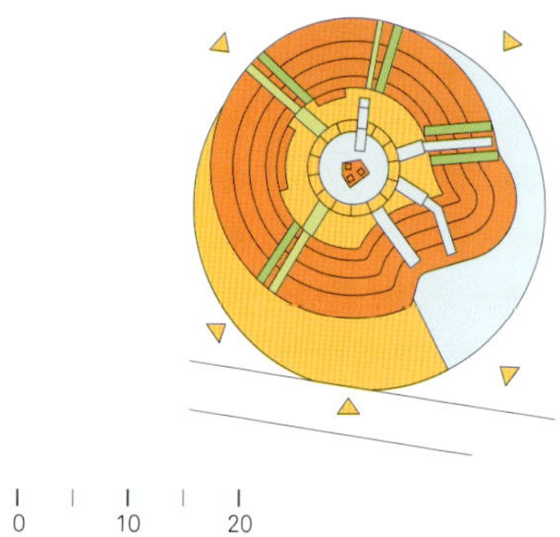


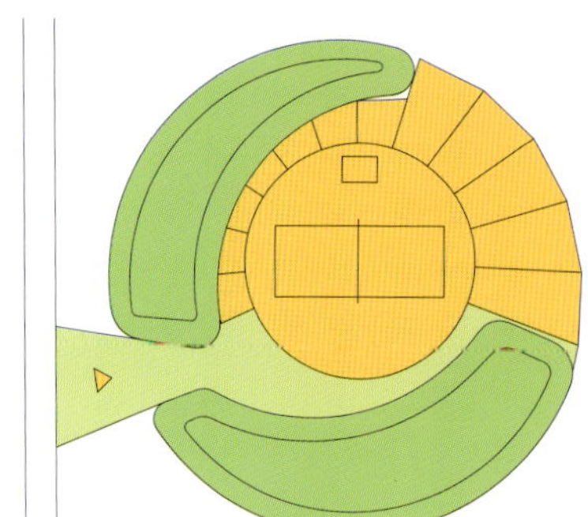

## 3 Family Island

The Island is characterized by a double looped small-scale circuit, which children can use for competing against each other riding bicycles and other children's vehicles. The black asphalt marked with pedestrian crosswalks and other symbols contrasts with the grass covering the rest of the island. A long slope with a circular shape on the northern part of the island creates a natural seating area where children and parents can sit to watch the races.

## 4 Zen Island

This garden island is divided into two parts. On the north side, a circular area can be used as an improvised stage that functions as a flexible zone where many different activities can be developed. On the south side, a slope serves as sitting area made of three rows of white concrete seats. Both parts of the island form an improvised open-air auditorium or theater where sand and grass, performance and observation, actors and spectators create the Zen Island's characteristic balance.

## 5 Explorers Island

This garden island is rather different from the rest. It is basically flat and is divided into three main zones: a central children's playground that is outlined by an irregular polygonal shape, an area of sand that surrounds the playground and a crescent-moon-shaped area, reserved for low vegetation. The playground area is designed as a playful space for small children to explore, in the form of a mini adventure park.

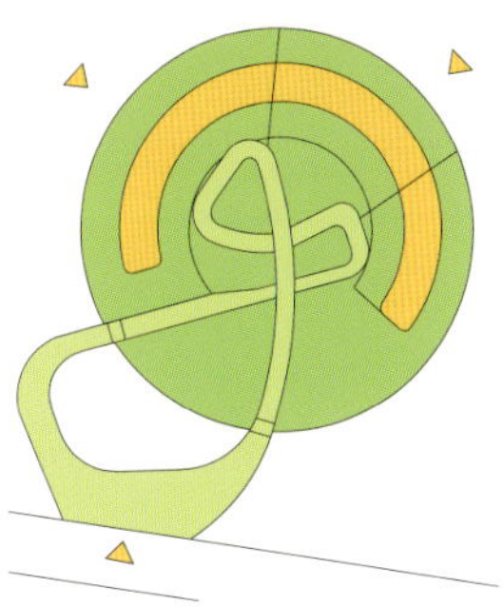

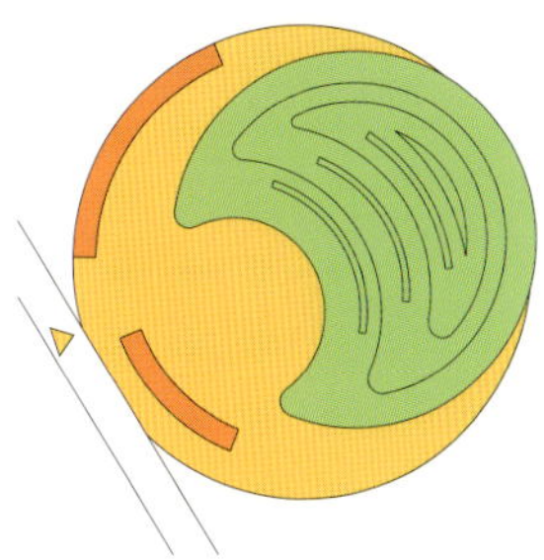

**Process** The Grundejerforeningen Ørestad City (Property Owner Association Ørestad City) and the Ørestadsselskabet (By&Havn, since 2007) together with the residents and other groups of interest played a major role in the development of the project. As a joint venture of all 25 private property owners involved in the urban development, Grundejerforeningen Ørestad City represented a collective client with a range of different interests and agendas. Ørestadsselskabet was responsible for developing all of Ørestad, acting as a representative for the client. Residents and groups of interest, including representatives of the future school and football clubs, were invited to participate in the project development process.

The City Park and the Kay Fiskers Plaza were the only two large public spaces planned for Ørestad City. In 2005, MUTOPIA was commissioned to develop a public space project for both of them, but the client decided to start developing the City Park project first, in response to the demand for recreational public space from a growing number of residents, while the Kay Fiskers Plaza project was put on hold.

Ørestadsselskabet was responsible for communication with the residents and groups of interest. MUTOPIA has been in charge of both the design development and the parallel participatory process. This process included a number of themed workshops during which the work in progress was presented as the basis for discussion, aimed at gaining input for the next design phase. In addition to this "large-scale" participatory process, a number of regular meetings with client representatives and the implicated groups of interest ensured an effective two-way communication throughout the entire design process, providing optimal solutions while respecting the agreed-upon budget.

## Citizen Participation

The strategy developed for Ørestad's City Park carefully integrated citizen participation during the design process. This participation was not related to the initiation of the project or to the physical realization of the interventions. It basically concerned the decision-making process to determine the programming of public space, the density of the interventions and their locations. For that reason, the main strategy was fragmented into several independent but connected participatory processes that focused on designing specific garden-islands, which were called "islands à la carte". Each island was designed by MUTOPIA in collaboration with a representative group of the users who live, work or study in the nearby blocks. Each "island à la carte" acquired a different dimension, different program, design, materialization and location depending on the decisions made during several discussion sessions with the residents.

A secondary objective of the citizen participation process was to promote the engagement of the new residents with public space. When citizens understand the potential and problems of their urban habitat, a shared sense of "collective ownership" of public space is developed. This has resulted in a visibly better physical state of the public space, with lower associated maintenance costs.

## Cost, Financing and Maintenance

The initial total cost of City Park was less than €200.000 which, for a park with an extension of 70,000m², comes to a cost of 2.6 €/m². The low cost of the park was only possible by dividing the strategy into two layers. On the one hand, an extensive low-budget gardening layer covers the whole site, and on the other hand, several island-gardens act as independent interventions which were allocated a larger budget per square meter. Debris produced by the excavations of the nearby buildings was reused to build the small hills and slopes that form some of the garden-islands. This is an environmentally friendly solution that allows for building small-scale visual landmarks without using expensive structures and considerably reduces the construction costs.

City Park was financed by the sale of the real estate property in Ørestad City. This means that for each m² of property sold, a certain amount of money was allocated for the public space project. The fragmented nature of the strategy provides enough flexibility to easily adjust the design to the available budget by controlling the number, size and materialization of the islands. The amount of interventions can increase gradually according to the growing number of residents in the neighborhood, optimizing the annual construction spending according to the available budget.

In general, the built interventions require a similar level of maintenance compared with other parts of the public space in the neighborhood, and only a few elements that were built with less durable materials in some of the garden-islands require a higher level of maintenance and a more frequent replacement of damaged parts.

## Timing

City Park was developed over a similar time span compared with other conventional public space interventions.

The integration of citizen participation did not have any adverse impact on the development process, and the construction of the interventions based on reusing debris from the excavations of nearby buildings did not create any delay in the construction; on the contrary, it simplified the realization.

The strategy takes into account the possibility of future changes to City Park, such as the construction of new garden-islands if needed or the physical and functional refurbishing of existing ones. This flexibility can work as a useful tool for renovating public space depending on the new demands of future residents, while the quality of its public life is maintained. The definition of a continuous and simple system for updating City Park allows for creating a highly sustainable strategy, especially when compared to traditional realizations that are designed for a specific situation, with a fixed program and using conventional materials.

## Use of the Public Space

Evaluations of the use of the public space from Ørestad's residents have been very positive. They appreciate the fact that several workshops let them to give their input concerning the content of the park and they think that the functioning of the park has been greatly improved since its original design, introducing spaces for several activities such as play, sports, barbecues and relaxation. The citizens and other users of Ørestad City perceive the park very positively and they use it frequently.

At the moment, one of the main problems of the park is that it is quite large and is located in a very open, windy area. The open system on which the park's design strategy was based took into account further meetings to improve the park after it was completed, and a decision has now been made to plant more trees in order to solve the wind problem. The space will undergo constant transformations.

## Impact on Citizens and in the Media

The strategy has produced a double positive impact on the citizens of Ørestad. The first one is that, because resident's suggestions were incorporated, the use of the public space has increased allowing them to engage in several outdoor activities that were not possible before. The concentration of single activities in closed circles reinforces the identity of each intervention and provides a clear reading of its use. At the same time, however, the specific program for each area promotes interaction only within affinity groups, excluding interaction among different groups. In that sense, the most neutral interventions, where many different activities can be developed, promote better global interaction among citizens.

The second positive impact of the strategy is the birth of a collective consciousness concerning public space, which developed during the participatory process in the design phase and has grown since the park was finished thanks to new meetings aimed at controlling and discussing the uses of the interventions and their possible improvement.

The urban development of Ørestad as a whole has had a large media impact. First of all, thanks to the ambitiousness of the plan, which became one of the city's largest urban expansions, but also due to the fact that architectural icons designed by the country's top architectural firms were used to generate an attractive image for Ørestad, which was widely diffused by the media. On the contrary, the concept and image for public space in Ørestad was not fully developed in the original master plan and did not receive as much attention from the media, partly because the ambitions for the public space were mainly related to the needs of the neighborhood itself, without any attempt to attract citizens from other parts of the city.

## LIJNBAAN URBAN COURTYARDS
## ROTTERDAM, THE NETHERLANDS

STRATEGY / INTERVENTIONS: **Casanova+Hernandez**
COMMISSIONER: **Municipality of Rotterdam**

This test case was commissioned by the Municipality of Rotterdam and co-sponsored by the Dutch Creative Industries Fund within the framework of wider research on Public Space Acupuncture conducted by Casanova+Hernandez in collaboration with the urban sociologist Arnold Reijndorp.

Analysis, diagnosis and intervention methodologies are tested in this project in order to define new flexible strategies for regenerating the city's public space, which integrate a mechanism of citizen participation. The intervention area selected by the municipality of Rotterdam was the public space in Joost Banckertsplaats and Jan Evertsenplaats. It includes a residential area of approximately 200 meters long by 100 meters wide located in the center of the city between the Lijnbaanstraat, a pioneer pedestrian commercial street which became an icon of modern urban planning in the 1960s, and the Schouwburgplein, where cinemas, auditoriums and a theater are concentrated creating a main cultural and leisure attractor of the city.

The site was designed in the 1960s following the famous renovation plan for the center of Rotterdam after its destruction during the Second World War. The plan lays out an orthogonal pattern of large open blocks mixed with large garden areas in between. Shops are located on the ground floor of the blocks facing the streets, with storage spaces that face the courtyards. These courtyards have a very ambiguous character, on the one hand because of the lack of shops or public program, which gives them a residential character, and on the other hand because they are actually public spaces that are visually open toward the city.

The lack of urban life in the courtyards, the maintenance problems and the feeling of insecurity, especially at night, have led to repeated suggestions that involve fencing them off to create collective spaces for the exclusive use of the inhabitants of the blocks. But the controversial plans to close the courtyards have generated much debate, especially among historians, urban planners and architects, who are in favor of preserving the city's modern planning.

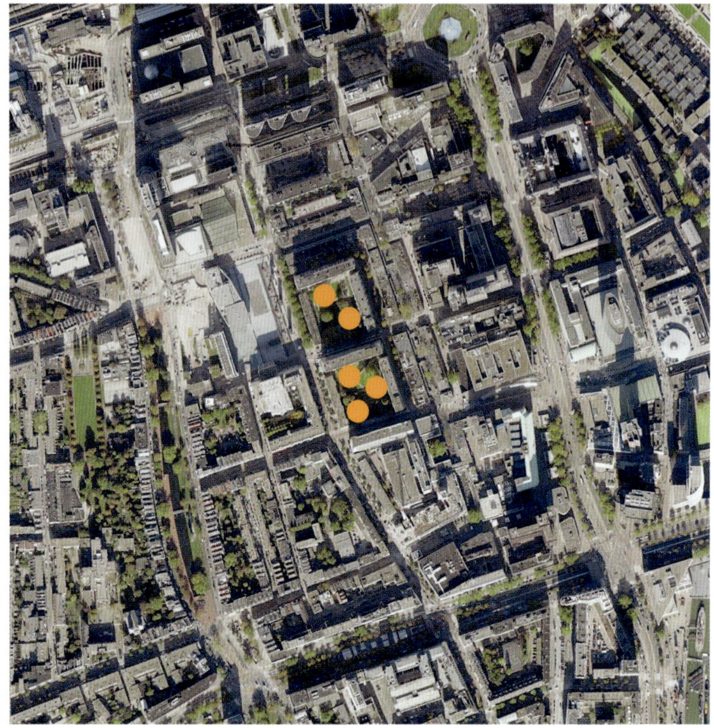

**Strategy** The proposed strategy rejects fencing off the courtyards to avoid public access and, on the contrary, defends the open character of the city's public space, positing the ambiguity of the open space around the urban blocks as an opportunity for activating the neighborhood's public and collective life.

The strategy Sharing Point seeks to promote neighborhood life in the area by creating a meeting point in public space where residents can share activities. Its goal is to redefine the identity of public space in this part of the city, while benefitting social life in the neighborhood.

The activation of the public space must be related to the needs of the citizens that live in the neighborhood. Different citizens have different hobbies and interests and they are naturally grouped into close-knit social circles. The Sharing Point strategy not only provides a location for these social circles to develop their activities in public space, it also promotes interaction among various circles, creating symbiotic combinations through shared activities, which reinforces social cohesion in the neighborhood.

## Citizen Participation and Programming

The strategy Sharing Point experiments with a process of citizen participation in some of its different phases. The actors involved are divided into three main categories: 7 existing neighborhood groups and citizens' associations, 5 professionals and business organizations that are already present in the area, and 2 housing corporations: Amvest (Joost Banckertsplaats) and Vestia (Jan Evertsenplaats).

First, it is interesting to learn about the different groups' needs as well as the suggested activities they might undertake in public space. Second, it could be very constructive to bring groups together that could share certain activities or that could even engage in a symbiotic relationship.

For instance, Fysiotherapie Rotterdam develops activities for children that could be shared with the children's group from the Kinderdagverblijf Dribbel. Sports activities can be combined with elderly activities by creating special rehabilitation zones for the elderly. Educational activities for children can be mixed with urban agriculture activities developed by the residents. In the end, many symbiotic combinations can be created by analyzing the needs of the different groups that play a role in the construction of the neighborhood's public life.

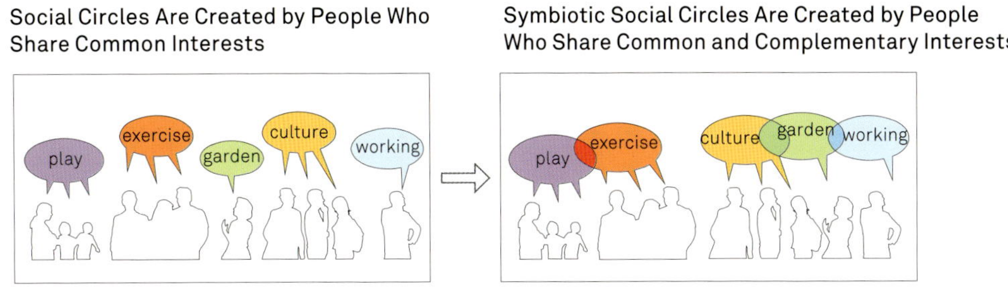


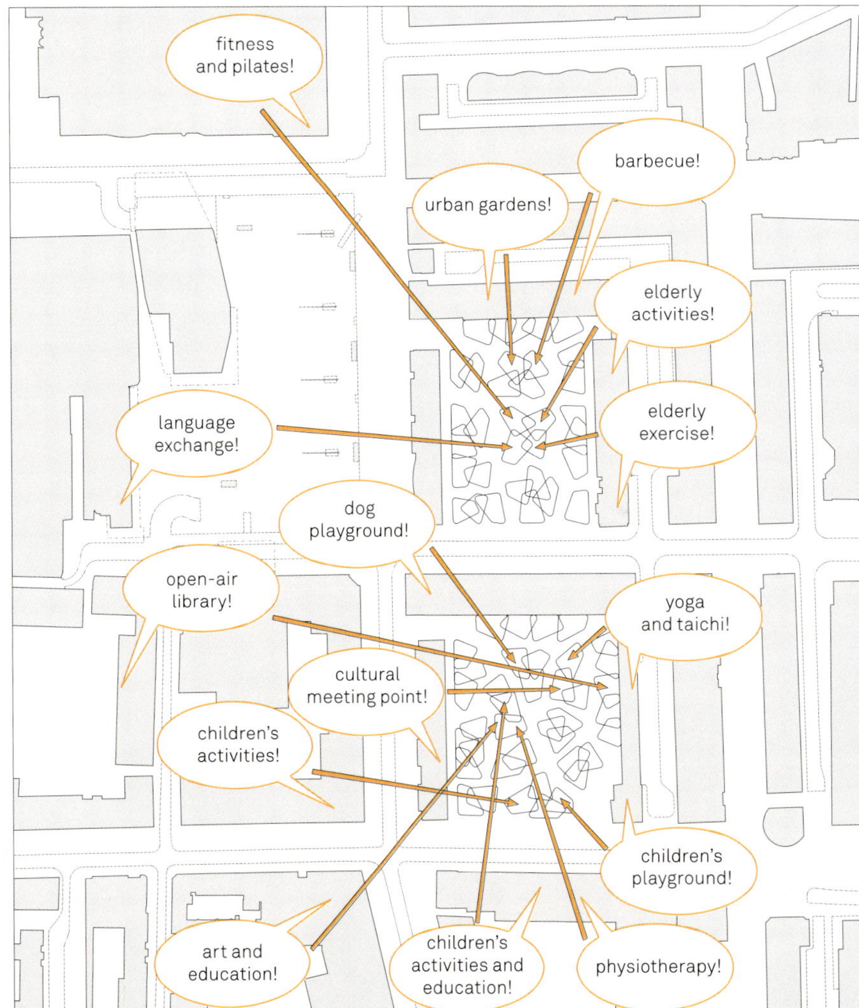

09

**Interventions** The strategy Sharing Point is a flexible system based on independent interventions called "sharing islands". The basic sharing islands are created by combining two, three or four modular elements. These islands are referred to as 2-clover, 3-clover and 4-clover. More complex compositions of sharing islands are located along the border of the courtyards near the buildings and are formed by combining five or more modular elements.

Each sharing island has a different perimeter, but they are all formed by the same modular elements, created by combining four main layers:

1. Edge material: steel border or pre-cast concrete seats.
2. Surface material: grass, flowers, green hills, urban gardens, soft rubber material for children's play-grounds, sand or wooden decks.
3. Singular elements: trees, sculptural lights or artwork some of which already exist.
4. Small constructions: greenhouses, garden storage units, cafés, kiosks or pavilions.

Each modular element adopts a different activity or function. The green areas are placed at the border of the courtyards near the houses. The playgrounds for children of different ages and the café pavilions are located near the streets. Other activities such as tai-chi and yoga areas, an outdoor gym, exercise areas for elderly people, lounge areas, picnic areas and game tables are given a central position.

A large catalog of activities can be implemented in response to the needs of different actors who are involved in the strategy, creating a solid yet balanced activity program for the public space.

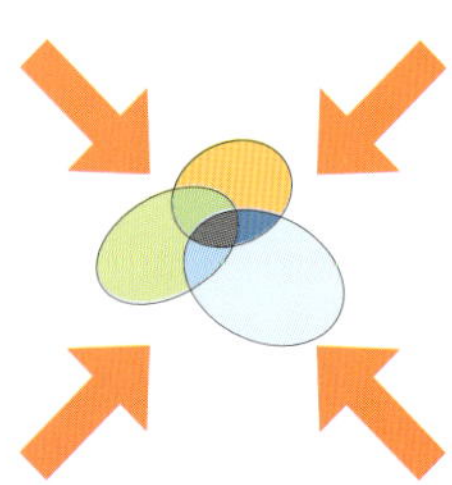


## Morphology of the Sharing Islands

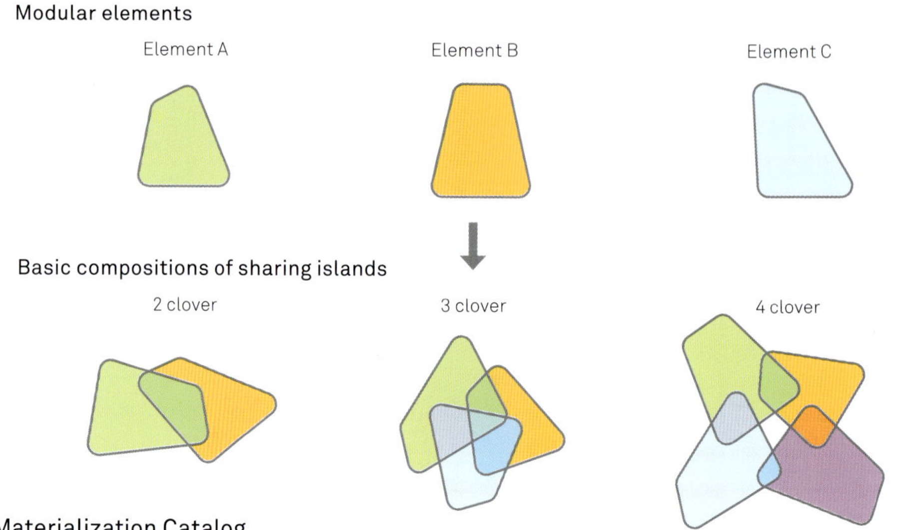


## Materialization Catalog

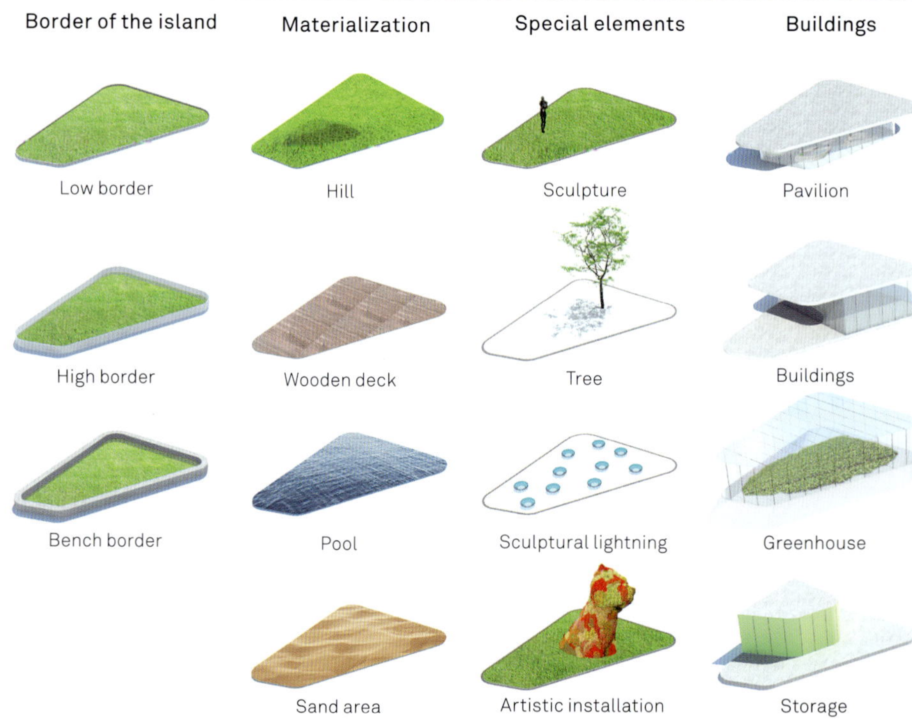

## Play

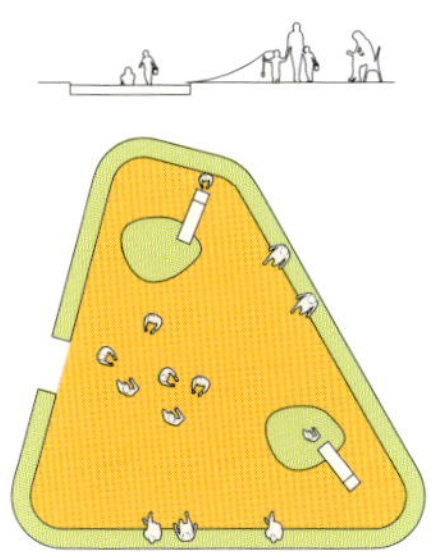

Playground children 0-3

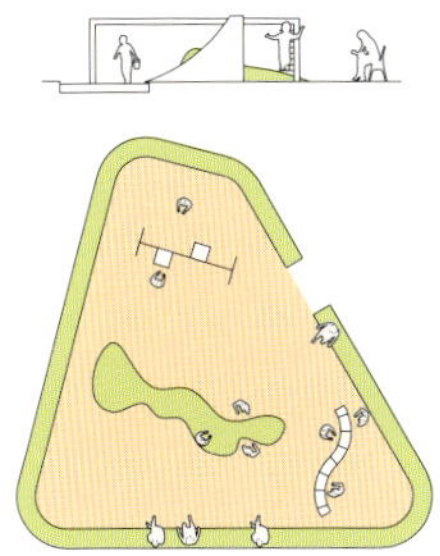

Playground children 4-6

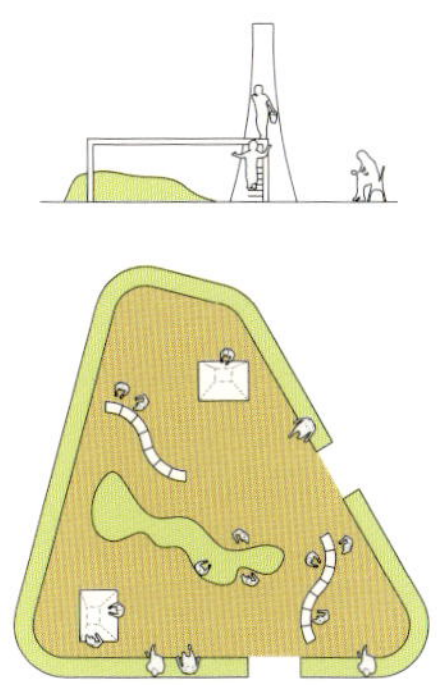

Playground children 7-12

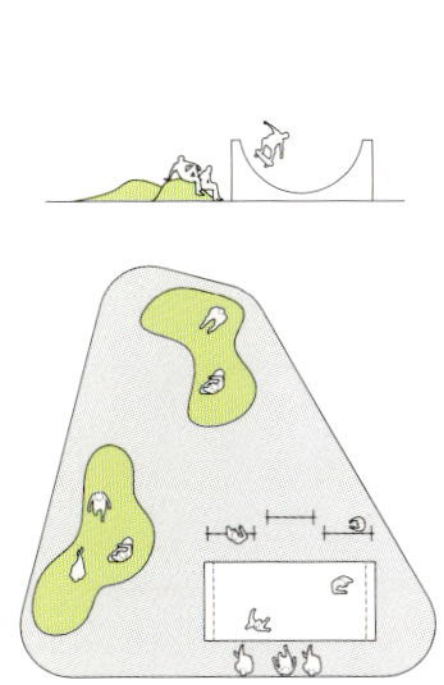

Playground children 13-16

## Exercise

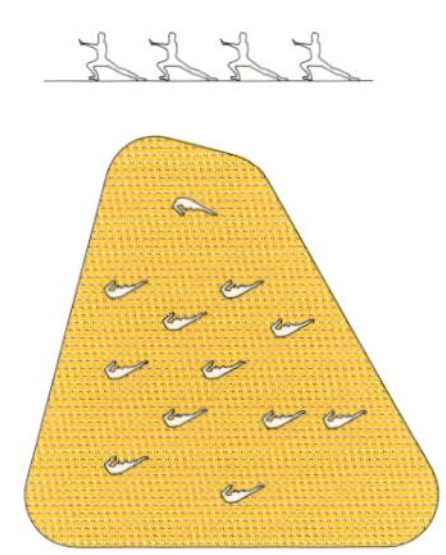

Tai-chi / Yoga / Pilates / Stretching / Dancing

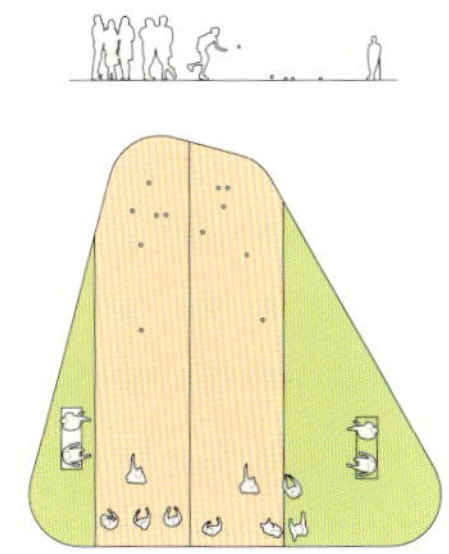

Petanque

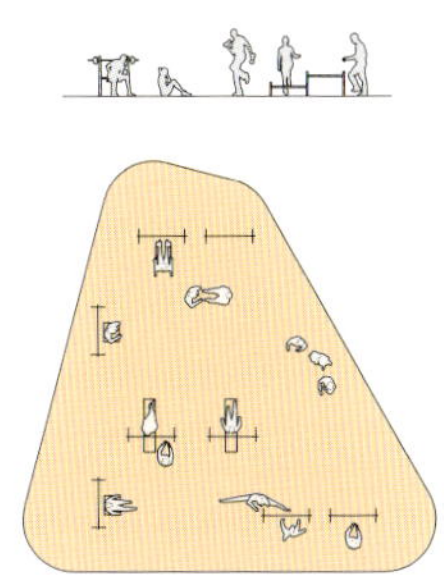

Outdoor gym

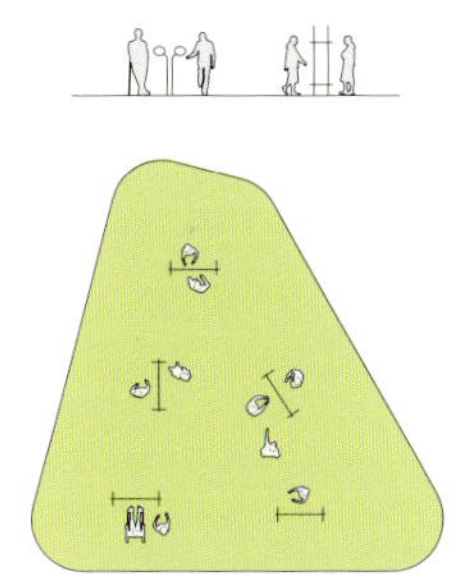

Gym for the elderly

## Games

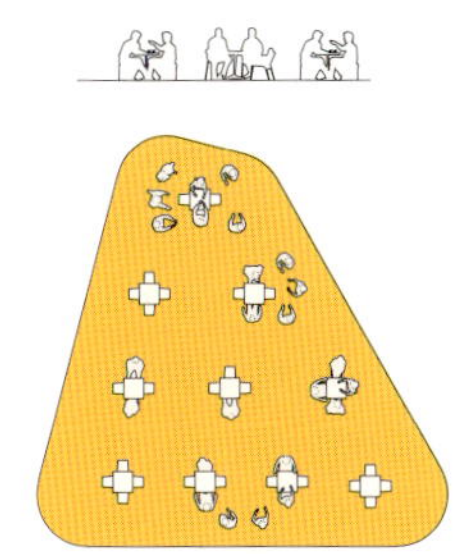

Board games

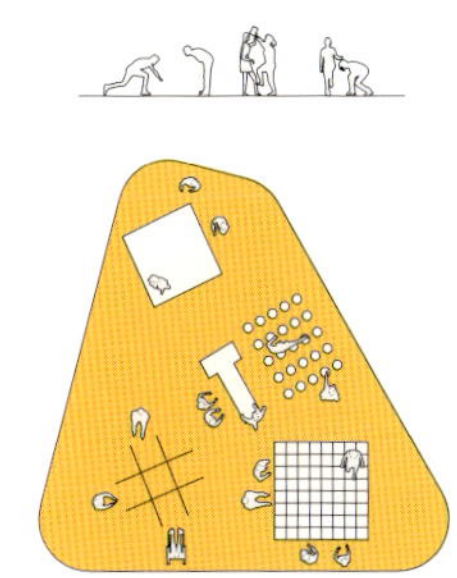

Giant board games

## Gardens

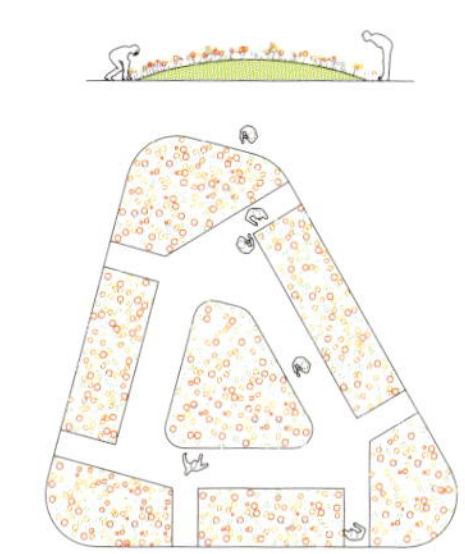

Flower gardening

Urban agriculture

## Working

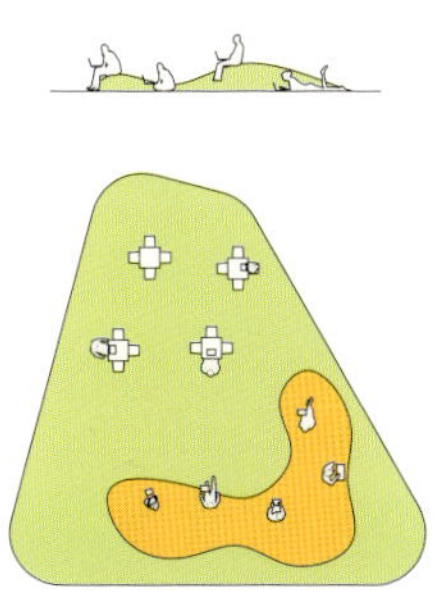

Wi-Fi area

## Culture

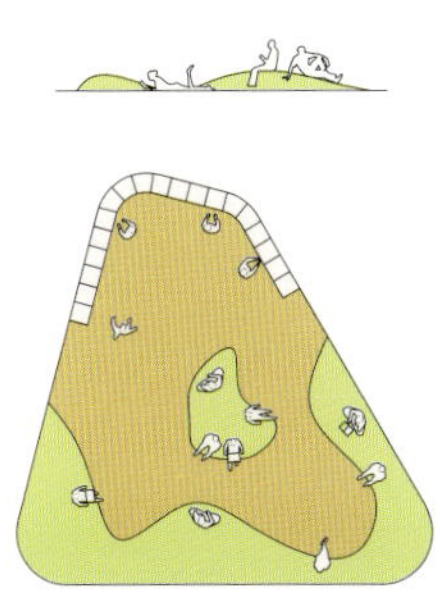

Open-air library

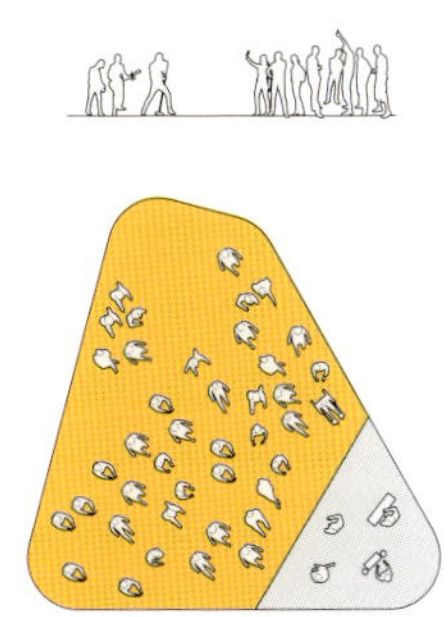

Street theater

## Leisure

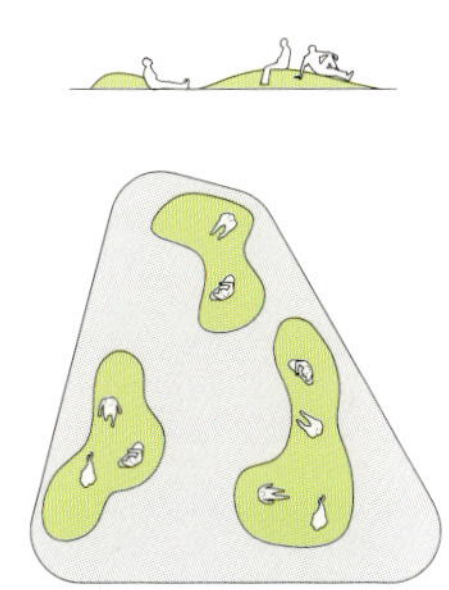

Lounge area

Cafe-Kiosk

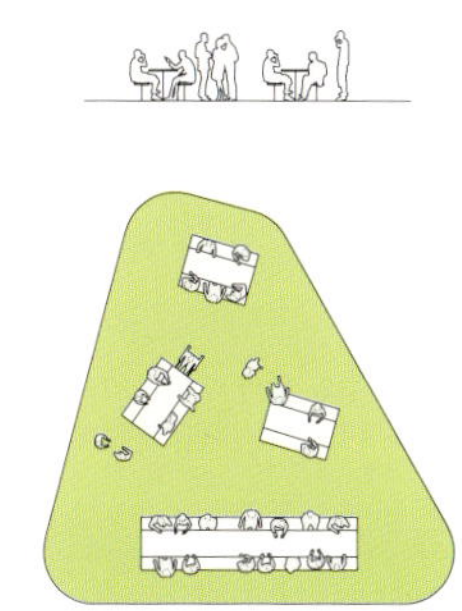

Picnic area

**Flexible Planing and Phases** The strategy Sharing Point is not conceived as a single intervention to be designed and built all at once, but on the contrary it is a strategy to be developed during several phases that can be adjusted in several ways over time to create a real and sustainable impact on urban life in the city.

The structural system created by the intersection of small plots, which are occupied by green areas or filled in with different activities, allows for implementing activities independently and at any point in the process, depending on the residents' needs. Each plot could be independently financed and maintained and some of them could have a more public use, while others are given collective uses, depending on the specific location.

The strategy can easily be implemented in one, two or more phases. The fact that the interventions can be developed independently makes gradual growth possible and also allows their future improvement.

Possible planning in four phases:

**Phase 1 (Planning the strategy)**
This phase consists of an urban and social analysis of the urban area, the selection of the possible program to be developed in cooperation with the different actors involved, a preliminary design and the debate about it.

**Phase 2 (Development of test interventions)**
Some test-interventions are designed and built on the basis of the outcome of the first phase. Recreational and educative programs can be tested, integrating citizen participation in an active way.

**Phase 3 (Definitive design of the interventions)**
The analysis of the effects produced by the test-interventions leads to modifications in some interventions and the creation of new ones in light of the experience acquired in the previous phase.

**Phase 4 (sustainable monitoring and maintenance)**
In this phase, the strategy is expected to take on a large degree of autonomy, including active citizen participation. Periodical evaluations of interventions' use lead to the modification of existing interventions or the construction of new ones.

## Phases

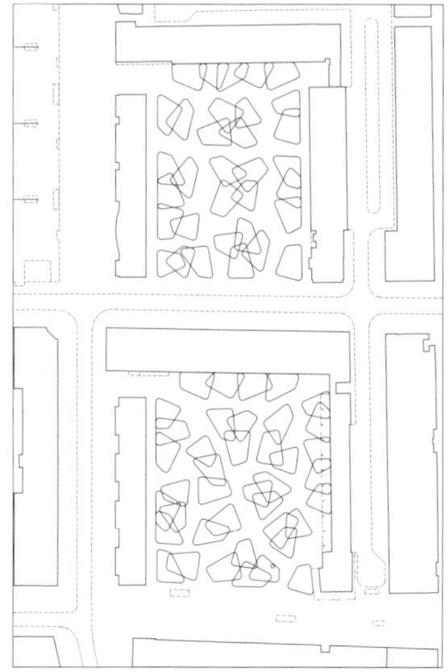

Basic structure

First phase - Green areas are combined with test interventions

Second phase - Evaluation, modification of existing interventions and realization of new ones

Flexible program ⟺

Future phases - all interventions can be adjusted to new necessities

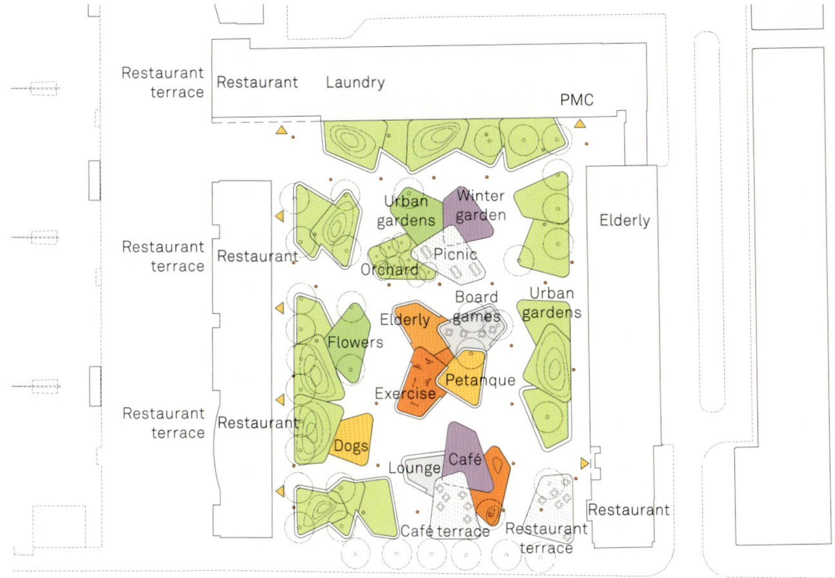
Restaurant terrace
Restaurant
Laundry
PMC
Restaurant terrace
Restaurant
Urban gardens
Winter garden
Elderly
Picnic
Orchard
Board games
Urban gardens
Elderly
Flowers
Petanque
Exercise
Restaurant terrace
Restaurant
Dogs
Café
Lounge
Restaurant
Café terrace
Restaurant terrace

Restaurant terrace
Restaurant
Flowers
Dogs
Zen-deck
Yoga/taichi
children's daycare
Auditorium
Open-air library
Stage
Physio-therapy
Pond
Restaurant terrace
Restaurant
(7-12)
(4-6)
(13-16)
(0-3)
(4-6)
Terrace
Ice cream
Children's playground
0
10
20

Winter
garden
Urban
gardens
Picnic
Orchard
Elderly
Board
games
Urban
gardens
Petanque
Exercise
Dogs
Café
Lounge
Wi-Fi
Café-terrace
Restaurant-
terrace

Dogs
Children's daycare
Zen-deck yoga tai-chi
Auditorium Stage
Open-air library
Physiotherapy
Pond
Playground (7-12 years)
Playground (4-6 years)
Playground (13-16 years)
Playground (0-3 years)
Playground (4-6 years)

## CENTRAL PARK.
RAJKA, HUNGARY

STRATEGY / INTERVENTIONS: **Casanova+Hernandez**
STRATEGY / COMMISSIONER: **CULBURB**

Rajka is a small Hungarian village, with a population of 2,700, located on the border between Slovakia, Austria and Hungary. The city is just 20 km from Bratislava and 75 km from Vienna. In recent years, its proximity to Bratislava has attracted 900 new Slovakian inhabitants who live in Rajka and work in Bratislava. As the Slovakian population grows, the Hungarian population has decreased, with residents selling their houses and land in order to move to larger cities nearby. This has caused segregation in the population according to age groups and geographic origins, which has affected social life in the village.

On the other hand, although current policy from the city council has prevented the construction of large-scale urban developments, residents are now calling for the creation of a park to protect the biggest green area in the center of the village, which runs the risk of being built over as a result of pressure from the real estate sector.

The CULBURB platform called for flexible strategies to provide a solution for the two afore-mentioned problems through the creation of public space interventions that foment interaction between the different groups living in the area, especially among young people, while at the same time the strategies should intervene in the village's central green area in order to transform it into a central park.

**Strategy** Community Circles is a strategy based on independent but coordinated small interventions that, on the one hand, provides new innovative and attractive spaces where different groups can share activities and, on the other hand, involves every citizen in a participation process that reinforces the collective identity of the village.

The strategy includes a process of citizen participation, in which representatives from different groups in the village's social structure can take part, focused on acting in the southern part of the existing green area. A total of 13 interventions are proposed for the park. The function and design for half of them will be defined through participatory processes created during round-table discussions with representatives of groups in the village. Interventions that generate the necessary spaces and activities for all groups as well as interventions that encourage citizen interaction will be especially promoted. The other half of the interventions will attempt to provide a response to the basic needs for recreation that affect Rajka's inhabitants, such as children's playgrounds or sporting fields, while rethinking their basic design principles and experimenting with the possibilities for increasing interaction among citizens.

The thirteen interventions are connected by a series of winding paths that direct the flow of pedestrians from the northern limits toward the southern end of the park. This network of paths invites residents to cross the park and to use it as a place for strolling, encouraging the use of the spaces for leisure and recreation. The open areas between the interventions and the paths are planted with native vegetation that has traditionally been used for pastureland, balancing out the higher cost of the interventions with the low cost and easy maintenance of the large surfaces.

**Interventions** The thirteen interventions that make up the strategy present a circular shape that creates a certain homogeneity among them, even though the size, the program and the materials used for each one are very different in order to create differentiation within the whole. The circle is a geometrical figure with no directionality, equally accessible from every point of the perimeter, which encloses a democratic space for sharing collective activities and works as a symbol of community.

Each intervention presents dimensions carefully tailored to the activity that takes place in it, which are also related to the dimensions of the other interventions. The circle encloses a portion of public space, creating a small-scale open-air room with a domestic character that is ideal for collective activities.

Each intervention works with everyday elements such as playgrounds, leisure areas or picnic tables, re-imagined through an unconventional design that breaks pre-established conventions that dictate how public space should be used. Breaking the codes of use and conventions is intended to awaken curiosity among visitors, who are invited to look for new ways of behaving in public space and, at the same time, to experience new ways of relating with others.

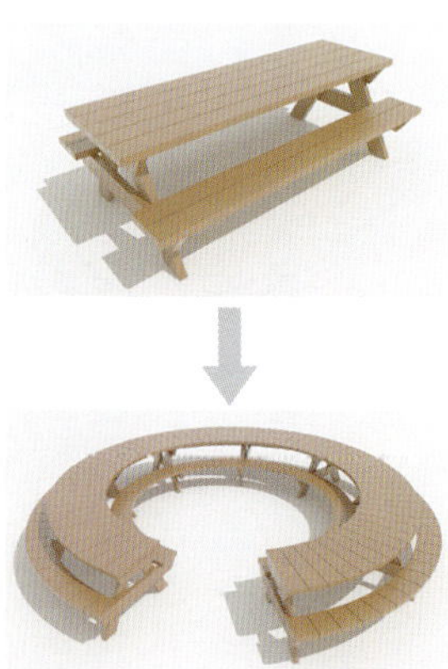

Standard picnic table

Round picnic table

## 1 Circular Seating Area

A conventional bench following a circular shape limits a space where visitors are seated in a position in which all of them can look at each other, encouraging communication.

## 2 Circular Picnic Table

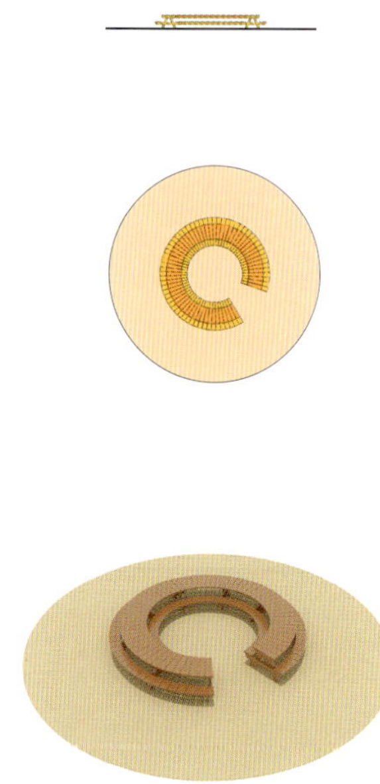

Conventional picnic tables are designed with long benches, which facilitates communication among people facing each other but makes communication difficult among people at the ends when the table is long. The circular design of the picnic table breaks the standard scheme and promotes interaction among all the people sharing the table.

## 3 Circular See-Saw

The classic seesaw design invites interaction between two children with two similar weights who sit on either side. Joining together three seesaws into a circle establishes new possibilities for play with six children, so that pairs of children of different ages can play together at the same time.

## 4 Circular Seating Hill

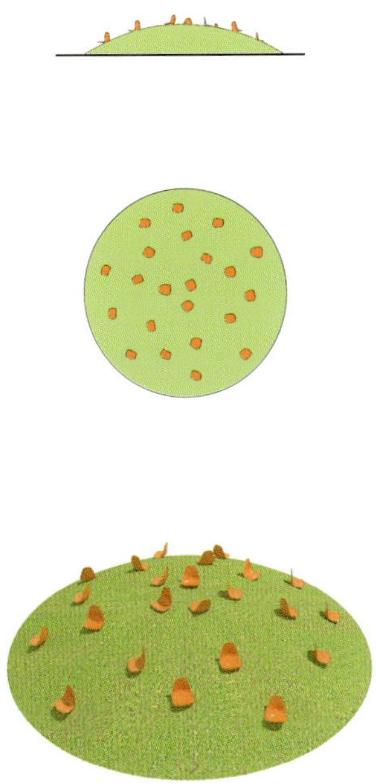

On the one hand, the circular hill is an extroverted intervention that allows for enjoying views across the park, but at the same time there are seats arranged randomly across the grass, which are situated at an appropriate distance to enhance the communication among the people sitting on them.

## 5 Circular Ping-Pong Table

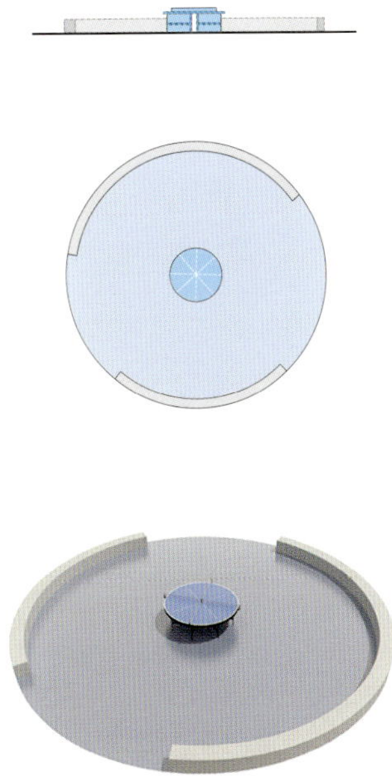

Conventional ping-pong is played on a rectangular table with a net that divides it into two sides and two players play against each other. Redesigning the table in a circular shape and with three nets changes how the game is played, allowing for six players to play at once, while reinventing the rules for a group game.

## 6 Spiral Slide Playground

The spiral slide transforms the mono-directionality of the ordinary slide, allowing for a different experience that can foster a greater versatility of use by children.

## 7 Circular Basketball Court

Basketball is traditionally played with two teams facing off and two hoops. Putting five hoops on the same court breaks with the traditional rules of the game and allows both for playing five independent games, one at each hoop, or for reinventing new ways of playing, where more teams can play in the same match.

## 8 Circular Soccer Field

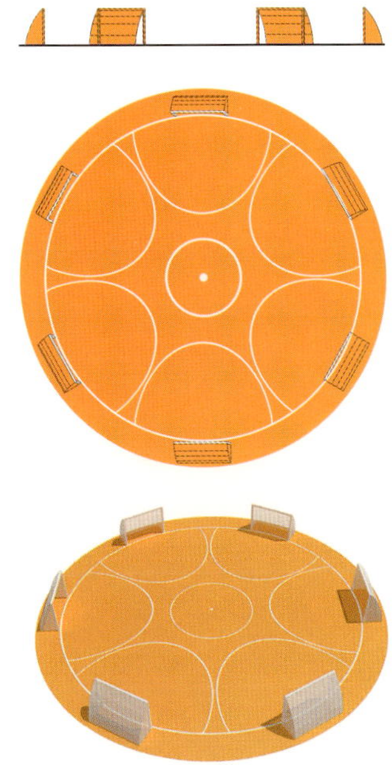

All games where goals are scored, like soccer and handball, involve two opposing teams. A playing field with six goals, in pairs of two within a circular field, permits conventional play, but it also facilitates new ways of playing with the possibility of combining more teams in the same match.

## CAN ESCANDELL PARK
IBIZA, SPAIN

STRATEGY / INTERVENTIONS: **Casanova+Hernandez**
COMMISSIONERS: **SEPES and Municipality of Ibiza**

As a result of the boom in tourism, Ibiza Town underwent rapid economic development in the 1960s and 1970s that prompted the urban transformation of the city. Although, in recent years, this transformation has led to the creation of new infrastructures for tourism, such as the marina, many restaurants, modern hotels and new housing blocks, the urban public space was still organized around small-scale squares. In 2011, the Ibiza Town Council and the state land agency (SEPES) decided to build a 17.35-hectare urban park located in the western part of the city, which will become the largest green area in the entire town.

At about the same time, in 2010, the Ibiza Town Council approved new regulations intended to boost citizen participation in the city's public affairs, which explicitly stated that citizens' implication in the successful operation of the city could not be limited to voting for representatives in the municipal elections. The new regulations were intended to foment a participatory democratic model according to which, citizens could use new channels for direct participation in decision-making concerning the city.

In this sense, public space in the city is a space for cohabitation that is open to all citizens, symbolizing the quintessential democratic space. The creation of a new public park constitutes an exceptional opportunity to try out a new model for creating and managing public space, which responds to the new policy supported by the Ibiza Town Council.

Hence, the new Can Escandell public park is not envisioned as the result of a closed design, but rather as an open strategy that experiments with incorporating citizen participation as a design tool. On the one hand, the strategy serves as a means for creating a popular park that is equipped with activities for all kinds of groups and, on the other, it serves as an experiment for trying out new participatory models that more directly involve citizens in making decisions about the city, according to the goals of the new regulations on citizen participation.

**Strategy** The open strategy is based on three central elements: the grid of paths that connects with the existing network of pedestrian routes through the city; the green areas defined by those paths, which are similar in size to the city blocks in the urban layout; and a series of interventions located within those green areas, which serve to complement the network of the surrounding urban facilities.

The strategy envisages that some of the elements will be fixed in the design, such as the grid of paths, the perimeters of the green areas, and some of the uses and locations of the most important interventions. However, the proposal allows for other elements to be defined through a process of citizen participation, such as the characteristics of certain green areas, as well as the locations and uses of some of the interventions.

The grid of paths through the park is designed to establish continuity with the network of adjacent streets, connecting with the urban residential zone to the south, the new Can Escandell urban development to the north and the historic center of Ibiza Town to the east.

The green areas are lounge zones for lingering that contrast with the grid of paths where the pedestrian flow takes place. Each green area is subdivided into a series of oval-shaped lots that form a mosaic of natural landscapes created using native island vegetation, such as pines, almond trees and wild grassland, in combination with cultural landscapes linked to agricultural activity and with fruit trees such as orange, lemon, fig and olive trees.

The use of native vegetation attempts to reinforce the island's cultural identity, to ensure rapid adaptation of the vegetation to the local climate and to minimize water consumption for irrigation, since the park is connected to a system for the recovery and reuse of rainwater.

Grid of paths + Green areas + Functional islands

## Connecting Existing Networks and Expanding Urban Facilities Within the Park

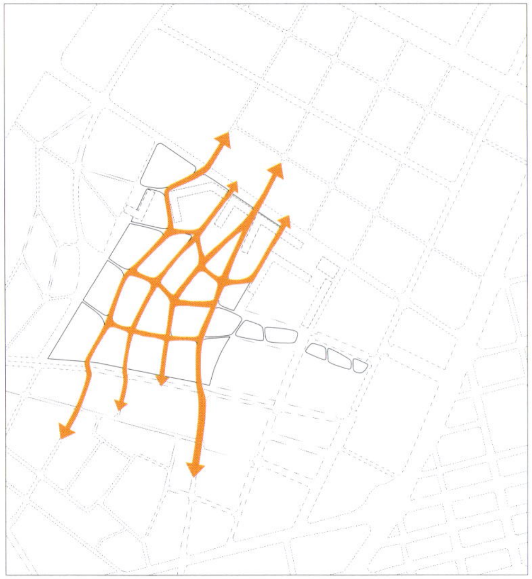

North-south pedestrian circulation

Urban fabric

Public facilities

East-west pedestrian circulation

Public spaces network

Public buildings and pavilions

**Interventions** Each green area incorporates one or more interventions, which are intended to animate the park with activity and uses. The spaces for the interventions are clearly outlined by an oval-shaped perimeter and function as rooms or lounge areas designed for specific activities, such as a children's playground, an exercise area for seniors, a small open-air auditorium or a cafeteria, among others.

All the interventions together establish a heterogeneous program of activities, which is open to citizens of all ages and socio-cultural origins. This program encourages cultural, sports and recreational activities, among others, and generates a place for meeting and gathering.

Each activity has been situated in a specific location in the park, where uses are tied in with the nearby urban surroundings. Three sizes of interventions lay out a hierarchy that corresponds with the importance of the activities' focus: the largest interventions are located in the park's

### Environmental Sustainability: Mosaic of Natural and Cultural Landscapes Created with Native Vegetation

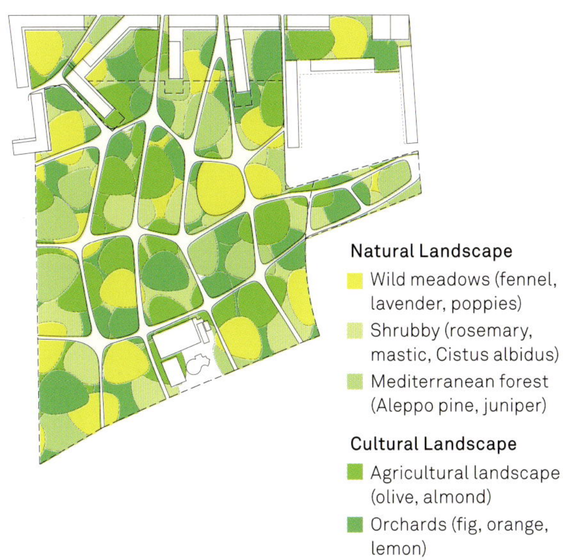


### Environmental Sustainability: Water Management

### Social and Cultural Sustainability

### Environmental Sustainability: Energy Efficient Lighting and Reduced Light Pollution

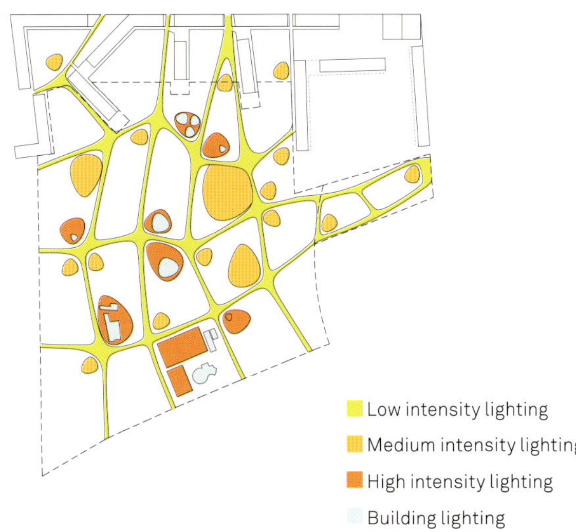


### Environmental Sustainability: Integration of Existing Elements Into the Park

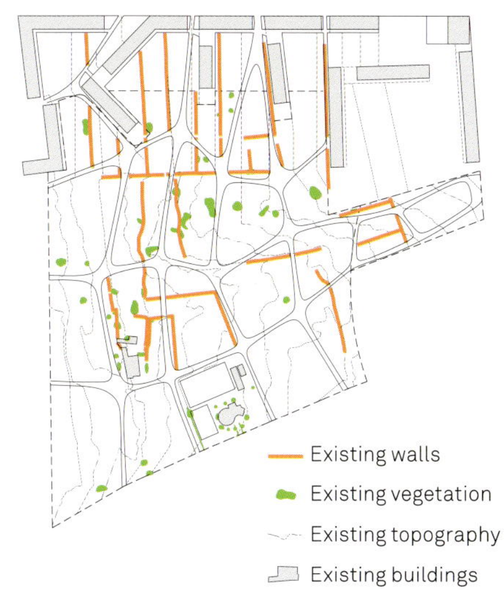

interior in order to encourage Ibiza's citizens to visit the park; the medium-sized interventions are located along the daily routes of the citizens through the park; and the smallest ones, which are intended to be designed through citizen participation processes, are situated along the park's perimeter, serving as facilities and recreational areas linked to the adjoining neighborhoods.

In this way, the children's playground areas can be located near the housing intended for families and the exercise areas for senior citizens can be situated close to the homes for elderly residents. Some of the interventions' function and design are defined in response to the needs of specific groups, but other meeting spaces have also been created to promote interaction among citizens of all ages and different social groups.

The organic and fragmented nature of the interventions adapts perfectly to the existing topography, reducing the need for earth works to a minimum and respecting the pre-existing conditions of the site. These site conditions are integrated into the park's design, using the existing slopes as part of the new topography, the existing trees as part of the proposed vegetation and the historic walls as part of the green areas.

The design strategy permits flexibility in defining the activities in the park through a network of open interventions that can incorporate the neighborhood residents' needs based on a mechanism of citizen participation during the design phase. Designing the interventions independently and assigning their uses autonomously makes the global strategy extremely flexible and easy to execute in phases. This also allows for the gradual extension of the park in the future toward the western unoccupied adjoining land.

Fragmenting the strategy into related yet independent interventions also makes the reprogramming for certain interventions more flexible in order to accommodate a response to future needs. This also makes it easier to control costs because larger investments corresponding to certain interventions can be compensated by the low execution and maintenance costs for other interventions.

The citizen participation process, structured in working groups made up of citizens who share common interests, helps to define the uses for certain interventions, to determine their ideal locations within the park, and to specify their design and materialization through what could be referred to as a multiple-level co-creative strategy.

### Playground Islands

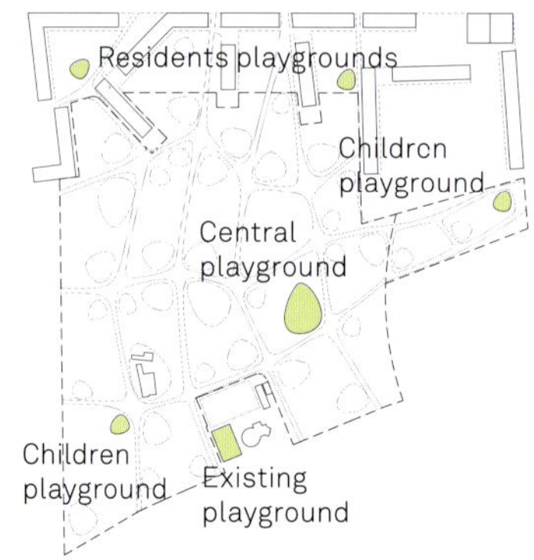


### Sports Islands

### Children's Playground

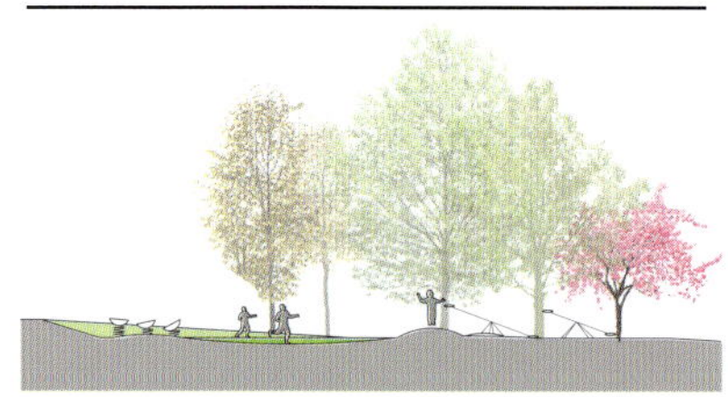

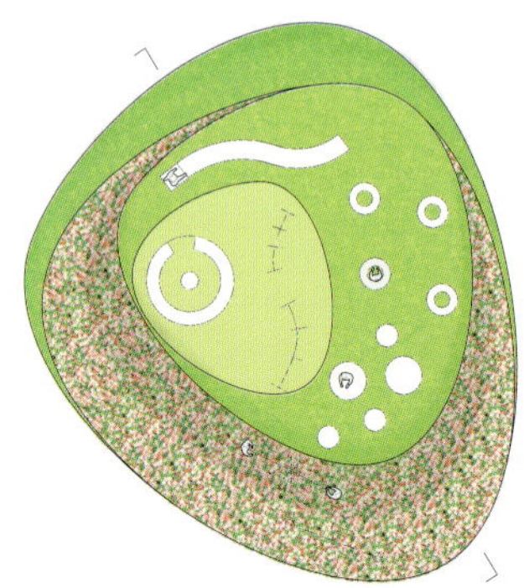

### Skating Rink

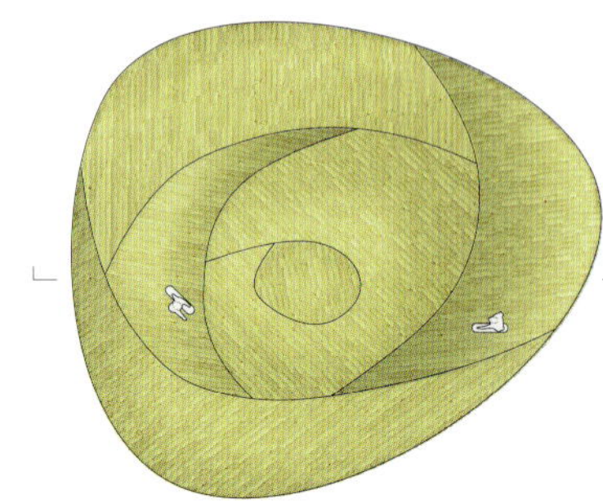

## Cultural Islands

## Gathering Islands

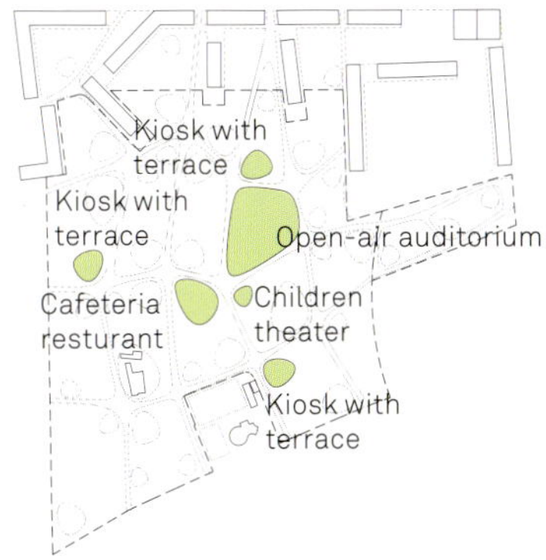


## Garden Islands

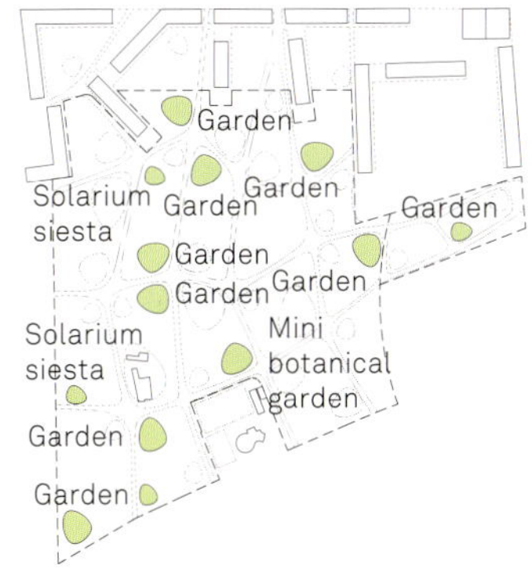


## DIY Do-It-Yourself Islands

## Kiosk With Terrace

## Children's Theater

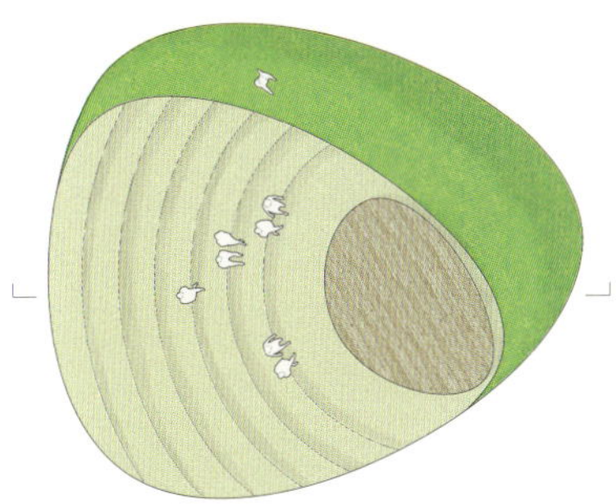

## Flower Garden

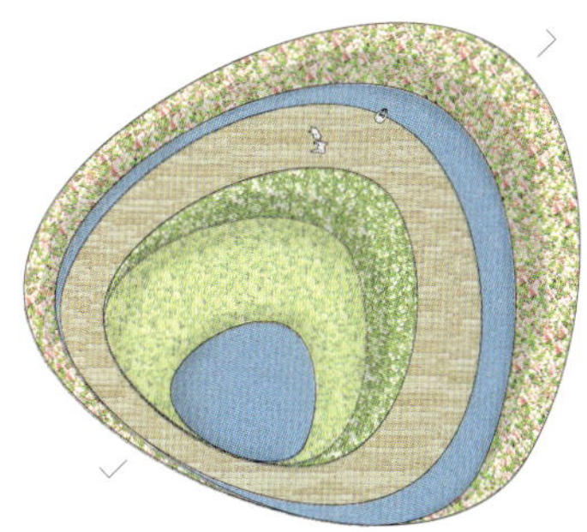

## Board Games

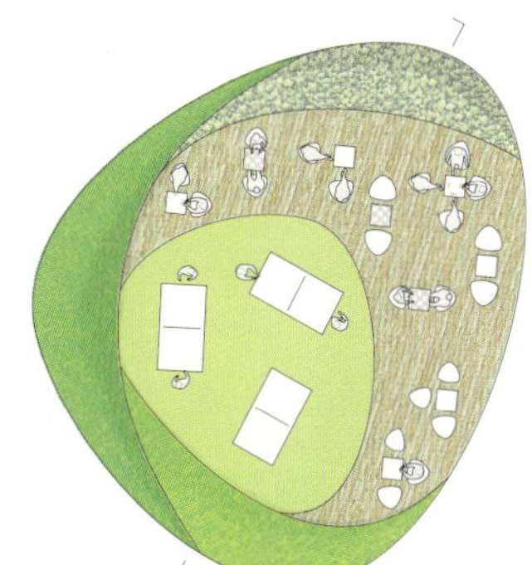

## Native Vegetation Integrated in the Park

## Educational Pavilions

## Sports Playground

## Café Pavilion with Terrace

## Skating Landscape

# Citizens as Builders: Co-production Strategies

Faced with the typical top-down model for planning public space promoted and developed by the local authorities, in recent years there have been a growing number of initiatives all over the world envisioned, realized and maintained entirely by citizens or citizens' groups. These initiatives include community gardens, artistic interventions or urban farms realized in deteriorated public places, abandoned lots, or interstitial urban spaces that have not been maintained by anyone. Sometimes they are realized with approval from the authorities, other times without their knowledge or consent. In many cases, the initial temporary nature of the interventions becomes permanent due to the passivity of local authorities or because they are finally permitted after they have been completed.

The motivations that lead so many citizens all over the world to intervene directly in public space autonomously and independently of the authorities are very diverse. In some cases this is due to simple aesthetic reasons, in the spirit of improving the urban environment they live in, or as a hobby shared collectively, or they have an economic motivation based on which urban spaces are used to produce food for direct consumption or for sale. In other cases the interventions have political motivations attempting to create a change in the urban environment through direct action, or they serve to denounce situations of neglect in order to provoke action from the authorities.

The fact that citizens or groups of citizens act directly on public land that is managed by municipal authorities can create situations of conflict between private and public interests when the interventions have not been approved or regulated, but it also has an enormous potential to regenerate urban life if the action is channeled using the appropriate strategy. The geographer Don Mitchell, author of numerous writings on the relationship between public space and democracy, questioned the traditional model of public space management with the following words: "Who has the right to the city and its public spaces? How is that right determined — both in law and on the streets themselves? How is it policed, legitimized, or undermined?"[1] Today more than ever it is important to ask ourselves these questions again, to rethink what kind of model of public space our cities need and to reevaluate the capacity of municipal bodies to regulate and legitimize the new ways in which citizens make use of public space.

Paradoxically, certain trendy movements involving direct citizen participation, such as urban farming, which are currently unregulated or disallowed in many cities, have been promoted by municipalities in the past. During the depression of 1890 in Detroit the city mayor, Hazen Pingree, began a program to transfer vacant lots owned by the municipality to citizens for the purpose of growing food as an economic aid to the high number of unemployed people in the city and to supplement their food supply. The movement was copied by many American cities and was revived during numerous

Citizens taking direct action to transform public space in movements such as guerrilla gardening or urban farming.

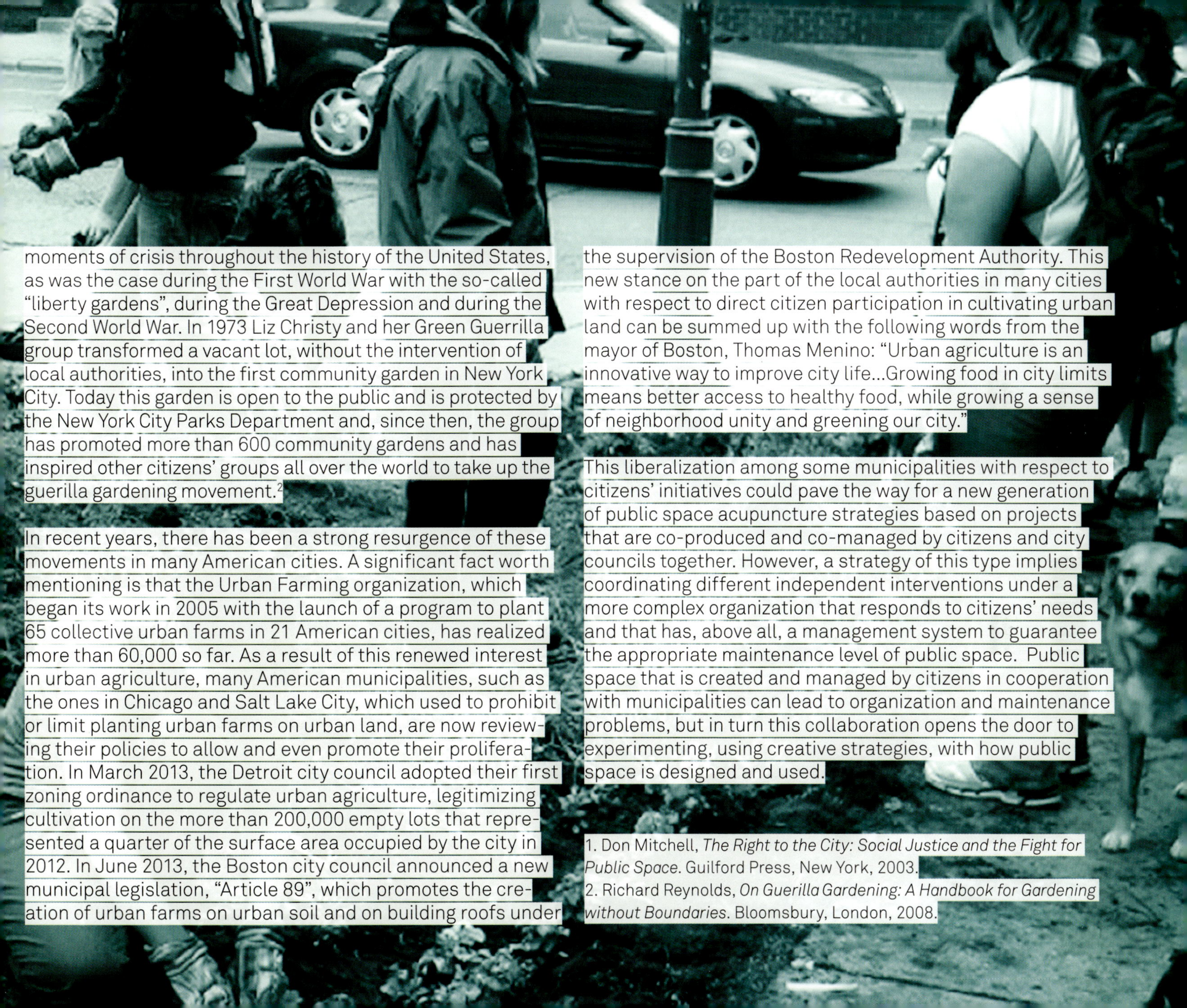

moments of crisis throughout the history of the United States, as was the case during the First World War with the so-called "liberty gardens", during the Great Depression and during the Second World War. In 1973 Liz Christy and her Green Guerrilla group transformed a vacant lot, without the intervention of local authorities, into the first community garden in New York City. Today this garden is open to the public and is protected by the New York City Parks Department and, since then, the group has promoted more than 600 community gardens and has inspired other citizens' groups all over the world to take up the guerilla gardening movement.[2]

In recent years, there has been a strong resurgence of these movements in many American cities. A significant fact worth mentioning is that the Urban Farming organization, which began its work in 2005 with the launch of a program to plant 65 collective urban farms in 21 American cities, has realized more than 60,000 so far. As a result of this renewed interest in urban agriculture, many American municipalities, such as the ones in Chicago and Salt Lake City, which used to prohibit or limit planting urban farms on urban land, are now reviewing their policies to allow and even promote their proliferation. In March 2013, the Detroit city council adopted their first zoning ordinance to regulate urban agriculture, legitimizing cultivation on the more than 200,000 empty lots that represented a quarter of the surface area occupied by the city in 2012. In June 2013, the Boston city council announced a new municipal legislation, "Article 89", which promotes the creation of urban farms on urban soil and on building roofs under the supervision of the Boston Redevelopment Authority. This new stance on the part of the local authorities in many cities with respect to direct citizen participation in cultivating urban land can be summed up with the following words from the mayor of Boston, Thomas Menino: "Urban agriculture is an innovative way to improve city life...Growing food in city limits means better access to healthy food, while growing a sense of neighborhood unity and greening our city."

This liberalization among some municipalities with respect to citizens' initiatives could pave the way for a new generation of public space acupuncture strategies based on projects that are co-produced and co-managed by citizens and city councils together. However, a strategy of this type implies coordinating different independent interventions under a more complex organization that responds to citizens' needs and that has, above all, a management system to guarantee the appropriate maintenance level of public space. Public space that is created and managed by citizens in cooperation with municipalities can lead to organization and maintenance problems, but in turn this collaboration opens the door to experimenting, using creative strategies, with how public space is designed and used.

1. Don Mitchell, *The Right to the City: Social Justice and the Fight for Public Space*. Guilford Press, New York, 2003.
2. Richard Reynolds, *On Guerilla Gardening: A Handbook for Gardening without Boundaries*. Bloomsbury, London, 2008.

Case Study F

# URBAN GARDENS
## ROTTERDAM, THE NETHERLANDS

STRATEGY / INTERVENTIONS: **Creatief Beheer**
STRATEGY: **Bureau Werkplaats**
COMMISSIONER: **Municipality of Rotterdam**

The Netherlands has a long tradition of allowing its citizens to install green interventions in public space, which they themselves propose and create without the help of the municipal authorities. The *geveltuin* (façade garden) is a common practice in small-scale urban gardening, which is permitted and regulated by municipal ordinances in many Dutch towns, allowing citizens to plant vegetation in the 30-centimeter-wide strip of public space adjacent to their building façades. This dimension is dictated by the size of the standard concrete tile generally used for urban pavement, which have to be removed in order to plant the gardens. To receive authorization from the municipality, the gardens need to follow specific regulations and must be properly maintained.

The emergence of urban farms and gardens on public land or in vacant lots has been common practice in cities like Amsterdam since the 1970s, making it necessary for municipal authorities to establish regulations and adopt innovative solutions to control their creation and maintenance. In recent years there has been a notable increase in the number of urban farms in cities like Amsterdam and Rotterdam. The reasons for this are very different from the case of other cities, since there is no shortage of fresh food and the cost of producing fresh vegetables in an urban farm is actually higher than their cost in a supermarket, in the opinion of some of the urban farmers. Some of the reasons behind the rise in urban agriculture in the Netherlands include the activity itself, that brings citizens into contact with the land, being able to eat natural foods, as well as social and educational aspects.

In this context, the Rotterdam municipality has launched various programs in recent years intended to promote non-conventional ways of planting vegetation in the city, from public subsidies for green roofs, to experimental urban farms on building rooftops or urban farm-restaurants. As part of this policy, there has been a rise in the number of requests from neighborhood groups for the creation of

gardens and urban farms on public land or in vacant lots in different areas of Rotterdam, which combine to form an extensive network of urban gardens. In order to control their growth and maintenance, the municipality launched a program to help with the creation of these initiatives, which includes their supervision.

The first intervention of this program was the Proefpark (pilot park) De Punt. It was a pilot project carried out in a neighborhood located in the western part of the city, which is going through a process of deep urban renewal. Many of the existing buildings have been torn down to build new residential complexes, which has led to the appearance of vacant lots in the middle of inhabited areas that may remain vacant for years before construction begins. The project, launched by residents in the area, was undertaken with the collaboration of the housing cooperative that owns the vacant lot, the Rotterdam municipality that subsidizes the creation and maintenance of the intervention, as well as Bureau de Werkplaats and Creatief Beheer, two independent organizations responsible for managing the communication between the municipality and neighborhood residents and for managing the project.

The project consisted not only in planting the urban farms, but also in building playgrounds, greenhouses, leisure areas and pavilions where residents can carry out various activities, transforming the area into a true public park and a meeting place for everyone in the neighborhood. After the intervention is completed, the organization Creatief Beheer mediates between neighbors and the municipality and is in charge of managing the gardens. They analyze the needs of the neighbors, provide help during the installation of the gardens and other small constructions, and control their maintenance and future growth.

The success of the pilot park led to the creation of a series of new interventions in other areas of the city, following the same model so that, all together, they make up an urban-scale strategy. Although each new garden or urban farm in Rotterdam tends to begin as a citizens' initiative, the fact that the city council monitors their construction and controls their maintenance helps to build a stable network of urban farms, which become part of an intentional, programmed strategy. This kind of public space acupuncture strategy combines bottom-up citizens' initiatives with the public interest in pursuit of a greener city and more vibrant public space with better interactivity among residents who share activities.

The strategy helps to intensify social cohesion in neighborhoods where there is a large degree of cultural diversity and it provides citizens with the possibility of acting directly on public space, while the municipal authorities also fulfill their responsibility for guaranteeing a public space in good condition, even if it is managed and maintained by the city's inhabitants. This way of creating public space lets citizens build their own urban environment, while the municipality collaborates to make it possible through a public space acupuncture strategy that is co-created and co-maintained.

**Urban Analysis** The western part of Rotterdam was not affected by the fire that broke out on May 14, 1940, caused by the bombardments that destroyed much of the city center. Bospolder is one of Rotterdam's pre-war neighborhoods, built from 1910 onward. Its urban structure is mainly formed by residential blocks that enclose private and collective gardens, with shops located on the ground floor along the main streets and squares. The area is mainly used by local residents and, only occasionally, is visited by citizens from other parts of the city for shopping purposes.

## Aerial View

## Users

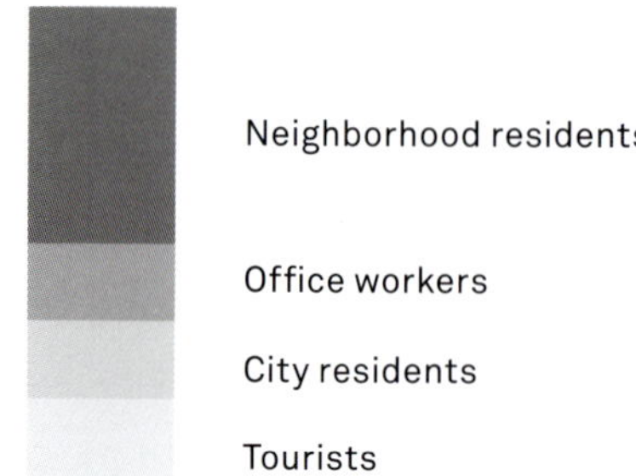


## Relation to the City

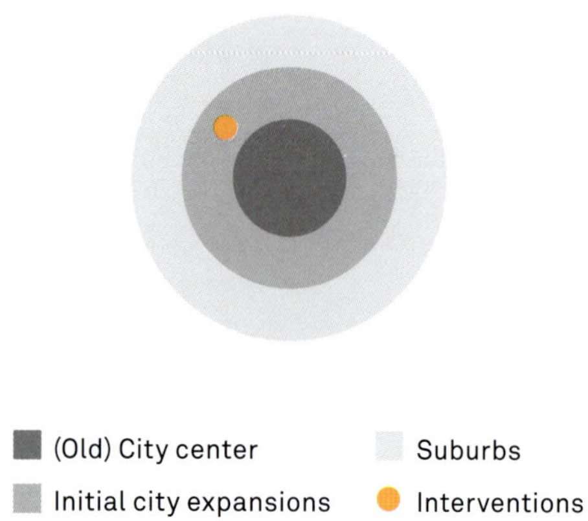


## Historic Urban Development

## Activities

**Social Analysis** The social structure of the neighborhood is strongly influenced by the large amount of immigrants, who represent 80% of the population, while in other areas of Rotterdam, although the presence of immigrants in general is very high, they represent only 48%. The unemployment rate in this area is 12%, much higher than the average rate for the city of Rotterdam, which was 8% in 2011. The percentage of family households present in the neighborhood is 37%, comparable to the 38% of households corresponding to singles.

## Age Structure

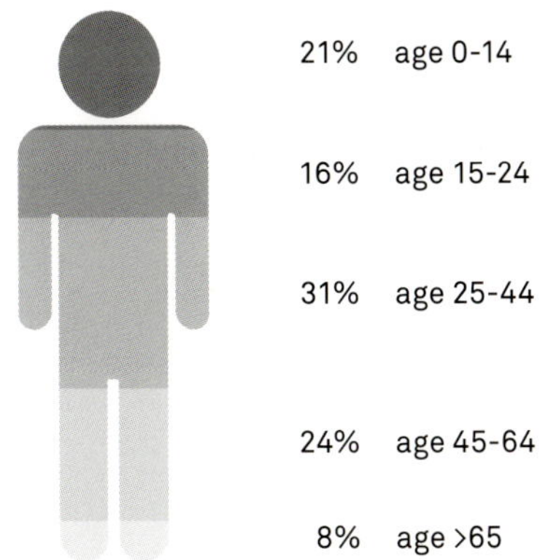


## Household Composition

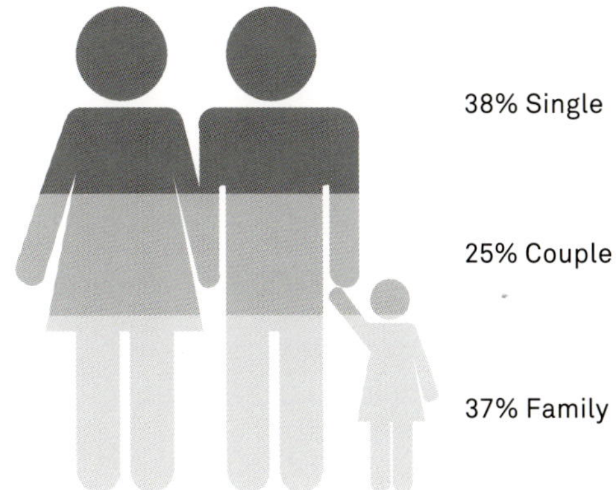

## Immigration

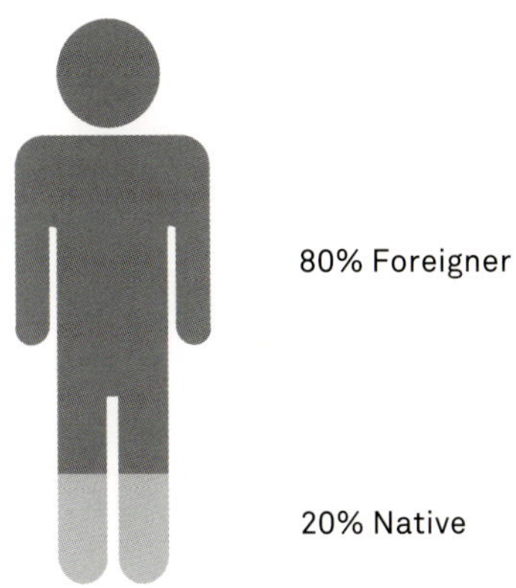


## Unemployment

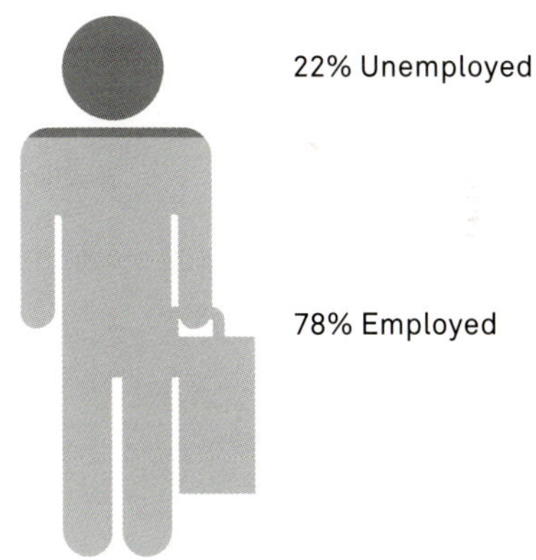


All the data is specific for "Bospolder" area. Source: COS 2011.

**Interventions** Many of the interventions are spread out over different areas of the city and have no real connection with the others, but in the western area of Rotterdam a few interventions are placed close to each other. Some are located in the central square of the Spangen district, while others are situated nearby in Bospolder. The latter will serve as a study area, where several urban gardens are mixed with small constructions such as greenhouses, garden houses, small pavilions, a hen house, a picnic area, and some playgrounds. The variety of small interventions presented in this case study shows some of the basic elements that have been used to create most of the interventions located in different parts of the city.

## 1 Urban Farms

There are several areas of the park that have been used as small urban farms. Many planting zones have changed position over the years. Collective gardens with circular shapes were located in the middle-north part of the park and, more recently, in the south-east and north-east zones as well.
Most of the collective gardens are created during planting events, when neighbors work together over a period of a few days. One of the first events involved planting grass on the vacant lot and was executed collectively. In 2007, the strip of land located in the north part of the park was divided into plots of 2x2 meters for individual vegetable gardens for the neighbors.

## 2 Winter Garden

Several small constructions have been built in the park to cover different needs. A small construction called the "Yellow Shed", which had served as a storage space or a coffee spot on rainy days since the beginning of the process, was removed in 2009. A wooden "Dice House" was built in 2009 as meeting point for young people. An old garden house made of timber was replaced by greenhouses made of steel and glass. All these buildings are constructions that mark the area and provide meeting spaces for the neighbors during winter, serving as the setting for different kinds of activities.

Accesses
Relaxation areas
Sitting areas
Circulation
Vegetation

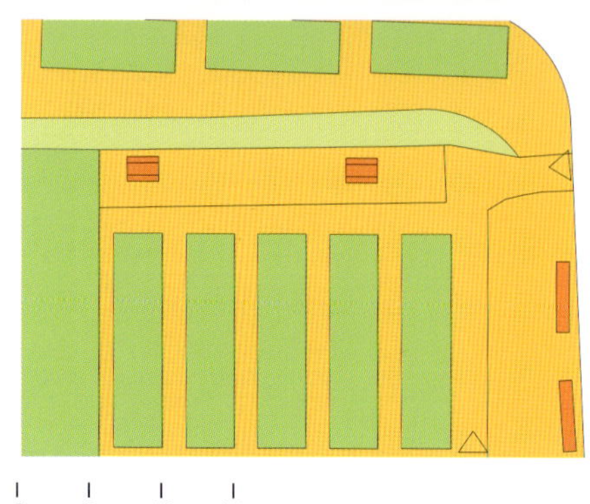


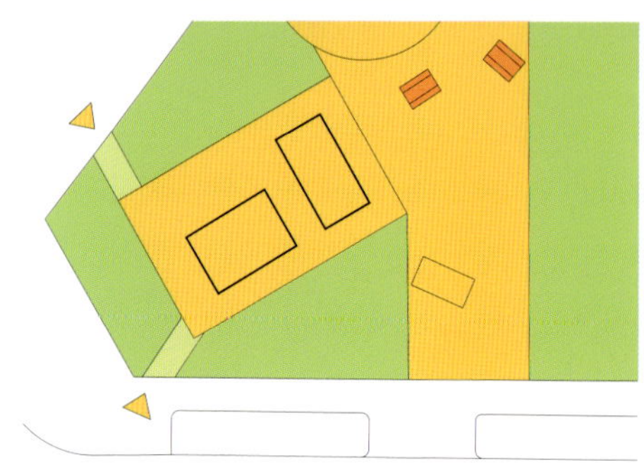

## 3 Playground

Several playground areas have been built in the park over time. In 2008, a wooden climbing tower for children was built and a small playground area surrounded by a few benches was installed in the north part of the park. Encouraging children to participate in the activities developed in the Pilot Park has been one of the main goals of the strategy. Games and children's activities are combined with planting in order to fulfill both recreational and educational aims. As a result, the project was nominated as one of the five most child-friendly projects in Rotterdam in 2005.

## 4 Bar

A tea house is located in a central position in the park, near the playing field. A small open-air gathering area with benches is located in front of the tea house. The tea house is equipped with a small storage area and a kitchen that is maintained by the neighbors. Several events take place regularly at the tea house, such as children's activities on Wednesdays, and the Pancake Day, which occurs from time to time.

## 5 Barbecue Area

In the past, the park had some isolated picnic tables. In 2007, a gathering area was added by installing a row of picnic tables and introducing a barbecue area in the central part of the park, near the soccer field. Creating a space for cooking and eating together is one way of encouraging interaction among residents, especially in a neighborhood made up of people from different cultures.

**Process** Proefpark De Punt was created in 2004 as an experimental project to test the possibilities of urban gardens built and managed by local residents in collaboration with the organization Creatief Beheer. It was commissioned by the Ontwikkelingsbedrijf Rotterdam, the Delfshaven district, the Com.Wonen housing corporation, and Bureau de Werkplaats.

Following its success, many other urban gardens have been built in different areas of Rotterdam creating a spontaneous, growing network. This network is organized by three main actors who are involved in generating the city's urban gardens: the residents of the different neighborhoods, who collectively request the gardens; the municipality of Rotterdam, which permits and facilitates their construction on public land; and Creatief Beheer as an independent mediator between the two of them.

The neighbors initiate each intervention and work on the construction and maintenance of the urban gardens. Creatief Beheer supervises the creation of the gardens and is ultimately responsible for their maintenance. The Municipality of Rotterdam makes the whole strategy possible and provides most of the economic support.

## Citizen Participation

First, the strategy encourages citizens to take the initiative in starting a project in public space, so citizens play the role of decision makers. Second, citizens are deeply involved in the development of the project, in what could be considered a co-creative strategy. Third, citizens are totally involved in the physical construction of the gardens and in their future maintenance with the assistance of experts and the supervision of local authorities. The projects are developed under a co-production strategy that takes into account a sort of co-maintenance mechanism as well.

This last point is especially remarkable because the urban gardens represent one of the few opportunities in which citizens can directly participate in the physical construction of public space by collaborating in its planting, irrigation and maintenance. Building something in public space frequently promotes a strong physical relationship between individuals and the urban environment, and a sense of ownership and pride in what they have created, stimulating its instinctive protection. In the case of a group, the participation process produces new ties among people and a sense of collectivity.

Direct citizen participation in the maintenance of the interventions also changes the typical concept of public space management. Maintenance, something that is frequently viewed as an unproductive expense wasted on repairing damages, is transformed into a creative activity in this strategy, which involves residents under the supervision of the organization Creatief Beheer, whose name literally means Creative Management.

## Cost, Financing and Maintenance

The municipality of Rotterdam and local housing corporations provide the annual funding for the whole strategy. In the case of the De Punt pilot park, an annual budget is approved every year. The assigned budget for the first year was €50,000, and €40,000 for the second year. Keeping a low budget usually requires the involvement of volunteers and neighbors to act as workforce to make the project feasible.

However, the active involvement of citizens in managing and maintaining public space carries obvious risks, such as the potential poor maintenance of collective gardens or the possibility that these areas could become abandoned or neglected in the future. To avoid these risks, Creatief Beheer is in charge of monitoring the construction of the collective gardens and teaching residents everything they need to know about planting and maintaining the gardens with the help of expert gardeners. Creatief Beheer is also in charge of managing the realizations, the communication with the neighbors, the coordination of the activities, and the control of the annual budget assigned to each garden.

## Timing

The network of urban gardens in Rotterdam has expanded rapidly in recent years. The means of defining the intervention method and the infrastructure have been developed empirically through trial and error. De Punt functions as a pilot park where many ideas have been tested and it has become a model for new interventions, although each new intervention has also subsequently undergone a specific development process, depending on the specific social and urban context.

Each new intervention can be started quickly once its budget is approved. The interventions are usually planned to remain for a period of at least a few years, which is a necessary condition for perceiving their impact on the physical and social structure of the neighborhood. It takes a while, not just to see nature growing in the streets, but also to overcome the initial skepticism, to involve neighbors in the project and to educate residents.

## Use of the Public Space

The strategy of urban gardens developed in Rotterdam, and especially the one put into play in De Punt pilot park promotes the use of public space, encouraging citizen interaction in many cases. Different levels of activation of public space can be detected. The urban gardens strategy stimulates a sporadic use of public space, involving specific periods of increased activity during the planting season, especially when the planting is organized through collective events. On the contrary there is a low level of activity in the gardens during the maintenance period.

Some of the interventions, such as the children's playgrounds, picnic zones and barbecue areas enjoy continuous use, comparable to the use of other public spaces in the city. Other interventions provide space for special events for families, children or adults that generate an extra use of the public space, gathering larger groups of people during specific moments, which does not happen spontaneously in other areas of the city's public space.

## Impact on Citizens and in the Media

The first consequence of the strategy is the creation of a feeling of community among the residents of the neighborhood that grows slowly by planting and building something together, and by sharing in many other collective activities.

Second, the fact that the interventions are initiated and developed by local residents with institutional help promotes a strong relationship between citizens and public space, understood as something they can use, work on and take care of. The management of public space is no longer seen as a problem, but as an opportunity.

Third, the strategy generates a change of perception concerning the use of public space, transforming unproductive areas of land into productive fields for growing vegetables and fruits, creating a direct link among people, work and land.

The usual criticism of this productive vision of public space comes from citizens who are not participants in the project and who complain about the natural appearance of public space, which changes through the seasons of the year and does not look like other conventional areas that are maintained by the municipality.

The strategy had a positive impact in the local media. Local newspapers, television and radio outlets drew attention to the project and to the fact that citizens could initiate new interventions themselves. One of the main direct consequences of the media attention can be seen in the fact that, in recent years, the amount of requests to create new urban gardens in Rotterdam has grown considerably and the De Punt pilot project has been deemed a success.

# AMSTERDAM NIEUW-WEST
## AMSTERDAM, THE NETHERLANDS

STRATEGY / INTERVENTIONS: **Researchers Berlage Institute**
COMMISSIONER: **Berlage Institute**
GUEST PROFESSORS: **Casanova+Hernandez**
LOCAL PARTNER: **Municipality of Amsterdam**

Nieuw-West is a neighborhood in Amsterdam that was built quickly after the Second World War in order to solve the housing shortage at the time. The new neighborhood was designed in accordance with the ideals of the Modern Movement, based on a clear urban structure that combined modern open blocks with large extensions of public space in between. Over time, the neighborhood suffered a severe physical, economic and social deterioration, and in 2007 Minister Vogelaar declared it one of the Netherlands' forty most problematic neighborhoods.

The health services and educational and recreational facilities became outdated. The excessive green areas were difficult to maintain, suffered from a lack of use and were unsafe. Houses were too small for new social demands, poorly preserved and did not offer enough typological diversity. As a result of this situation, social problems arose due to a concentration of people with low incomes and little education, and a large proportion of ethnic minorities who suffered from discrimination and exclusion, as well as from self-imposed isolation. The area was characterized by a large concentration of poverty and unemployment and the inhabitants suffered from a general feeling of insecurity. The general image people had of the area was negative, and residents whose socio-economic position improved began moving out of the area, resulting in a worsening of the situation and generating the beginning of a vicious circle.

Since 2001 the neighborhood has been undergoing a large-scale transformation process of urban renewal. The plan "Towards Park City 2015" defines how the urban transformation is being carried out, through the demolition of thousands of houses which are being replaced by new ones, radically transforming the original urban structure in what is presently considered to be one of the largest urban renewal projects in Europe.

On the one hand, the site, which has undergone an extraordinary physical and social transformation in recent

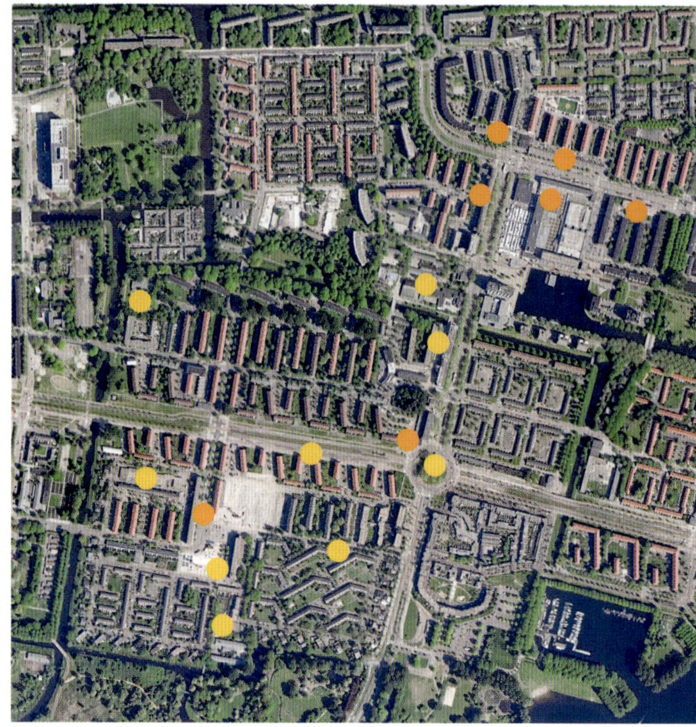

Interventions research project 1

Interventions research project 3

times, serves as an open field for experimentation with long-term strategies for regenerating urban life in the area and for stimulating a vibrant public space that can act as a meeting point for citizens, with the potential to strengthen social cohesion in the neighborhood.

On the other hand, the current specific situation resulting from the economic crisis has paralyzed a large part of the plans for construction, leaving behind many vacant lots in the area, which increase the negative image of the neighborhood and impact on possible future social problems. In this context, short-term strategies that act on public space, or even on the vacant lots in the neighborhood, provide a quick answer for solving existing social problems and preventing new ones.

The site also has a very diverse social background due to the fact that 50% of the population is of non-Dutch origin, providing the neighborhood a multi-ethnic and multicultural character by mixing people from very different origins such as Moroccans, Surinamese, Turks and Antilleans. In such a multicultural society, what could the role of public space be? What is the influence of a public program and public space design on the cohabitation of different groups? Can Public Space Acupuncture promote social sustainability?

**Strategy** The urban regeneration of Amsterdam Nieuw-West was the topic of a one-year research studio directed by Helena Casanova and Jesus Hernandez with postgraduate researchers at the Berlage Institute in Rotterdam, in collaboration with the Municipality of Amsterdam as a local partner.

The participants in the studio were Kwang Hyun Baek, Sung Bin Jung, Jaewon Lee, Han Lin, Haw-Wei Liou, Lei Mao, Jinyeong Seo, Jinlefu Su and Joo Youn Yoon.

The aim of the studio was to develop research focused on the critical analysis of the use of public space in order to design innovative strategies for regenerating urban life by promoting the active use of public places and social interaction among citizens.

Many of the projects proposed by the researchers included citizen participation as a tool in the strategy, to be employed in one or more phases of the process, through citizen collaboration in the tasks of decision-making, creation, management or even in the production of the interventions.

The researchers' direct contact with the different groups of people in the neighborhood, the residents' associations, and the housing corporations that are responsible for maintaining the buildings and, together with the municipality, for managing the many green areas, encouraged the development of ideas based on the co-production of interventions which the residents themselves are meant to be responsible for maintaining.

The external experts invited to the research studio were Jaume Barnada (Deputy Chief Architect of the City of Barcelona) Josep Bohigas (BOPBAA architects, Barcelona), Peter Kuenzli (urban development Manager of Gideon consult), Jan Liesegang (Raumlabor Berlin Architecten, Berlin), Patrizia di Monte (director of 'estonoesunsolar' / Gravalos di Monte architects), Michelle Provoost (CRIMSON architectural historians, director at INTI International New Town Institute), Francis Rambert (director Institut Français d'Architecture), Arnold Reijndorp (urban Sociologist), Stefan Rettich (Karo Architecten, Berlin), Maria Solé Bravo (designer and director STAP-BCN), Dietmar Steiner (director Architekturzentrum Wien) and Neeltje Westenend (social researcher and designer).

The Amsterdam Nieuw-West stakeholders invited were Arnold M.M. Paalvast (chairman residents' platform Geuzenveld-Slotermeer), Perry Hoetjes (housing coorporation Stadgenoot), Klaas van de Meer and Hilde Grundemann (housing coorporation IJmere), Gertjan Koele and Bart Bozelie (housing coorporation Eigen Haard), Edwin van Dijk, Maarten van Ettekoven and Dogan Oorthuis (representatives of the municipality of Amsterdam), Vannia Stonner (team leader Green Design, Amsterdam Nieuw-West) and Zef Hemel (Deputy director Spatial Planning Department City of Amsterdam).

**Research Project 1:** Scenario Acupuncture
**Authors:** Jaewon Lee, Jinyeong Seo, Kwang Hyun Baek and Sung Bin Jung

Scenario Acupuncture proposes a complete public space acupuncture strategy for Amsterdam Nieuw-West, taking into account the important factors involved in the development process and strategy management such as timing, phasing and the actors involved in each stage in order to promote a gradual regeneration of public life. The strategy experiments with concepts such as temporariness and durability to provide a wide range of interventions suitable for each phase of the process, from visual, temporary and mutating interventions to permanent ones. Different levels of citizen participation have been integrated into several phases of the strategy promoting initiatives from residents' associations, artists' groups, shop owners and all kind of citizens' groups by creating a program of possible collaborations with the municipality, the housing corporations and other private or public stakeholders.

## Positioning of Main Interventions by Phases

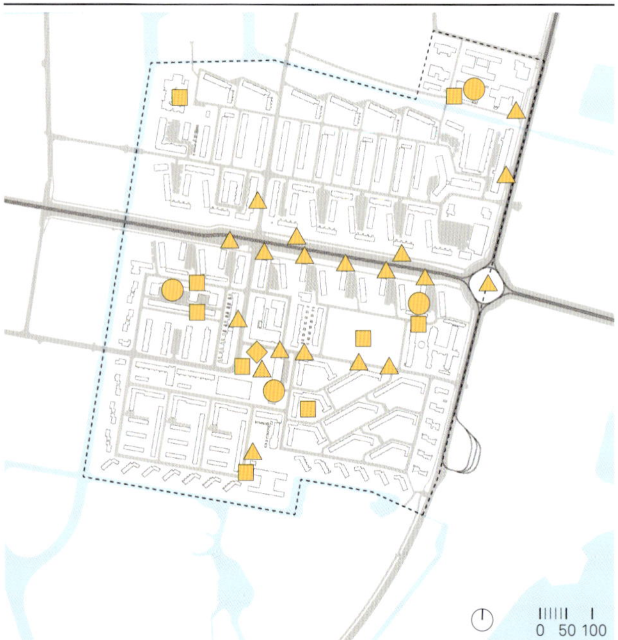


△ Phase 1 - Advertising
○ Phase 2 - Educational program
□ Phase 3 - Small interventions
◇ Phase 4 - Large interventions

## Strategy Phases Relating Actors Involved, Type and Location of Interventions and Citizen Participation

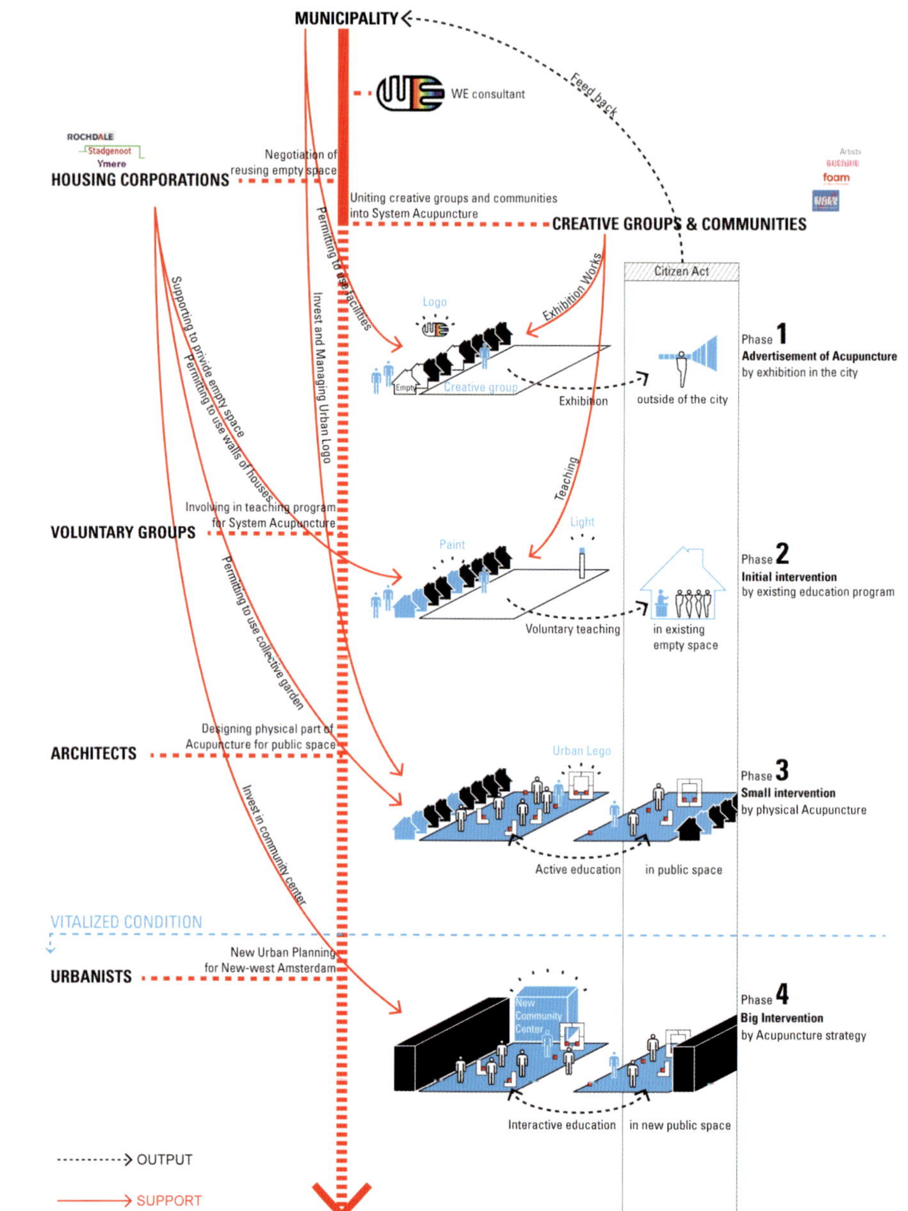

# Different Intervention Levels in Each Phase of the Strategy

Phase 1 - Advertisement in the city

Phase 2 - Educational program in empty buildings

Phase 3 - Small physical interventions in public space

**Research Project 2:** Participation Platforms

**Author:** Han Lin

The project Participation Platforms experiments with citizen participation and hybrid bottom-up strategies as tools to intensify the use of public space (especially the vacant lots located in between residential buildings) and to improve social cohesion in the neighborhood. The exclusive use of recycled materials in every intervention reinforces the low-cost character of the strategy, questioning the need for large investments to generate public life instead of using social capital and promoting citizens' initiatives.

## Positioning of Main Interventions in between Urban Blocks and Vacant Lots

## Combination of Different Models of Citizen Participation in Different Interventions

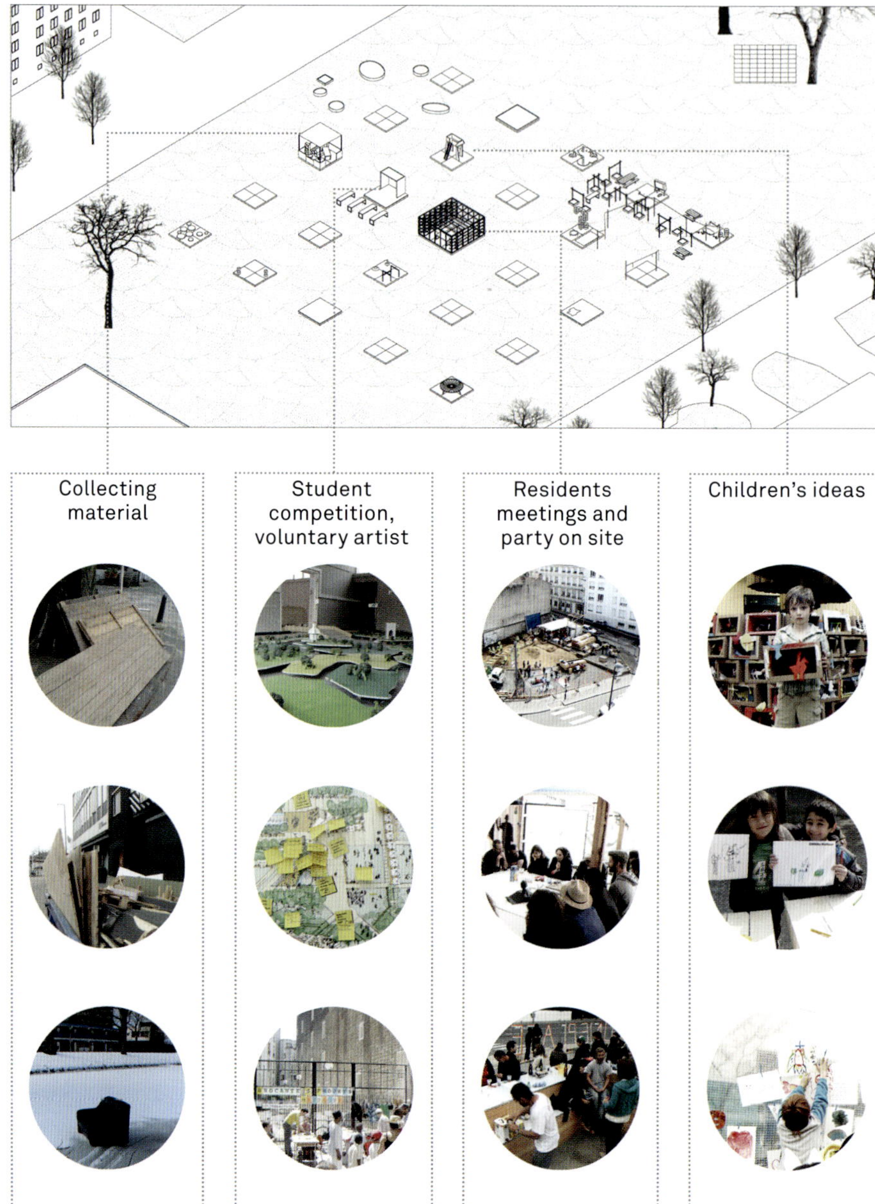

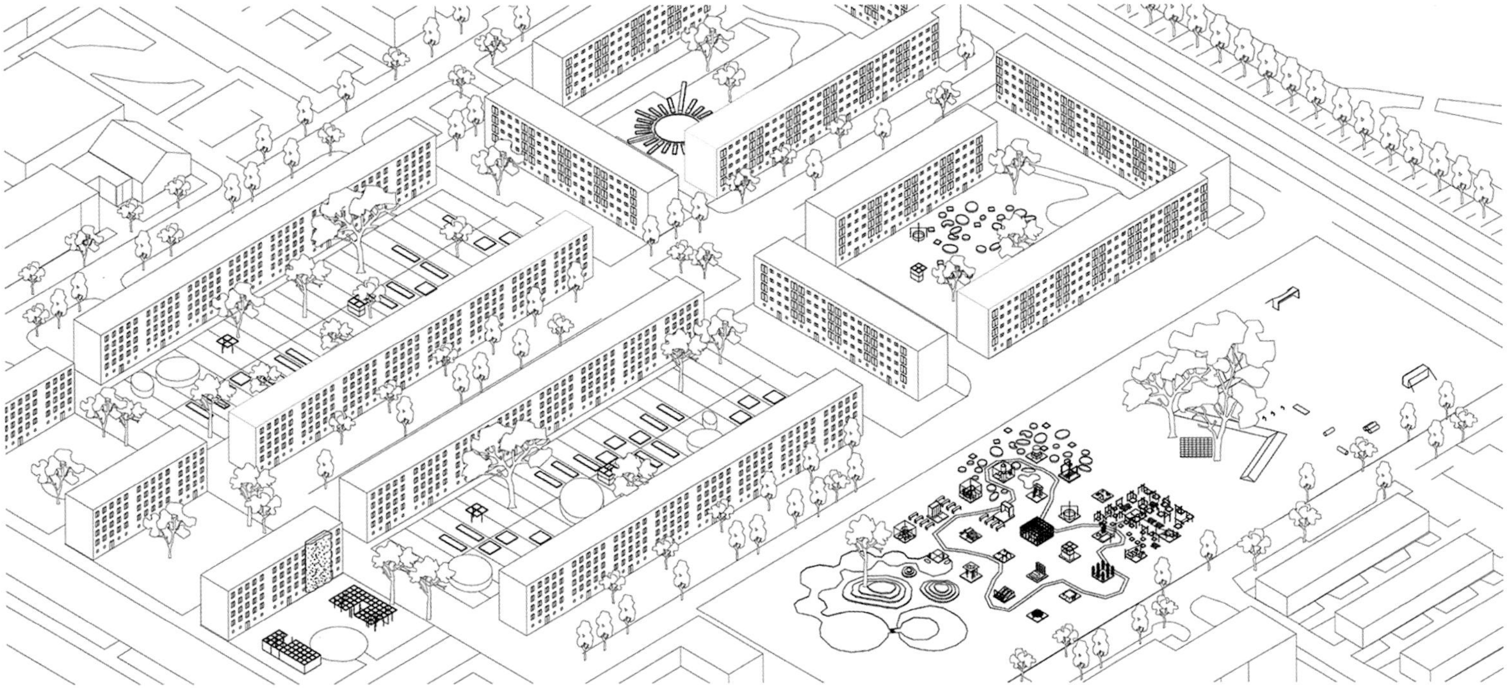

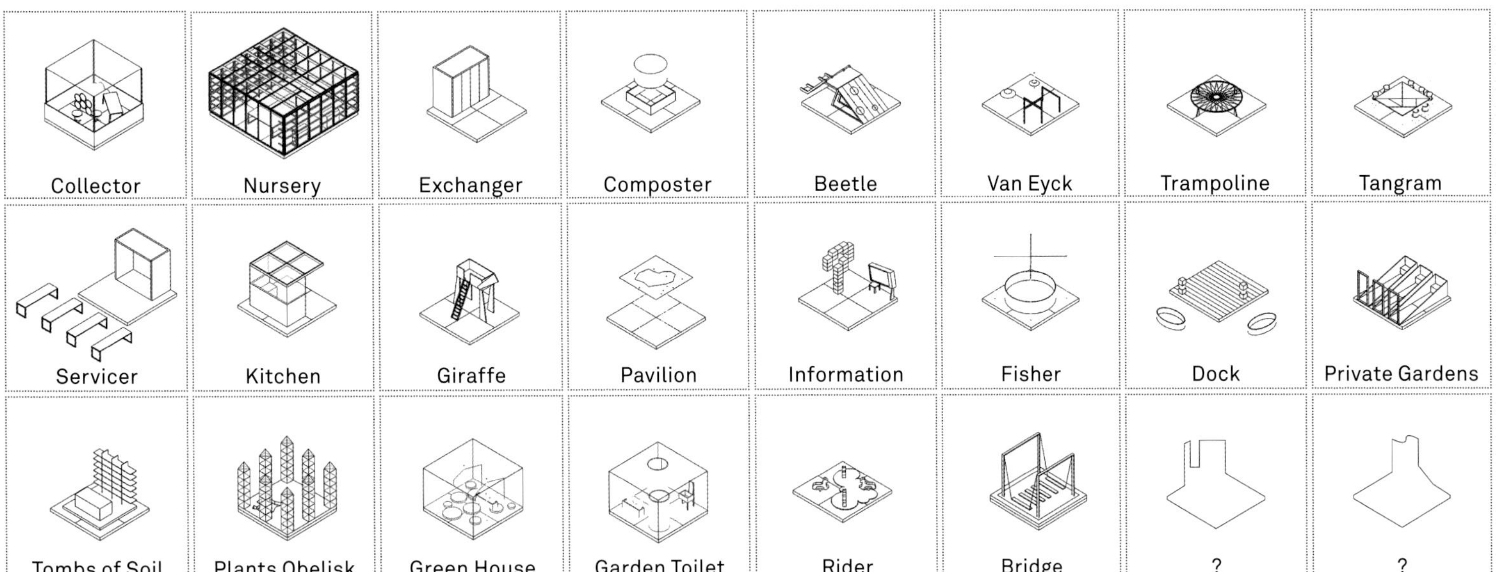

Collector
Nursery
Exchanger
Composter
Beetle
Van Eyck
Trampoline
Tangram
Servicer
Kitchen
Giraffe
Pavilion
Information
Fisher
Dock
Private Gardens
Tombs of Soil
Plants Obelisk
Green House
Garden Toilet
Rider
Bridge
?
?

**Research Project 3:** Market Space Public Place
**Author:** Haw Wei Liou

The project Market Space Public Place focused on experimenting with commercial activities to regenerate the use of public space in Amsterdam Nieuw-West. By linking the existing local production of ecological products in urban agriculture practices to new ways of commercializing and consuming these products, the conventional social habits dictated by our consumer society are questioned and new models are proposed for the use of public space to reinforce public life.

The project activates the use of public space and promotes citizen interaction with a system based on co-production and co-management strategies that involve local citizens and local shops, supported by the Municipality of Amsterdam.

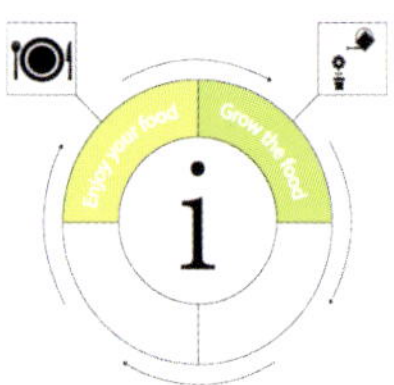


Public space: food production-consumption

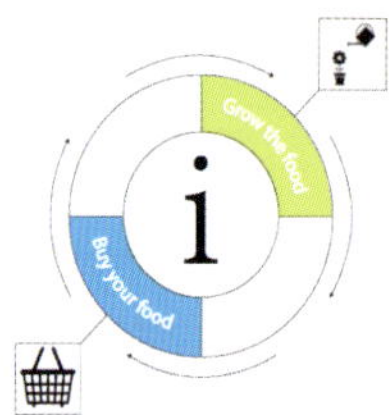


Public space: food production-distribution

Public space: food production-distribution-consumption

## Activation of the Use of the Public Space Close to Commercial Spaces

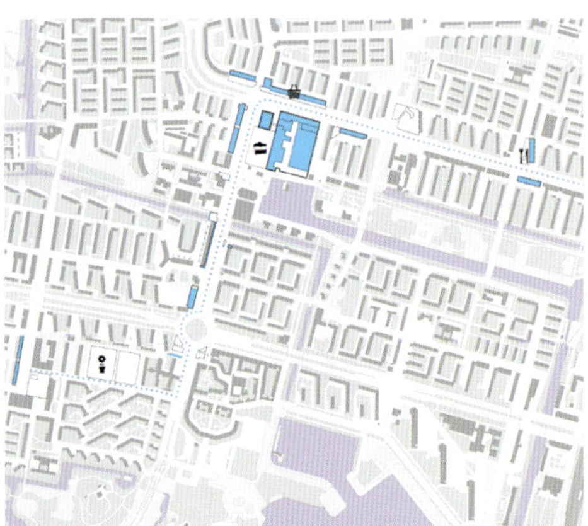

## Location of Existing Urban Gardens and Main Commercial Areas

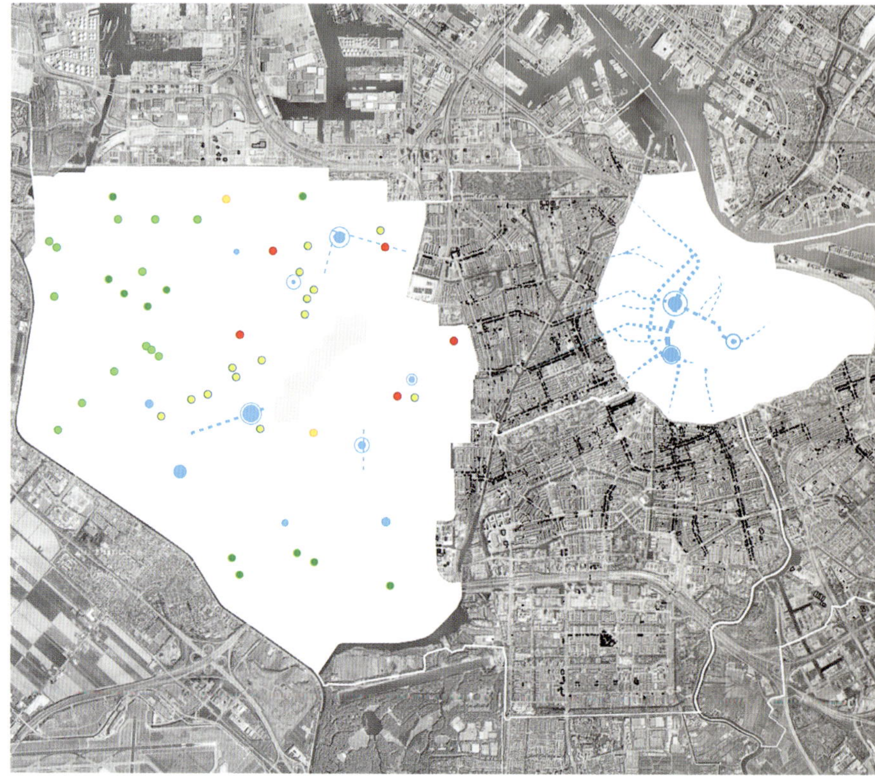

## Components and Elements of the Modular System

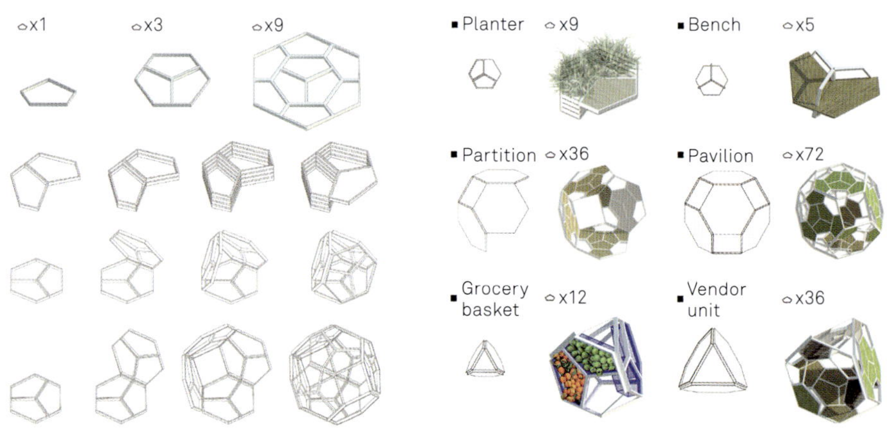

## Farming Festival at Plein 40-45

## Citizen as an Urban Farmer and Public Space as a Place for Production, Distribution and Consumption of Food

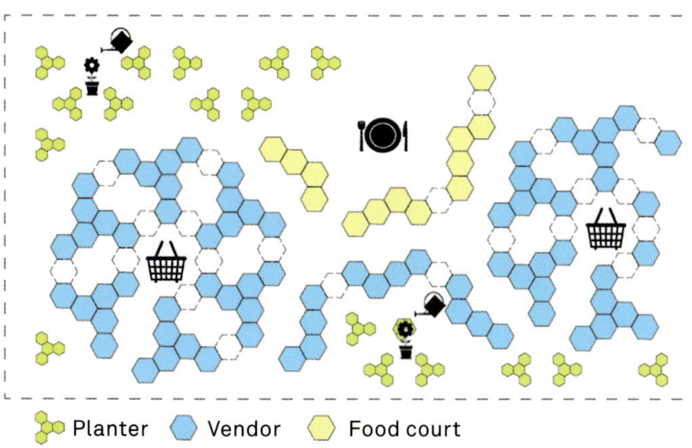


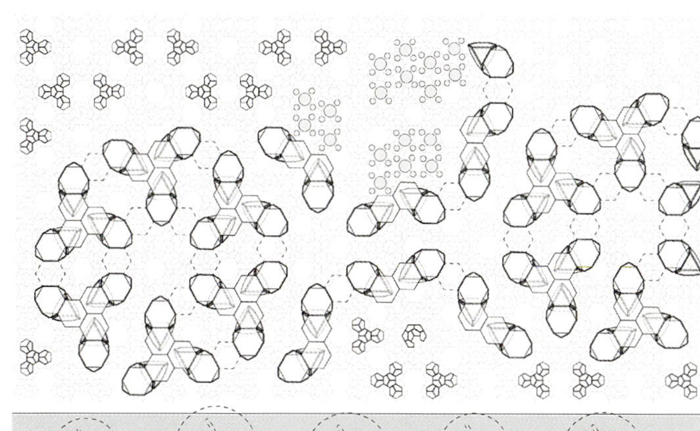

## RUSOVCE
## BRATISLAVA, SLOVAKIA

STRATEGY / INTERVENTIONS: **Casanova+Hernandez**
STRATEGY / COMMISSIONER: **CULBURB**

Rusovce is a suburban area with 2,700 inhabitants that emerged as a result of the expansion of Bratislava. The real estate boom at the beginning of this century caused its rapid urban sprawl made up of large single-family houses combined with sparse and poorly equipped public areas, which did not contribute to creating a sense of community among the inhabitants.

The fact that Rusovce has belonged to different countries in the past (Hungary in the years following 1920, Czechoslovakia after World War II and Slovakia in the present) and that it is located bordering three countries has caused Rusovce's population to be strongly divided among Slovaks, Hungarians and Austrians. On the one hand, the social segregation stemming from the population's different cultural and linguistic origins translates into a lack of social cohesion, but on the other hand, this segregation is structured around certain "socio-cultural circles" which could be the foundation for a stable social structure if they were connected.

Physical and programmatic improvements in public space could help to promote interactivity among citizens. But can the reactivation of public space really help to eliminate the invisible barriers that separate different social groups? In contexts characterized by a strong cultural and even linguistic segregation, it is predictable that incentivizing communal use of public space will not necessarily mean that the different groups will spontaneously interact. Other mechanisms are necessary to provoke this interaction, and the inclusion of citizen participation programs in the strategies can be one option.

**Strategy** The strategy for regenerating public space in Rusovce not only proposes the construction of various interventions in public space which encourage interaction among citizens from the three different nationalities, but also proposes transforming the construction process into a public event in which members of all three communities can participate.

Urban Sprawl and Social Segregation

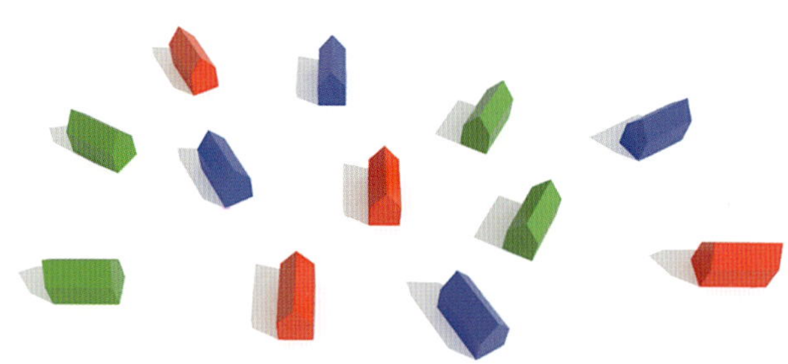

In the same way that members of each cultural group acquire a sense of belonging over time through sharing experiences, the way to create a certain amount of unity among the different groups in the village is for them to share experiences as well, something which does not generally occur spontaneously. To that end, the strategy is centered on a participatory process with the aim of debating, designing and creating meeting points in public space where citizens from the different groups can have the experience of building something together, which can then be used by everyone.

Obviously, any participatory process requires a minimum level of interest among citizens. There are citizen platforms in Rusovce, like Mame radi Rusovce (We Like Rusovce), concerned with the development of public space and the protection of existing green areas, which favors an optimistic outlook about the possible level of citizen participation in the strategy. But reinforcing social cohesion is a long-term process that also needs time to be consolidated. Therefore, the strategy emphasizes the educational role of the citizen participation process, with special programs for children and youth from each of the different groups. These programs rely on the collaboration of local schools to combine the strategy with educational activities, in order to promote a long-term sustainable plan.

The strategy concentrates the construction of interventions at different points of a green area located in the center of the village, where sports and educational facilities coexist. Each intervention is created by joining a series of circular elements that serve to virtually limit a small portion of public space, which acquires the dimensions of an outdoor room.

The distinct interventions, which are created by one, two or three circular elements, present different spatial characteristics and functions. The strategy consists of fifteen interventions distributed throughout the site so that the specific conditions of each location are answered by the specific characteristics of each intervention.

**Interventions** The interventions are designed as multi-functional spaces created with platforms at various heights. They are hybrid elements that can be used for different purposes, such as relaxation, playing board games, outdoor workshops, children's playgrounds, an open-air neighborhood meeting room or a picnic area for sharing the culinary specialties of the three different cultures. Long, curved tables and

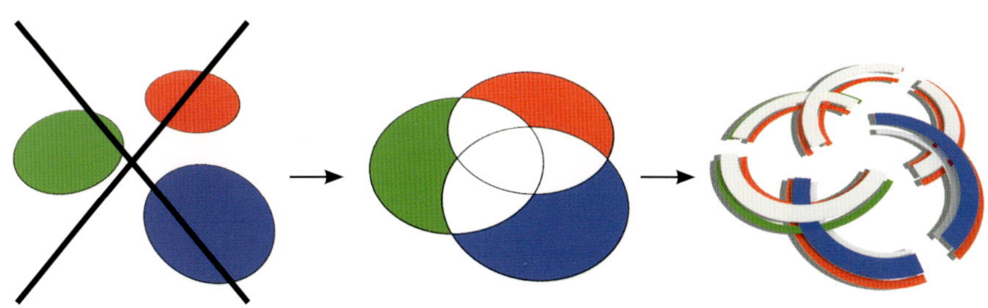

Isolated social circles → Hybrid social circles → Hybrid interventions

benches located at different heights can also be used as a small makeshift auditorium for performances, or as bleachers for watching the matches held on the playing fields. Each intervention becomes a multi-use space where citizens of different ages and origins can share certain activities.

In some interventions, the platforms form a circular space. This space is composed of an interior area, with an introverted character to promote interaction among users and an exterior area with an extroverted character, visually connected with all the activities taking place in the surroundings. The mixed introverted and extroverted character of the intervention favors flexibility of use and attracts different groups that share the same space.

Other interventions are organized using the intersection of two or three circular elements, generating more complex compositions that are characterized by increased spatial richness and more possibilities for use. The use of colors from the flags that represent Slovakia, Hungary and Austria for the seats and tables in each circle creates a fragmented, multi-colored composition that, like a new flag, symbolizes the existing multicultural mix, but also reminds users that the intervention is the result of the collective work of all three groups.

**Participatory Process** The interventions are built during participatory workshops with residents of all three different nationalities, which also function as forums for debate about each group's need as well as about the activities that they can share. The workshops combine participants who are related either by age group or because they have hobbies in common, but they are always made up of citizens from the three nationalities.

The aim of the workshops is the physical construction of the interventions, such that each intervention not only represents the creation of a new urban element or the contribution of a new program to public space, but also serves as a working experience shared by citizens of different origins, which plays an educational role.

The strategy envisages monitoring the participatory workshops via a website and specialized blogs designed to attract citizen participation and disseminate the results. As a result of the participatory process, each intervention contains its own story, which all citizens can comment on, so that aside from a functional and artistic value, each work takes on a symbolic value as well.

## Interventions

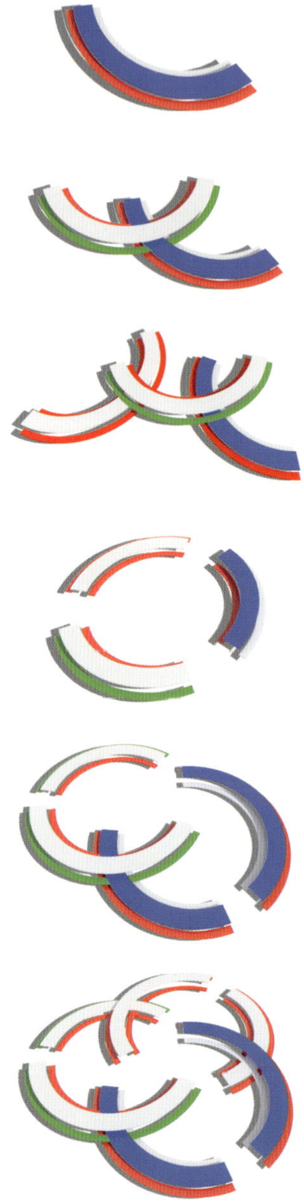

## Site Plan with Intervention Clusters

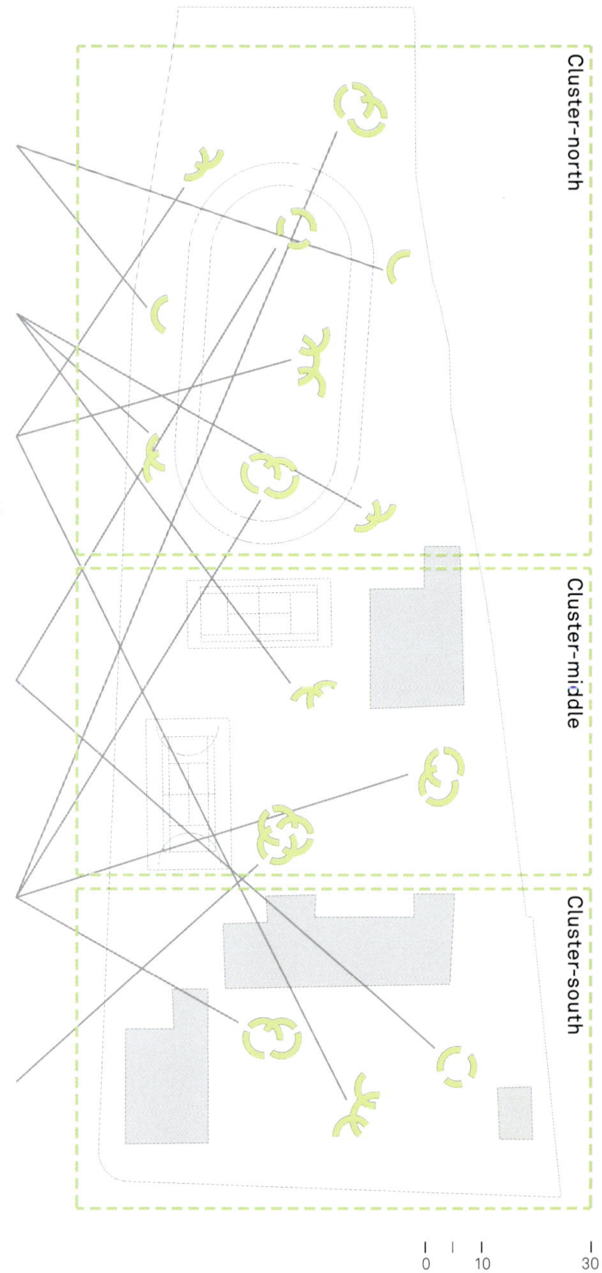

Cluster-Middle

Cluster-South

Cluster-North

# 3

# Re-Placemaking

# Re-placemaking

The traditional concept of "place" is in crisis. The generic city is replacing the specific city. Similar shopping centers are cloned all across the planet, where the same commercial chains sell identical products. Bustling traditional Chinese hutongs are demolished to build gated communities that all look the same. Aseptic shopping malls replace the traditional souqs in the Arab world. And every year nearly identical skyscrapers crop up in very different places on the planet. The rhythm at which "places" are destroyed is directly proportional to the creation of man-made spaces that have no special relationship with their location and, therefore, could be anywhere. Marc Augé calls them "non-places" to emphasize that these new spaces do not hold enough significance to be considered "places".[1]

However, globalization destroys not only the specific identity of a place, but also the "sense of place" that marks some sites with a special significance for some people and which, in the words of the geographer Yi-Fu Tuan means that certain places "have been given stronger meanings, names or definitions by society than others".[2] The sense of place is what creates a link between citizens and a location, what provides certain sites with a strong identity that is felt deeply by its inhabitants. The sense of place is, therefore, an interesting social phenomenon that exists independently of any individual perception.

The acceleration of the effects of globalization in recent years has caused increasing international interest in concepts such as placemaking and place identity, with the re-edition of books like The Death and Life of Great American Cities by Jane Jacobs[3] and works by authors such as Lewis Mumford[4], Kevin Lynch[5] and William H. Whyte.[6] The significance and the importance of places for their inhabitants have become central issues for many professionals who play a role in designing cities. Urban planners, urban designers and landscape architects collaborate with urban sociologists and environmental psychologists to develop methodologies that help to understand the identity of a place through interviews with inhabitants and by mapping the social and urban context. This analytical process is often combined with a participatory design process in direct collaboration with local communities in an effort to acquire tools that will help maintain or create a sense of place.

But, despite certain exceptions, the fact is that the rapid growth of many cities all over the planet is grounded in the persistent construction of non-places and the systematic destruction of existing places. The nostalgic desire to create, protect or recover the sense of place collides repeatedly with pragmatic laws dictated by market-oriented urbanism. All this means that, although we recognize the benefits of traditional placemaking in the creation and regeneration of urban life, we have to rethink this concept, seeking out new alternative ways of implementing it. This reconsideration should be based on a critical analysis of the current situation, by openly formulating the following questions: If globalization, as different authors have argued, has reached a point of no return that invades all aspects of our lives, what are the opportunities, in the present day, for creating urban spaces with a sense of place? If the cultural singularities of sites and the diversity that characterizes different cities are progressively diluted by the implementation of imported urban planning schemes and generic buildings that could exist anywhere in the world, what alternative mechanisms to the traditional ones could be applied in this context to generate a sense of place?

In any case, in new cities created through rapid urban developments that are immediately inhabited by citizens of different origins who have no prior relationship with each other or with the place, what mechanisms can help foment a sense of place in the future that will link citizens and the place where they live, while generating a collective feeling within the community?

If we understand the sense of place as a collective feeling that exists in society and is therefore independent from the place itself, could certain sites without a sense of place be redefined in the collective memory of the inhabitants as locations that do possess a sense of place? What kind of strategies could be applied in cases where it is not possible to recover a link with the past or where that link never existed in the first place?

Both in the case of new urban developments that have been built over a short period of time and in regenerating abandoned parts of the city that have no urban life, new strategies are needed for creating or recreating a certain sense of place among residents. Some strategies transform the city into a stage where citizens can carry out a public function linked to the place. Others understand the city as a place for celebrating events where programmed or spontaneous activities can be shared by citizens. Lastly, there are strategies that transform public space that has already lost its sense of place into art-scapes with their own meaning. In one way or another, all these strategies share the concern for placemaking, most of the time not necessarily with an eye to the past, but looking toward the future in what could be called “re-placemaking”.

1. Marc Augé, *Non-Lieux, Introduction à une Anthropologie de la Surmodernité*. Éditions du Seuil, Paris, 1992.
English edition: *Non-Places: Introduction to an Anthropology of Supermodernity*. Verso Books, London & New York, 1995.
2. Yi-Fu Tuan, *Space and Place: The Perspective of Experience*. University of Minnesota Press, Minneapolis, 1977.
3. Jane Jacobs *The Death and Life of Great American Cities*. Random House, New York, 1961.
4. Lewis Mumford, *The City in History*. Harcourt Brace & World, New York, 1961.
5. Kevin Lynch, *The Image of the City*. MIT Press, Cambridge,1960.
6. William H. Whyte, *The Social Life of Small Urban Spaces*. The Conservation Foundation, Washington D.C. 1980.

# City as a Stage

The concept of the Theatrum Mundi, the simile that compares society with a giant theater and human beings with actors, has been repeated in many works of philosophy, literature and theater throughout history; from Plato's myth of the cave, Petronius's Satyricon, Balzac's The Human Comedy or Calderón de la Barca's The Great Theater of the World. Richard Sennett[1] attributes to Rousseau the conception of the city as a great theater where citizens are actors who put on the performance of public life. In this performance, public space serves as a stage, architecture as the scenery, urban furniture as the props and the script of public life determines our behavior and even the way we dress, which is defined to a certain extent by context just like the costumes in a play.

The architecture of the city has always been an important component of this urban stage, serving as the backdrop for the performance of public life. According to legend, in 1787 the Russian minister Grigory Potemkin ordered the construction of a series of fake villages along the route taken by Empress Catherine II in her visit to recently conquered Crimea. The so-called Potemkin villages were therefore just a stage set meant to hide a desolate landscape, which lent a theatrical dimension to the passage of the imperial procession passing in front of cheering crowd dressed in their finest clothes. Reality or fiction, the Potemkin villages temporarily transformed empty space into a performance space, in a similar way that, a century later, Haussmann's plan for the renovation of the center of Paris used a comparable technique to cover the new boulevards, opened within the dense urban structure of medieval Paris, with new façades. Those façades, containing arcades, cafés and commercial spaces, are now representative of the image of Paris's vibrant urban life. To a certain extent, Haussmann's street-wall is part of the urban scenery where Parisian public life is performed and, consciously or unconsciously, citizens play a role in accordance with that scenery while, at the same time, they enjoy being spectators at the performance.

If the sense of place is a collective feeling that is associated with a location, when we transform inert urban space into an "urban stage" where citizens perform certain aspects of public life, a site can take on a certain sense of place. Artifice can help to create a new reality, although it could be argued that the reality in question is not "authentic". But, if the city itself is seen as the largest man-made artifact, how can one place be considered less authentic than any other? Is not the city itself an enormous stage that has been built throughout history, where each building is a new element in the set?

The transformation of the urban stage constituted by public space has been throughout history and continues to be one of the necessary instruments for promoting urban life. One of the purposes of urban planning has been to create the urban façade of streets and squares that stimulate the performance of public life. But at the same time the city is, by definition, a plural space where different types of people

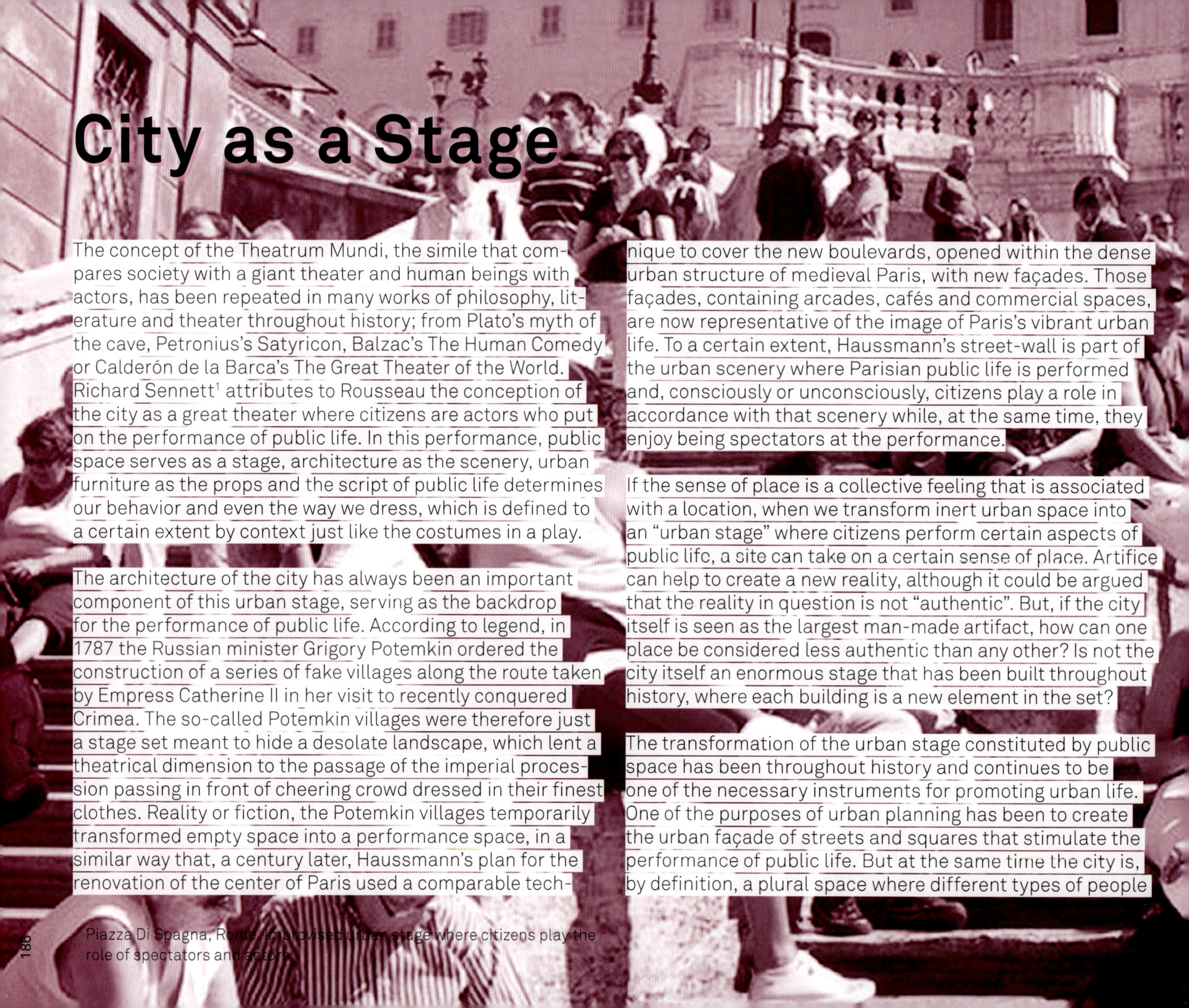

Piazza Di Spagna, Rome. Improvised urban stage where citizens play the role of spectators and actors.

live and work together and different kinds of activities take place, which means it is logical that there should be differentiated urban stages associated with different ways of performing public life.

The urban sociologist Arnold Reijndorp illustrates this diversity of urban stages with allegorical images of the three different types of stage sets, described by Serlio in his second book,[2] for the theatrical performance of comedy, tragedy and satire. Neighborhood social life is performed on the comedy set, leisure on the forested set for satire, whereas the most public and representative acts take place on the monumental set of tragedy. In Reijndorp´s interpretation of the old metaphor of the city as theater, beyond emphasizing the need for scenographic diversity in order to develop a rich urban life, he underlines the importance of a suitable relationship between the script and the scenery to ensure the semiotic coherence of the performance.

In the metaphor of the city as theatre, the theatrical performance is, above all, a system of communication and its success depends on its ability to communicate. The difficulty in constantly keeping up this communication comes from the complications that arise from citizens' double role as both spectator and actor in the performance. On the one hand, the success of the urban play depends on whether the citizen-actor is willing and able to play a role on each different stage; to that end, it is important that the script to be performed is attractive to the citizen. On the other hand, it is important that the citizen-spectator understand and enjoy the performance, which makes the coherence between the urban sets and the scripts to be performed by the citizen-actor a crucial factor.

Transforming public space into an urban stage or a space intended for the performance of public life is still a plausible strategy today that can activate urban life by promoting the role of citizens in it. The character of this set and the role played by the actors has to be updated in accordance with the social reality of the moment, making this a significant subject for experimentation in public space acupuncture strategies aimed at achieving a vibrant urban life.

1. Richard Sennett, *The Fall of Public Man*. Knopf, New York, 1977.
2. Sebastiano Serlio Bolognese, *Il Secondo Libro di Prospettiva*. J. Barbé, Paris, 1545.

# HARBORFRONT
# COPENHAGEN, DENMARK.

STRATEGY: **Municipality of Copenhagen**
COMMISSIONER: **Port of Copenhagen**
INTERVENTIONS: **Multiple designers**

The development of Copenhagen's harborfront can be considered an integral strategy for regenerating public life along the water, which has been subdivided into several parts, due to its scale and complexity. The elements that provide functional and spatial unity to the strategy are the public transportation network (water taxi and water bus) that transforms the water into a virtual street, the landscape projects developed along the waterfront, and the water promenade along the quay, which, together with the construction of new bridges, allows for continuous pedestrian and bicycle circulation along both sides of the harbor. Several independent interventions located at strategic points along the harborfront have been implemented to add specific activities to the place and to work as visual landmarks that link the citizens' experience of the public space with the history of the site.

The different interventions articulate pedestrian movement along the harborfront by creating visual and functional tension along the waterside. Among them, some of the harbor baths work as a series of floating interventions that can be cloned and easily transported along the water to different points. The harbor bath located in the north, near Langebro bridge, serves to attract citizens and is conceptually linked to the harbor pool in the south, close to the pedestrian and bicycle bridge that leads to Fisketorvet. The People's Park and its harbor beach work as visual and physical connectors that link the two bridges. The beach steps, located in the southern part of the park create an area for resting close to the water, which relates to the terraces of the public square to the north, located in between the café terrace of the National Library and the water bus stop nearby. The strategy for regenerating public space along the harborfront consists of separate, nearly independent interventions, some of which were realized in different periods, yet they all relate to each other to create a balanced and coherent whole.

Aside from regenerating the public space from a spatial and functional point of view, the strategy seeks to integrate the harbor into the urban life of the city and to provide a sense of

Former harbor of Copenhagen and current housing buildings along the waterfront

place. Although some interventions establish a certain dialogue with the history of the place, the strategy does not try to provide a sense of place by looking back into its past as a harbor, but by creating a new type of public space for the city, characterized by its own identity. By cleaning the water in the former harbor area and building floating interventions, an unused space of the city is transformed into a performance space. The many seating areas, café terraces and gathering spaces around the water characterize the public space as an urban stage where citizens play the role of actors and spectators in the performance of public life.

It stands to mention that building a new architectural backdrop, like Haussmann did in Paris in the 19th century, was not necessary to transform in this case public space into an urban stage. On the contrary, it was enough simply to promote new aquatic activities, such as swimming, canoeing and different water sports, supported by a series of scenographic elements, like the floating pools, to shift the focus of attention onto the water front. In this sense, the typology of the created urban stage does not adhere to the principles of the classical theatrical tradition, initiated by Greco-Roman theater, where the action is framed by an architectural background or a backdrop that reproduces the illusion of being in a different place. Instead, it resembles certain plays or contemporary dance pieces that lay bare the undressed back wall of the theatre or the real nature of the place where the performance happens.

The architectural background does not play the role of a figurative urban stage, recreated with industrial buildings, old ships and out-of-service cranes that could cause visitors to perceive the urban space as part of a port that no longer exists, but rather it is an abstract stage formed by modern buildings, facilities and green areas that enable the port to be perceived as a river.

The water functions as a theatrical stage, and the spectators line up in front of it on both shores. As opposed to the layout of classical theater where the audience faces the stage so that their attention is concentrated on the performance, this arrangement, adopted in more contemporary theater, places the stage in the middle of the audience, involving the spectators, to a certain extent, as part of the performance. This fact reinforces the citizen's role as actor and spectator at the same time, one who watches and is watched. It also lends depth and dynamism to the urban stage, augmenting its attractiveness and inviting people to cross over to the other shore to experience what others are experiencing, to see what they are seeing.

In conclusion, the strategy identifies public space as a representational space, transforming the city into a theater with the objective, in this case, not only of activating public life in a disused part of the city, but also of providing meaning for the place itself.

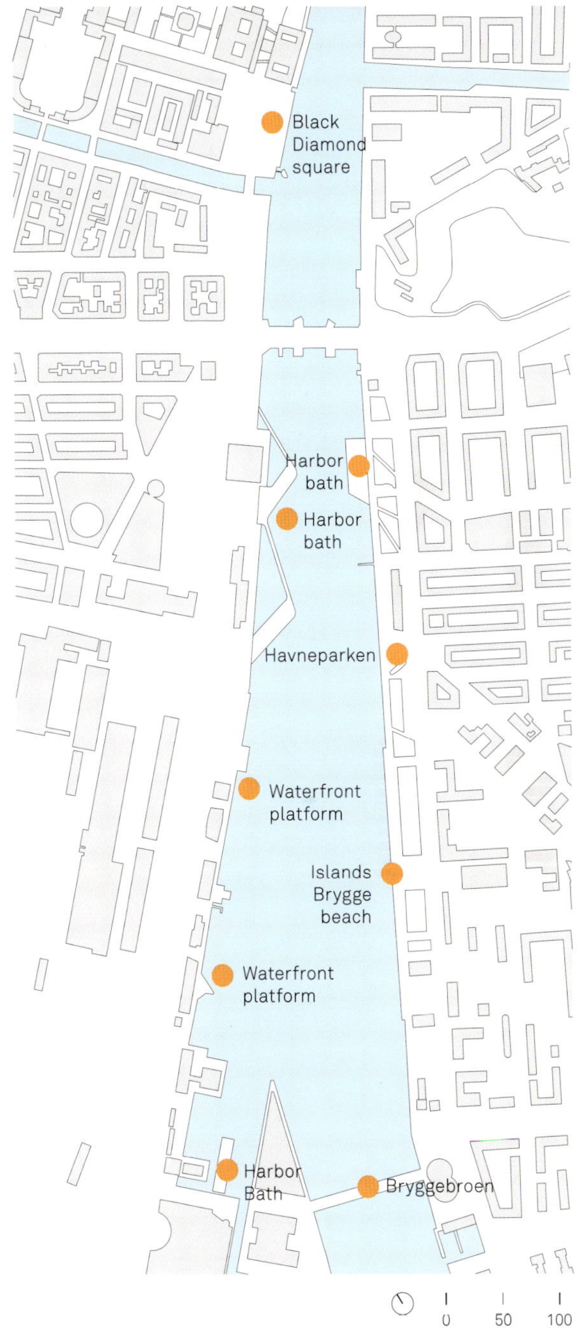

**Urban Analysis** The Copenhagen harbor was active until the 1980s when many industries closed down. Since then, a large transformation of the sites along the harbor has been combined with major investments in sewage treatment to improve the water quality. The new neighborhoods mix residential and office facilities with new public spaces along the harbor, acting as a new leisure center for the city. Its excellent location at the edge of the historical city and the mix of activities that combines housing and offices with restaurants and cafés make this fragment of the Copenhagen harborfront a very popular new area of the city. New transportation systems along the harbor such as four water bus lines and a large variety of recreational facilities such as green areas for sunbathing, two restaurants, children's playgrounds, the Harbor Baths, water polo areas and sports facilities have resulted in extensive use of the harborfront, both by local residents and by other citizens of Copenhagen alike.

## Aerial View

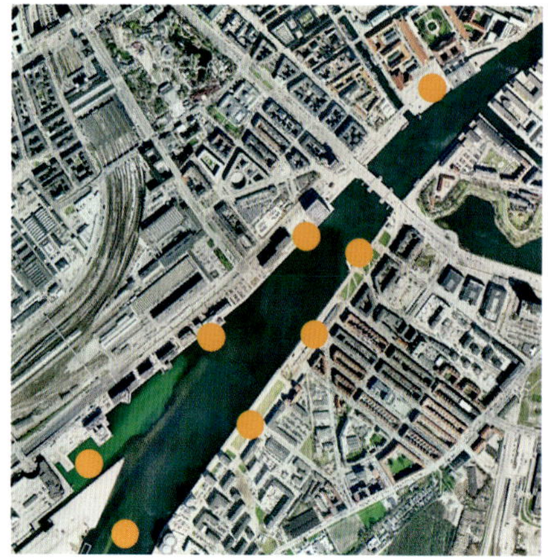

## Users

## Relation to the City

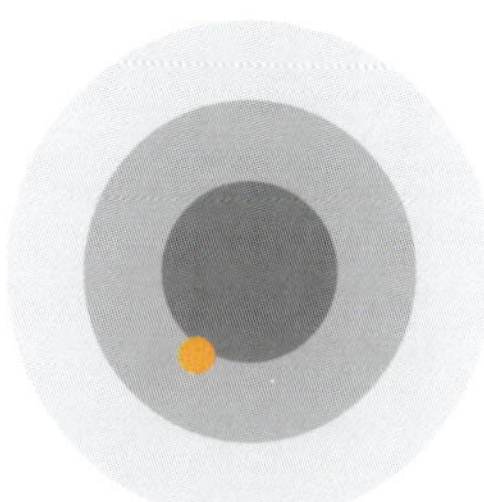

(Old) City center
Initial city expansions
Suburbs
Interventions

## Historic Urban Development

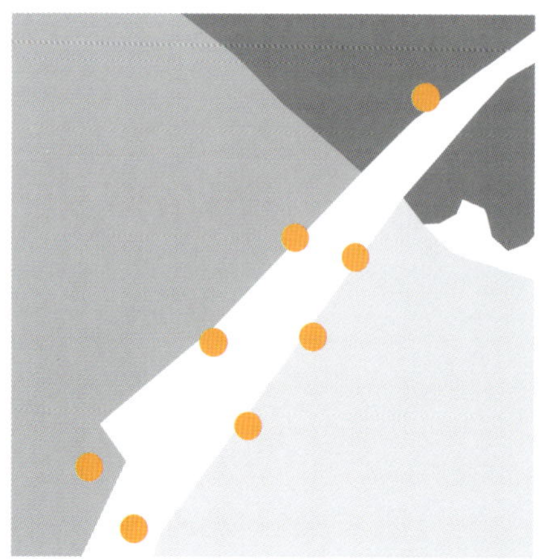

Medieval city
Post-18th century
Late 20th century
Interventions

## Activities

Residential
Public buildings
Offices
Industrial
Shops
Hotels

**Social Analysis** The city of Copenhagen has a large population of singles living alone, who occupy half of the city's apartments, while only a third of them are occupied by couples. That means that more than three quarters of the residential units are inhabited by just one or two people, while only 22% of the houses are occupied by families. Immigrants represent 17% of Copenhagen's population, and the unemployment rate was 8% in 2011.

## Age Structure

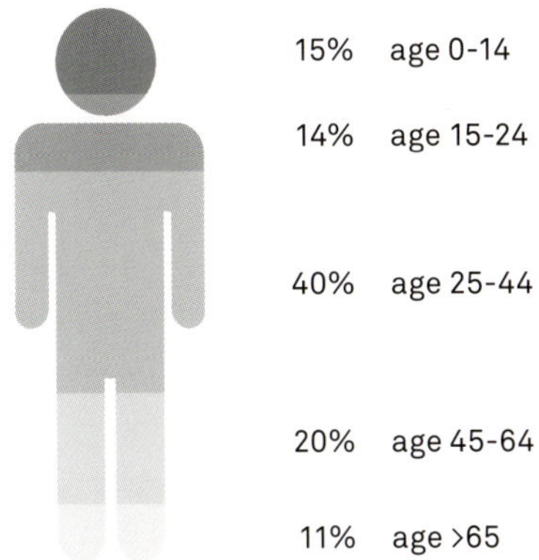


## Household Composition

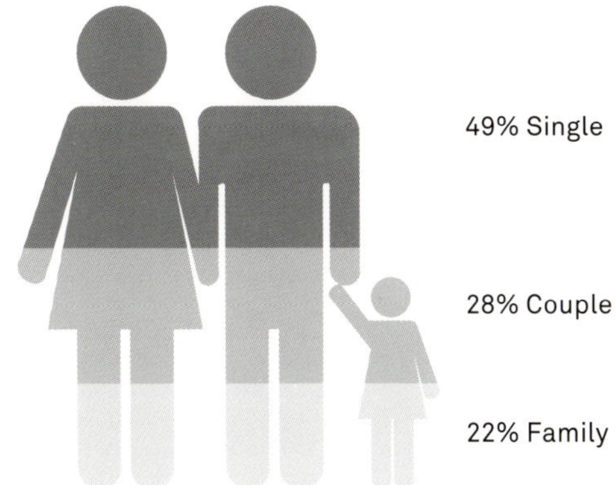

## Immigration

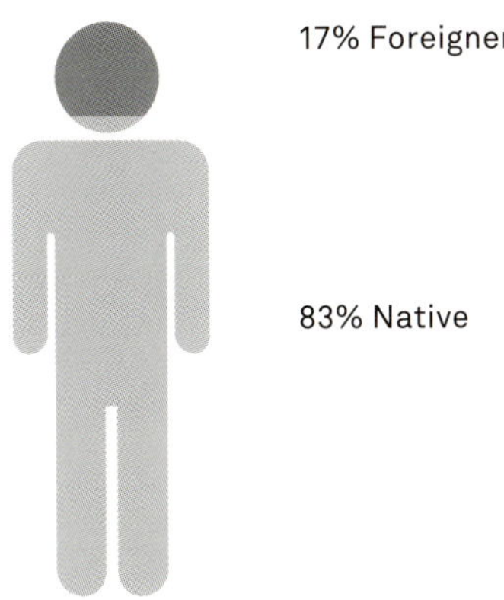


## Unemployment

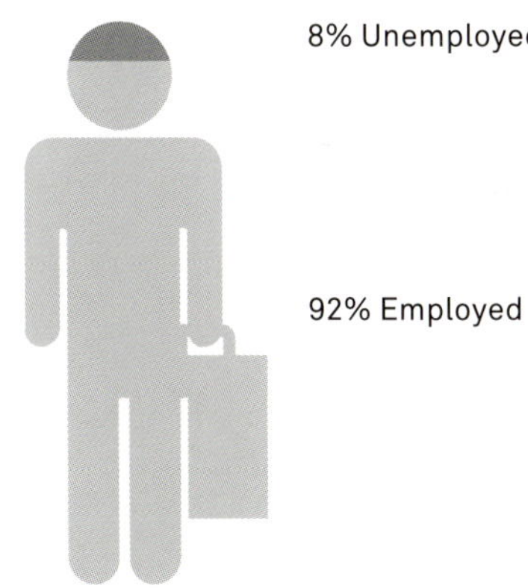


Source for all data: Copenhagen city source Statistics Denmark 2011.

**Interventions** The interventions realized to regenerate urban life in the public space along Copenhagen's harborfront are many, built in different periods and spread across many kilometers of waterfront.

This study has been reduced to five main interventions located along a small 1.5-kilomter stretch of the harbor, which is limited by the National Library building at the north end and the Bryggebroen Bridge to the south. Some of the interventions were specifically designed for their locations, while others, such as the Harbor Baths, are generic interventions that are repeated at several points along the waterfront.

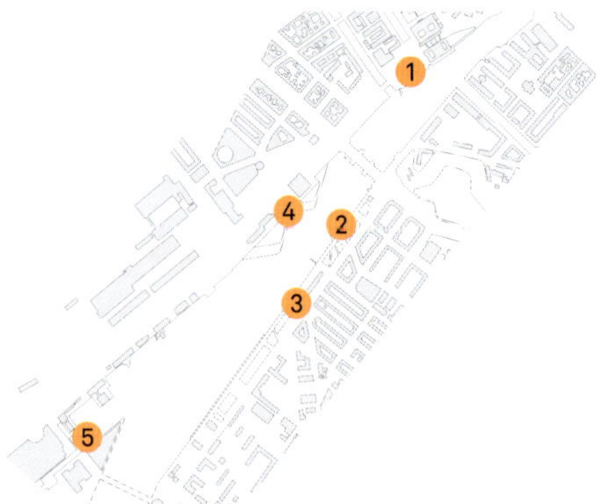


Accesses
Relaxation areas
Sitting areas
Circulation
Vegetation

## 1 Black Diamond Square

The National Library, popularly known as the Black Diamond, is a city landmark that visually marks this zone of the harbor. The café-terrace outside the Library has become a popular public place on the waterfront. Its wooden platform is connected with a square to the south where a few long benches are placed adjacent to the café entrance and there are several long wooden steps for sitting on that face the harborfront, acting as a small theater for observing the life of the harbor. The strategic location close to the library and easy connection with other parts of the city, via a nearby water bus stop, make this place a popular space to meet, read, and sunbathe in summer.

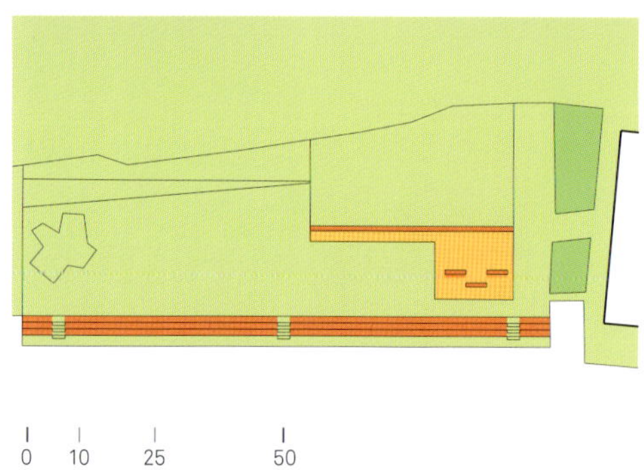


## 2 Harbor Bath at Islands Brygge

Designed by the architects Julien de Smedt and Bjarke Ingels and built in 2003, the Harbor Bath has a total of 5 pools and a capacity for 600 people. There are two 50-meter-long swimming pools, two children's pools and a diving pool with three- and five-meter springboards.

The Harbor Bath was not only designed as a place for exercise, but as a place to socialize, play and enjoy the sun. It was built following the improvements of the water quality in the harbor and it soon became a symbol of the harbor's regeneration.

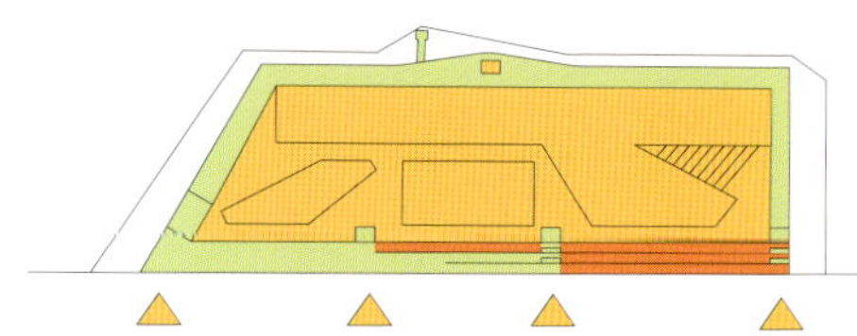

## 3 Havneparken in Islands Brygge

The urban renewal in Islands Brygge contains a long waterfront park named Havneparken. The main landscape intervention, located at the center of the park, integrates a fragment of a railroad track and an old train car to remind visitors of the site's industrial past. A bandstand, built by reusing a former ship's hull, refers to the former function of the place as dockyards. Some old steel structures that have been left behind now serve as pergolas, and fragments of demolished industrial buildings have also been kept. The intervention, aside from transforming a former industrial harbor into a meeting area for citizens, plays a role in commemorating the history of the site.

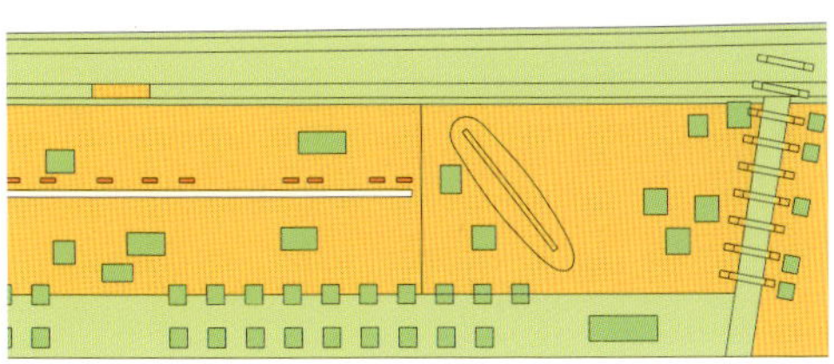

## 4 Kalvebod Waves

The new Harbor Bath located at Kalvebod Brygge was designed by JDS architects and occupies an area of 8,500 m2. A sinuous wooden promenade connects the edge of the pier with the water enclosing two plazas, several facilities and swimming pools. The waving promenade also connects the harbor level with higher belvedere platforms fitted with seats for enjoying panoramic views. Walking promenades, resting zones and sport areas are intertwined into a three-dimensional sculptural intervention characterized by a hilly silhouette.

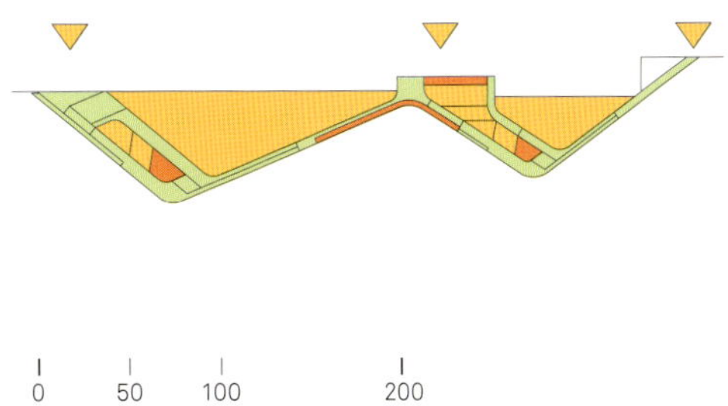

## 5 Harbor Bath at Fisketorvet

In 2002, this Harbor Bath was located at Islands Brygge. When a new Harbor Bath, designed by PLOT, was built for that location in 2003, the old one was moved to its current site.

It is located in a frequented area in front of Fisketorvet shopping center and close to the Bryggebroen bicycle and pedestrian bridge, which is used daily by 9,000 cyclists to cross the harbor. The Harbor Bath contains three separated pools: a 0.70-meter-deep children's pool, a diving pool equipped with three diving boards, and a swimming pool. Access to the pools is free and lifeguards oversee the facilities.

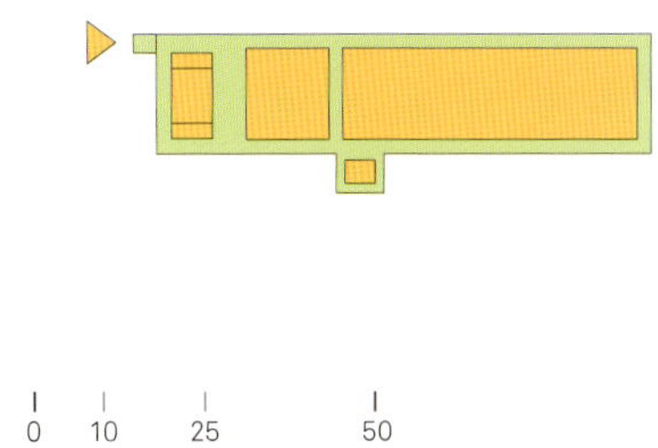

**Process** Copenhagen's harborfront has been developed through a long process divided into several phases, focused on different areas. In the 1970s there were no parks in the area of Islands Brygge. The commercial and industrial harbor had always stood as a barrier between the existing residential area and the water. In 1978 local residents organized an action committee directed by the architect Poul Jensen and his wife, the landscape architect Annelise Bramsnæs, to prevent a new vacant area from being built, proposing its transformation into a park. In 1983, the Harbor Authority finally granted the use of 1 hectare of land located just south of Langebro and hundreds of residents planted trees and grass to create a park, which opened in 1984. In 1995, the municipality of Copenhagen provided economic support for an extension of the park by 2.8 additional hectares of waterfront located to the south of the original area. Finally during the 1990s, the municipality of Copenhagen took measures to improve the quality of the harbor water significantly and other interventions were built along the waterfront, such as three Harbor Baths built in 2002, 2003 and 2013.

The main actors involved in the regeneration of public life along the Copenhagen harborfront are the municipality of Copenhagen and the Port of Copenhagen (today By & Havn) which originally owned the land. The interventions have been planned by the Municipality of Copenhagen in collaboration with independent architecture and landscape architecture offices that are in charge of developing the specific design for each intervention. Although there is a clear spatial and functional relationship among the different interventions built along the Copenhagen harborfront, at the same time they are quite independent, maintaining a specific identity.

## Cost, Financing and Maintenance

Due to the fact that the whole strategy is fragmented into several independent interventions developed in different phases and by different parties, the cost of each intervention is independent and adjusted to the specific objective to accomplish. On the one hand, the budget for some interventions, such as the People's Park and the public space adjacent to the National Library, which cover large extensions of public space, is similar to the cost of other public space interventions in the city. On the other hand, some special interventions such as the Harbor Bath at Islands Brygge have been built with a higher budget per square meter.

The Harbor Bath designed by PLOT architects (today BIG and JDS architects) in Islands Brygge had a total cost of €520,000 for 1,600 $m^2$ of built area, the equivalent of €325/$m^2$, which can be considered a modest cost for a very popular intervention that works as a landmark in the area and has become the icon of the regeneration of the Copenhagen harborfront.

The municipality of Copenhagen is in charge of maintaining all the interventions realized along the harborfront. Some of them, such as the large parks and squares facing the water, require similar maintenance as other public spaces in the city, and the tasks are carried out by the regular cleaning service, gardeners and other maintenance staff employed by the municipality. Other interventions, such as the Harbor Baths, which are free to the public, require special staff like lifeguards to oversee the facilities and control the basic maintenance of the pools. The municipality is also in charge of the management and of keeping the Harbor Baths in good condition, which is very intensive in summer because of the many visitors that use the waterfront areas.

## Timing

The long process of renovating the public space along the waterfront in the Copenhagen harbor has been ongoing over a period of 30 years and continues up until today. Although this long process began with the construction of infrastructures to improve the water quality in the harbor, the public space interventions have been developed later, in parallel to the growth of new urban developments and the construction of iconic buildings along the water.

Some of the interventions such as the first Harbor Bath designed for Islands Brygge, have been designed as temporary elements that are easy to move to other locations, serving as prototypes for more permanent designs. However, most of the interventions have been designed for long-term use.

## Use of the Public Space

Obviously, the transformation of the industrial areas on both sides of the harbor into public areas linked to the new urban developments has greatly impacted the regeneration of urban life in that part of the city. The new leisure areas facing the water, the playgrounds and the varied program located in the new squares and parks have activated the use of public space along the water.

In addition, as the result of improving the water quality and the construction of the Harbor Baths, the water areas have become part of public space. The new "aquatic public space" is concentrated in several interventions located in different points of the harbor, which function as floating squares where the urban life is highly dynamic.

Copenhagen's Harborfront can be catalogued as a successful strategy for activating the use of public space in the area, both inside and outside the water. Perhaps this symbiotic combination is what makes the area attractive not only to local residents, but also to other citizens that live in other parts of the city.

## Impact on Citizens

The public space along Copenhagen's harborfront created to support the new urban developments was, first of all, a real need of the neighborhood. Improving the water quality and cleaning up the soil in the area before the new residential blocks, offices and hotels were built was also a must.

This development, which allowed for the emergence of new open-air recreation areas, was well received by the local residents. Over time, the strategy also became very popular among other citizens of Copenhagen, attracting different kinds of people, especially in summer when the area becomes an urban beach alternative to Amager Beach.

One of the few complaints from local residents is that, at times, the public space becomes so crowded that it no longer belongs to the neighborhood. In any case, the harborfront has become one of the favorite public spaces among the citizens of Copenhagen: it has a clear, strong identity and has become a landmark both for residents and for tourists.

## Media Impact

The whole strategy has received a lot of attention from the media. On the one hand, because the strategy reinforces the already solid image of Copenhagen as one of the cities in Europe with the best and most vibrant public spaces. On the other hand, because of the iconic character of the Harbor Baths, which have become successful elements for branding the whole strategy. The Harbor Baths have been the focus of attention for local newspapers, and the photos of Copenhagen's residents using the waterfront as an urban beach is the image that sums up their success, without the need for words.

The interventions along Copenhagen's harborfront have also been extensively published in many specialized publications for architecture, urbanism and landscape architecture and they have been awarded with several prizes, such as a special mention in the European Prize for Urban Public Space in 2004.

**Københavns Havnebad Islands Brygge**

Claus Bjørn Larsen

**Vandet i Københavns Havn er lige så rent som vandet i Øresund. Dette er en glimrende grund til at smutte forbi Københavns Kommunes 'strand' på Islands Brygge, som giver byboerne mulighed for at køle kroppen midt i byens hjerte.**

**Badevand i byens havn**
Københavnerne har en badestrand, som ligger lige midt i byen med fri udsigt til byens tårne og havnefrontens liv.

Vandet i Københavns Havn er lige så rent som vandet i Øresund. Derfor har Københavns Kommune og Københavns Idrætsanlæg realiseret ideen om at gøre havnens vand tilgængeligt for byens borgere.

**Københavns første havnebad**
Til badesæsonen i 2002 åbnede havnebadet på Islands Brygge som det første af byens havnebade. I 2003 blev havnebadet sejlet over til Havneholmen ved Fisketorvet, mens der til gengæld på Islands Brygge siden er blevet bygget et permanent og større havnebassin med plads til 600 badegæster.

**Bassinerne**
Der er fem bassiner i alt, og to af dem er til børn. Der er et til de små og et til de lidt større børn. Alle børn under otte år skal dog følges med en voksen.
Der er to svømmebassiner på hver 50 meter og et udspringsbassin med tre- og femmeter vipper.

**Klart blåt vand**
Havnebadet har åbent alle ugens dage, så længe miljøkontrollen tillader det. Det er nemlig sådan

CASE

**Copenhagen: From sewer to harbour bath**

**In Copenhagen, Denmark, many years of investments in the sewage system has revitalised the harbour. The revitalisation is mainly due to a remarkable reduction in the discharge of wastewater during rainfall. This case focuses on how municipal strategies and investments towards cleaning up the harbour have resulted in a water quality so high that people can now swim in the harbour. In 2002, a public harbour bath opened in the area of Islands Brygge. Today, the harbour bath is a striking urban oasis that marks Copenhagen's position as a clean and liveable city.**

For many years, the discharge of wastewater from sewers and industrial companies had a major impact on the water quality in Copenhagen harbour. The water was heavily polluted with sewage, algae, industrial waste and oil spills from commercial harbour transport.

In 1995, 93 overflow channels fed wastewater into Copenhagen harbour and the adjacent coastlines. Since then, the municipality has built rainwater reservoirs and reservoir conduits, which can store wastewater until there is space again in the sewage system. This has resulted in the closing of 55 overflow channels. Today, wastewater is only discharged to the harbour during very heavy rainfall.

## SCHUYTGRAAF
ARHNEM, THE NETHERLANDS

STRATEGY / INTERVENTIONS: **Casanova+Hernandez**
COMMISSIONER: **GEM Schuytgraaf**

Schuytgraaf is a newly founded urban development to the southwest of Arnhem, which had some 7,000 inhabitants in 2010, and it is eventually expected to reach around 15,000 in the coming years. It was developed within the framework of the Vinex program, approved by the Dutch Ministry of Housing in 1991 to concentrate the construction of new residential areas on the outskirts of certain Dutch cities, from 1995 on.

Schuytgraaf is divided into 25 neighborhoods that are allocated different parameters in terms of density and program according to their location with respect to the new train station area, the center for most of the commercial activity in the whole urban development.

GEM Schuytgraaf was the joint venture in charge of managing Schuytgraaf's urban development, and KCAP were the urban planners responsible for the general planning and supervision of the whole area. In 2007, Casanova+Hernandez was commissioned by GEM to develop the master plan and the public space design for one of the 25 neighborhoods.

The intervention area is sector 2a of Schuytgraaf, which comprises an extension of 6.4 hectares. The plan is developed along a central circulation axis that links four pedestrian squares, around which are located four residential clusters containing an educational facility and 200 dwellings. The central axis and the pedestrian squares articulate the collective and public life in the new neighborhood and the squares become the main places for interaction among its inhabitants.

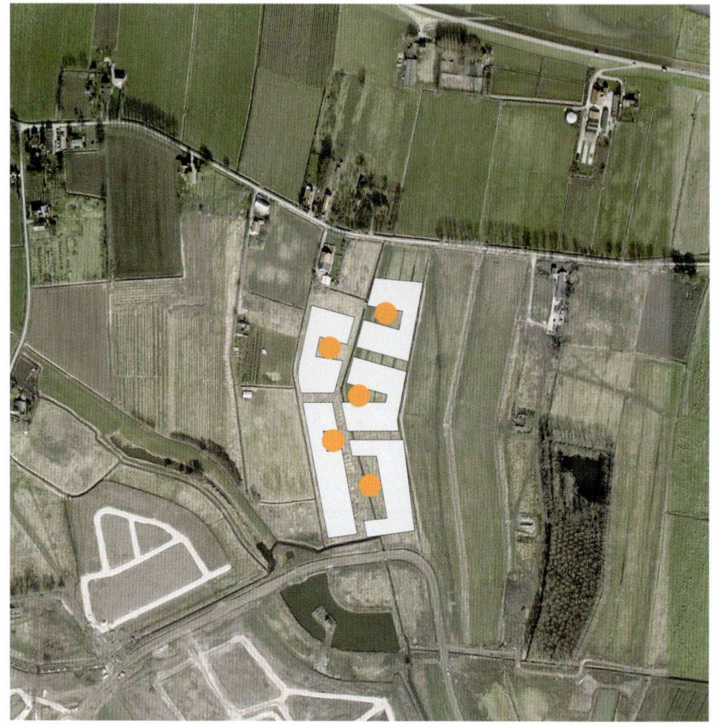

**Strategy** The new neighborhood, like any suburb based on a low-density residential program and a lack of diversity of uses, is characterized by homogeneous public space. The absence of commercial premises on the ground floor has an impact on the urban life in the public space, and in parallel the fact that the neighborhood will be developed in a single phase means that the future residents will not have well-established ties with the place or with their neighbors.

The proposed public space strategy attempts to create a sense of place among the new inhabitants, providing the area with meeting places where the new residents can interact, generating a sense of community. To that end, the public space is devised as an open house with different outdoor rooms, connected by a central hallway. Each room, or pedestrian square, though it is similar to the others in terms of its dimensions and the architecture that surrounds it, is differentiated from the rest in terms of use and appearance, creating a rich spatial and functional sequence which can be clearly perceived as pedestrians circulate along the main transit axis.

An independent intervention is built in each square, characterized by a distinct dominant color in the pavement, the street furniture and the vegetation. At the same time, each intervention is associated with a special feature from Schuytgraaf's landscape, whether it is the fruit trees, the fields of flowers, the dikes or the Roman ruins nearby. The set of interventions aims to create a differentiated public space thanks to a variety of spaces characterized by a strong individual identity, but which share certain features belonging to a common strategy.

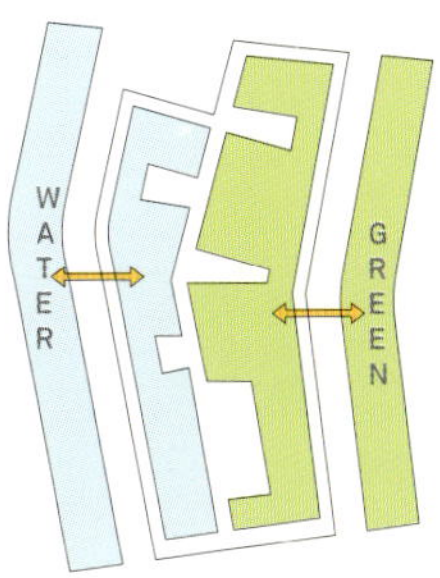


1
Central axis dividing water strip and green strip

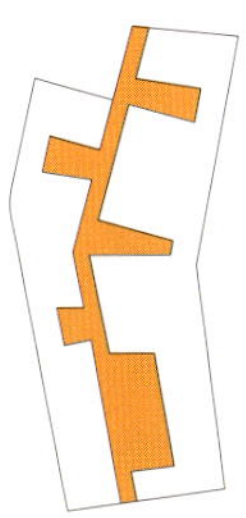

2
Central axis and sequence of squares

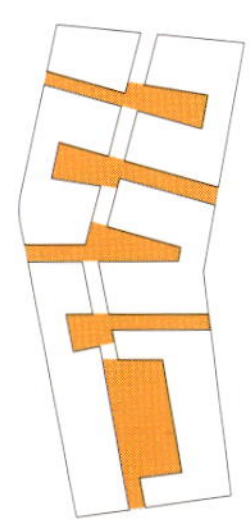

3
Relationship squares-streets

## Interventions

Four principal interventions in public space articulate the strategy.

### Intervention 1. Roman Remains Square

The violet intervention, located in the north, is structured using the fanciful outlines of Roman mosaics, which make reference to the Roman history of the site. The circulation area of the square grows wider and narrower following the meandering border created by green zones planted with native vegetation. At some points, the curved edge of the flower bed is bordered by long benches and the circulation area widens, creating small-scale lounges where residents sit to contemplate fragments of the wild landscape.

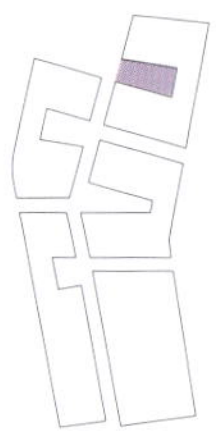

Section

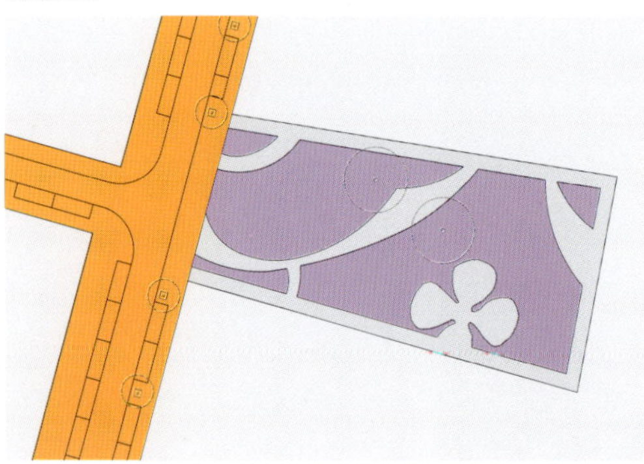

Plan

0 5 25

## Intervention 2. Dike Square

The green intervention, located in the central area, displays a topography of green flat slopes that recall the landscape of the area's dikes. These hills limit a space at the center of the square where a children's playground is located, protected from traffic and immersed in a calm and intimate atmosphere.

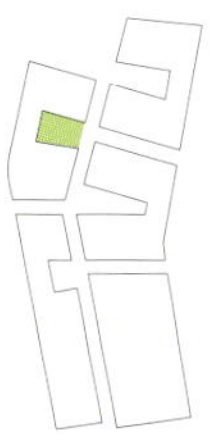

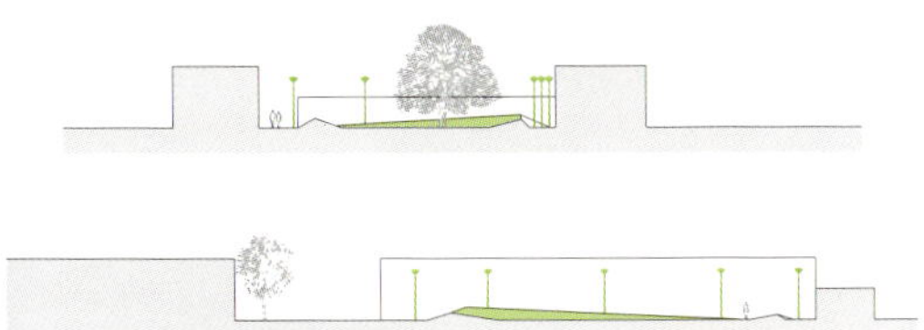

Section

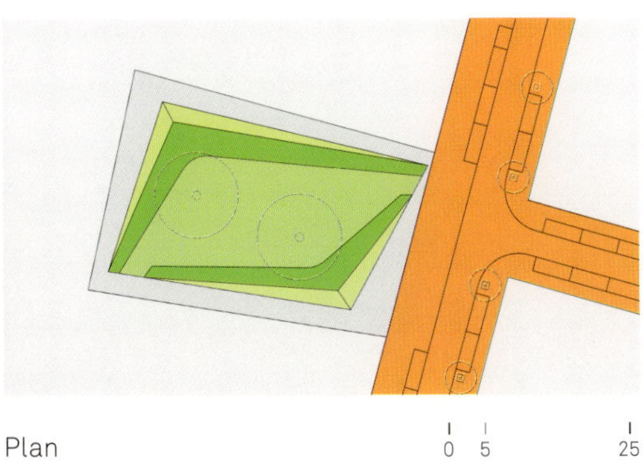


Plan

## Intervention 3. Wildflowers Square

The red intervention, located next to the previous one, is formed by two large oval-shaped hills planted with red geraniums, envisioned as two plant-covered islands that emerge from the pavement of the square. The recycled cork pavement, which is also red, incorporates circular tree pits made with a dark reddish granulated resin that lets rainwater filter through. The square as a whole is characterized by its chromatic richness, which recalls the intense color of the region's flower fields during the blooming season.

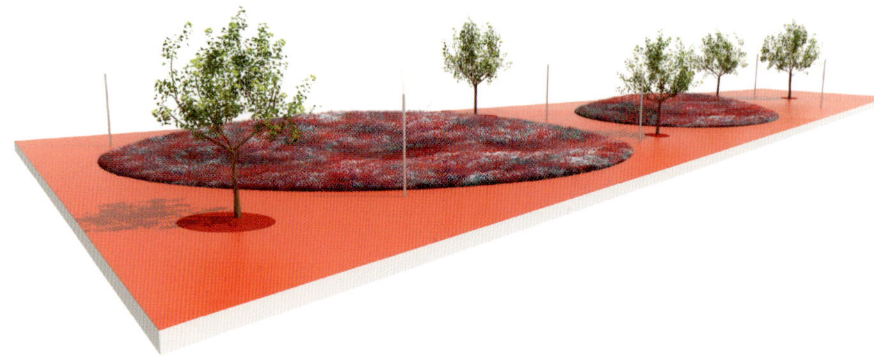

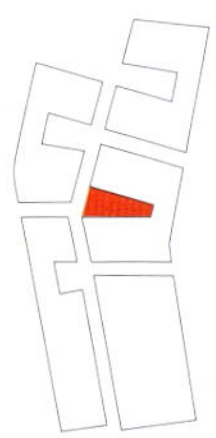

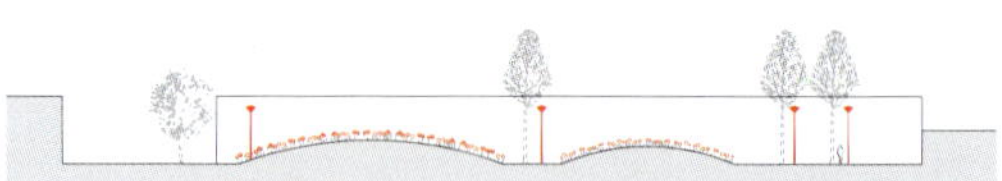

Section

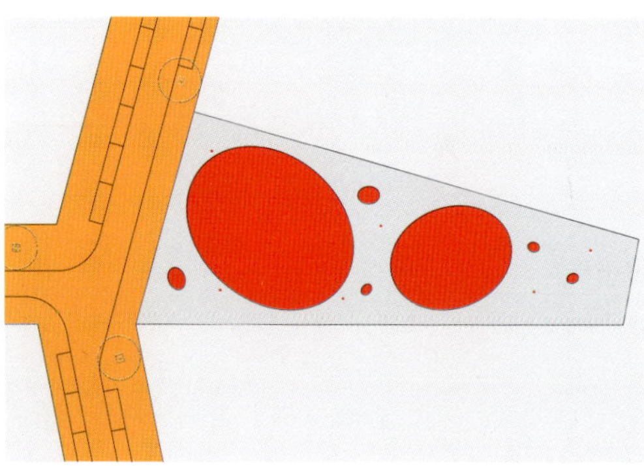

Plan 0 5 25

## Intervention 4. Orchard Square

The dark green intervention located in the southern area of the plan is provided with a central zone created by a dense group of fruit trees arranged in parallel lines. A lounge area is set up under the trees using different pieces of urban furniture.

The set of interventions as a whole seeks to create a specific sense of place by relating the new public space to the landscape and to the history of the place and the surrounding area. The urban plan divides the urban space into residential clusters, articulated around pedestrian squares that function as small-scale urban stages. These domestic-scale urban stages are used mainly by the inhabitants who live in the adjacent cluster, but the fact that each cluster hosts a different intervention provides it with a different appearance and function to attract residents from other clusters, encouraging more interaction among the neighborhood residents.

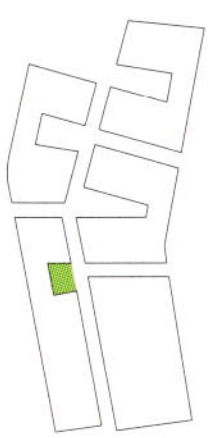

Section

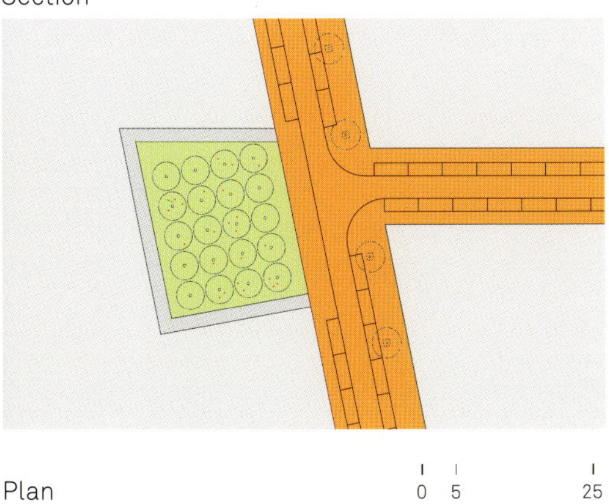


Plan

# ØRESTAD SOUTH
## COPENHAGEN, DENMARK

STRATEGY / INTERVENTIONS: **Casanova+Hernandez**
COMMISSIONER: **Ørestad Development Corporation**

Ørestad is the most extensive urban plan in Danish history. It covers a total area of 120 hectares with residential buildings, commercial facilities and public institutions in a new urban zone located in the Øresund region, south of Copenhagen. In 2007, the Ørestad Development Corporation launched an international competition for the design of the urban spaces in Ørestad South in order to create a vibrant city district with an alive public space.

The intervention area has an extension of 14.1 hectares, distributed along three boulevards that run through Ørestad South from north to south and seven squares that are connected to the boulevards, sometimes used for transverse circulation among them. All these public spaces are conceived as a network of urban voids, which are spread throughout a compact urban layout.

**Strategy** The strategy is made up of two independent overlapping layers. The first layer consists of paving, planting trees and installing basic urban elements that lend uniformity and homogeneity to public space. A second layer consists of a series of interventions on top of this basic layer. They are situated in key points of public space to reinforce the programmatic differentiation, the spatial qualities and the identity of the seven squares and three boulevards. The interventions transform these boulevards and squares into improvised urban stages where different aspects of Ørestad South's public life can play out.

The implementation of this second layer of the strategy can be easily divided into phases allowing for the independent realization of each intervention when necessary, so that public space facilities grow in relation to the construction of new blocks and the increasing amount of residents.

The strategy combines the unique, differentiated identity of each intervention with a varied program of activities that brings each square to life specifically. However, achieving vibrant urban life is not only dependent on the one-dimensional programming of activities in public space, it also requires a multidimensional coordination of the following parameters:

**Activity gradient**
The highest level of activity happens in the three main squares, while a medium level of activity is created in the park boulevard and in the interventions located on the wooded boulevard.
**Citizen interaction**
The location for a higher level of interaction among citizens is planned on Cliff Square and at the southern end of the Park boulevard, where there are two main attractors for large-scale events. A medium interaction level happens in the sports fields and the areas designed for open-air activities located in the three main squares as well as in several spots along the boulevards.
**Dynamics**
A sequence of similar or complementary activities generates the movement of citizens following a series of circuits: a training circuit that runs along the entire area connecting with the sports fields located to the north, the Andersen's stories itinerary designed along the wooded boulevard, the history line along the canal boulevard, and the cultural itinerary that connects the main squares.
**Adaptability over time**
The strategy stimulates the alternation of activities during the day, throughout the week and during the different seasons of the year in order to preserve a constant vibrant urban life. In particular, the marked difference in weather conditions between summer and winter gives the opportunity for implementing a series of transformable spaces in the design, such as a roller skating rink (summer) - ice skating rink (winter), summer and winter training circuit, water games area (summer) - winter games area (winter), relaxation area (morning) - sunset lounge (evening), children's story-tellers space (morning) - social gathering place for elderly people (afternoon), or outdoor cinema (summer) - ice hockey field (winter).

**Interventions** Spreading out the poles of activity in public space over seven squares and three boulevards avoids a centralized urban structure, but could also run the risk of creating uniform and undifferentiated public space. In order to avoid this, the interventions are characterized by a well-defined identity and are provided with a strong variety of activities to create clear differences between areas within the urban development. Indeed, the strategy tries to promote public life in Ørestad South by transforming the public space into an urban stage formed by a wide range of interventions with different characters, where public life is performed. The activities programmed in the interventions work as a stimulating script that attracts citizens to become performers. In order to create successful interventions both aspects, identity and activity, are defined as follows:

### 1. Identity

The major problems associated with large-scale new urban developments built over a short period of time, when compared with the natural growth of the historical city, are the lack of sense of identity and the difficulty in generating a balanced urban life.

The current urban plan assumes its artificial generation and articulates a language based on the combination of different pieces of contemporary architecture to create a specific artificial identity. The strategy is a reflection on the power of artificiality to generate identity in the contemporary city.

The interventions in public space recreate seven typical Danish landscapes that are present in the collective memory of the Danish people: the fiord, the cliff, the dunes, the forest, the fields, the meadows and the islands. These landscapes assign an iconic identity to each square, which helps to differentiate the different parts of the neighborhood and creates a coherent narrative for the whole area.

Squares

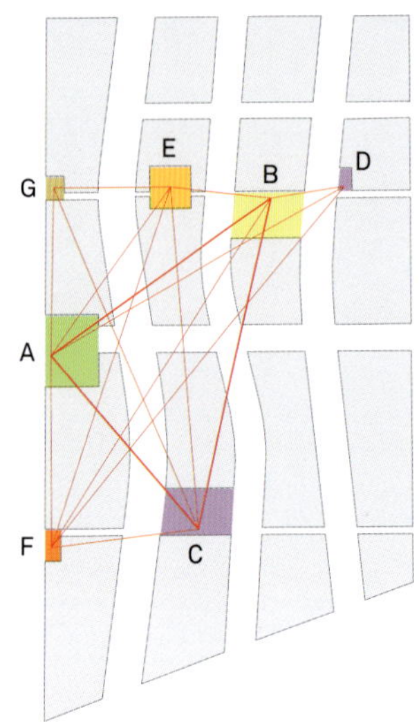


Relaxation Areas

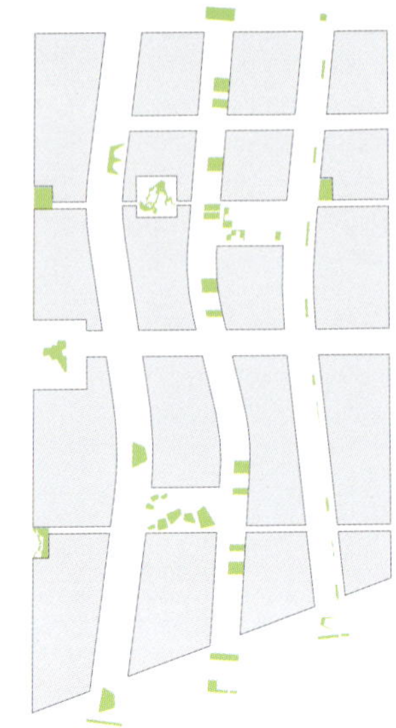

Boulevards

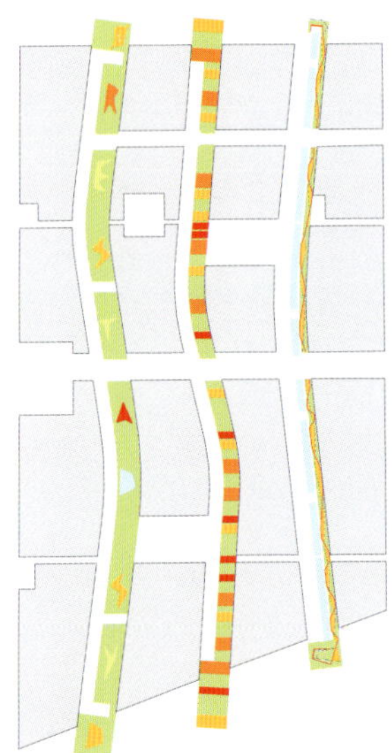

Outdoor Activities

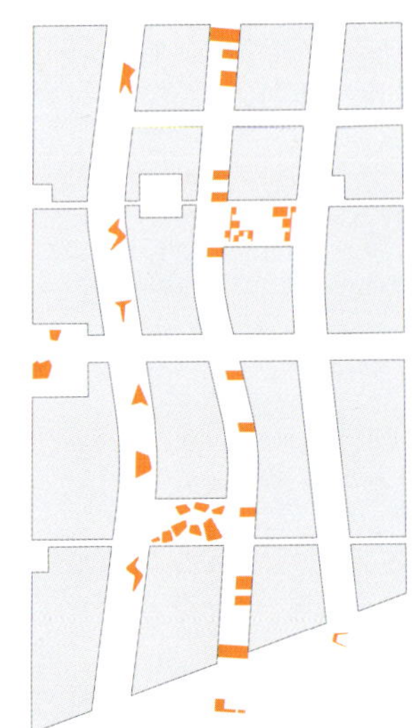

## 2. Activities

A wide variety of activities have been located throughout the public space. First, the location of each activity is related to the surrounding conditions, such as the characteristics of the site, its solar orientation and the functions of the nearby buildings. Second, each new activity pays special attention to how it relates to other activities nearby in order to create a balanced and structured activity map.

A functional classification of the activities can be resumed into: relaxation, outdoor activities, games, sports, food and services. The relaxation activities are spread homogeneously over the whole area, with special attention to the squares and the southern areas in contact with the water. The outdoor activities and games, such as pétanque, table games, the children's playground or the outdoor library, are located in the three main squares: Cliff, Dunes and Islands Square. The most dynamic activities and playing fields are located basically along the Park Boulevard and the Wooded Boulevard.

To complement these activities, outdoor cafés, restaurants and snack-bars are placed in the three main squares and in the Forest Square, close to the shops that are located on the ground floor. There are also a few cafés and restaurant pavilions along the Wooded and Park Boulevards.

The adequate relationship identity-activity and stage-script for the performance of urban life is what allows for building a vibrant and dynamic urban life, converting public space into a space for citizen interaction and, finally, stimulating the birth of a neighborhood feeling and a sense of place in Ørestad South.

Activity Index

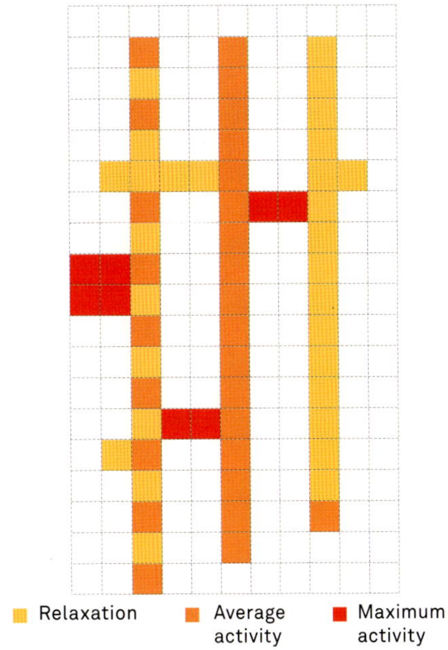


Sports

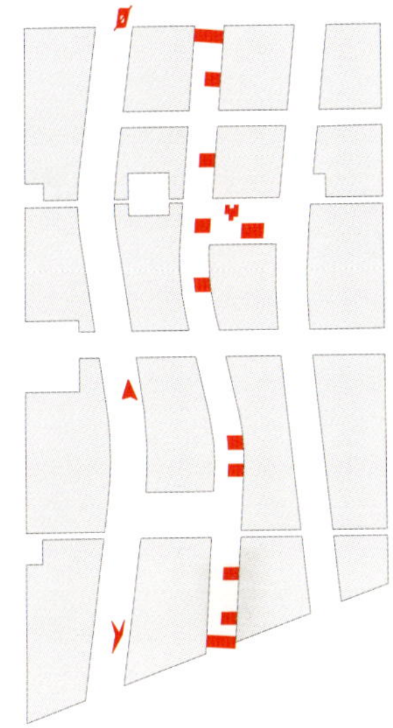

Interaction Zones

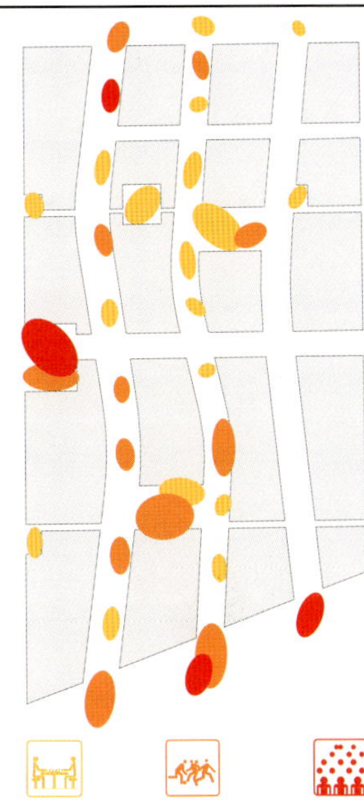

Food

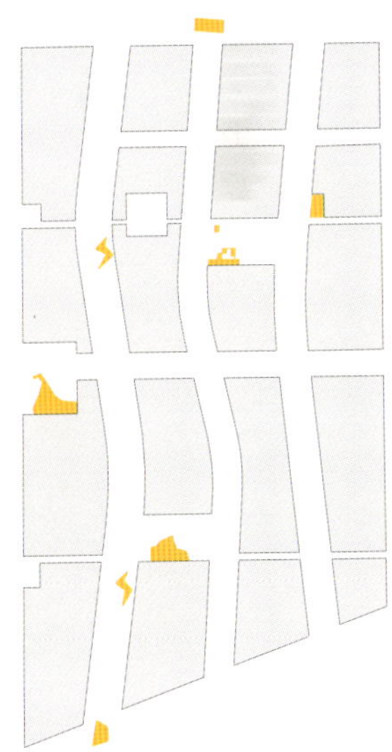

1 Wooded Boulevard

2 Park Boulevard

3 Canal Boulevard

Plans:
Southern
interventions

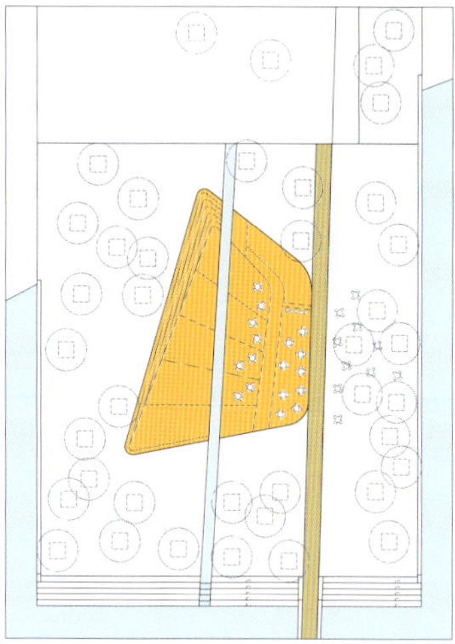

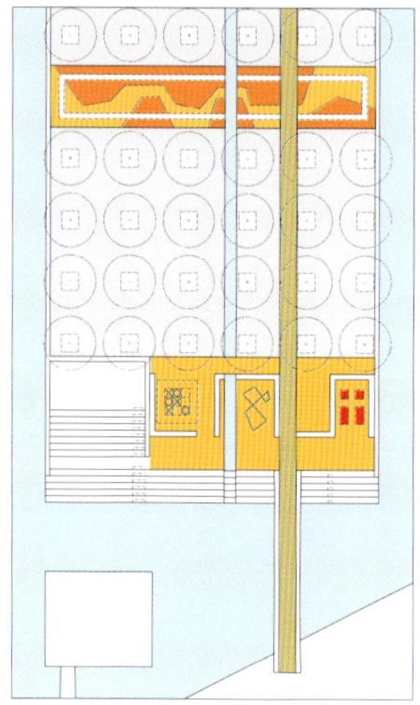

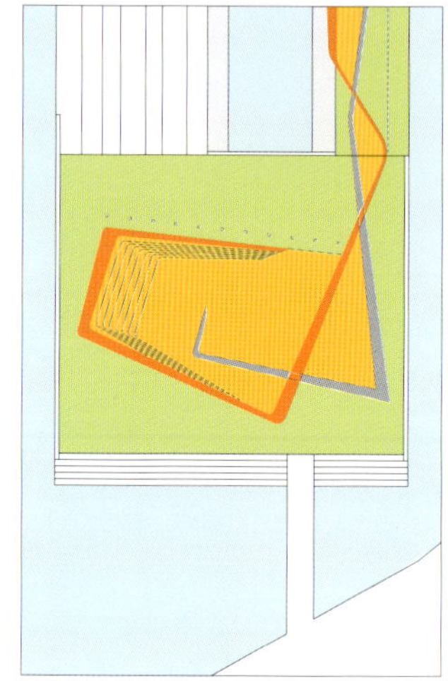

Sections

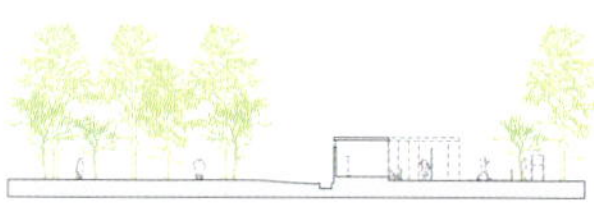

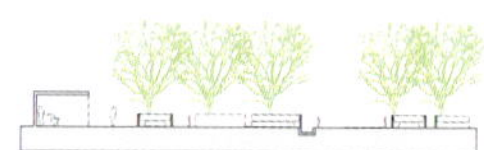

Plans:
Northern
interventions

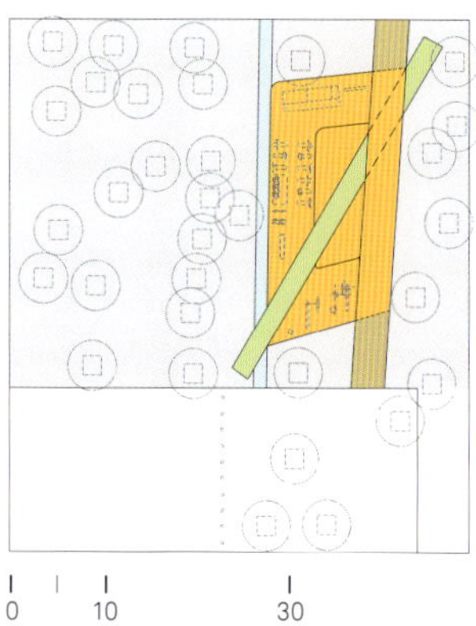


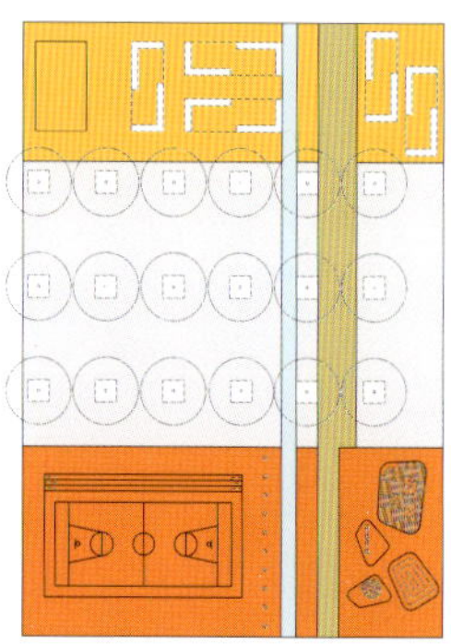

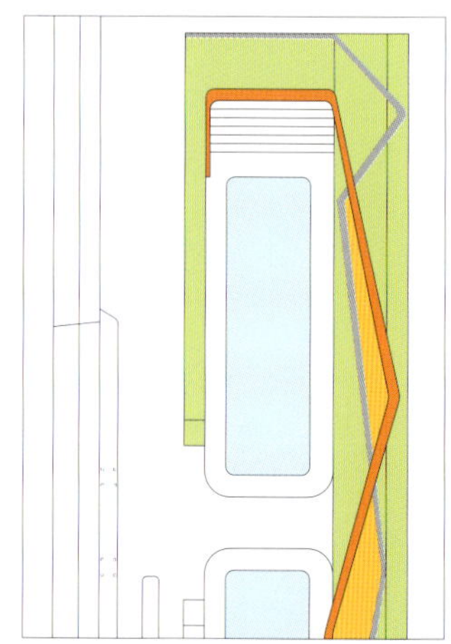

# A Cliff Square

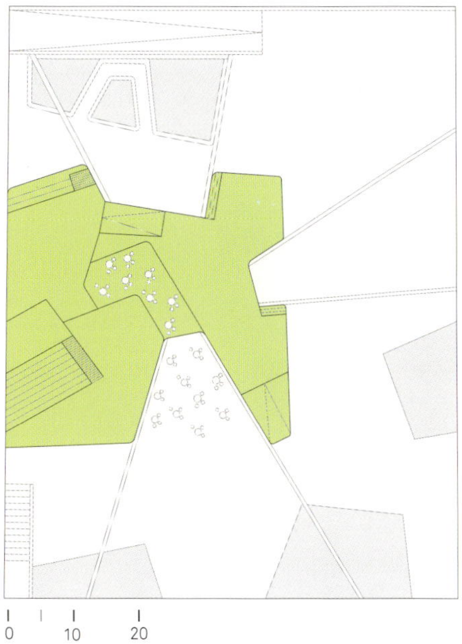


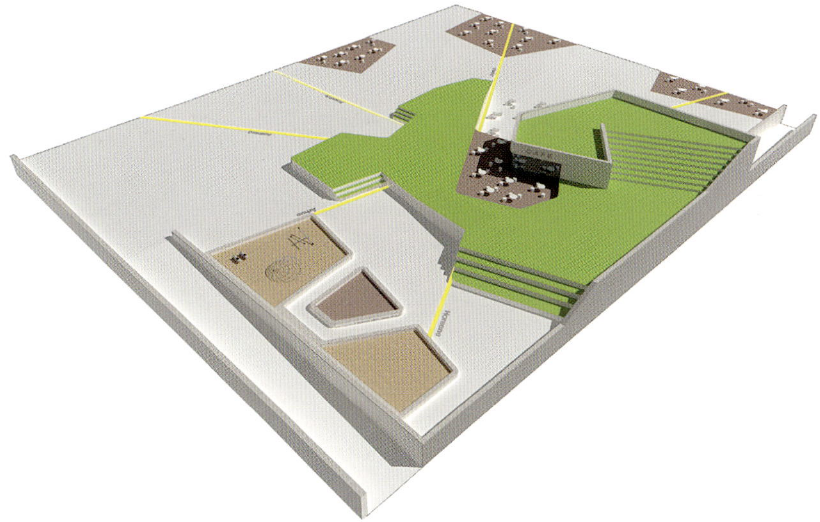

## B Dunes Square

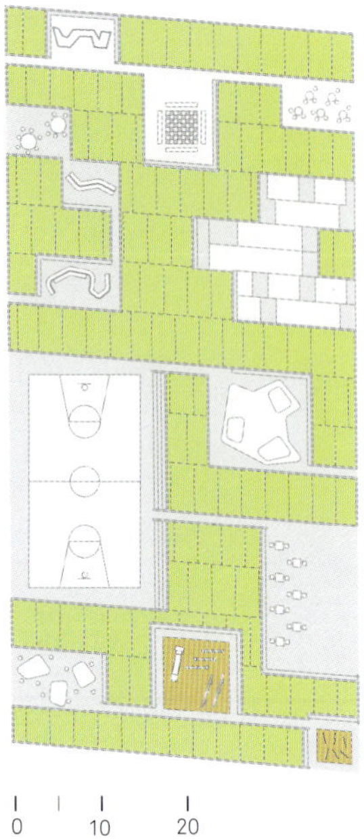

## C Islands Square

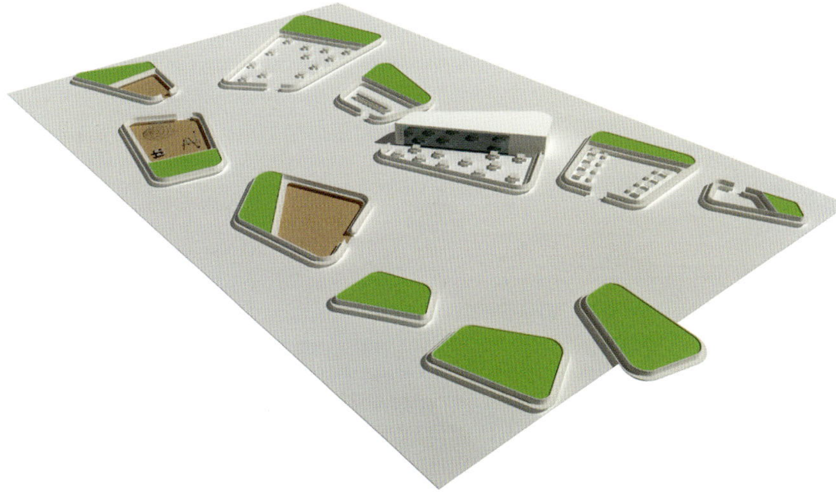

0
5
10

## E Fiords Square

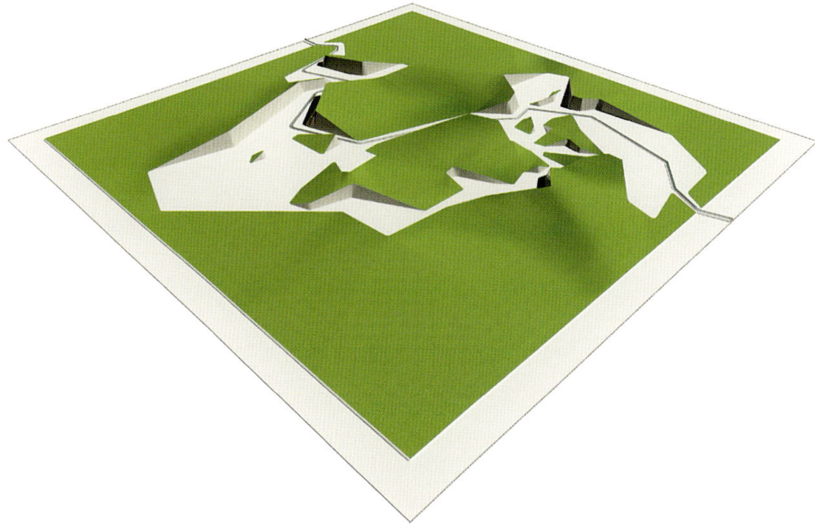

# F Meadows Square

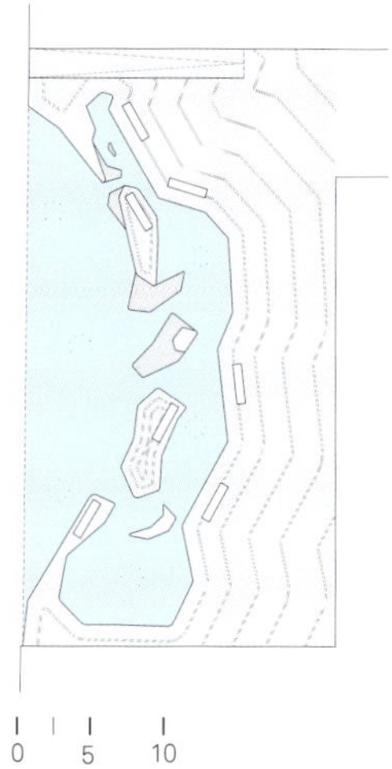


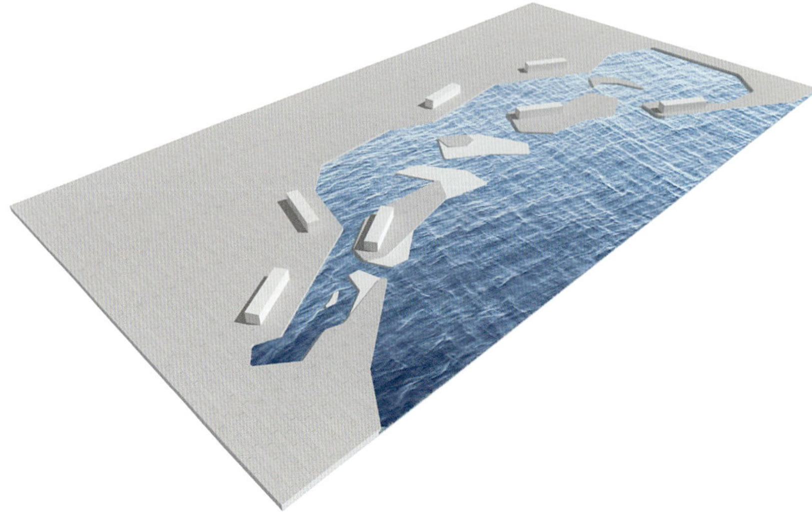

# G Fields Square

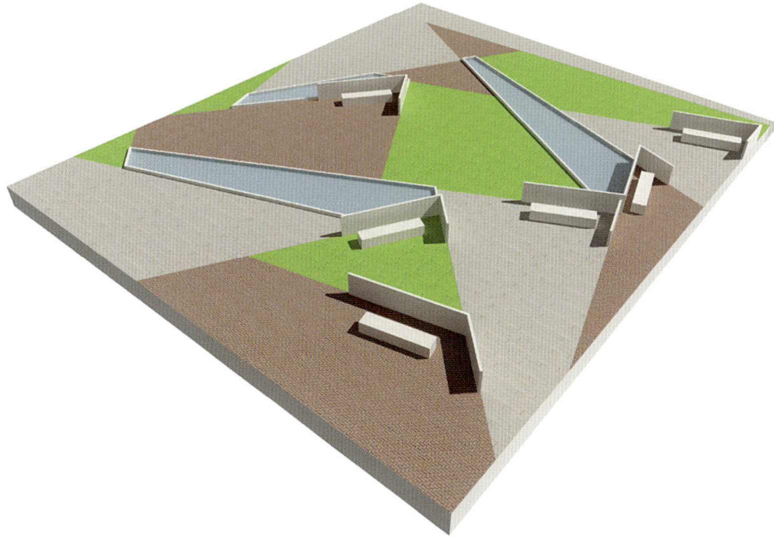

# City as an Event Place

Rituals and festive events have been a part of human culture for tens of thousands of years, dating back to the oldest known evidence from burial rituals from the Upper Paleolithic. Some of them are seasonal celebrations that mark the beginning of the spring, the end of the harvest season, or the New Year and others have a religious nature. They all contribute to giving a special meaning to the places by hosting games, sports, music, dancing, parades and the culinary traditions characteristic of each community. Rituals and traditional celebrations are a fundamental part of public life; they structure community life and help reinforce the collective identity.

An event, as opposed to rituals and traditional celebrations, is a special organized occurrence that does not necessarily have to follow any particular tradition, but which does have the capacity to bring people together, for instance, by assembling crowds in a stadium or a small group of people around a street performance. Today, many cities program a considerable calendar of macro-events to "activate" urban life. Events have become a municipal branding mechanism through which cities compete with each other to demonstrate their cosmopolitanism. Numerous events held in cities around the world, such as jazz, rock or classical music festivals, sporting competitions, and theater, dance or film festivals, although they really only promote the use of public space during a few days a year, serve to stimulate a dynamic and active image of public space in the eyes of citizens.

These mass events organized in public space do not have the profound meaning of a ritual, nor do they share the historical connotations of traditional celebrations, rather they are the product of a type of society that Guy Debord described as "the society of the spectacle". Paradoxically, the event-spectacle also generates social ties because, as Debord himself argues: "The spectacle is not a collection of images, but a social relation among people, mediated by images".[1] But, can a rich program of events scheduled in public space somehow create a sense of place by itself? To what extent is it relevant whether the activity in public space was artificially created, independently of local cultural traditions?

Many sites have acquired a sense of place thanks to the celebration of a specific type of event, and man has always felt the need to mark those places using architecture. That is why the place used for the celebration of Neolithic rituals was marked with menhirs, leading to the subsequent construction of altars and temples by different religions on the five continents. The construction of auditoriums on the hills above the Greek polis that designated the civic places for the celebration of theatrical events, gave rise to the Roman theaters and amphitheaters that have evolved into the modern stadiums where sporting events are held today. Architecture and landscape architecture have helped characterize the space for celebrating the event, giving it meaning and a sense of place.

Centre Pompidou Square, Paris. Street performances transform public space into an event place.

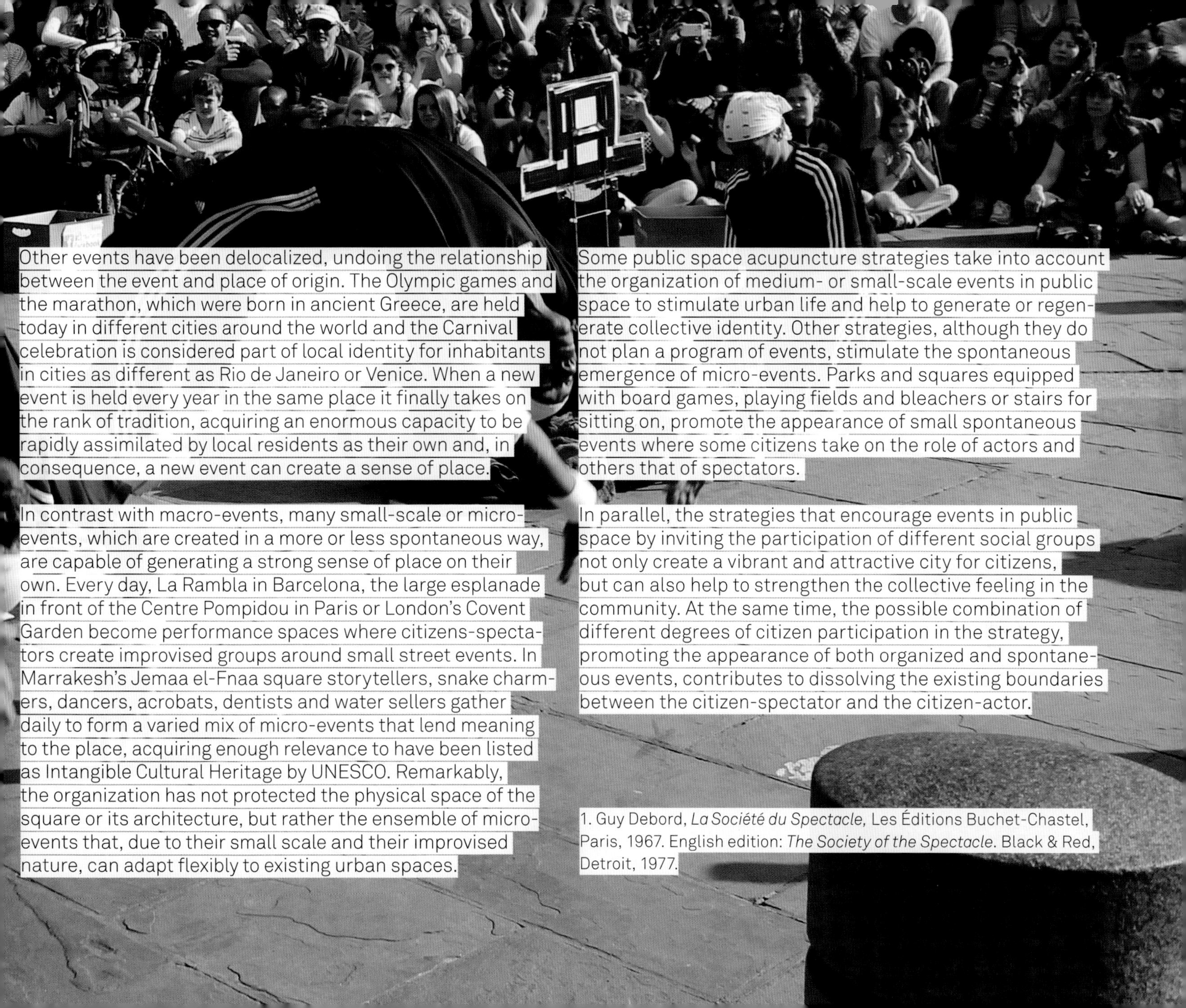

Other events have been delocalized, undoing the relationship between the event and place of origin. The Olympic games and the marathon, which were born in ancient Greece, are held today in different cities around the world and the Carnival celebration is considered part of local identity for inhabitants in cities as different as Rio de Janeiro or Venice. When a new event is held every year in the same place it finally takes on the rank of tradition, acquiring an enormous capacity to be rapidly assimilated by local residents as their own and, in consequence, a new event can create a sense of place.

In contrast with macro-events, many small-scale or micro-events, which are created in a more or less spontaneous way, are capable of generating a strong sense of place on their own. Every day, La Rambla in Barcelona, the large esplanade in front of the Centre Pompidou in Paris or London's Covent Garden become performance spaces where citizens-spectators create improvised groups around small street events. In Marrakesh's Jemaa el-Fnaa square storytellers, snake charmers, dancers, acrobats, dentists and water sellers gather daily to form a varied mix of micro-events that lend meaning to the place, acquiring enough relevance to have been listed as Intangible Cultural Heritage by UNESCO. Remarkably, the organization has not protected the physical space of the square or its architecture, but rather the ensemble of micro-events that, due to their small scale and their improvised nature, can adapt flexibly to existing urban spaces.

Some public space acupuncture strategies take into account the organization of medium- or small-scale events in public space to stimulate urban life and help to generate or regenerate collective identity. Other strategies, although they do not plan a program of events, stimulate the spontaneous emergence of micro-events. Parks and squares equipped with board games, playing fields and bleachers or stairs for sitting on, promote the appearance of small spontaneous events where some citizens take on the role of actors and others that of spectators.

In parallel, the strategies that encourage events in public space by inviting the participation of different social groups not only create a vibrant and attractive city for citizens, but can also help to strengthen the collective feeling in the community. At the same time, the possible combination of different degrees of citizen participation in the strategy, promoting the appearance of both organized and spontaneous events, contributes to dissolving the existing boundaries between the citizen-spectator and the citizen-actor.

1. Guy Debord, *La Société du Spectacle,* Les Éditions Buchet-Chastel, Paris, 1967. English edition: *The Society of the Spectacle*. Black & Red, Detroit, 1977.

Case Study H

## BEYOND LEIDSCHE RIJN
## UTRECHT, THE NETHERLANDS

STRATEGY: **Bureau Beyond**
COMMISSIONERS: **Utrecht City Council, Property Development Leidsche Rijn**
INTERVENTIONS: **Multiple designers and artists**

Leidsche Rijn is a new neighborhood in Utrech developed over a very short period of time. Like many other new large-scale urban developments, it is inhabited by new residents who have no historical ties to the place and who do not know each other. In consequence, the social links are fragile, social cohesion is limited and the new district lacks identity.

The strategy Beyond refers to "beyond the normal planning habits". When Leidsche Rijn was being planned, culture was a layer that was ignored at the beginning of the urban planning process. However, shortly after the development began, it became clear that culture could serve as a tool to generate public life in the area. Beyond Leidsche Rijn is a long-term strategy initiated in 2001, based on a series of actions and artistic interventions in public space, that on the one hand aims to strengthen the relationship between citizens and place, and on the other hand attempts to enrich public life in the new neighborhood.

The strategy presents a varied group of interventions. Some of them, like the Sculpture Park in the Leidsche Rijn Park, consist of a series of art pieces commissioned to several artists to strengthen the relationship among the new residents, the landscape and the history of the site. Others, like the several parasite pavilions located at different places around the neighborhood which were frequently moved into different positions, create a cultural network to house exhibition programs, debates, concerts, movie projections and all kinds of cultural performances to stimulate citizen participation and social interaction. Other temporary events like the ones developed for the Nomads in Residence program, invited artists to host gatherings such as "Everyone is an expert" by Silke Wagner, who invited residents to share their knowledge with others, thus creating a platform for strengthening social ties in the neighborhood.

One of the strategy's most remarkable aspects is the attempt to activate public life by programming a series of small- and medium-scale events that are linked to physi-

cal interventions in public space, such as the "parasite pavilions" or other temporary constructions. Public space becomes an event place, comparable to a market square or a central square in the historic city. In contrast to these spaces which are already recognized by all citizens as event places, Leidsche Rijn has to be programmed from scratch, symbolized through architecture and promoted using a parallel informative strategy.

Unlike cities with a long tradition in staging events, whether they are spontaneous or previously programmed, one of the main problems in newly developed urban areas is the initial difficulty in involving new residents in participating in events within the neighborhood, and another one has to do with how to create a participatory dynamic that can generate a feeling of belonging. Some of the events planned by Bureau Beyond in the context of the Nomads in Residence program, such as "Everyone is an expert", served as pilot activities with the aim of generating other spontaneous events in the future, organized by the residents themselves.

In this sense an important part of the strategy's role, and the specific objective of certain interventions, was to create new links among citizens. The other central task of the strategy was to create connections between the citizens and the place. To this end, other interventions, like those undertaken in the Sculpture Park or the parasite built as a presentation space for the Center for Nature and Environmental Education, serve to bring citizens into contact with the nature and the history of the place, with the aim of rooting the population, especially the younger members, in the place and of promoting the growth of a true sense of belonging over time.

If for Marc Augé "a Non-place is a space devoid of the symbolic expressions of identity, relations and history", new towns are born as non-places. The public space acupuncture strategy, which transforms a new town into an event place, is the first step to promote relationships between the neighbors and the place and to endow it with a symbolic expression.

"Nomads in Residence"
Bik van der Pol and Korteknie Stuhlmacher Architecten

"Viva el monopatín"
Maurer United Architects

"Land"
N55

**Urban Analysis** Leidsche Rijn is located to the west of the old city of Utrecht and is still under construction. The new urban development is separated from the old city by the A2 highway, which connects Utrecht with Amsterdam. In 2001, the inhabitants of Leidsche Rijn numbered around 16,000. By 2011, the population had grown to 25,000 and is still growing. It is already the largest new urban development in the Netherlands in recent years.

The extraordinarily rapid growth of Leidsche Rijn was the result of a strong demand for housing within the residential sector in the Netherlands. It took the form of a large-scale mono-functional housing development, based mainly on the construction of two- to three-story family houses, some of which are detached, though most of them are grouped into clusters of row houses with back gardens. There are no shops or other functions on the ground floor. The necessary retail areas, offices and other cultural or educational facilities are concentrated at specific points within the plan.

## Aerial View

## Users

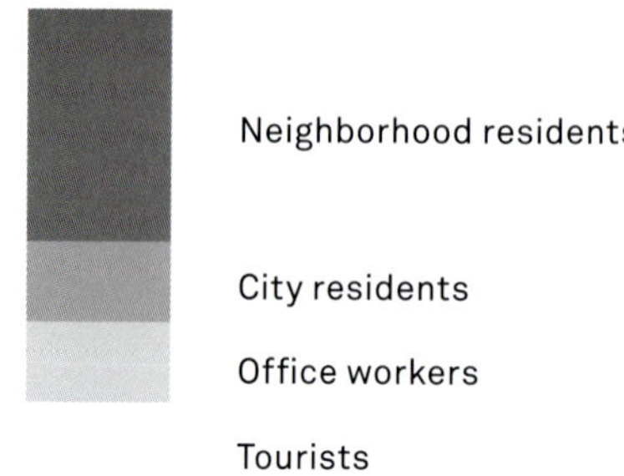


## Relation to the City

(Old) City center
Initial city expansions
Suburbs
Interventions

## Historic Urban Development

Before mid-20th ct.
Late 20th century
21st century
Interventions

## Activities

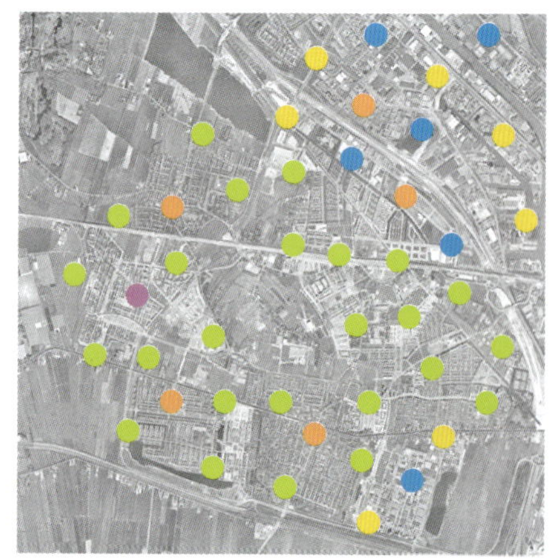

Residential
Public buildings
Offices
Industrial
Shops
Hotels

**Social Analysis** Leidsche Rijn presents a strong residential character with a large amount of dwellings that follow the row housing typology. Almost 80% of the dwellings are occupied by families or young couples who need space for children to play in the garden. As a result, the percentage of children in the area is very high (25% of the population) compared to a traditional city neighborhood, while the amount of people over 65 is still very low (6% of the population). Foreign residents represent 30% of the population, lower than the average rate for the old city center of Utrecht. The unemployment rate in 2009 was about 5%.

## Age Structure

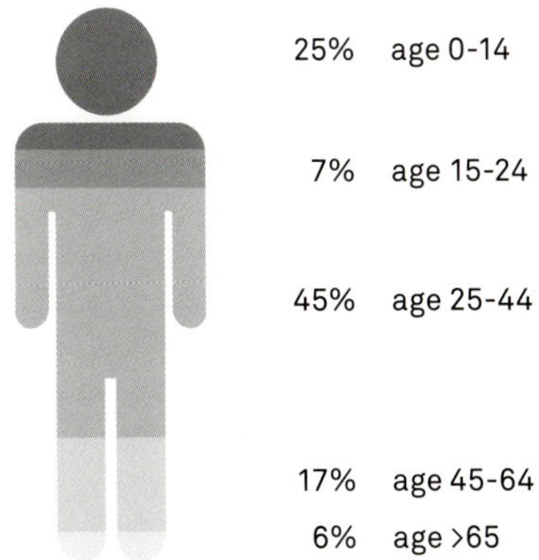


## Household Composition

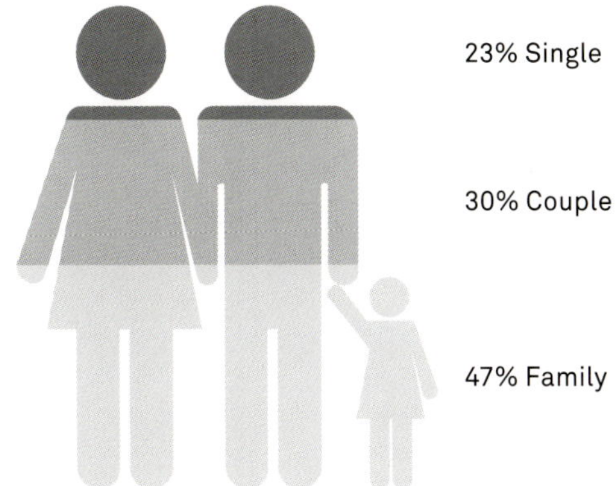

## Immigration

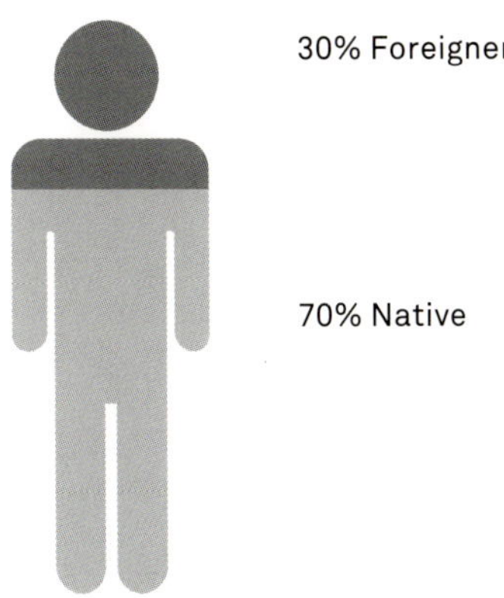


## Unemployment

Age Structure, Household Composition, Unemployment: specific for Leidsche Rijn. Source GBA 2011. Immigration: specific for Leidsche Rijn. Source: Projectbureau L. R. 2011.

**Interventions** The strategy Beyond is based on many different kinds of interventions that overlap one another. Some of the interventions are ephemeral, some are actions that involve local inhabitants, some are nomadic interventions that move around the area, and others have become permanent interventions. Five interventions have been selected for analysis, which combine iconic constructions and work as local landmarks with a cultural or social program.

## 1 The Parasol

Artists: Daniel Milohnic & Dirk Paschke, Architect: Resonatorcoop

The Parasol was a parasite pavilion built in Vleuterweide that functioned as a community center managed by the welfare organization De Haar. It was designed by Daniel Milohnic & Dirk Paschke in collaboration with the architectural firm Resonatorcoop. It consists of two modified shipping containers that create a meeting space and a sanitary unit. Outside, a wooden deck for outdoor events was covered with a canopy made of bamboo parasols, which connected the different sections of the pavilion. Several events were hosted at the pavilion, such as the Christmas market, until it was finally dismantled in 2007 and its hosting function was moved to the Weide Wereld neighborhood center.

## 2 Sainte Bazeille

Artist: Dominique Gonzalez-Foerster

The parasite designed by the French artist Dominique Gonzalez-Foerster was originally conceived as a modular system for mobile living and working spaces. The mobile architecture consists of two perpendicularly intersecting volumes: a horizontal cylindrical volume and a standard steel container.

The pavilion was placed in Hoge Woerd on June 21. It was used as a presentation space for the Center for Nature and Environmental Education, and as space for displaying archaeological finds. The intervention works as an interactive instrument where residents meet together and learn about the local nature and the history of the place.

Accesses
Relaxation areas
Sitting areas
Circulation
Vegetation

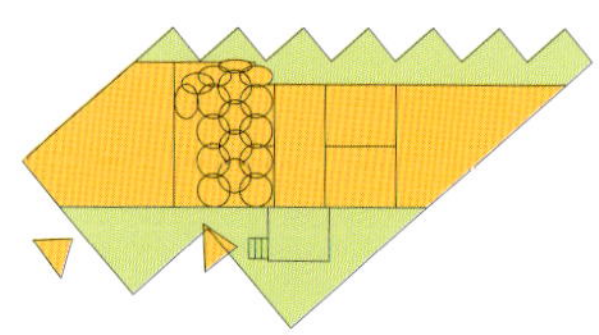

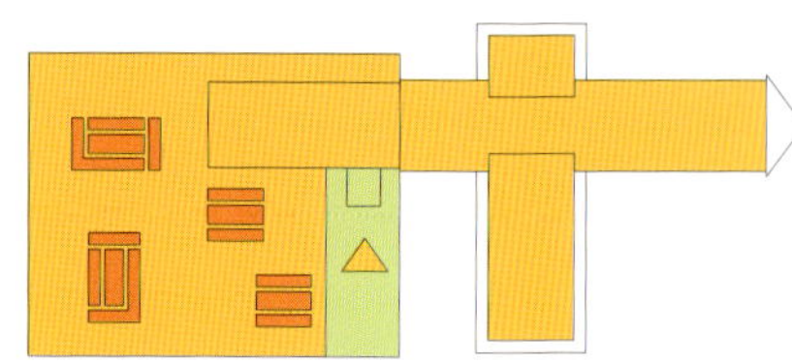

## 3 Nomads in Residence

Artists: Bik Van der Pol, Architects: Korteknie and Stuhlmacher

Nomads in Residence is a parasite pavilion located in Terwijde, conceived by the artist duo formed by Liesbeth Bik and Jos van der Pol as a gathering environment for artists and residents.

The pavilion was designed by the architects Korteknie and Stuhlmacher as a prefabricated prismatic black volume (18.0m long x 4.0m wide x 3.4m high) that can be transported on public roads as a single piece. It turns into an open house when all the flaps are opened. The flaps themselves can function as a podium or café terrace, a performance venue or a hangout zone. The interior is a spacious, flexible living and working space for guest artists to develop a specific cultural program over a period of one or two weeks.

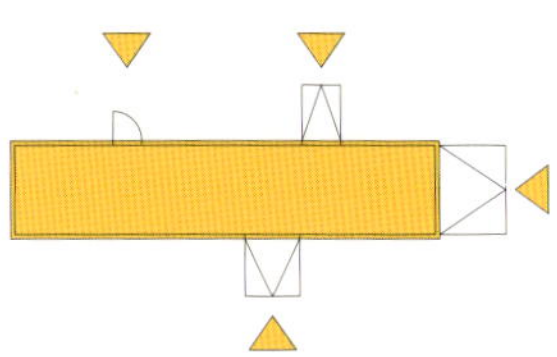

## 4 Het Gebouw

Artists: Stanley Brouwn, Architect: Bertus Mulder

The pavilion consists of two white rectangular volumes (27.30m long x 3.90m wide x 3.90m high) that lie across each other and it serves as an exhibition space, or eventually as a working space for artists.

The building was designed by the Dutch artist Stanley Brouwn in collaboration with the architect Bertus Mulder and it was opened to the public in September 2005 with the visual arts event "The pursuit of happiness". The pavilion is located close to the Paper Dome where the future center of Leidsche Rijn will be and it has become a visual landmark that brands Leidsche Rijn's cultural zone.

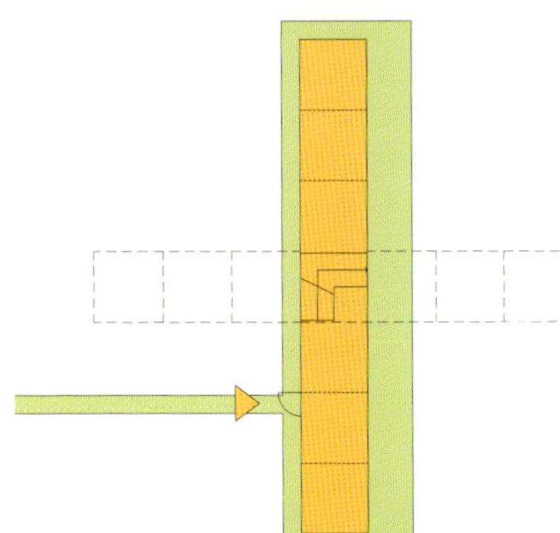

## 5 Paper Dome

Architect: Shigeru Ban

The Paper Dome was built in the area of Parkwijk and was opened to the public in July 2004. It is a temporary multifunctional building that works as gathering center for many different kinds of events, such as concerts, dance, theater, skating or the Art Market.

The building, designed by the Japanese architect Shigeru Ban, consists of a lightweight structure made of more than 700 cardboard tubes, which form a dome that is 25 meters in diameter and nearly 10 meters high. The delicate structure and translucent textile skin create a "floating" interior by day, while at night it is perceived from the exterior as a lantern that marks the cultural center of the new neighborhood.

**Process** The mayor and aldermen of the Utrecht City Council commissioned Beyond and delegated it to the director of Property Development Leidsche Rijn and the head of the department of Cultural Affairs.

The city council had decided to make funding available for the development of an art project in the public space of Leidsche Rijn as early as 1997, but finally commissioned the development in 2001.

The Beyond strategy was devised by a study group led by Peter Kuenzli, former director of Property Development Leidsche Rijn. The group consisted of an artist (Jan van Grunsven), an architecture critic (Bernard Colenbrander), artistic consultants from SKOR - Foundation for Art and Public Space (Tom van Gestel, Govert Grosveld), and a former representative from the department of Cultural Affairs (Mariette Dölle).

Beyond was implemented by Bureau Beyond, a compact project organization of around 10 people. Among them, the Artistic Team formulated the commissions, the project coordinators realized the projects in collaboration with the artists and a program manager oversaw the whole operation.

Beyond also aimed to stimulate the public's involvement in a variety of ways. There was a platform through which visitors were able to contribute their ideas. Residents' meetings were held regularly in order to offer everyone the chance to express their thoughts, for instance, discussions about the role that the parasite buildings could play in Leidsche Rijn. A broad information strategy was also designed to inform residents about new projects and events via specific websites, regular newsletters and folders.

## Cost, Financing and Maintenance

Beyond enjoyed a budget of €7 million over 15 years. Of this total amount, around €3.5 million was provided by the Utrecht City Council. The remaining amount was obtained through sponsorships and subsidies. The Ministry of Housing, Spatial Planning, and Environment (VROM) contributed €900,000 through the IPSV program (Innovation Program for Urban Renewal). The Foundation for Art and Public Space (SKOR) contributed €550.000 and also participated by providing an expert to become part of Beyond's Artistic Team. The K.F. Hein Foundation and the Elise Mathilde Fund made also financial contributions.

All the assignments commissioned to the different invited artists and the subsequent management of the different projects were carried out by Bureau Beyond. This included oversight of construction, movement and dismantling of the artistic installations, parasite pavilions or buildings.

The temporary and experimental character of many interventions led to the use of ephemeral materials, which in many cases required frequent maintenance. Working within the yearly assigned budget, Bureau Beyond had the autonomy to make decisions with regard to extending the life span of the more successful projects and modifying or dismantling others.

## Timing

The major challenge for a strategy to promote public life in a new and expanding neighborhood lies in how to create the adequate programs and interventions at the right moment. The strategy needs to guarantee a flexible structure capable of reacting quickly to developments in the neighborhood. At the same time, the program has to evolve continuously in order to obtain a certain impact from this type of work-in-progress situation.

The strategy Beyond was conceived to span a period of fifteen years, but the fragmentation of the whole program into independent yet related interventions was intended to provide flexibility for the development. The temporary character of some of the interventions responds to the fact that many of the areas under construction needed certain facilities for relatively short periods of time and that those facilities would no longer be useful once the whole development is completed. Temporality was combined with mobility through the use of nomad interventions that respond to the temporary needs of different areas in the neighborhood during specific periods of time, while multiplying the presence of the interventions in a virtual way throughout the site.

## Use of the Public Space

Interventions such as Sculpture Park stimulate the public use of the park, and the temporary projects create a surprise effect among the residents, promoting temporary use of the public space in specific locations. In general terms, however, according to the opinion of the citizens' organizations and other parties involved the impact of the strategy on improving the use of the public space was very limited.

One of the reasons was that most of the interventions and art programs only attracted people who were already interested in art, but did not succeed in involving other groups. Although the starting point for the art program was to select artists who incorporated the social strata of the place into their works, in most cases, such as in "Nomads in Residence", the artists who lived and worked in the parasite pavilions did not manage to attract many different kinds of people to visit their work.

The interventions where artists carried out actions in public space or organized attractive participative programs were more successful. In those cases, art played an active role in the cultural enrichment of the public domain.

## Impact on Citizens

In global terms, the strategy Beyond improved the perception of this new urban development among the citizens of Utrecht and Leidsche Rijn. However, the evaluation of the impact of the interventions on urban life in Leidsche Rijn is very irregular.

On the one hand, certain interventions promoting interaction among people via collective events have worked as a successful way to create a feeling of collective identity. Some of the artwork and pavilions also served as local landmarks, which gave identity to the place, helping it become quite popular and well accepted. On the other hand, according to the opinion of some neighbors' organizations, the direct impact of the interventions in citizens' public life was low. Citizens perceived that they were not sufficiently involved in the process of organizing the strategy, proposing the content or selecting the artists and therefore some of the projects did not attract a large group of residents.

Another important factor that, in the opinion of some of the actors involved, caused the relatively low impact of the strategy was that some of the program was implemented during an early stage of the urban development when there were not many people actually living in the area.

Aside from the short-term direct effects of the strategy, there were some long-term effects that are still difficult to evaluate. One of them is directly linked to the role of art in public space as an educational tool. The implemented art interventions are now influencing the children in the neighborhood and might produce some positive effects in the future.

## Media Impact

The media attention for the Beyond project in Leidsche Rijn was rather big. Several interventions and projects were in the news and were covered by local newspapers and magazines, in addition to reports on TV programs. The project became very popular, not only among the inhabitants of Leidsche Rijn, but also among the inhabitants of Utrecht. Leidsche Rijn was visited by the majority of the citizens of Utrecht and the strategy fulfilled one of the municipality's main objectives, which was to connect, at least virtually, the populations of Utrecht and Leidsche Rijn, although they are physically separated by the motorway.

Most of the interventions were published in many specialized publications for art, design and architecture. Several art exhibitions and events such as Parasite Paradise enjoyed national repercussion and the Beyond project received attention from many international publications.

ACHTERGROND

**KUNST ›** *De beeldende kunst in de wijk Leidsche Rijn moest iets bijzonders worden. Utrecht wilde op de grootste Vinexlocatie van Nederland geen serie beelden of een fontein in een park. De gemeente koos voor 'culturele interventies' die het stedelijk leven moeten stimuleren. Het kunstprogramma Beyond loopt in september ten einde.*

**Het Gebouw, de bijzondere expositieruimte voor uiteenlopende musea in de Utrechtse wijk Leidsche Rijn**

# Van babykunst tot beeldenpark

ANKA VAN VOORTHUIJSEN

Het spermabombardement ging niet door. Het voorstel van de Amerikaanse kunstenaar Adam Kalkin om zoveel mogelijke vrouwen in Leidsche Rijn te bezwangeren en zo een soort *founding father* te worden van een generatie Vinex-baby's, ging projectbureau Beyond te ver. Als het plan bekend was geworden, had het ongetwijfeld tot veel reacties geleid, voor 'reuring' gezorgd, zoals Tom van Gestel, lid van het artistieke team van Beyond, het noemt.

Want dat was het voornaamste doel van Beyond: de stedelijkheid aanjagen. Levendigheid tot stand brengen die er in een bestaande stad van nature is, maar die in een zee van nieuwbouwhuizen aanvankelijk ontbreekt. Door in een vroeg stadium, tijdens het ontstaan van de wijk, kunstenaars te vragen een project te bedenken of bijvoorbeeld tijdelijk in de wijk te komen wonen, kon er iets spannends ontstaan, hoopte Beyond. Binnen bepaalde grenzen natuurlijk.

Ook teruggefloten werd de kunstenaar die het (verzonnen) gerucht wilde verspreiden dat er een schietbaan in de wijk zou komen, wat naar zijn verwachting zou leiden tot demonstraties en onrust, kortom stedelijk leven. 'Dat

# MEŽAPARKS
## RIGA, LATVIA

STRATEGY / INTERVENTIONS: **Casanova+Hernandez**
COMMISSIONER: **Municipality of Riga**

Mežaparks is a large forest park built in the early 20th century. It is located seven kilometers north of Riga and stretches across 430 hectares. In 1901, construction began in the park of what is now considered one of the world's first garden cities, called Keizarmezs, which contained around 100 villas before World War I. Several cultural and recreational facilities, such as an open-air stage and an amusement park were built in the park after the war.

The park has significant historical value due to the fact that the Kaiserwald concentration camp was located there during the Second World War, and many Jews, Gypsies and Communists were murdered in those woods. But it has also a symbolic meaning for the Latvian people because, when national sovereignty was reinstated after the Singing Revolution in 1990, the historical first Latvian Song Festival concert was celebrated on Mežaparks' open-air stage.

Since that event, every four years the park has hosted the Latvian Song and Dance Festival in late July. Mežaparks is also home to the Riga Zoo, various water sporting activities on its lakeside, and an amusement park, which makes the area a popular summer destination for Riga residents.

During the 1990s, after Latvian independence, the Mežaparks residences began to be returned to their pre-war owners. Many of the houses were renovated, stimulating the construction of new ones as well. At present, the park is under pressure because it has become an attractive place for building new urban developments, which means that new regulations are needed and new strategies must be envisioned to regenerate public life in the park and to promote its cultural, historical, environmental and social role in the city of Riga.

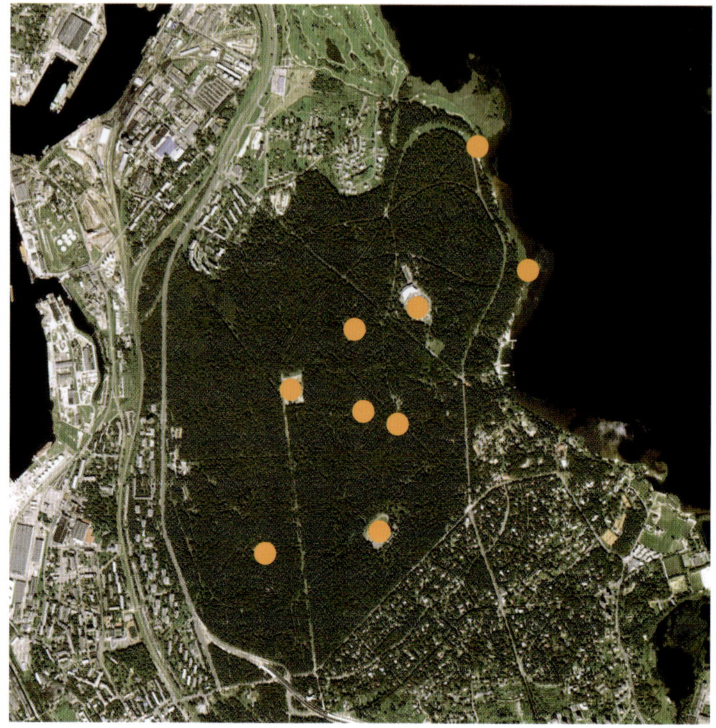

**Strategy** In 2005 Casanova+Hernandez was invited by the Municipality of Riga, together with seven other international teams, to participate in an international workshop to develop a vision for the future development of Mežaparks. After the fall of the Berlin Wall, Latvia, like many Communist bloc countries, experienced a building boom triggered by the sudden emergence of a free-market economy. At the same time, it was coupled with the political will to eliminate the State's control over the city's urban development as it existed under the former Communist system. At this high point for optimism, rapid urban development was associated with ideas as varied as progress, modernity, the future, and freedom. It was therefore not surprising that many of the visions presented by local and guest international teams promoted fast-paced medium- or large-scale urban developments that implied significant loss of woodland areas within the park.

However, an analysis of the situation, accounting for the broader context of the city's scale and the long-term consequences of a large-scale development in the area, led Casanova+Hernandez to submit an alternate proposal based on a public space acupuncture strategy that aimed to revive public life in the park and consolidate its identity as a venue for events. To this end, residential construction is limited to the perimeters of the park, protecting all existing trees, and a series of independent interventions are proposed within the existing network of forest clearings, where buildings existed in the past or where obsolete facilities could be refurbished.

This strategy proposes revitalizing public life in the park by promoting the role of its public space as a place for events that plays a similar role to that of a central park on a city-wide scale. The strategy is a symbiotic one, in which the first phase focuses on detecting and protecting the park's most valuable elements based on their ecological, historical or cultural value, and in the second phase these assets are remodeled and complemented with new interventions to encourage activity in each of the areas.

The symbiotic understanding of the strategy is applied at different stages of the intervention, from aspects of planning, environmental sustainability, strategy financing, functional aspects and activity programming, to design aspects.

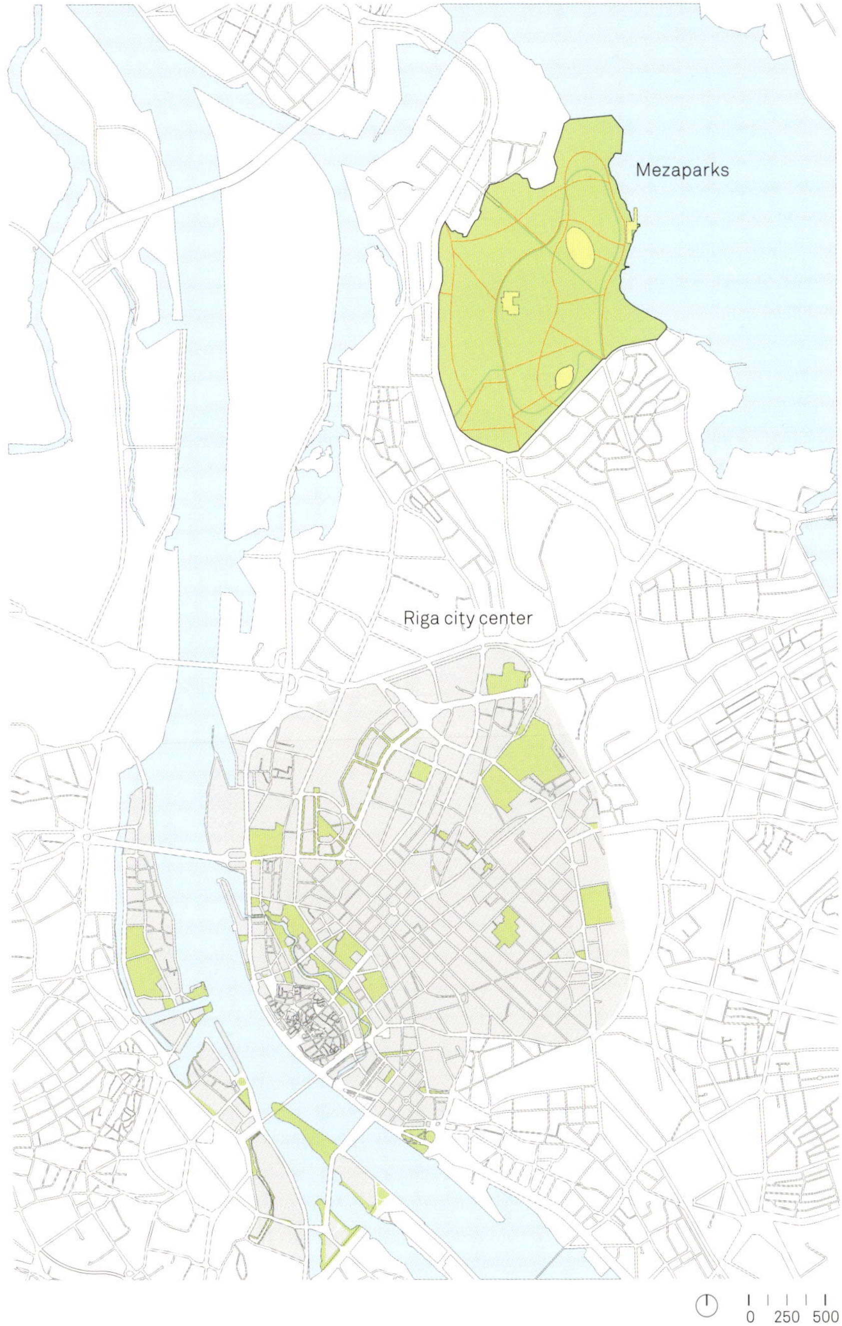

This symbiotic strategy is developed in three overlapping levels:

1. Existing natural environment. Mežaparks literally means “forest park”, and the forest is indeed its most valuable element. The strategy proposes recognizing the forest as an element to be fully protected, complemented with specific interventions to enrich its public life.

2. Infrastructures. The existing network of trails and entrances to the park is renovated and supplemented with new accesses and paths. The road network is diversified to accommodate different types of users such as pedestrians, cyclists, horse riders and visitors in cars. Sometimes these specialized routes run parallel to each other and other times they converge to work symbiotically, so that users of the different routes come into contact.

3. Facilities. Some of the existing facilities are preserved and new ones are built in order to diversify the leisure activities offered by the park and to attract a broader range of people from the city. The existing facilities that are currently only used during certain hours of the day and seasons of the year are complemented with new activities. In this way, the park becomes an active place throughout the week and the year, working as a magnet to attract a greater number of visitors.

## Strategy Layers

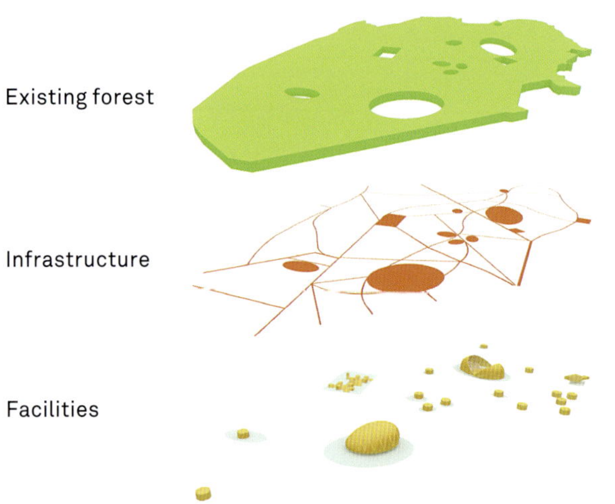


## Positioning of Main Interventions and New Activities in the Park

**Main interventions** The strategy envisages a series of larger-scale interventions in existing forest clearings that act as urban landmarks on the scale of the park and as an attraction for the citizens of Riga as a result of the varied program of events.

## Intervention 1. Song Festival Music Hall

The proposal suggests remodeling the auditorium that currently houses the Latvian Song and Dance Festival and supplementing its programming with all kinds of large-scale events. A new retractable roof, to cover the auditorium in winter, will allow for its use year-round and will help to transform its image, thus becoming the building a new landmark for the city of Riga, tied in with Latvia's national identity.

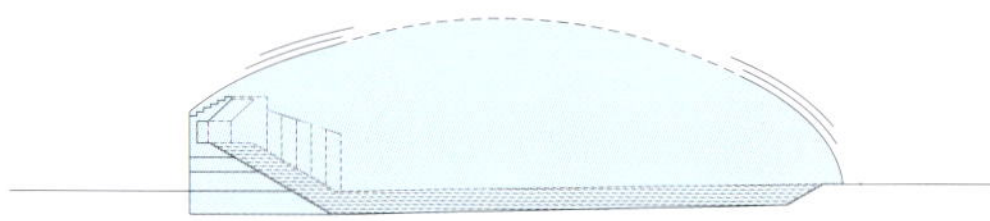

Section

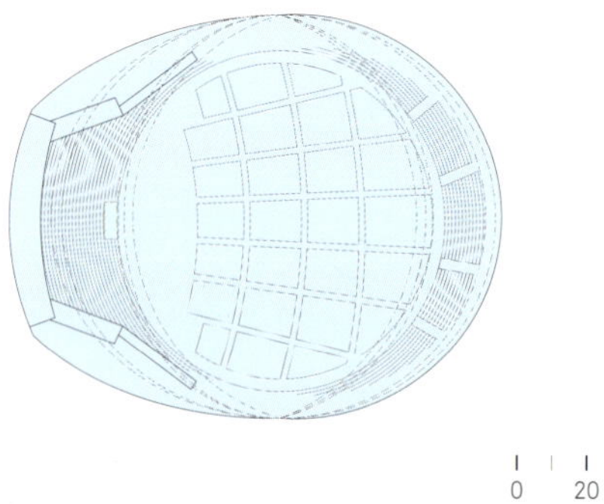


Plan

## Intervention 2. Theater & Song Museum

This hybrid building is created by combining two architectural elements: a transparent glazed element and a massive one built in wood. The wooden part is related visually and conceptually to the surrounding forests. Its architecture echoes traditional Latvian construction and houses an inviting auditorium in its interior. The glazed element is visually and conceptually related to the lake that reflects the building. It houses the Song Museum, acting as a display window where visitors can discover the role of the Latvian Song Festival in the country's history.

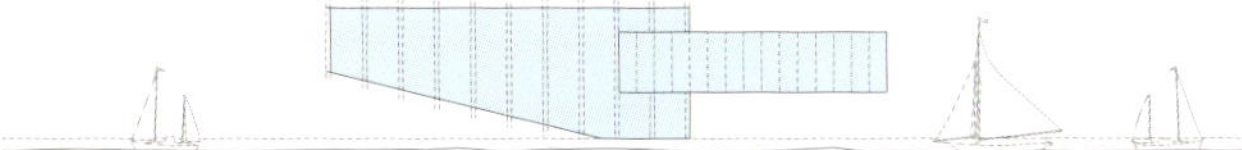

Section

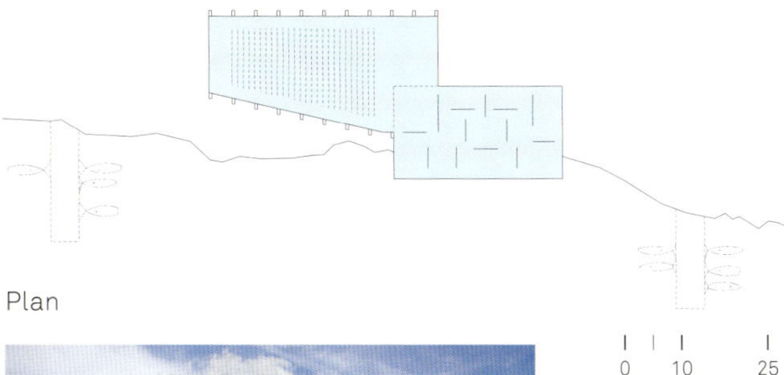

Plan

## Intervention 3. Children's City

This children's playground hosts all sorts of attractions so that families can spend an entire day in the forest. Water activities, playgrounds for younger children and adventure games for older ones are interspersed with picnic areas, coffee shops and restaurants.

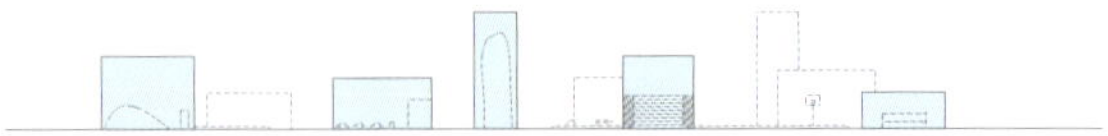

Section

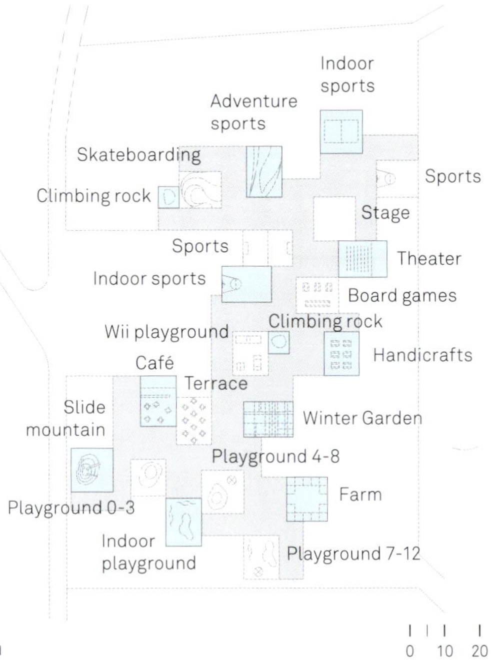


Plan

<u>Intervention 4. Sports Hall</u>

The sports hall is located in the old equestrian buildings, refurbished and upgraded with new facilities for a wide range of sports. Some smaller facilities are sprinkled around in various locations in the park, linked to a series of themed trails that run throughout. These trails can be used for jogging, biking, skating and other sports.

These four major interventions serve as large-scale regenerators of activity in the park, while reinforcing the image of Mežaparks as a new public space and as a meeting point for the citizens of Riga. The public space in the park reasserts its identity as a venue for events and at the same time strengthens its historical and symbolic value for all citizens.

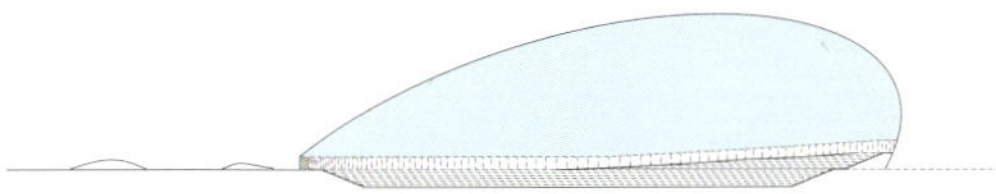

Section

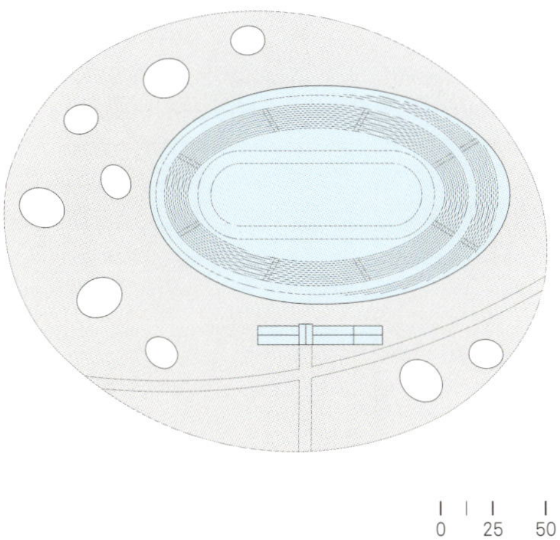


Plan

## WII-PLAYGROUNDS
AMSTERDAM. THE NETHERLANDS

STRATEGY / INTERVENTIONS: **Casanova+Hernandez**

As part of a study on Child Friendly Neighborhoods in the Netherlands, Casanova+Hernandez conducted research on the decline in use of public space by Dutch children and on the new strategies for promoting attractive play spaces capable of encouraging physical activity. The study took place in parallel to research into the disappearance of children's playgrounds designed by Aldo Van Eyck in Amsterdam's Oud-West district. These studies were tested in the practice through the design of a public space acupuncture strategy to promote innovative play areas in public spaces that could respond to the needs of our current social context.

After the Second World War, Aldo van Eyck revitalized the use of the public space in the center of Amsterdam by transforming inactive urban spaces like vacant lots or unused spaces into children's playgrounds, which acted on an urban scale as venues for microevents. Microevents are a kind of events which, due to their small size and limited number of participants, tend to go unnoticed during everyday life in the city. Many microevents happen every day in cities and among them, children's games have always been emphasized as spontaneous activities that emerge without the need for complex facilities or an organized program. In fact, children's games have their own rules that have been passed down from generation to generation. These rules evolve according to the specific conditions of each place, and children themselves fix and manage the rules of play. It is common for certain active groups to lead the games while others follow or look on, similarly to what happens with larger-scale events.

The playgrounds designed by Aldo van Eyck can be understood as microevent icons from the pre-technological age, which consisted of simple and abstract elements that fostered children's imaginative capacity and encouraged them to play by inventing their own events.

More than 60 years after the program began, few of these playgrounds remain. Many of the lots have been occupied by buildings and others have been taken over by parking lots. This disappearance is due in part to the declining number of

1970s, Children playing on a playground, Hasebroekstraat

2013, Children playing with technology

children in Dutch families, especially in cities. But it is also the result of changing social habits, linked to the fact that children are now more likely to play at home with technological devices, hence making less use of public space as a place to play.

Given this new situation, could Aldo Van Eyck's playgrounds somehow be brought up to date (Van Eyck playgrounds 2.0) so that playing outside could become popular again? Could a new playground typology somehow give rise to a strategy for revitalizing Amsterdam's public space, like Van Eyck did after the war?

**Strategy** Based on a study by Jantje Beton in 2008, the main reason, according to Dutch parents, why children do not use public space as a place to play is because they prefer to watch TV and play video games at home instead of playing on outdoor playground facilities. According to this research, children's lack of interest in playing in public space may be partly motivated by the failure of children's outdoor games to evolve, many of which are identical to those installed by Van Eyck in the 1940s.

Furthermore, as happens in many other Western countries, most children and adolescents in the Netherlands do not get the minimum exercise that pediatricians recommend for ensuring healthy growth. Experts recommend at least 60 minutes of daily physical activity for children, but there is a growing trend for children to spend their time engaged in sedentary activities such as surfing the Internet, watching TV or playing video games at home.

The conclusions of a study with 320 children led by Simons, Bernaards and Slinger in 2012 reveal that the new generation of video games that require body movements to play (active games) may promote an active lifestyle in adolescents, contributing substantially to the daily time spent in physical activity.

Modernizing playgrounds in public space using new technologies could be a way to entice children to play outdoors, to get more physical exercise and to socialize with other children. Unlike games played at home, playing in public spaces educates children socially by forcing them to develop negotiation strategies in unfamiliar environments and to develop their public persona.

Maximizing Exercise in Children's Play Activities

Children playing video games (passive games)

Children playing active games

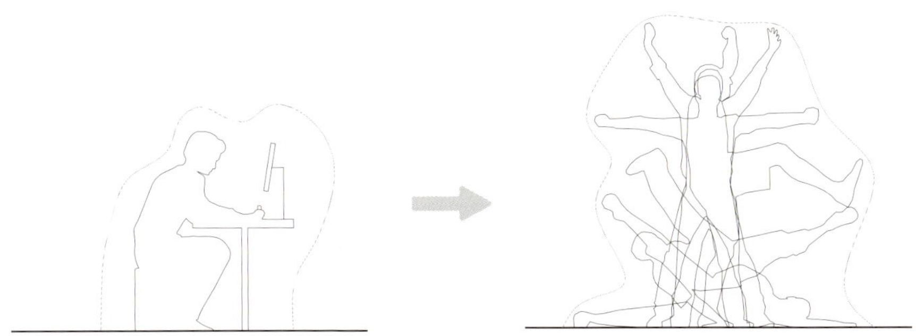

Another factor that has changed in recent years, from a social standpoint, as a result of how the Internet has evolved, is the ability or the need to share activities with a group of friends, colleagues or even strangers who are part of our social networks. New technologies have the potential to broadcast every little daily action, which becomes a public event that can eventually be viewed by thousands of people on YouTube. Many activities and events that were once private now only make sense if they can be published to a broad group of viewers so that they can respond with a "Like". Playing has therefore gone from being considered an individual or collective activity to being an activity that can be narrated or broadcasted. The public dimension of the event can be included in the game and, like with events that involve professional athletes or rock stars, images can be projected onto big screens and even broadcasted on the Internet.

The devised strategy takes these factors into account by proposing interventions made up of a group of urban elements that combine active video games, controlled by body movements, with video screens that allow a wider audience to follow the game. The video game attracts children to public space. Since it is an active game, it encourages them to do the physical activity they need to stay healthy and the screens transform playtime into a public microevent which can be followed by a small audience. Since the activities developed in the physical world have moved into the virtual world in recent decades, this strategy returns them to the physical world by combining the virtual and physical dimensions into a new "hybrid reality " that is attractive to children and, at the same time, activates urban public space.

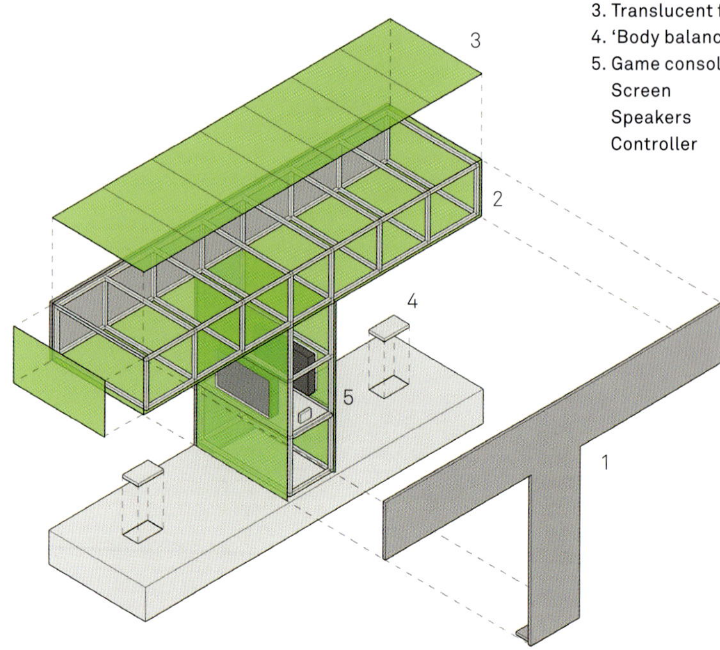


1. Steel construction
2. Sub-construction
3. Translucent finishing
4. 'Body balance board'
5. Game console
   Screen
   Speakers
   Controller

## Maximizing Open-Air Exercise in Children's Play Activities

Children playing at home alone or in small groups

Children playing in public space in wii-playgrounds

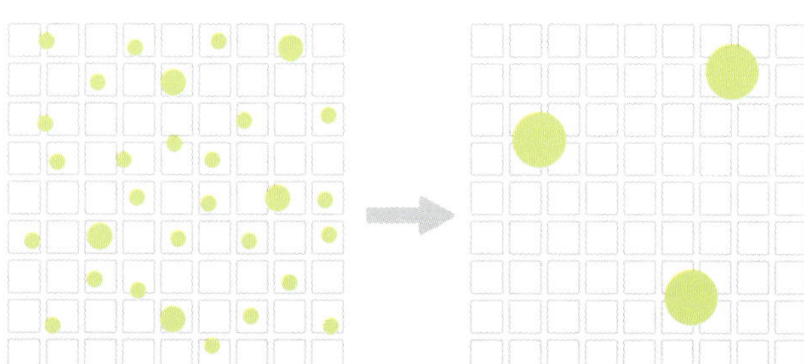

## Maximizing Different Social Relationships in Children's Play Activities

Direct Social Interaction (by Playing at the Playground)

Semi-direct Social Interaction (Spectators and Future Players)

Indirect Social Interaction (Spectators and Followers via social networks)

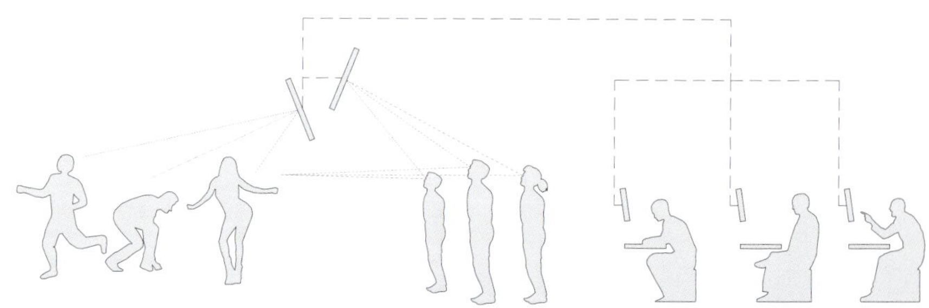

## Four Device Types for Practicing Different Sports - Competing Alone, in Groups or Facing Off Two Teams

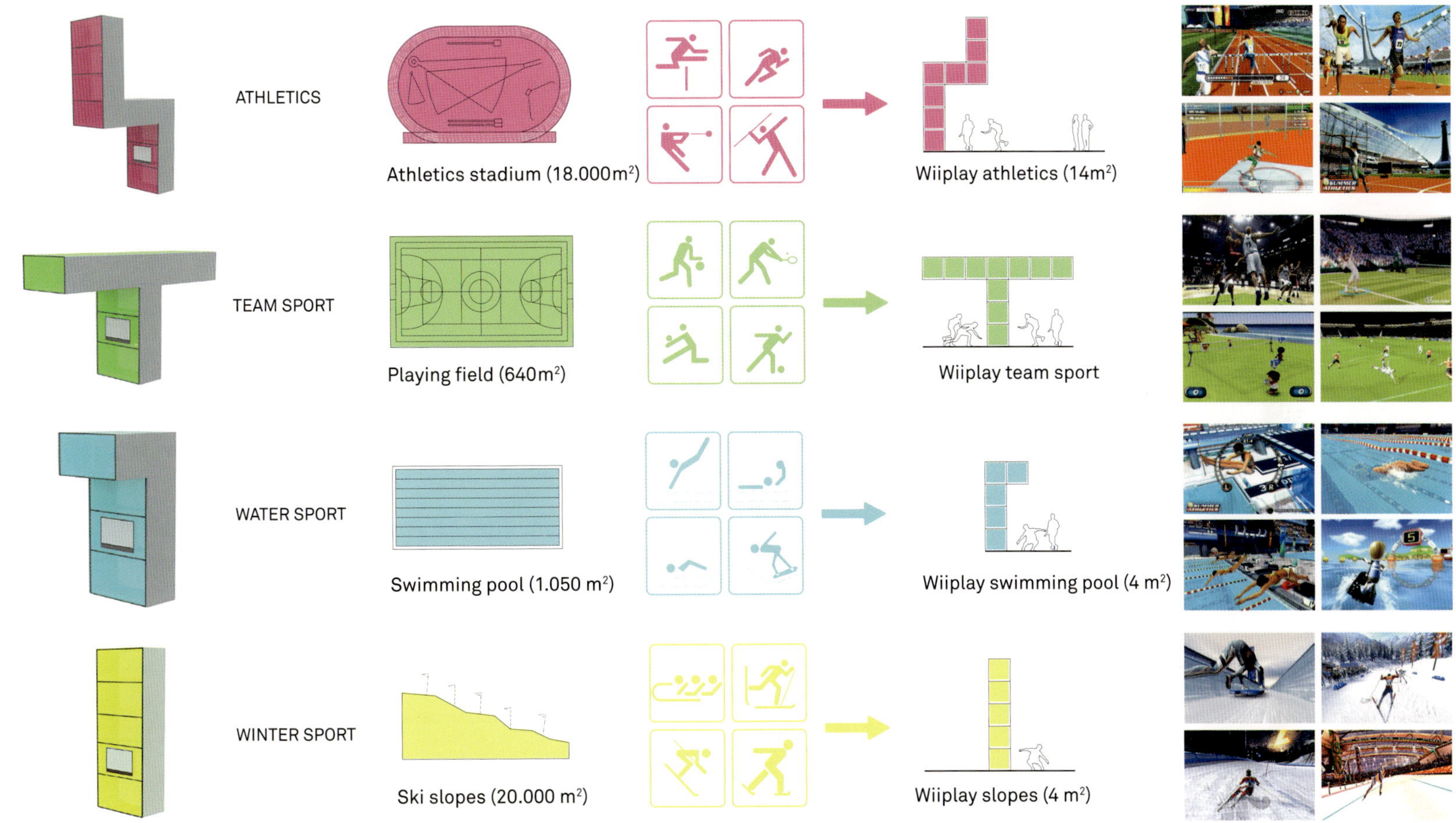


## Clusters: Variety of Spatial and Functional Combinations of Basic Elements

Hasebroekstraat. Amsterdam Oudwest, 1954

Aldo van Eyck children's playground.
Hasebroekstraat, 1995

Hasebroekstraat, 2013

0
20

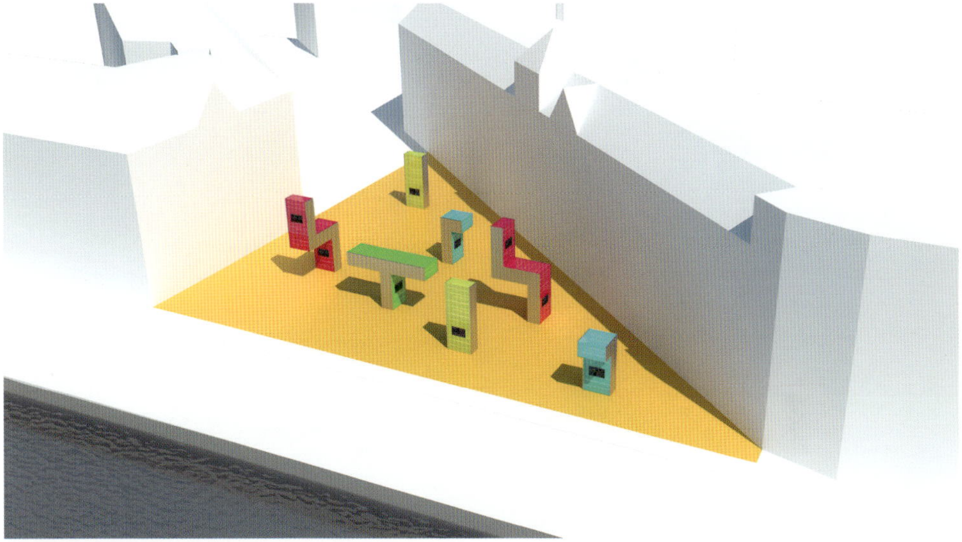

# PUBLIC SPACE FOR THE ASIAN CULTURAL COMPLEX (ACC)
## GWANGJU, SOUTH KOREA

STRATEGY / INTERVENTIONS: **Casanova+Hernandez**
COMMISSIONER: **Korean Ministry of Culture**

Given the success in the media and among tourists of the Guggenheim Museum in Bilbao designed by Frank Gehry, which brought international fame to the city, many other cities around the world have tried to mimic this urban regeneration strategy in order to achieve what has been called the "Bilbao Effect". However, the Bilbao Effect would not have been possible without a larger-scale urban operation called Bilbao Ría 2000 which, aside from introducing emblematic buildings, reconverted the city's inactive industrial landscapes into vibrant public space.

The plan to create a large-scale cultural complex, the Asian Cultural Centre (ACC), sought "collateral" urban regeneration similar to that achieved by large cultural complexes in other cities, such as the Guggenheim Museum in Bilbao, the Centre Pompidou in Paris, the MACBA in Barcelona and the Tate Modern in London. If we study the transformation of the use of public space around these well-known buildings carefully, it is possible to conclude that, in all cases, there is a considerable increase in the number of visitors to an area of town that was not previously a popular destination. Therefore, as a result of the new leisure/cultural program, spontaneous activities emerge based on the use of public space as an urban stage. In the esplanade in front of the Centre Pompidou in Paris spontaneous groups are formed every day to watch performances by musicians, acrobats, mimes, dancers and all types of entertainers. In the square in front of the MACBA in Barcelona, a crowd of skateboarders practice their stunts daily, before the eyes of large numbers of citizens who adopt the role of anonymous spectators at an unscheduled performance. Public space becomes a setting for improvised events that energize urban life in the neighborhood.

The Gwangju initiative involved creating a huge cultural complex, encompassing a large number of museums and cultural institutions, with the aim of transforming the Geum-dong district. The question then becomes how to develop an effective strategy for creating vibrant and dynamic public space, which will not only serve the new cultural center but will also have a regenerative effect on public life in the neighborhood as a whole.

광주광역시
GWANGJU CITY

**Strategy** The strategy maximizes the effect of "collateral regeneration" that can be created by the construction of the new ACC arts complex in Gwanju. To this end, a diverse and segmented public space is created, which mixes together with the fragmented arrangement of the new cultural buildings and benefits from the inertia created by the activities programmed by each center.

Whereas the various cultural buildings within the ACC serve to promote the performative aspect of the city, the proposed strategy aims to spread this effect using a series of independent interventions scattered throughout public space that are in charge of reinforcing its public dimension. This public space becomes the setting for holding various events that transform the city into a large-scale outdoor theater, where improvised and scheduled events join together to revitalize public life.

**Interventions** Given the enormous scale of the cultural complex, comprising nine buildings including museums, theaters, exhibition halls and auditoriums, the interstitial public space among buildings has been subdivided into circular squares. Each circular square acquires a unique character and function that promotes an activity that may be related to the purpose of the adjoining buildings. For example, the square in front of the museum becomes a free outdoor museum and the squares located near the auditoriums become different-sized outdoor theaters that can house miscellaneous performances such as plays, puppets or chamber music. Other circular squares house art markets, auctions or other commercial activities to create a link between the ACC museums and the art galleries that are already opening in the area in preparation for the future creation of the cultural complex. As a result, public space not only acts as an activating agent for public life within the ACC, but it also acts as a vehicle that conveys this activity to the nearby neighborhoods.

Each intervention in public space acquires a specific size, activity and character depending on several parameters such as:

**1. Position within the site**

Spaces on the perimeter of the site (A, D, F, H, M, O, S, U and V) facilitate pedestrian access, working as an extension of the adjacent streets.

Spaces on the interior of the site develop activities that require physical protection such as the Children's Playground (E, G, I, J and K), the Reading Area (N), and the Performance Plaza (C).

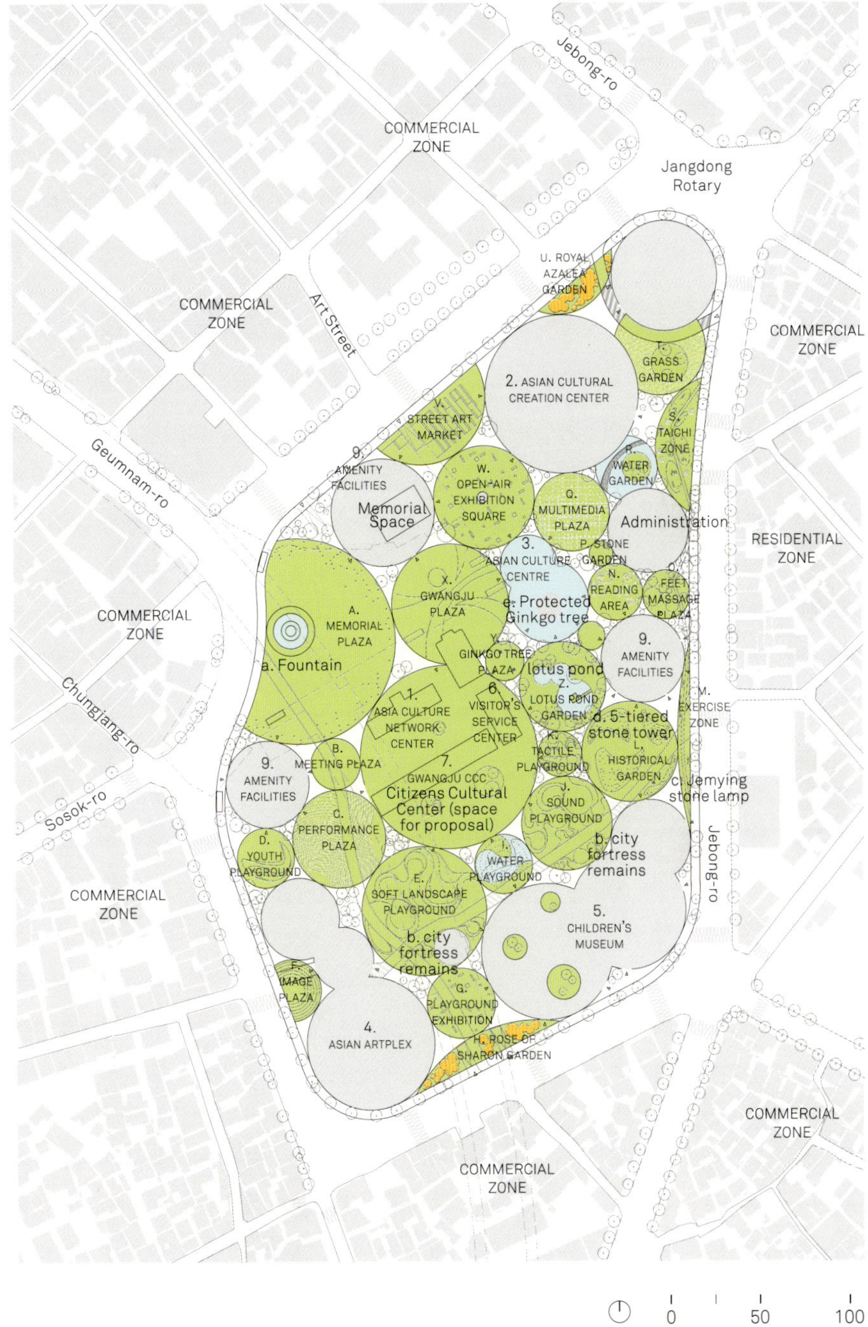

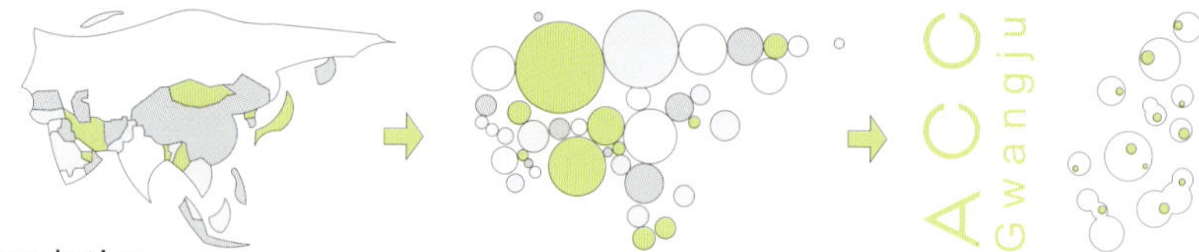


### 2. Adjacent function

Spaces on the perimeter of the site are related to the activities in the surroundings. For example, the Art Street to the north of the site is extended into the site through the Art Market (V), the Open-Air Exhibition Plaza (W) and the Multi-Media Plaza (Q).

Spaces located close to an existing or historical building are associated with its function. For example, the Memorial Plaza (A) includes the existing fountain (a); the Historical Garden (L) includes the City Fortress Remains (b), the Jemyong Stone Lamp (c) and the 5-tiered stone tower (d); and finally, the Meeting Plaza (B) houses the existing subway entrance (f).

Spaces that share related activities are located close to each other such as, for example, the Art Activities (Q, V, and X), the Children's Activities (E, G, I, J, and K), the Sport Activities areas (M, O, and S) and the meditation and contemplative zones.

### 3. Function associated to the ACC buildings

Open-air spaces work as extensions of the adjacent building program. For example: the open-air amphitheatre as an extension of the Citizens' Mini Performance Hall at the Asian Artplex (4); the open-air Reading Room (N) as an extension of the Asian Cultural Center (2); the open-air Exhibition Playground (G) as an extension of the Children's Creative Workshop; and the open-air Exhibition Square (W) as an extension of the Asian Cultural Creation Center (3).

### 4. Intervention related to the urban context

The careful selection of the program and location of each intervention in the ACC seeks to establish a strong urban relationship with the adjacent surroundings and with the wider urban context. The food court and restaurants are located close to the commercial areas in the surroundings, and the playgrounds and exercise zones are planned close to the residential areas.

Urban relationships are also established via several thematic axes. For example, an eco-environmental axis passes through the site connecting the Green Road of the Obsolete Railway, located in the northern and eastern sections of the site, with Sajik Park and Gwangju Park. This path is created by several open-air pedestrian areas that are connected to the main routes and reinforced by open-air activities such as exercise areas. A symbolic Democratic Movement axis will also connect Jeonnam National University, Chosun University and the ACC. The main buildings and open-air spaces related to the Democratic Movement will be restored and unified, thus creating the May 18 Demostration Movement square, which will act as the main representative public space of the ACC with a strong historic and symbolic value.

#### Circulation

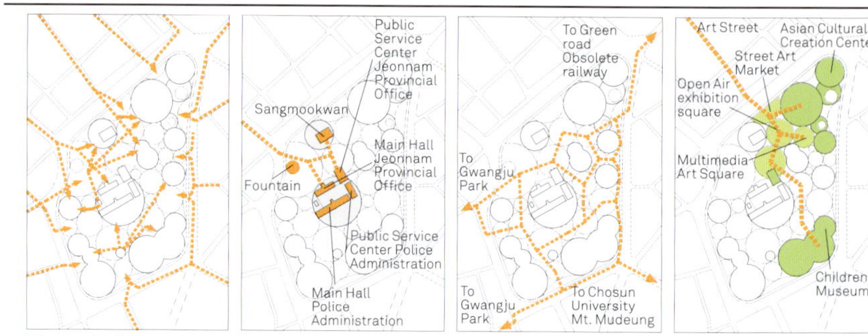


Flow of citizens | Democratic movement axis | Eco-environmental axis | Art path

#### Spatial Organization

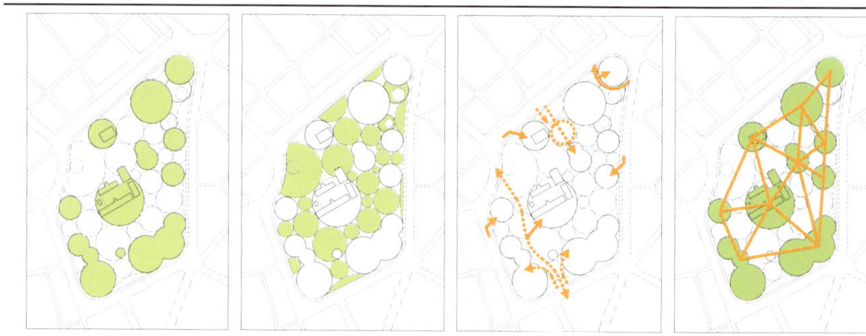

Buildings | Open-air spaces | Vehicle accesses | Buildings spatial relationships

#### Environmental Aspects

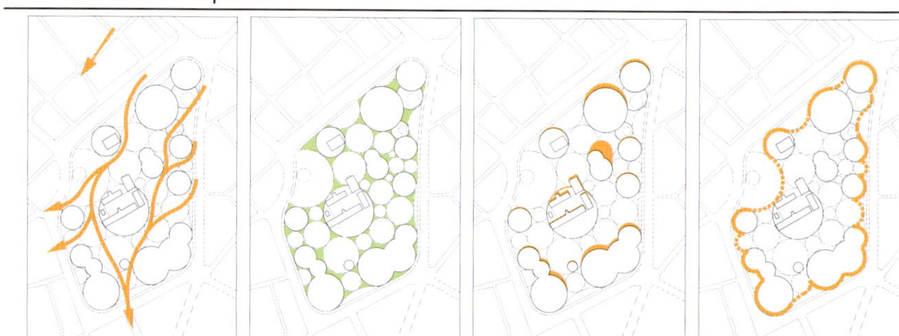

Ventilation | Green areas | Shady areas | Noise buffer zone

## Character of the Interventions in the Public Space of the ACC

Intervention K: Tactile Playground Plaza

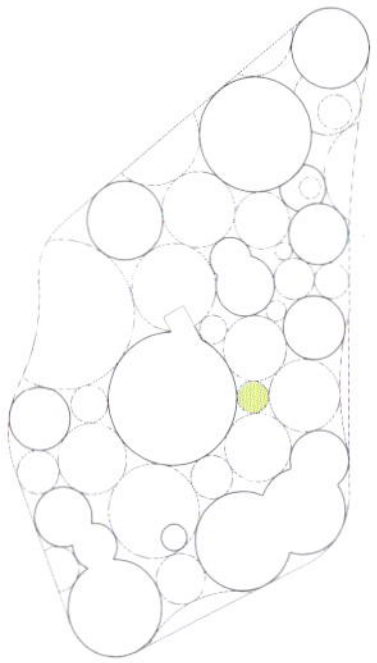

## Intervention G: Outdoor Exhibition Plaza

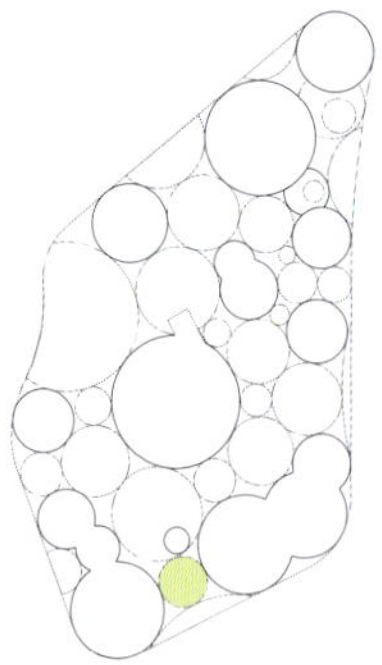

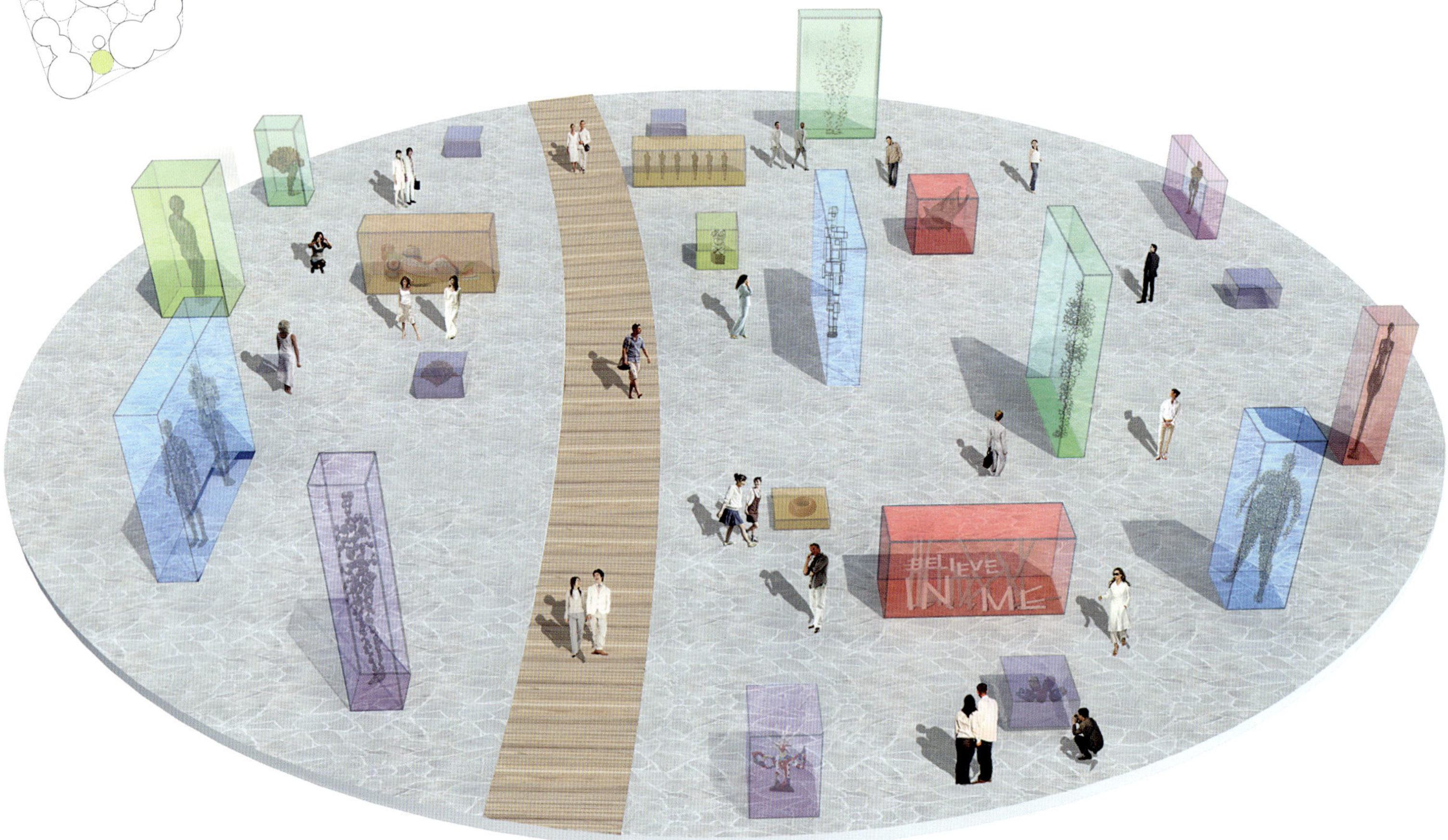

# City as an Art-Scape

Since prehistoric times, art, understood as a form of human expression, has been used by man as a tool for marking places and providing them with a special meaning. Franz Boas, with his book Primitive Art,[1] was a pioneer in introducing the study of art into the field of anthropology and paved the way for many anthropologists to follow him in investigating the development of artistic activities through different civilizations in distinct areas of the planet. Beginning with the rock paintings done in caves during the Upper Paleolithic period some 40,000 years ago, art has served as a tool for marking cultural identity through the history of great civilizations as varied as the Egyptians, Mesopotamians, Greeks, Romans, Persians, Indians, Chinese, Inca and Maya.

This need to provide symbolic content for public places fostered the birth of public art, which has historically been understood as an additive operation in charge of incorporating artistic elements onto building façades and into the streets, squares and parks that form public space. At the same time, public art has a strong political dimension because, since it is located in the public domain, it has the virtue of communicating directly with citizens. Although on many occasions urban art has had a merely decorative and beautifying function, other times it has taken on a symbolic role that has been used by power as an educational tool, as a mechanism to extol certain values or as a mere vehicle for spreading ideological propaganda.

After the Second World War, many public institutions established permanent programs responsible for commissioning public artwork that did not adhere to the classic concept of monument, but which experimented with new ideas from the artistic avant-garde. In the 1960s, public art based on site-specific works created to interact with a particular place emerged, so that work and context formed an indivisible entity. Simultaneously, the expansion of the term "art" stimulated collaboration between different disciplines as well as experimentation with different formats such as video art, land art or artistic installations. In addition, public art was no longer considered only a permanent work made with long-lasting materials, and experiments began with the concept of temporariness in the form of ephemeral artistic interventions or performances. The emergence of anonymous urban art and new media like graffiti have promoted a phenomenon that we might call the democratization of urban art, leading a new generation of young artists to use public space as a means of expression, without intermediaries like galleries or curators to decide the content to be exhibited. This has facilitated the direct contact between the artist and the citizen-spectator, greatly incrementing the diffusion of the artwork, but at the same time also increasing the variety of messages.

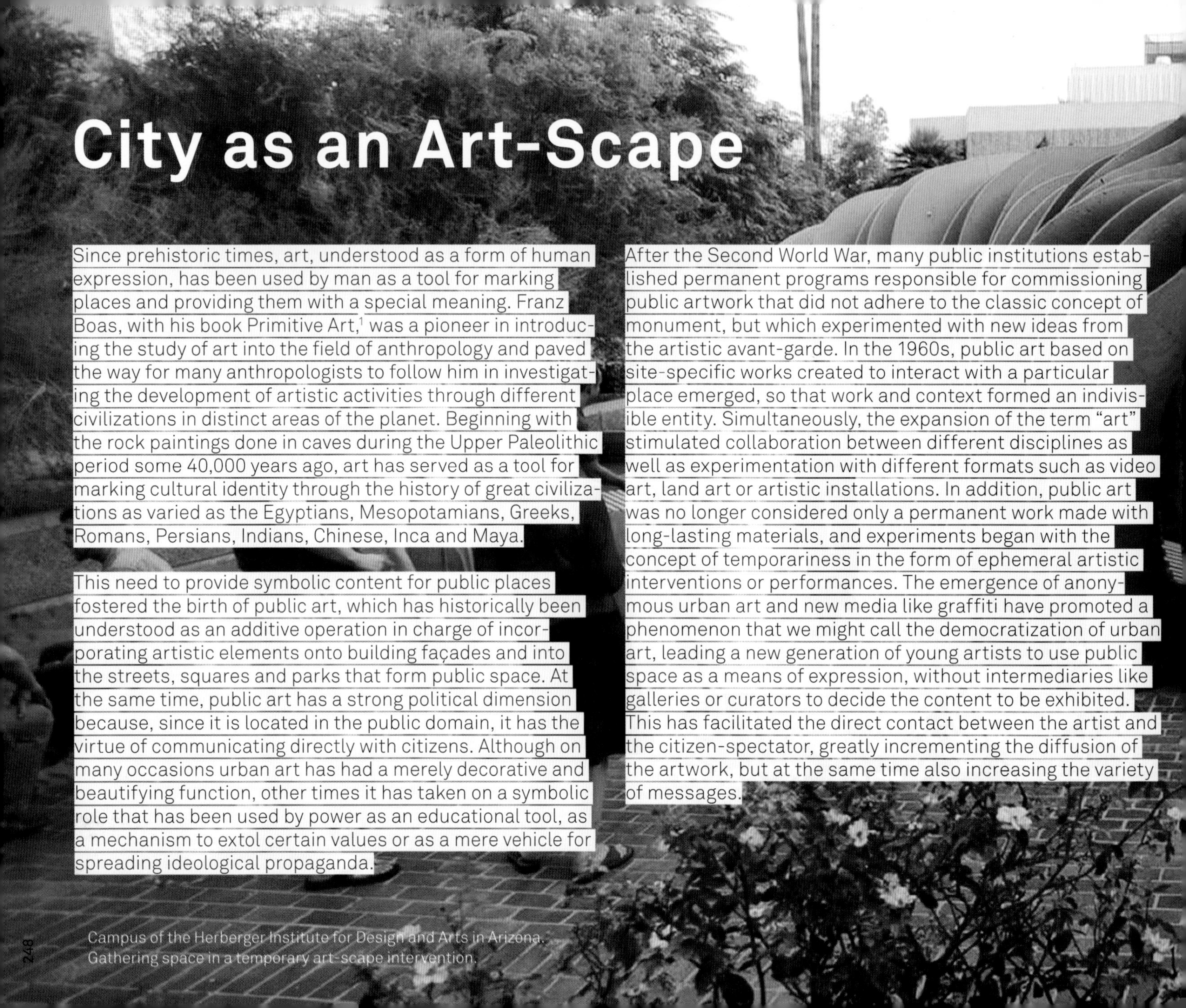

Campus of the Herberger Institute for Design and Arts in Arizona. Gathering space in a temporary art-scape intervention.

The hybridization process of public art does not just intertwine different disciplines, like landscape architecture and art; it has also promoted collaboration between numerous artists, landscape architects and designers in hybrid urban interventions that we might call art-scapes. This has led to the transformation of numerous public places into memorable pieces of public art that remain in the collective memory of city residents and visitors as places with a special identity, which acquire a sense of place in some way. Although some of these creations draw inspiration from the history of the site to lend it meaning, what is especially remarkable is the independence with which works of art are able to generate a new sense of place independently of the places themselves. In this way, sites with little or no sense of place can take on a new meaning for citizens thanks to art. At the same time, many of those art-scapes seek to promote interaction with citizens by reinforcing the community's sense of place.

This interconnection between public space, art and citizens opens up a new field for experimentation in which the artistic interventions can be combined with public space acupuncture strategies to promote interaction among citizens, as well as between citizens and the place. Although public art has been used on numerous occasions throughout history to extol the institutional values that reinforce collective identity, whether on a national, regional or local level, at present it can be used in our increasingly individualized society as a tool for communication that relates individuals with one another, or that brings groups together in a society that is becoming more and more segregated. Similarly, a new way of understanding art, not just as a top-down process but as a participatory activity, can create new avenues for experimenting with the role of public space.

Paraphrasing the Russian poet Joseph Brodsky's famous words: "Art is not better, but an alternative existence; it is not an attempt to escape from reality, but the opposite: an attempt to animate it", we can conclude that public space acupuncture strategies that transform urban landscapes into urban art-scapes can generate a different perception of urban reality, creating an alternative public space that encourages citizens to experience the city in a different way and which helps to infuse new energy into urban life.

1. Franz Boas, *Primitive Art*. H. Aschehoug and Company, Oslo, 1927.

Case Study I

# CITY LOUNGE
## ST. GALLEN, SWITZERLAND

STRATEGY/ INTERVENTIONS: **Carlos Martinez, Pipilotti Rist**
COMMISSIONERS: **Municipality of St. Gallen, Schweizer Verbandes der Raiffeisenbaken**

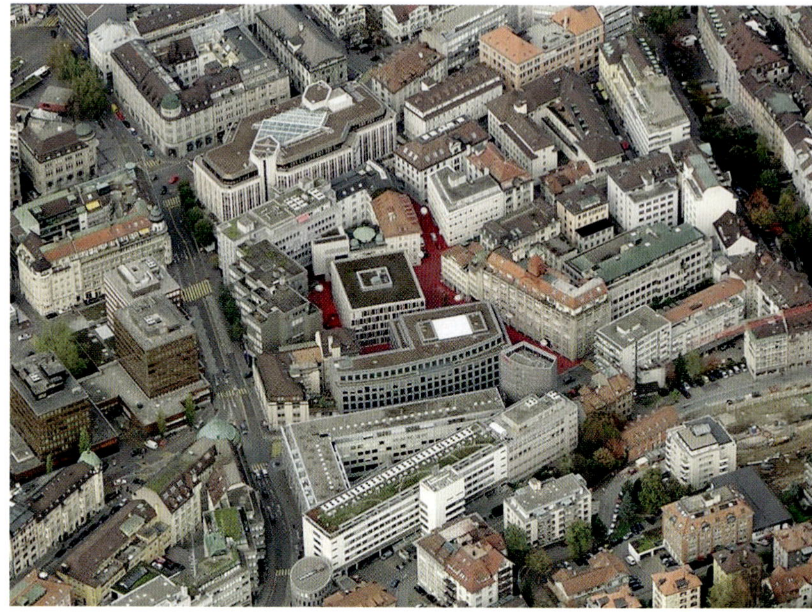

The process of transforming the former industrial neighborhood of Bleicheli Quartier in St. Gallen into a financial district consisted of reusing abandoned textile factories and other existing buildings as modern banks and office buildings. This transformation raised the question of how to create vibrant public space in places like the intervention site, with almost no commercial activity and the atmosphere of an abandoned backyard, without character or a sense of place. A competition was launched to upgrade the public space and stimulate urban life in the neighborhood. The winning proposal was designed by the architect Carlos Martinez together with the visual artist Pipilotti Rist. "City Lounge" thoroughly explores the visual and sculptural possibilities of the public space to create an attractive place for citizens, defined by a strong identity.

First of all, the strategy clearly marks the area of the intervention using a color code, which is applied in every element of the public space: pavement, street furniture, and sculptural objects. The red color works as a visual link to unify the whole intervention. Second, a few independent yet interlinked interventions are positioned in strategic points within the area, marking the visual and functional highlights of the public space. The interventions group different kinds of urban furniture in clusters. Each cluster has its own character, working as an open living room situated throughout the public space.

The strategy is devised as a large-scale work of art installed in public space, not only because it was created by an architect in collaboration with an artist, but also because it stands out from its context to gain some autonomy, as though it had been added into the urban landscape without belonging to it.

This autonomy of the artwork becomes evident by using concepts such as "the red carpet" which suggests that the pavement of the intervention works as an added element, like a carpet on top of the city's real pavement. Certain details, such as the lack of difference in height between the street level and the sidewalk, which are differentiated by a subtle

change of material that is not perceived visually, or the material continuity between pavement and the street furniture, result in the intervention being experienced as a continuous surface which sometimes folds like a carpet.

On the other hand, in the same way that recoding everyday objects and giving them new meaning is a very characteristic feature of contemporary art, City Lounge experiments with redesigning standardized urban elements such as street furniture and lighting fixtures so that they acquire an artistic dimension. The signage in the public space has also been recoded, substituting codes that are familiar to all citizens, such as the symbol for parking spaces, by new ones printed on the red carpet to build a unique visual language that is distinct and differentiated from what is used in the rest of the city's public space.

The strategy differentiates a fragment of the city's public space with a strong identity thanks to the colorful and sculptural character of the interventions, thus configuring an attractive new urban language. Recoding the city arouses the curiosity of citizens, who have to reinterpret reality by using their imagination. The artistic aspect of public space frees citizens from their everyday behavior and encourages them to perceive and use the city in a different way.

But art also holds the great potential of manipulating our perception of the urban environment and creating emotions. "City Lounge" carefully plays with the use of color, materials, shapes and scale to influence our perception of public space. Subconsciously, we do not relate the different interventions that form the strategy to parts of the city's public space, but rather to small-scale and intimate domestic spaces such as a living room, dining room, entrance hall or study, which stimulates the paradoxical feeling of being in an open-air house and invites citizens to use it in an informal way.

If one of the goals of art is to make us see reality from a new perspective that awakens our imagination, the strategy that understands public space as an art-scape shows us public space under a new light, stimulating its use so that new relationships can be built between individuals and their urban environment, at the same time encouraging different kinds of interaction among citizens.

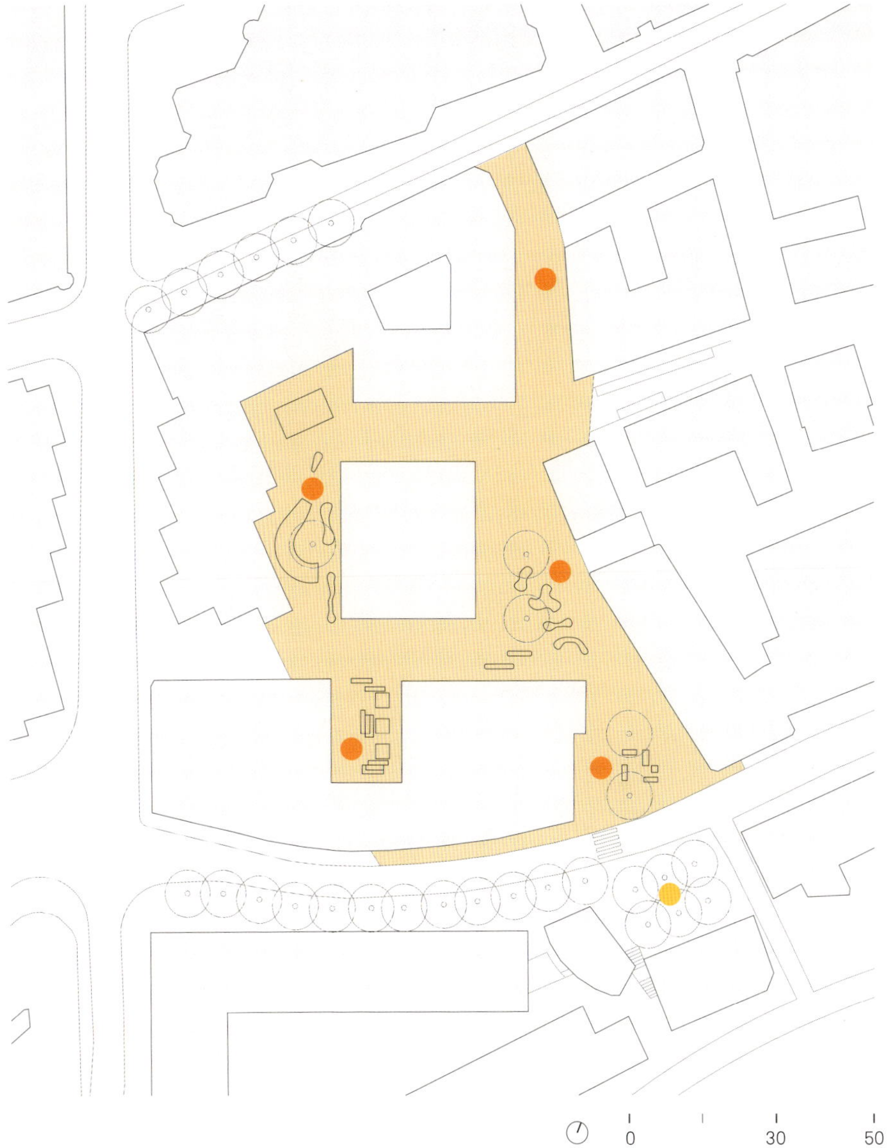

**Urban Analysis** The City Lounge project is located in the Bleicheli Quartier in St. Gallen, a district to the west of the medieval city. The Bleicheli Quartier was one of the world's leading centers for embroidery production in the 19th century and it has recently become St. Gallen's financial district. The neighborhood enjoys a central position in the city, between the St. Gallen train station and the historical cathedral complex.

Banks, insurance companies and offices established in the area create the main urban activity in the neighborhood. This working activity is combined with retail activities that take place in spaces located on the ground floor. Local residents frequent restaurants and shops, and many office workers use the public space daily.

## Aerial View

## Users

## Relation to the City

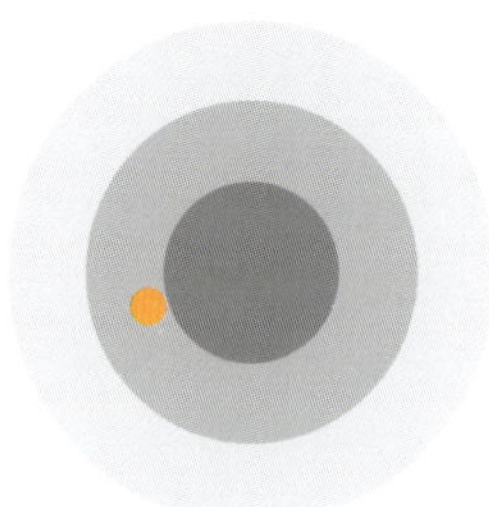

(Old) City center
Suburbs
Initial city expansions
Interventions

## Historic Urban Development

Medieval city
Post-19th century
Interventions

## Activities

Residential
Industrial
Public buildings
Shops
Offices
Hotels

**Social Analysis** In 2010, St. Gallen had a population of 73,000 inhabitants, 28% of whom were immigrants from ex-Yugoslavia, Italy, Germany, Turkey and Austria. The unemployment rate was very low, just 3% in 2011.

There is a very balanced mix of couples, families and people who live alone in the city, each group constituting a third of the total population.

## Age Structure

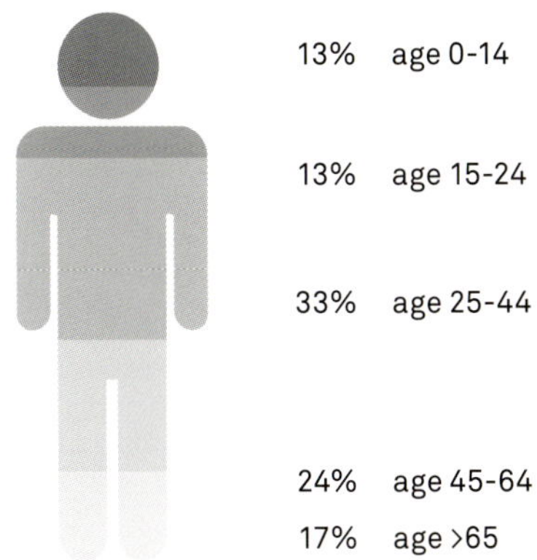


## Household Composition

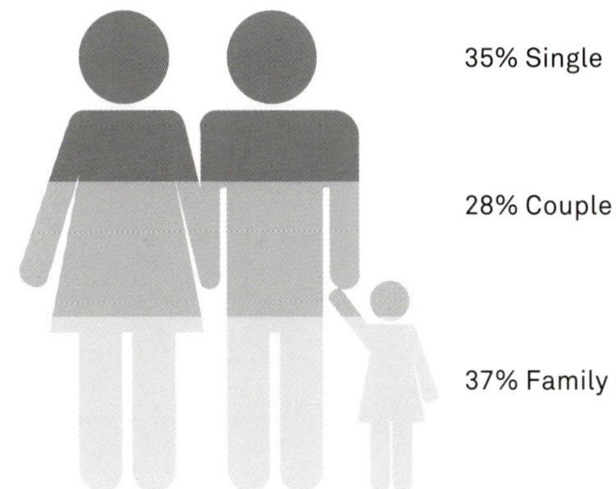

## Immigration

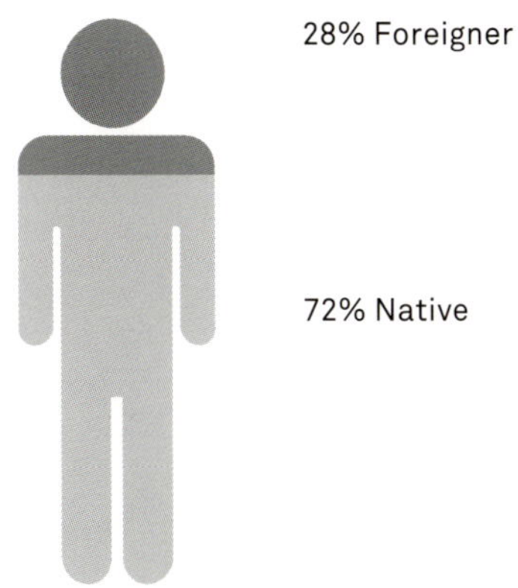


## Unemployment

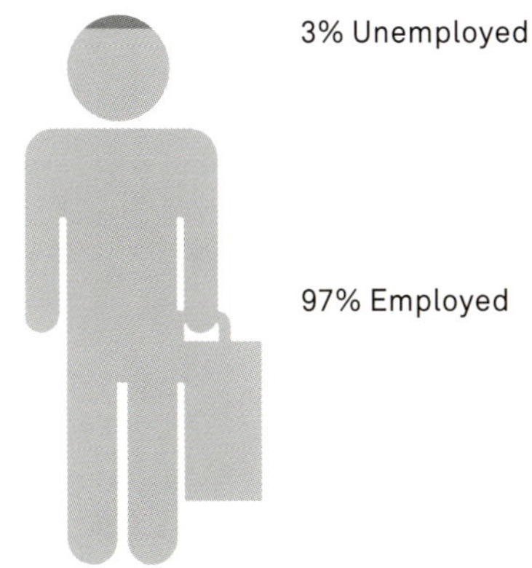


Age Structure, Immigration: St. Gallen. Source STATPOP 2010. Household Composition: Source Swiss Statistics. Unemployment: Canton St. Gallen. Source SECO 2011.

**Interventions** The irregular morphology of the site's urban structure fragments the public space into several open spaces. A specific intervention has been designed for each urban space, using different sculptural urban elements. Each intervention has a nickname that identifies its function and character, such as Reception Area, Café, Relaxation Lounge, Sculpture Park and Business Lounge.

At the same time, besides its conceptual and functional fragmentation, the continuity of the red pavement and the repetition of hanging sculptural street lamps over the entire area provide unity to the whole.

## 1 Sculpture Park - Reading Corner

The irregular perimeter of the nearby buildings and the circular shape of the existing parking ramp generate an interstitial outdoor space, which enjoys a certain character of quietness and intimacy. The intervention consists of several seating elements designed with organic shapes, which are adapted to fit the irregular spaces while working together as pieces of the sculpture park. The intervention is conceived as an open-air reading room inspired by the quiet atmosphere of the context, hidden away from the most frequented zones, and furnished with seating elements specially designed for the place.

## 2 Business Lounge

The Business Lounge is placed at the back of the new SVRB building. The intervention consists of a group of long benches designed in the form of sofas and long tables that transform the space into an outdoor meeting area with conference rooms. In this way, the meeting activities that are usually carried out inside the building can be celebrated outside as well, while at the same time, the public space can eventually serve as a gathering area where visitors and office workers from the nearby buildings can interact at break time.

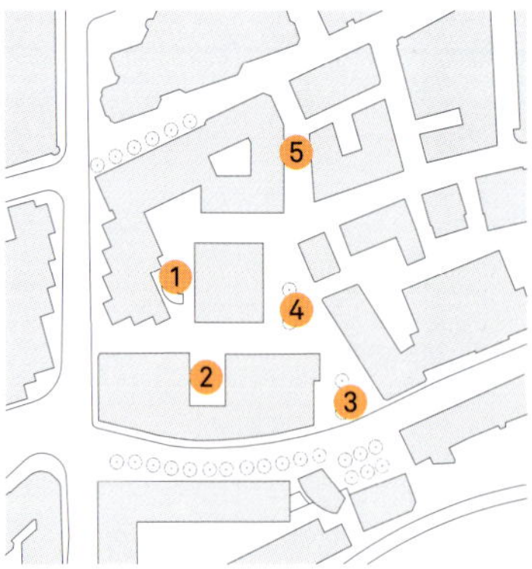

Accesses
Relaxation areas
Sitting areas
Circulation
Vegetation

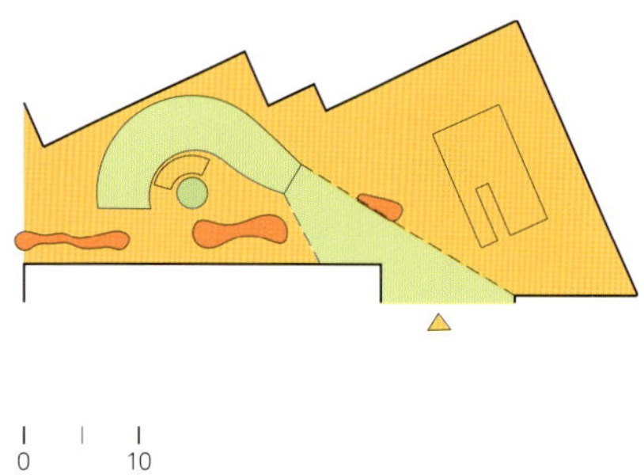


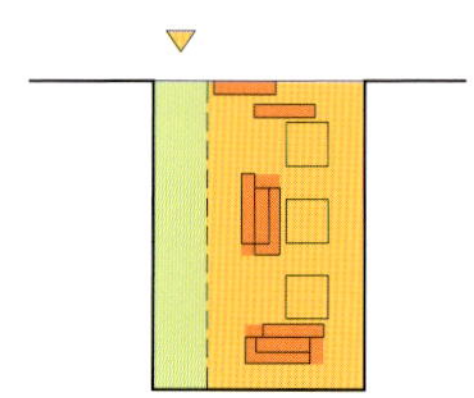

## 3 Reception Area

The triangular open space located at the southern end of the site works as an outdoor reception zone for the City Lounge. It also plays the role of a small entrance square for the SVRB building, for receiving visitors. A few long backless benches create an informal area, which works as a waiting area and a meeting point for the bank staff and for visitors to the educational center during the day. In the evening it becomes a lounge area for all kinds of users.

## 4 Relaxation Lounge

The Relaxation Lounge acts as a central living room located in a large central open space of the complex. Several sculptural seating elements have been placed around existing trees and one of them is combined with a fountain. The organic design of the seating elements and their proximity to each other stimulate interaction among visitors and create a gathering area near the café terrace located to the south.

## 5 Parking

The continuous red pavement that mixes circulation spaces for pedestrians and vehicles encourages citizens to use the entire surface of public space regardless of its function. According to this concept, the assigned parking areas are not strongly visually differentiated from the pedestrian zones or the circulation areas for cars. Indeed, they are simply marked in a subtle way by printing yellow symbols on the red pavement. A sculptural element located on the north side of the area depicts the shape of a car emerging from the red pavement to indicate the position of the car parking rows.

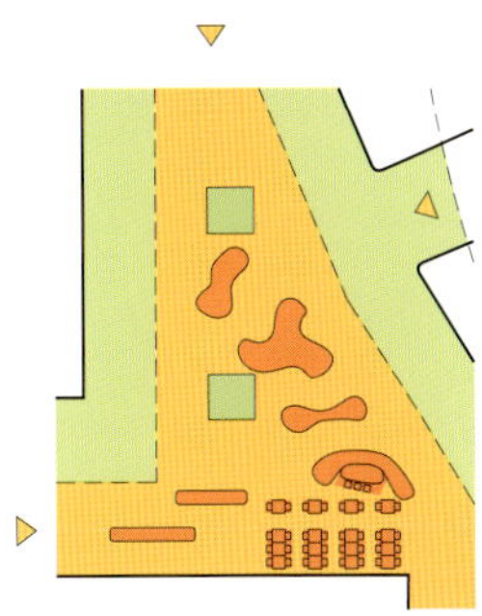

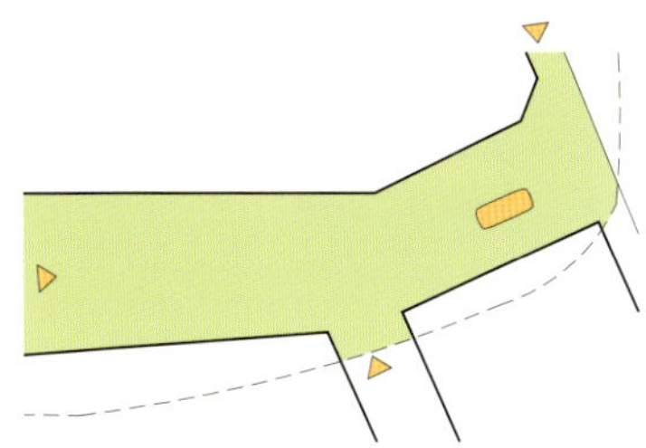

**Process** The project was initiated by the Municipality of St. Gallen and by Schweizer Verbandes der Raiffeisenbaken (SVRB). SVRB promoted and financed the renovation of the public space around the new bank building and the municipality of St. Gallen supported the competition, thereby ensuring that the winning entry could be built in accordance with the urban requirements of the city.

The aim of the competition was the renovation of public space in an area of the Bleicheli neighborhood in order to transform it into an outdoor public living room that could, in turn, stimulate urban life in the area. The architect Carlos Martinez and the visual artist Pipilotti Rist won the competition with their proposal entitled Stadtlounge (City Lounge) which was finally built in 2005 and opened to the public on November 3 that same year.

## Cost, Financing and Maintenance

The average cost of the intervention was 850 CHF/$m^2$ and it was financed by Schweizer Verbandes der Raiffeisenbaken (SVRB) of St. Gallen.

The management and maintenance of the area is carried out by the Municipality of St. Gallen, as is the case for most of the public space in the city. The innovative use of materials, such as rubber EPDM in the pavement and fiberglass in the urban furniture and sculptural objects, had to be approved by the municipality during the design phase and the municipality of St. Gallen is now responsible for any future reparation and maintenance of the interventions. EPDM requires no special maintenance for a period of 10 years but any oil, tire stains, and chewing-gum marks on its surface need to be removed or repaired manually, something that will increase the maintenance costs to keep it in good condition, compared with the maintenance costs of other standard public space interventions in the city.

## Timing

The time required for the development and construction of City Lounge was very similar to the time invested in other special landscape projects developed in the city's public space.

Although the project was built with materials that are not commonly used in public space in the city, City Lounge was not designed to be a temporary intervention, but rather as a long-term project with similar durability to other interventions in public space. In any case, as with many other innovative projects, it presents several long-term challenges due to the higher cost of maintenance and its possible deterioration over time.

## Use of the Public Space

City Lounge has become a successful strategy for activating the use of public space, especially among residents and office workers in the area. The fragmentation of the strategy into several interventions with different characters helps to attract different kinds of citizens who use the public space at different times of the day.

The variety of seating elements, in terms of identity and design, and the strategic location of the interventions in relation to the different activities that are undertaken nearby stimulates a flexible and spontaneous use of the public space. Seats for waiting in the so-called City Lounge reception area, long tables in connection with the meeting rooms for the offices, relaxation and reading areas in the quietest spots, and sculptural benches close to cafés and restaurants promote the use of the public space. On the one hand, this suggests a specific activity for each part of the City Lounge zone, while at the same time the interventions are abstract enough to be used in different ways.

## Impact on Citizens

City Lounge has become a well-known place in St. Gallen, mainly due to the combination of architecture and visual arts used to characterize the place with a peculiar strong identity. First, the use of the red color to identify an area of public space in the city clearly indicates the scope of the intervention and contrasts with the neutrality and homogeneity of the rest of the public space. Color works as an element to designate a lounge area in public space, in a similar way as green marks the presence of a park. Second, the sculptural character of the urban furniture and the lighting system, very different from the urban elements in the rest of the city, helps to differentiate this part of the city and to reinforce its special identity.

As a result, visitors have the impression that they are entering a special part of the city, which is easy to recognize, where the public space is transformed into a sculptural landscape designed to fulfill its functional role, but also to provoke a different sensory experience. City Lounge remains in the collective memory of the citizens of St. Gallen as an iconic and attractive public space associated with the renovation of Bleicheli Quartier into a financial district.

## Media Impact

City Lounge received a lot of local media attention. First, because the combination of an innovative image and a simple nickname such as "City Lounge" creates a coherent story that associates art and innovation with a trendy public space, something that is easy to communicate in the media and can be easily remembered by the citizens. Second, because the collaboration of the well-known visual artist Pipilotti Rist in the project transforms what in principle was supposed to be just a conventional public space intervention into a work of art, eliciting strong media attention as well. The city became an active open-air museum and the media promoted this fact.

The media impact of City Lounge has also reached international levels and the project has become a tourist attraction for the city, recommended in tourist guidebooks.

Bild: Ralph Ribi

### Roter Teppich wird ausgegossen

Das Bleicheli-Quartier wird nach Plänen von Pipilotti Rist und Carlos Martinez im Auftrag der Raiffeisen-Banken in eine «Stadt-Lounge» – ein öffentliches Wohnzimmer – verwandelt. Als Erstes wird nun der rote Teppich ausgerollt beziehungsweise ausgegossen: Mit Hilfe von Schaufeln, Besen, Spachteln und Kübeln tragen Mitarbeiter der St. Galler Bauunternehmung Müller AG Schicht um Schicht Granulat auf. Zuerst Schwarz, dann Rot, dann wieder Schwarz und wieder Rot. «Insgesamt sind sechs Arbeitsgänge nötig», sagt Bauführer Eugen Pollat. Man liege mit dem Projekt im Zeitplan. Und das Publikum? Passanten bleiben interessiert stehen. Zu hören sind aber auch diverse «Wäää, da stinkt aber». (mar)

## GREEN ROOM
ROTTERDAM, THE NETHERLANDS

STRATEGY / INTERVENTIONS: **Casanova+Hernandez**
COMMISSIONER: **Municipality of Rotterdam**

Since 2008, Casanova+Hernandez have collaborated with the municipality of Rotterdam on several urban studies. One of these studies focused on the analysis of the use of public space by the citizens of Rotterdam, the selection of urban areas with the potential for activating citizens' interaction and finally the design of a number of Public Space Acupuncture strategies that could breathe new life into public space.

The selected study area was the section of downtown Rotterdam limited by the so-called "fire line" (Brandgrens). The zone has a surface area of 283 hectares and corresponds with the sector affected by the devastating fire that occurred on May 14, 1940 after the German air force bombed the city during World War II. The affected zone was almost completely demolished due to the significant structural damage that the fire caused to the existing buildings. The reconstruction of downtown Rotterdam was carried out following the ideas rooted in the Modern Movement, based on a rational urban structure, an efficient circulation system and a new model for public space which was very different from that of the old part of the city.

The comparative analysis between the public space limited by the "fire line" and an adjacent zone of the historic city reveals that the existing public space in the modern area accounts for 71% of the total surface, whereas in the old area it accounts for only 44%. This means that Rotterdam's modern planning considerably oversized the surface area of public space in comparison to the compact layout of the historic city.

The general view is that the modern area of Rotterdam was designed for vehicles and not for pedestrians, but if we compare the surface areas of public space set aside for the circulation of vehicles, they are similar in both parts of the city. There is, however, a major difference in other types of public space that are not strictly roads, such as sidewalks, roundabouts and areas for tram circulation, as well as in other large extensions of public space such as open spaces

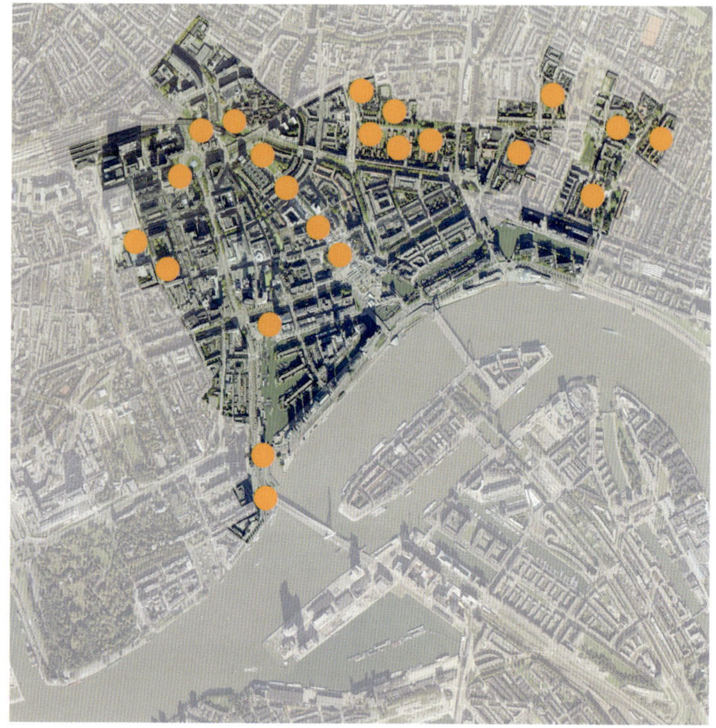

Rotterdam's city center after the bombing in May 1940 and its reconstruction

near the canals and the river, public space between open residential blocks and the multitude of large-scale urban interstitial spaces.

One of the proposed strategies for revitalizing the use of public space focuses on acting on empty interstitial spaces in the city that are only occasionally used to house outdoor activities such as markets, outdoor concerts and all kinds of festivals, but which remain empty most of the time. While on the one hand these unused interstitial spaces can create a sense of insecurity among citizens, especially at night, and have an ambiguous identity, on the other hand they are "extra" public spaces with great potential that can be envisioned as important urban elements characteristic of the city of Rotterdam, which no other Dutch city has.

**Strategy** The strategy analyzes and catalogs the city's interstitial urban spaces and plans a series of independent alternative interventions that, on the one hand, activate their use as public spaces and, on the other, erase their ambiguous character to provide them with their own identity.

Many of the interventions are mobile and easy to transport, making it possible to remove them when public events are celebrated in the interstitial urban spaces where they are installed.

All the interventions, regardless of their location, respond to the question of how to create a "sense of place" in urban spaces that do not have a use or a character of their own, which are often residual spaces derived from the planning process. The proposed solutions are based on transforming the public space into an art-scape, in which each intervention decodes how to use and perceive public space to give it a new meaning.

## Relationship Between Built and Public Areas in Old and New Rotterdam

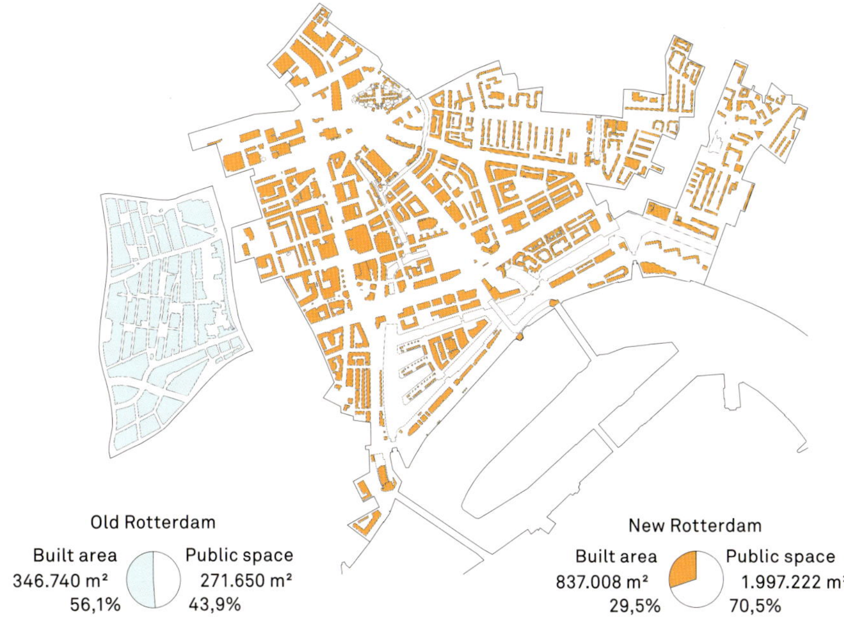


## Categories of Interstitial Public Spaces

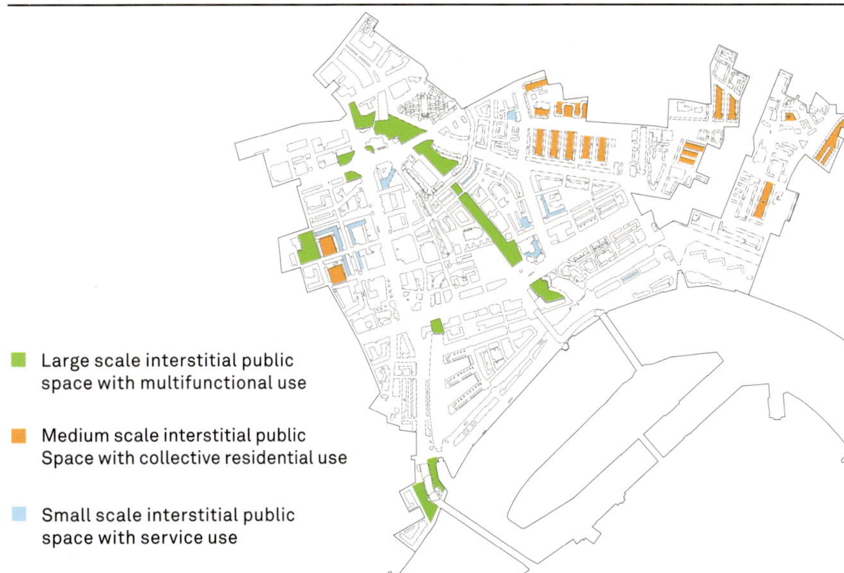

19

**Interventions** The strategy proposes a series of interventions in different points of the city. The first one to be realized was a test-intervention called “The Green Room” located in Willemsplein, a square that acts as an urban void limited by the Erasmus bridge, the Maas river and few buildings. Despite its central location in the city and its stunning views over the river and the Erasmus bridge, which has become the main icon of the city, the square is a large unused space without urban activity.

The Green Room is a hybrid intervention that blends landscape architecture, architecture and sculpture to create a unique urban element that redefines the way we behave in public space, activating its use and providing it with meaning. It consists of two main elements: the prefabricated green walls and the seating platform.

The prefabricated green walls are made of ivory plant (Hedera helix) that grows on a three-dimensional wire mesh, forming a green wall that is 60 centimeters wide and three meters high. Three square windows integrated into the green walls at different heights encourage interaction between visitors of different ages and the walls. The corner formed by the two green walls protects visitors from the strong prevailing westerly winds, while the open corner on the opposite side allows for sunlight to enter the room. The intervention combines the feeling of protection and intimacy with the sense of an open public space forming a pleasant place to stay, which many visitors often prefer to other ones in the area.

The seating platform functions as a topography created by prisms of different heights, which, due to their abstraction, can be used in many different ways, becoming stools, chairs or tables that can acquire different uses, such as a children’s playground, a working area, an exercise area or other ones that can be decided spontaneously by users. The smooth finishing of artificial grass makes these elements appealing to the touch and encourages citizens use them.

All together, the green walls and the seating platform create a hybrid urban element that is half natural and half artificial, which invites citizens to colonize it in many different ways, using it as a lounge zone, play area, meeting point or workspace, among others.

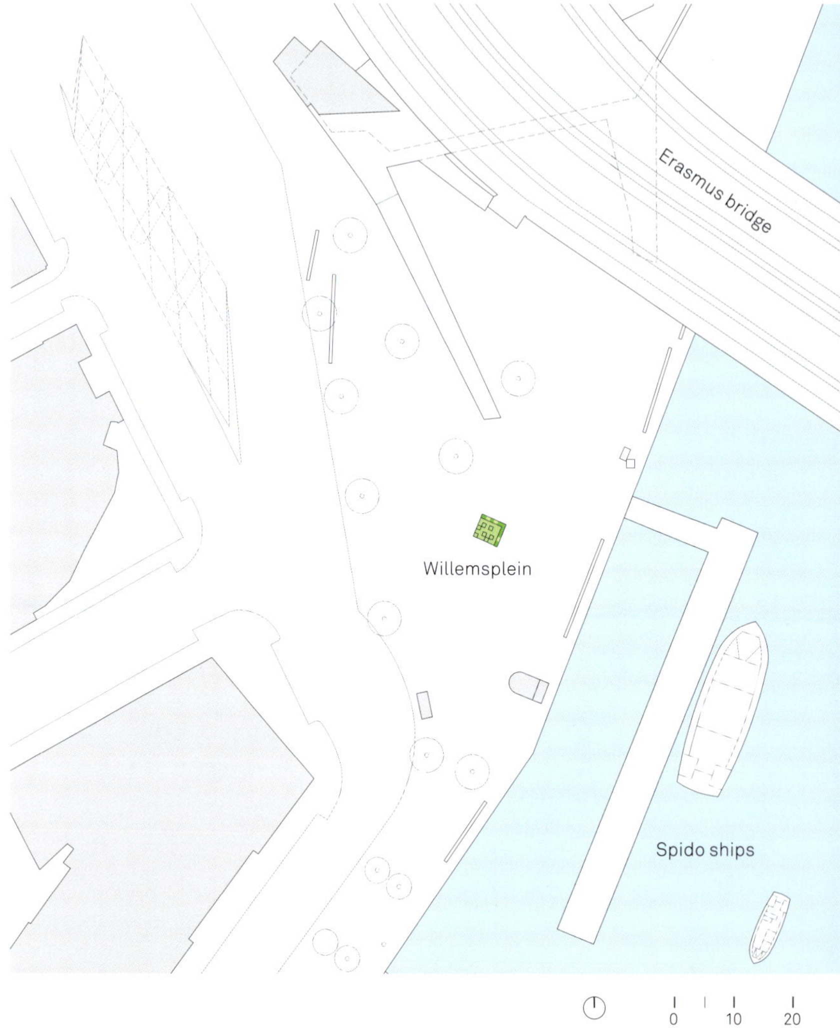


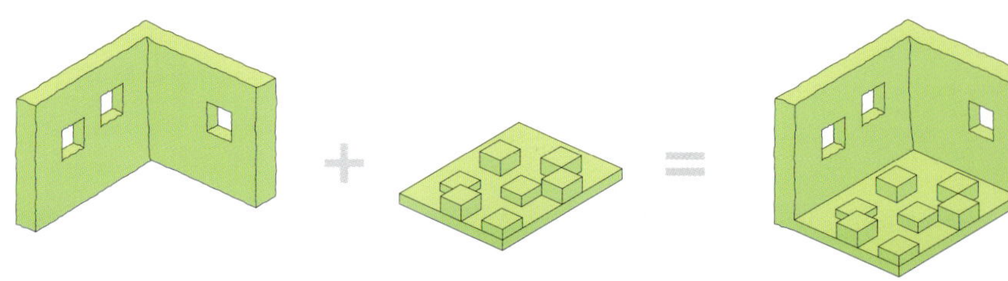

26
TULIP INN

The intervention transforms a portion of the city's unused public space into a room open to citizens marked by a domestic feel. In fact, its dimensions are very similar to that of a real domestic room and its green walls create a sense of privacy while the windows in the walls provide views over the river area, framing unique elements in the surroundings, like the Erasmus bridge.

The Green Room creates an urban space on a human scale that contrasts with the huge scale of the surrounding context. The new space is perceived as a quiet green island floating in the public space of the city, generating an oasis effect that attracts citizens.

The Green Room was conceived as an artistic intervention not to be looked at, but to be used. It is an open installation that makes sense when the public uses it: installation and citizen become a complete set that works as an urban stage with improvised actors. This theatrical dimension has transformed the intervention into a favorite place for visitors to take group and wedding pictures, where the people being photographed tend to devise special poses.

The vegetation gives the intervention a living, colorful and temporary character, which contrasts with the cold aspect of the surroundings created using hard pavements, concrete and glass. Likewise, the innovative use of vegetation to build the walls, floor and seats of the room gives the intervention a strong particular identity that contrasts with the anonymous appearance of the surrounding public space. Public space understood as an art-scape that combines identity and functionality, is perhaps what has made the Green Room very popular among visitors, activating the use of the square and characterizing the space as a vibrant place with a new meaning.

Sections, plan and axonometry

Construction and installation of the intervention

# Activity Study According to the Amount of Users

Rotterdam
TICKETS
FAHRKARTEN
BILLETS

19

# BENCH ISLANDS
## GRONINGEN, THE NETHERLANDS

STRATEGY / INTERVENTIONS: **Casanova+Hernandez**
COMMISSIONERS: **Nijestee Housing Corporation, Municipality of Groningen**

Stadswerven is a neighborhood in Groningen, designed by Berlage in the 1930s. Its urban structure is composed of long residential blocks arranged around communal courtyards, sometimes in combination with industrial buildings, which were located along the canals to take advantage of them as transportation routes.

The disappearance of industrial activity along the canals, as it has moved to the outskirts of the city, has led to the appearance of new residential complexes. Some of these complexes have maintained the structure based on long residential blocks, combining them with taller buildings located in front of small urban squares. This transformation has caused part of the collective life of the residential blocks to no longer concentrate in the interior courtyards, but rather it has moved into the squares in public space, thus providing the opportunity for developing a strategy based on landscape interventions in public space with the aim of enriching urban life in the neighborhood.

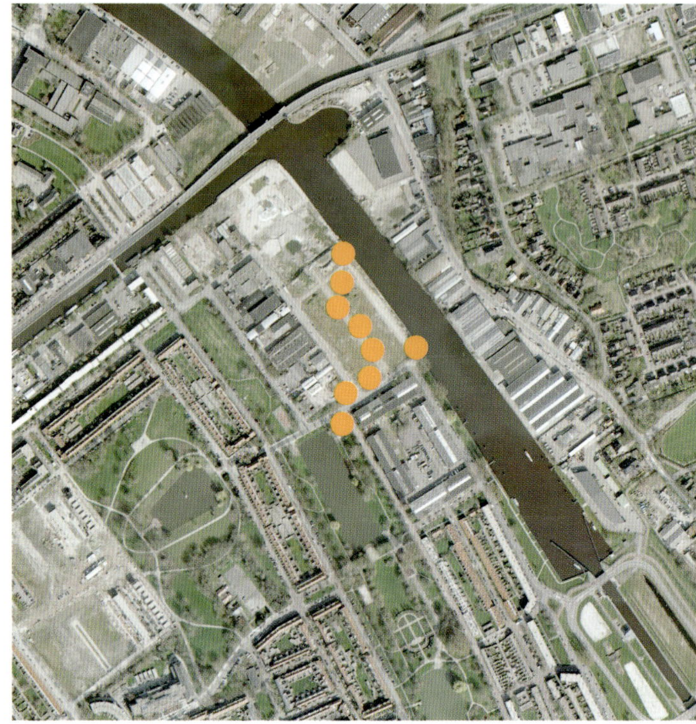

**Strategy** Given the residential character of the neighborhood and its distance from the city center, the strategy is not focused on promoting the more public side of its public space, but rather its collective aspect. To this end, the strategy is broken up into small interventions located near each other, establishing a strong visual and functional relationship among them. The spatial fragmentation of public space into oval areas responds to the need for encouraging interaction among small groups of residents and for creating more intimate places that function as collective satellite outdoor spaces for the new blocks, which are integrated into the public space instead of being located in the interior courtyards. In the absence of commerce or public facilities to attract all kinds of citizens to the area, the strategy aims to collectivize public space so that, although these spaces are open to all citizens, the residents of nearby blocks may subliminally consider them as their own.

In this way, the interventions create clearly defined spaces where children can play and parents can interact with each

Long urban blocks with collective courtyards

New residential blocks and public squares

other. At the same time, the elderly residents of nearby homes can socialize outdoors and the disabled people who live in the adapted dwellings in one of the blocks can use the interventions as outdoor gathering places. The strategy promotes activity in public space by creating areas to house activities that can be shared in by members of particular circles, reinforcing public space as a parochial domain. But at the same time, the fact that some interventions are located very close to each other not only promotes interactivity between groups that share affinities, but also opens the door to interaction among the different groups.

**Interventions** The interventions that form the strategy are built using a versatile system based on four standardized modular concrete elements, which can be combined in a wide variety of ways to generate a host of proposals with very different geometric shapes and sizes.

Each intervention marks off a small part of the city's public space using a long bench and is given the name "island". The modular system provides the opportunity for creating many different types of islands, from closed ones with regular geometric perimeters to open ones formed with curving wavy perimeters. These islands can be classified into three main types: closed islands, clover islands and clip islands.

### Versatile System Based on Standardized Modular Elements

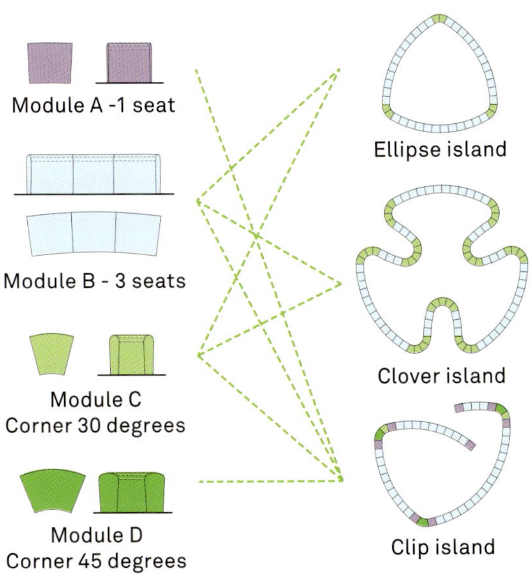


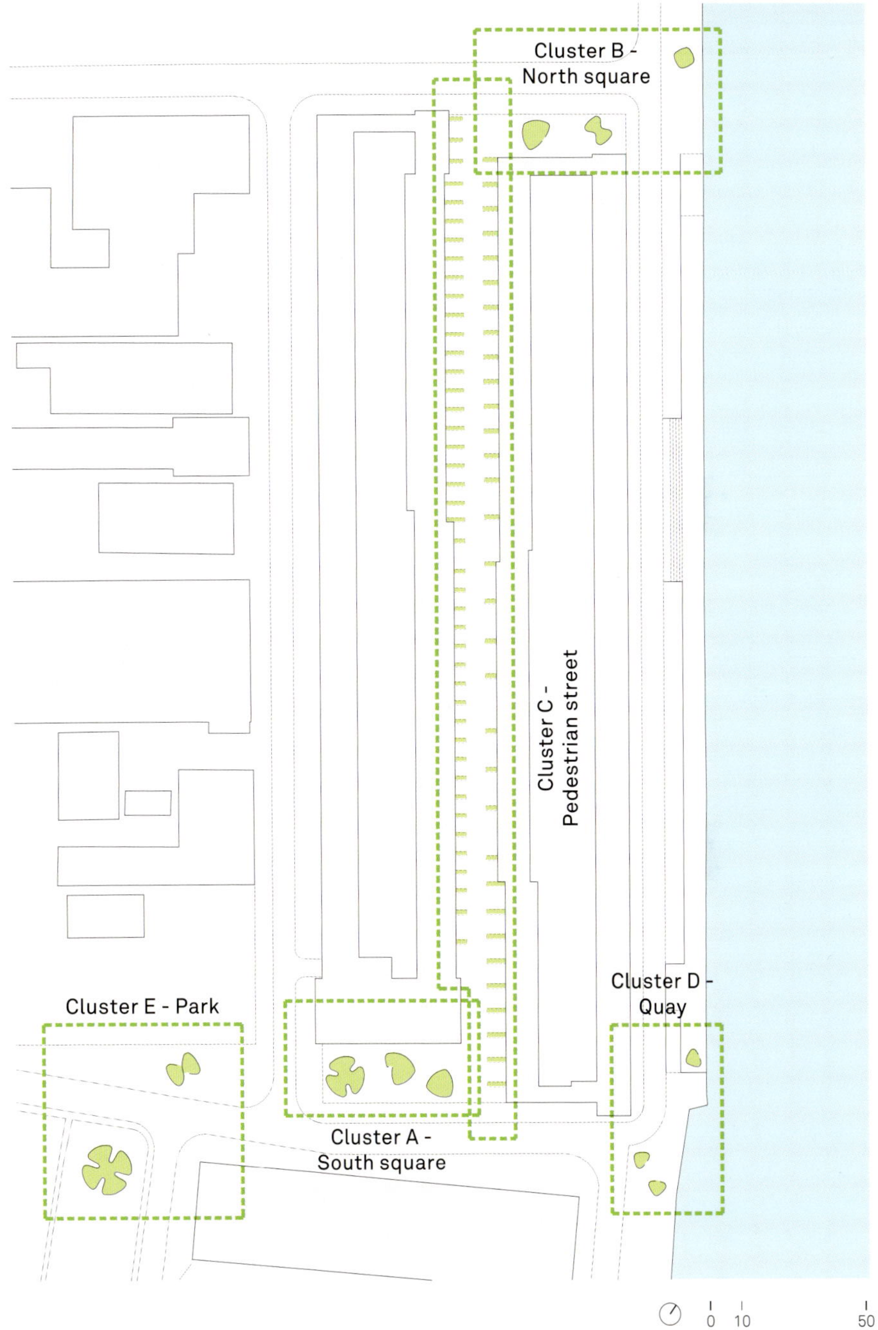

The interior of the island can be used for various purposes such as a children's play area, an area for playing board games or an exercise area. In other interventions this space is landscaped with grass, flowers or trees, transforming the intervention into a garden island. Hybrid interventions such as the zigzag islands or clip islands can combine a space to host open-air activities with a gardened area.

The system offers a wide range of possible interventions to be included in the strategy, which can take on very different shapes (elliptical, round, square, rectangular, clover, clip or zigzag) and, in turn, different sizes. Each intervention is defined by the combination of an element selected from the catalog, which determines its size and shape, with a specific use and a social purpose. In this way, each intervention can adopt a more introverted or extroverted character, in order to promote either individuality or interaction among citizens.

## Variety of Spatial Qualities in Three Main Intervention Types

Open intervention - People inside

Closed intervention - People outside

Open and closed intervention - People inside and outside

## Ellipse Island

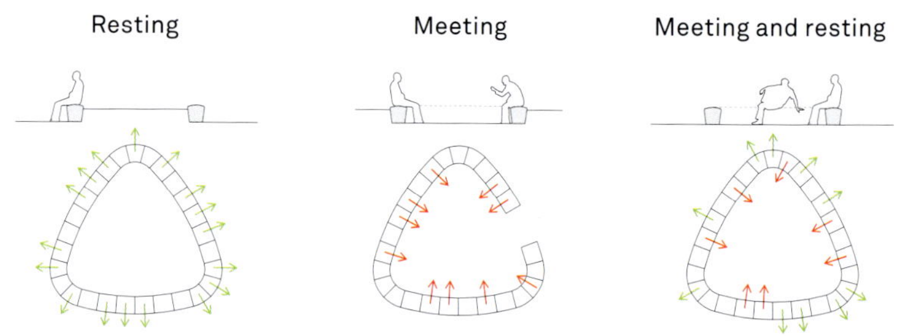


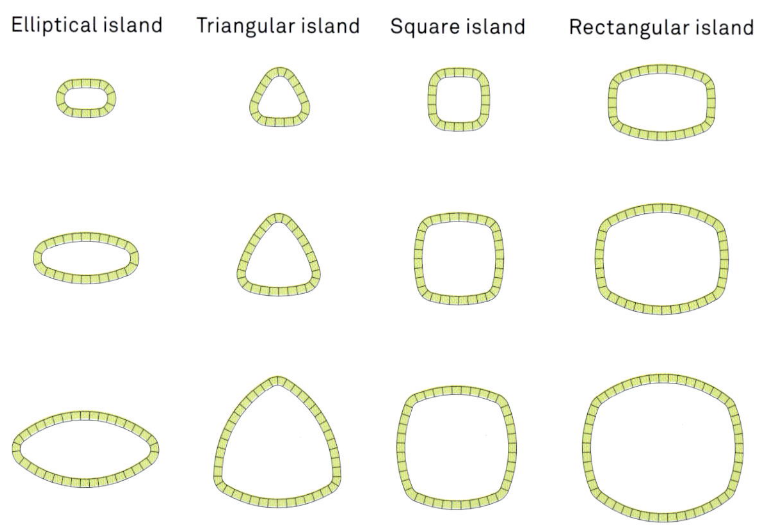

## Clover Island

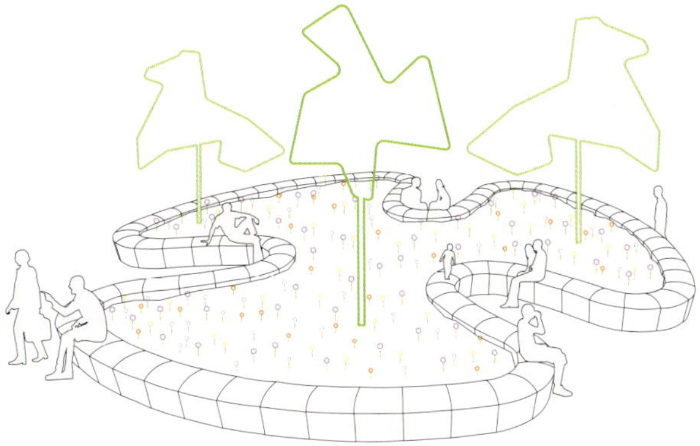

Meeting points

Resting areas

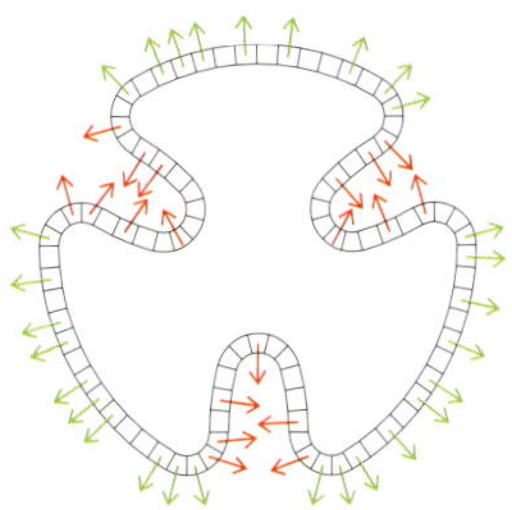

2-Cloverleaf island | 3-Cloverleaf island | 4-Cloverleaf island

## Clip Island

Children's playground | Board games for adults | Symbiotic Children-elderly

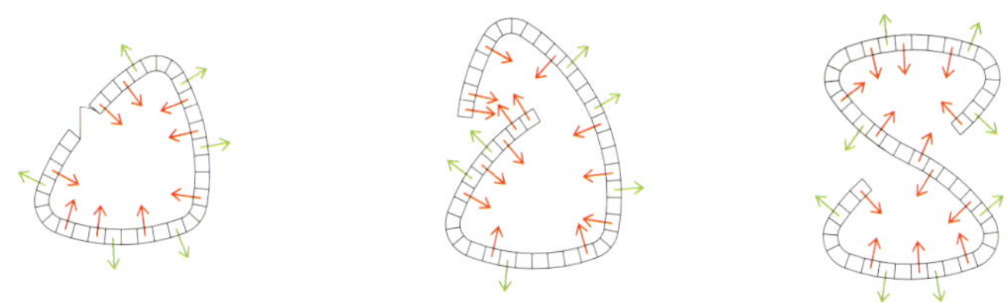

Open island | Clip island | Zigzag island

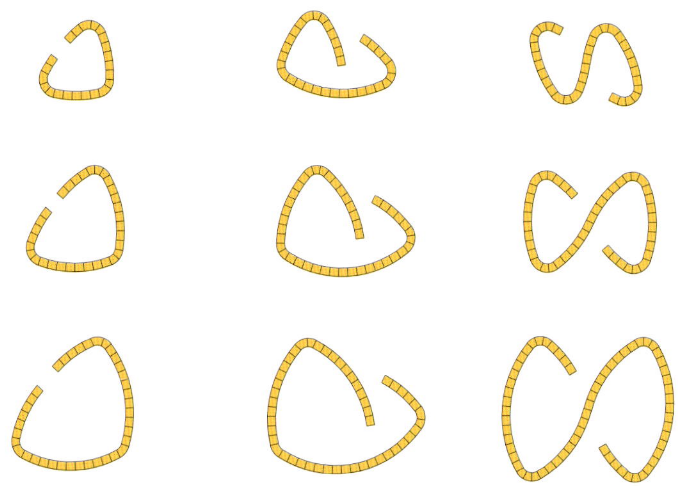

## Intervention Cluster A at South Square

Cross section

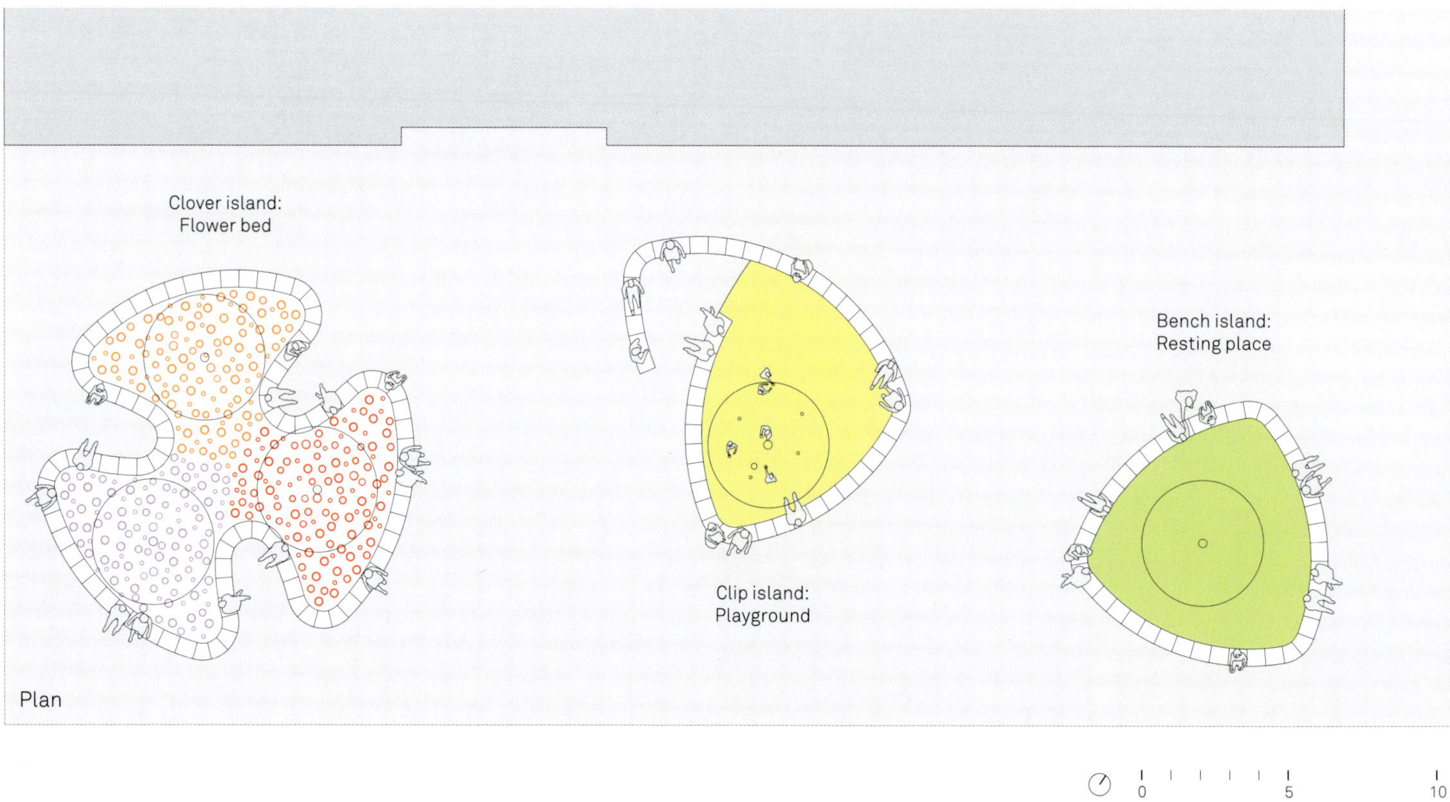


Plan

Test Case 21

## MOSAIC PARK & CERAMIC MUSEUM
## JINZHOU, CHINA

INTERVENTION: **Casanova+Hernandez**
STRATEGY: **J-COM, IFLA**
COMMISSIONER: **Jinzhou City**

The tremendous growth of the Chinese economy in recent years has been accompanied by rapid urbanization, as a result of which many cities have grown enormously in order to house the large number of people who have migrated to the city from the countryside. After an initial phase in which, due to this strong growth, urban planning policies focused on offering rapid responses to the most pressing needs, a second stage has begun in which the focus has shifted to increasing the quality of urban life.

The new needs of today's China are qualitative rather than quantitative. As a consequence, the task of urban design professionals has shifted from just providing quick answers to thinking about what the relevant questions should be. In this context, public space is attracting the interest of politicians, urban planners and citizens as a new territory with a huge potential for developing strategies that tackle the problems of environmental quality, social sustainability and collective identity from a different perspective.

**Strategy** A strategy that experiments with the new role of public space in urban growth has been implemented in Jinzhou, a city with a population of three million people, located 500 kilometers northeast of Beijing. The future development of the city has been planned around the creation of high-quality public space in the form of a large-scale 176-hectare park. The park was built on land reclaimed from the sea. Initially intended to house an international landscape exhibition, in the future it will become the central park in a new urban development.

As with any rapid, large-scale urban development, the problem that arises is how to generate an urban identity in a place that has no history, even more so if it is built on land reclaimed from the sea, where there was initially no human landscape at all. The strategy developed by the Jinzhou municipality conceives the park as a series of independent but related landscape interventions. These interventions

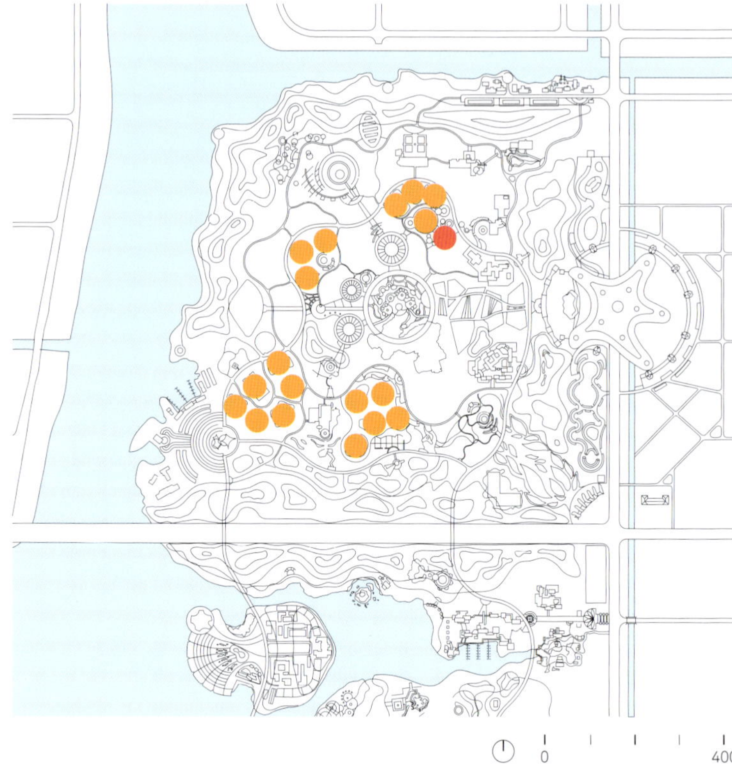

Jinzhou city and construction board for the 2013 World Landscape Exposition at the building site

share the same circular shape and similar dimensions, where a series of different programs are undertaken to stimulate activity in the park.

Within the unitary design of the park, the strategy included the creation of a series of 20 interventions developed by international designers from all over the world who were asked to reflect on the program and the identity of each intervention, tying the projects in with the designers' cultural origins.

However, although the creation of an imported landscape, like a French Baroque garden, a Renaissance Italian garden or an Arabic garden, can provide character and a strong identity to any place, nonetheless it is still something alien to the citizens, something far removed from local cultural roots that transforms the landscape into a simple curiosity, a source of entertainment, but not a place with deep meaning. The signifier may have a clear signified, but at the same time it can be irrelevant to the citizens.

On the other hand, it is also true that the move toward globalization has been hugely successful precisely in introducing global products into very different cultures, which may initially have held no meaning for the local cultures but have subsequently acquired their own meaning in relation to concepts such as progress and modernity.

In this case, the interventions are not seen as mere functional instruments, but as artistic elements that provide special meaning to the place. It is precisely the reflection on the relationship between signifier and signified, between the object and what it represents, that opens the door to creating a sense of place, which citizens can somehow recognize.

## Intervention #36

### Mosaic Park as Symbol of Cultural Hybridization

Intervention #36, designed by Casanova+Hernandez, consists of the Mosaic Park and the Ceramic Museum. It aims to go beyond the Expo's initial goal of providing an imported landscape to lend the park a globalized identity, and seeks to create a connection between the citizens of Jinzhou and the location, giving deeper meaning to the place.

In order to achieve this goal, the intervention experiments with the concept of cultural hybridity, an ancient phenomenon developed over centuries in the history of exchanges between the West and the Far East. It is formalized as a polysemic landscape, where the signifier acquires different signifieds, connecting the place to European culture as well as to the local one.

On the one hand, the ceramic materials used for the park and the museum establish a relationship between the intervention and the Mediterranean mosaic tradition, which was spread across Europe by the Roman Empire. This tradition has evolved throughout history to the present day, crystallizing into interesting regional variations such as the trencadís technique used in Catalan modernist architecture and landscape architecture, which characterizes the work of renowned designers such as Antoni Gaudí.

On the other hand, the geometry of the park is inspired by the crackle glaze of Chinese porcelain pieces, developed during the Song Dynasty in Ge Ware pottery. The intervention reminds citizens that the Jinzhou region was once a ceramic and porcelain production area, although this tradition was lost and forgotten centuries ago. However, the intervention does not just attempt to give meaning to the place by connecting citizens with their historical roots, it also aims to create future links between citizens and the place through the construction of the Ceramic Museum, which is conceived as a center opened to local artisans to promote the diffusion of contemporary ceramics and porcelain art.

Roman mosaic

Ge ware vase, Song Dynasty

Trencadís, mosaic technique using broken ceramic pieces. Gaudí, Park Güell, Barcelona.

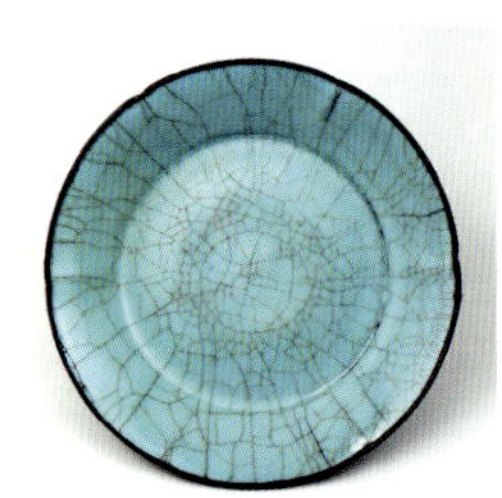

Crackle glaze in Ge ware plate

## Mosaic Park and Ceramic Museum as Three-Dimensional Crackled Landscape

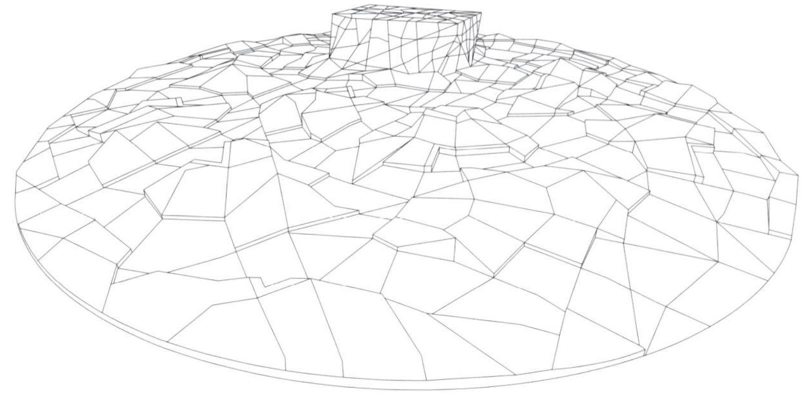

## Plan of Mosaic Park as Mosaic of Ceramic Surfaces and Flower Beds

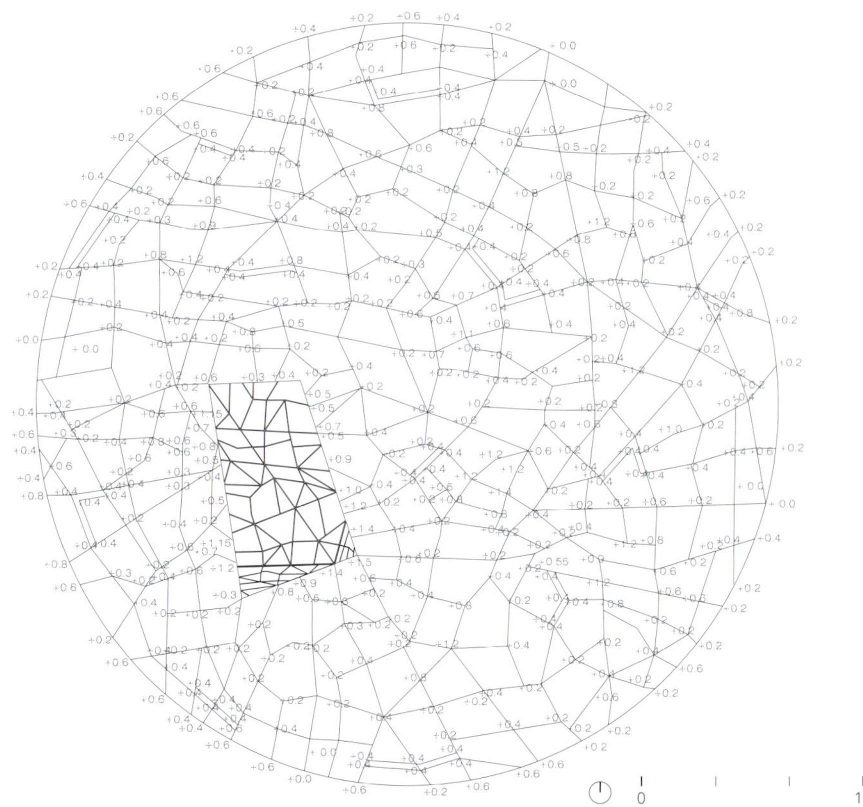

### Hybrid Artscape: A Blend of Architecture and Landscape

The intervention represents the synthesis of the contemporary urban park, which is not a fragment of the natural landscape or a protected landscaped piece of the city, but a mixture of both. Mosaic Park has a hybrid character that blends architecture with landscape architecture, and nature with artifice.

On the one hand, the geometry of the intervention is developed as a three-dimensional crackled landscape, where landscape and architecture merge into a continuous topological surface comprising 884 irregular planes. On the other hand, this geometry takes shape in a multicolored mosaic that combines four different species of flowers with mosaics made from broken local Chinese ceramic tiles. The vegetation and the ceramic tiles merge into a polychromatic mosaic that brings together nature and local crafts.

The geometry of the Ceramics Museum building is designed as a continuation of the park's crackled geometry, and its façades are made of the same ceramic tiles used in the park's pavement and benches, combined with glazed openings also following irregular patterns.

The mosaic formed by the combination of gardened areas and ceramic surfaces distributed across the entire surface of the intervention provides visual unity to the park, avoiding the classic separation between hardscape and softscape and between constructions and landscape. The intervention becomes an artistic work that blends in with the landscape of the place, creating a hybrid identity with its own meaning that we can call "artscape".

### Hybrid Landscape

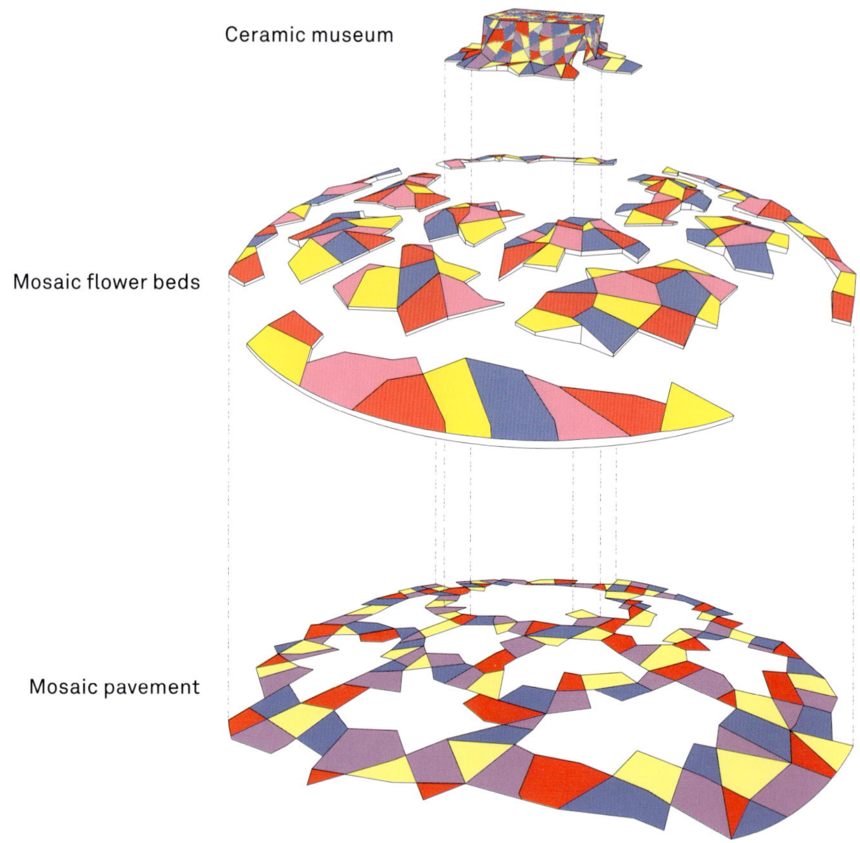


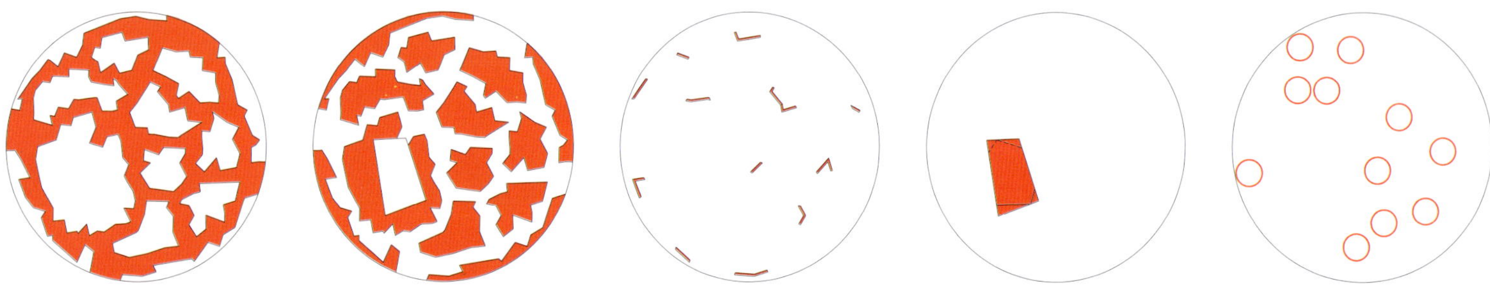

Mosaic pavement | Flower beds | Benches | Building | Trees

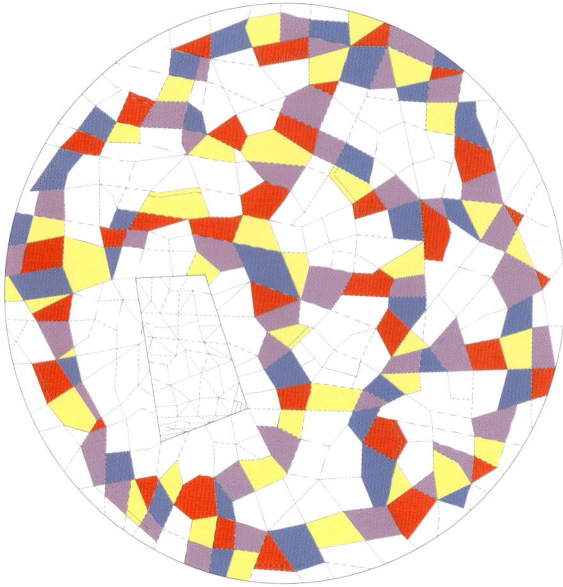

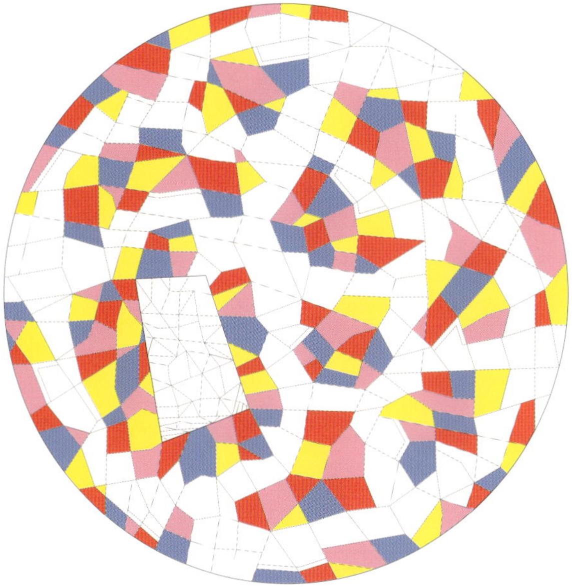

### Intervention as public life activator

The intervention works as a catalyst for public life in two ways. On the one hand, Mosaic Park activates the use of public space. The intervention is an attractive and colorful landscape that invites visitors to enjoy a multi-sensory experience. It was designed with proportions related to the human scale, offering spaces for walking, sitting and playing, and it is equipped with long benches that create a setting for spontaneous informal encounters.

On the other hand, the Ceramic Museum activates cultural and social life. It aims to awaken visitors' curiosity about the place's history, to provide information about a lost tradition, and finally to create a meeting place for citizens through a program of exhibitions and public events.

The iconic nature of artscapes such as Mosaic Park also helps to attract visitors to the park, while its image has been widely disseminated in newspaper articles, television programs and even on postage stamps. The media potential of architecture, although indirectly, also plays an important role in activating the life of public space by increasing the value of its image.

Public awareness campaign: media and postage stamps

21

### Social platform

The Ceramic is conceived as an open structure, where the program evolves over time and serves as a social platform to showcase the work of local artists, designers and artisans who work and experiment in the ceramics and porcelain tradition.

On the one hand it seeks to incite citizens' interest in their own traditions, but even more importantly, it attempts to stimulate the local creative industry and contemporary design by building an iconic and modern space for the dissemination, exhibition and sale of local crafts.

In short, the intervention aims not only to bolster the public use of the park, but also to strengthen the cultural life of the city and the local economy as well, looking beyond the direct physical impact toward creating a social impact.

### Museum as Platform to Exhibit the Work of Local Artists

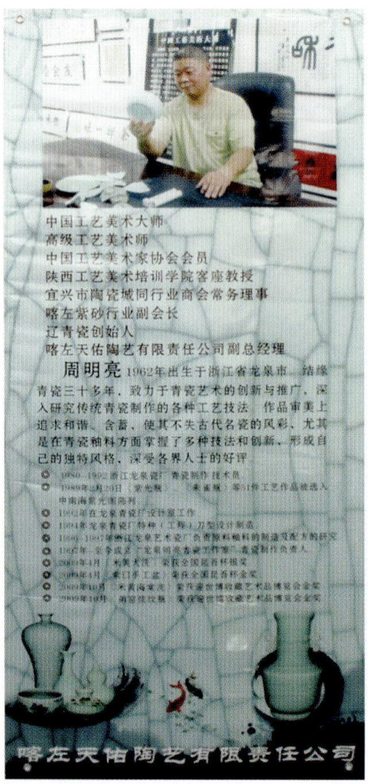


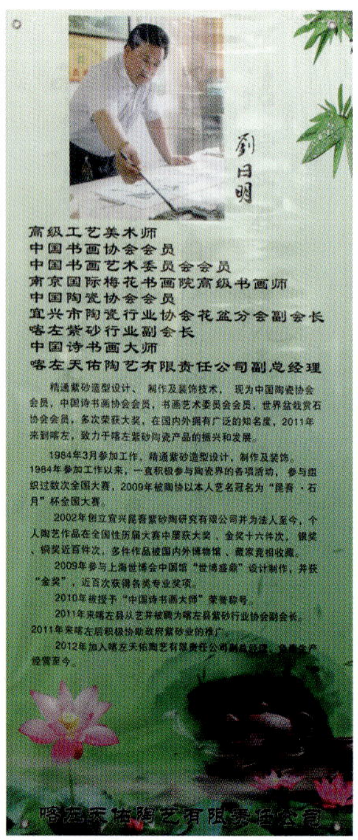

## Museum as a Symbolic and Flexible Cultural Platform to Showcase Different Temporary Exhibitions

# Comparative Graphic Tables

## CHAPTER 1: TIME-BASED STRATEGIES

### 1.1 Short-Term Strategies

**CS A**
Lausanne Jardins 2009. Lausanne, Switzerland

**TC #01**
Temporary Intervention "Green Windows". Lausanne, Switzerland

**TC #02**
Temporary Intervention "Senses Cocktail". Appeltern, The Netherlands

### 1.2 Mutating Strategies

**CS B**
Museumsquartier Courtyard. Vienna, Austria

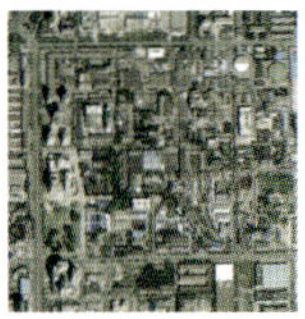

**TC #03**
Morpheus, 798 Art Zone. Beijing, China

**TC #04**
Grassscapes. Antwerp, Belgium

### 1.3 Long-Term Strategies Based on Temporary Interventions

**CS C**
"This is Not a Vacant Lot". Saragossa, Spain

**TC #05**
Temporary Interventions in Vacant Lots. Madrid, Spain

**TC #06**
Floating parks. Rotterdam, The Netherlands

## CHAPTER 2: CITIZEN PARTICIPATION

### 2.1 Co-management Strategies. Citizens as Decision Makers

**CS D**
I Love to Play! & Painting Initiative. Tirana, Albania

**TC #07**
Velluters Citizen Strategy in Vacant Lots. Valencia, Spain

**TC #08**
Sandleiten. Vienna, Austria

### 2.2 Co-creative Strategies. Citizens as Designers

**CS E**
City Park Ørestad. Copenhagen, Denmark

**TC #09**
Lijnbaan Urban Courtyards. Rotterdam, The Netherlands

**TC #10**
Central Park. Rajka, Hungary

**TC #11**
Can Escandell Park. Ibiza, Spain

### 2.3 Co-production Startegies. Citizens as Builders.

**CS F**
Urban Gardens. Rotterdam, The Netherlands

**TC #12**
Amsterdam Nieuw-West. Amsterdam, The Netherlands

**TC #13**
Rusovce. Bratislava, Slovakia

## CHAPTER 3: RE-PLACEMAKING

### 3.1 City as a Stage

**CS G**
Harborfront. Copenhagen, Denmark

**TC #14**
Schuytgraaf. Arhnem, The Netherlands

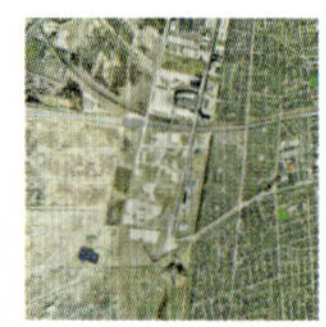

**TC #15**
Ørestad South. Copenhagen, Denmark

### 3.2 City as an Event Place

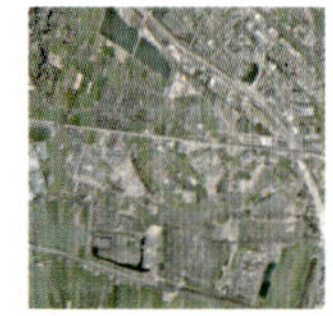

**CS H**
Beyond Leidsche Rijn. Utrecht, The Netherlands

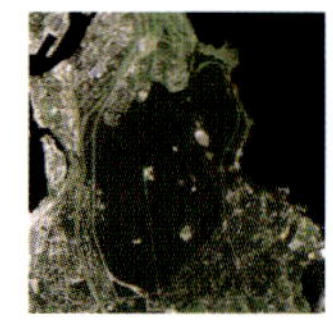

**TC #16**
Mezaparks. Riga, Latvia

**TC #17**
Wii-Playgrounds (Van Eyck Playgrounds 2.0). Amsterdam. The Netherlands

**TC #18**
Public Space for the Asian Cultural Complex (ACC). Gwanju, South Korea

### 3.3 City as an Art-Scape

**CS I**
City Lounge. St. Gallen, Switzerland

**TC #19**
Green Room. Rotterdam, The Netherlands

**TC #20**
Bench Islands. Groningen, The Netherlands

**TC #21**
Mosaic Park & Ceramic Museum. Jinzhou, China

## CHAPTER 1: TIME-BASED STRATEGIES

### 1.1 Short-Term Strategies

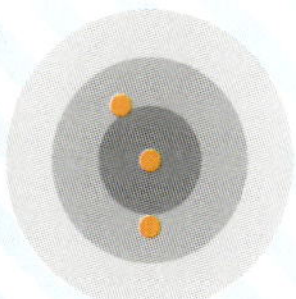

**CS A**
Lausanne Jardins 2009. Lausanne, Switzerland

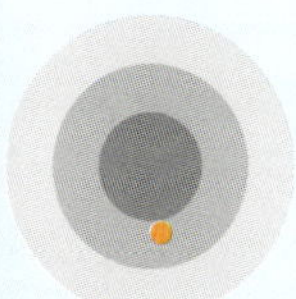

**TC #01**
Temporary Intervention "Green Windows". Lausanne, Switzerland

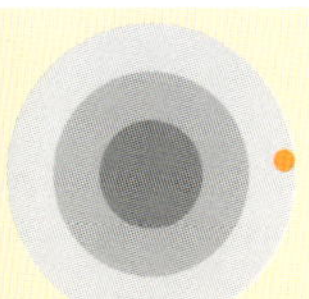

**TC #02**
Temporary Intervention "Senses Cocktail". Appeltern, The Netherlands

### 1.2 Mutating Strategies

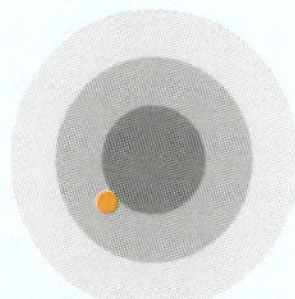

**CS B**
Museumsquartier Courtyard. Vienna, Austria

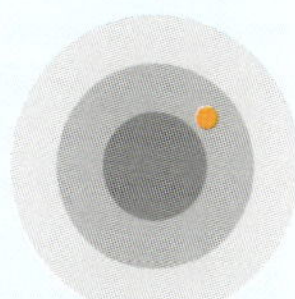

**TC #03**
Morpheus, 798 Art Zone. Beijing, China

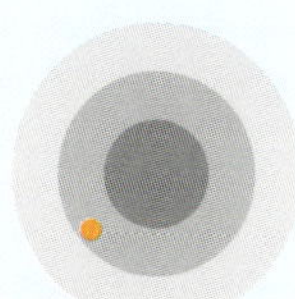

**TC #04**
Grassscapes. Antwerp, Belgium

### 1.3 Long-Term Strategies Based on Temporary Interventions

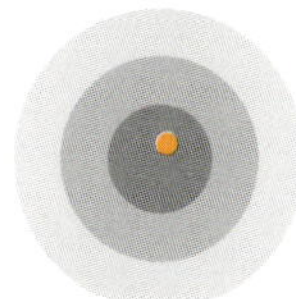

**CS C**
"This is Not a Vacant Lot". Saragossa, Spain

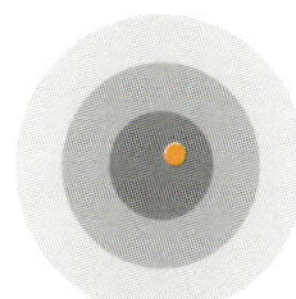

**TC #05**
Temporary Interventions in Vacant Lots. Madrid, Spain

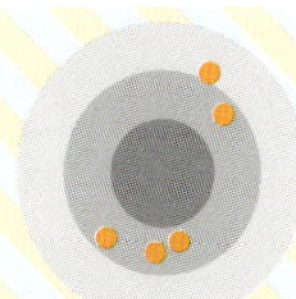

**TC #06**
Floating parks. Rotterdam, The Netherlands

## CHAPTER 2: CITIZEN PARTICIPATION

### 2.1 Co-management Strategies. Citizens as Decision Makers

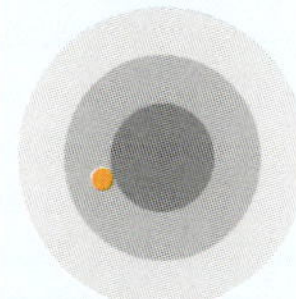

**CS D**
I Love to Play! & Painting Initiative. Tirana, Albania

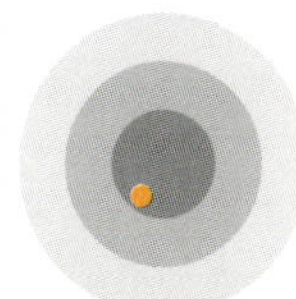

**TC #07**
Velluters Citizen Strategy in Vacant Lots. Valencia, Spain

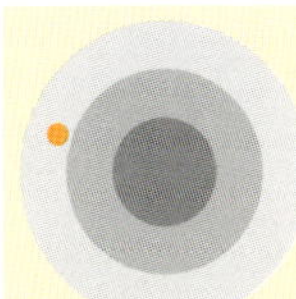

**TC #08**
Sandleiten. Vienna, Austria

### 2.2 Co-creative Strategies. Citizens as Designers

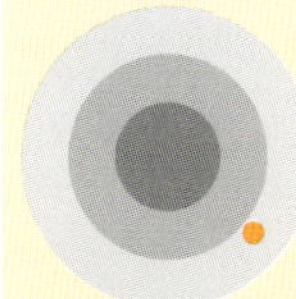

**CS E**
City Park Ørestad. Copenhagen, Denmark

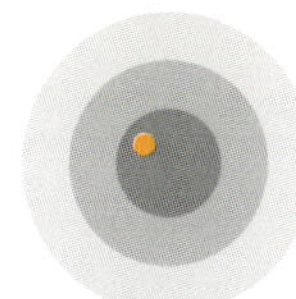

**TC #09**
Lijnbaan Urban Courtyards. Rotterdam, The Netherlands

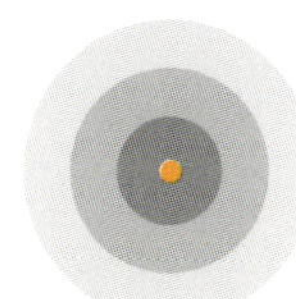

**TC #10**
Central Park. Rajka, Hungary

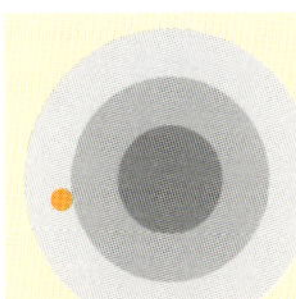

**TC #11**
Can Escandell Park. Ibiza, Spain

### 2.3 Co-production Startegies. Citizens as Builders.

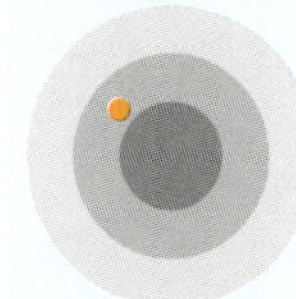

**CS F**
Urban Gardens. Rotterdam, The Netherlands

**TC #12**
Amsterdam Nieuw-West. Amsterdam, The Netherlands

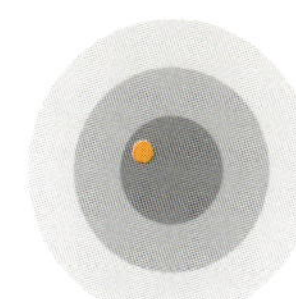

**TC #13**
Rusovce. Bratislava, Slovakia

## CHAPTER 3: RE-PLACEMAKING

### 3.1 City as a Stage

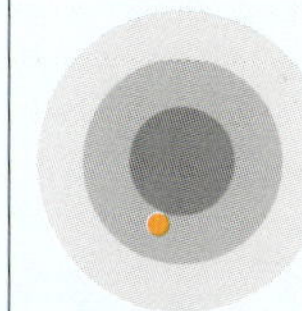

**CS G**
Harborfront. Copenhagen, Denmark

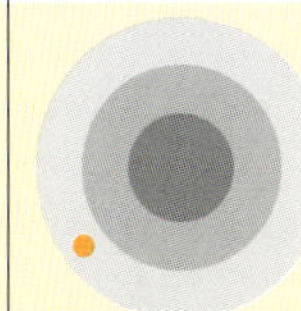

**TC #14**
Schuytgraaf. Arhnem, The Netherlands

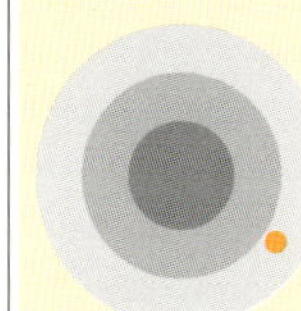

**TC #15**
Ørestad South. Copenhagen, Denmark

### 3.2 City as an Event Place

**CS H**
Beyond Leidsche Rijn. Utrecht, The Netherlands

**TC #16**
Mezaparks. Riga, Latvia

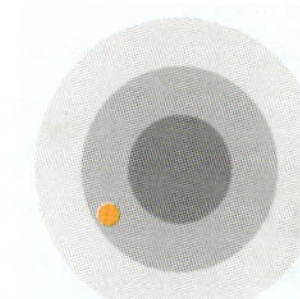

**TC #17**
Wii-Playgrounds (Van Eyck Playgrounds 2.0). Amsterdam. The Netherlands

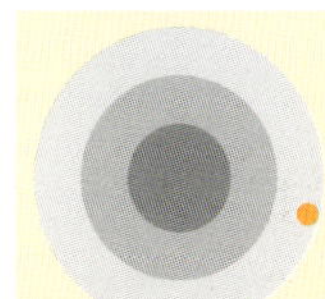

**TC #18**
Public Space for the Asian Cultural Complex (ACC). Gwanju, South Korea

### 3.3 City as an Art-Scape

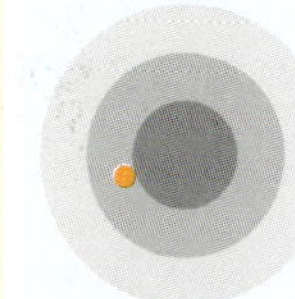

**CS I**
City Lounge. St. Gallen, Switzerland

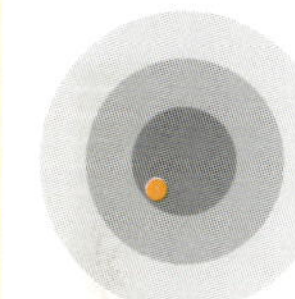

**TC #19**
Green Room. Rotterdam, The Netherlands

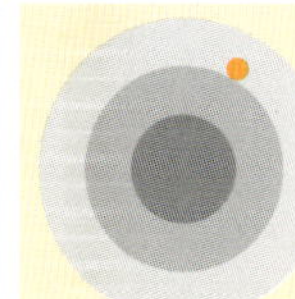

**TC #20**
Bench Islands. Groningen, The Netherlands

**TC #21**
Mosaic Park & Ceramic Museum. Jinzhou, China

## Medium Scale Concentrated

**CS B**. 95,27 Ha
Museumsquartier Courtyard.
Vienna, Austria

**TC #01**. 28,23 Ha
Temporary Intervention "Green Windows".
Lausanne, Switzerland

**TC #02**. 14,00 Ha
Temporary Intervention "Senses Cocktail".
Appeltern,
The Netherlands

**CS E**. 78,68 Ha
City Park Ørestad.
Copenhagen,
Denmark

**TC #09**. 39,33 Ha
Lijnbaan Urban Courtyards.
Rotterdam,
The Netherlands

**TC #04**. 54,40 Ha
Grassscapes.
Antwerp, Belgium

**TC #11**. 112,71 Ha
Can Escandell Park.
Ibiza, Spain

**CS F**. 26,26 Ha
Urban Gardens.
Rotterdam,
The Netherlands

**TC #10**. 19,34 Ha
Central Park.
Rajka, Hungary

**TC #18**. 106,13 Ha
Public space for the Asian Cultural Complex (ACC).
Gwanju, South Korea

**TC #20**. 12,49 Ha
Bench Islands.
Groningen,
The Netherlands

**CS I**. 21,97 Ha
City Lounge.
St. Gallen,
Switzerland

**TC #13**. 25,23 Ha
Rusovce.
Bratislava, Slovakia

**TC #19**. 17,40 Ha
Green Room.
Rotterdam,
The Netherlands

0 500 1000 2000

## Medium Scale Spread

**TC #03**. 92,10 Ha
Morpheus, 798
Art Zone.
Beijing, China

**CS C**. 147,33 Ha
"This is Not a Vacant Lot".
Saragossa, Spain

**TC #05**. 27,36 Ha
Temporary Interventions in Vacant Lots.
Madrid, Spain

**TC #08**. 15,28 Ha
Sandleiten.
Vienna, Austria

**TC #12**. 142,50 Ha
Amsterdam Nieuw-West.
Amsterdam,
The Netherlands

**TC #07**. 17,85 Ha
Velluters Citizen Strategy in Vacant Lots.
Valencia, Spain

**TC #14**. 6,97 Ha
Schuytgraaf.
Arhnem,
The Netherlands

**CS G**. 149,44 Ha
Harborfront.
Copenhagen,
Denmark

**TC #17**. 17.44 Ha
Wii-Playgrounds
(Van Eyck playgrounds 2.0).
Amsterdam. The Netherlands

**TC #15**. 53,32 Ha
Ørestad South.
Copenhagen, Denm

## Large Scale Spread

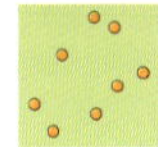

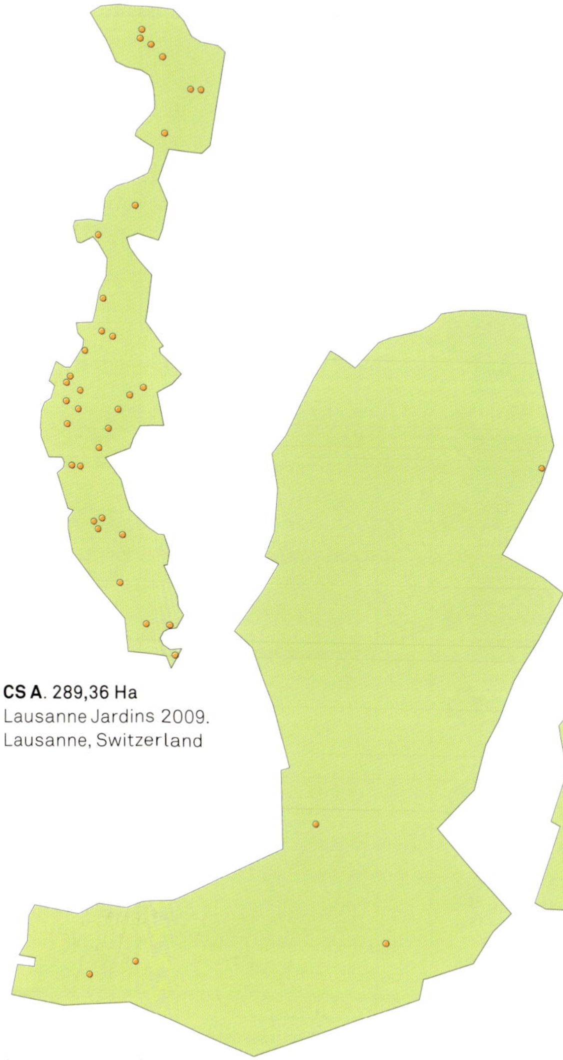

**CS A**. 289,36 Ha
Lausanne Jardins 2009.
Lausanne, Switzerland

**TC #06**. 1213,77 Ha
Floating Parks.
Rotterdam, The Netherlands

**TC #16**. 617,70 Ha
Mezaparks.
Riga, Latvia

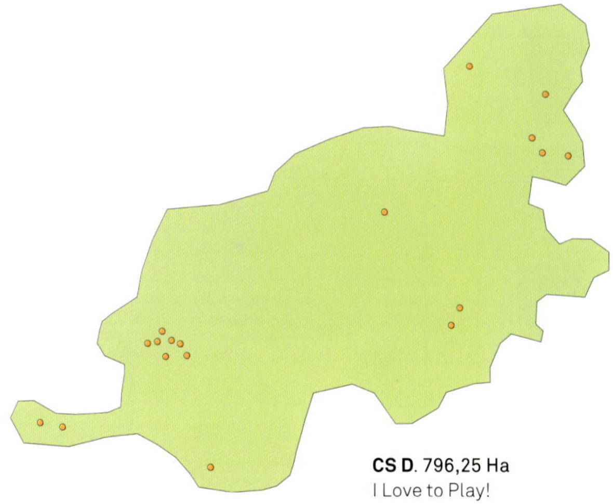

**CS D**. 796,25 Ha
I Love to Play!
& Painting Initiative.
Tirana, Albania

**CS H**. 1907,42 Ha
Beyond Leidsche Rijn.
Utrecht, The Netherlands

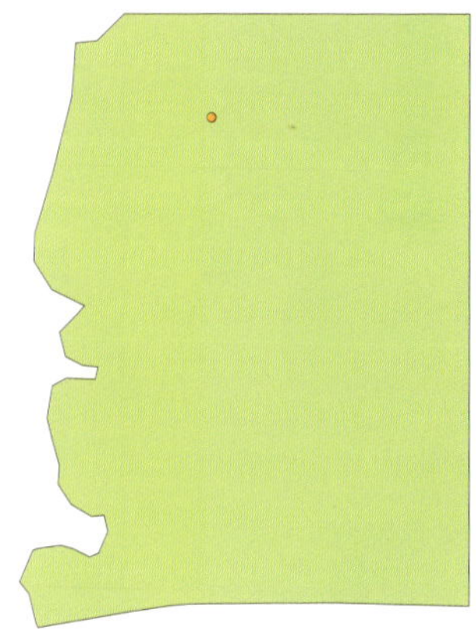

**TC #21**. 660,43 Ha
Mosaic Park & Ceramic
Museum. Jinzhou, China

the approach in the harbor area, the park in Ørestad was developed as an ensemble. However, the chosen strategy resembles that of the harbor: several unique and independent small-scale interventions combine to form a park. The problem with the execution of the chosen strategy is that the interventions are very much designed for specific activities. Each "island" creates a specific stage for a specific performance, where spectators and actors belong to the same familiar group of beach volleyball players, or parents and children that come together only for this specific activity. The islands don't interact with a larger public.

In addition, the participation of residents and office workers from the area is restricted to the design process. The chosen design strategy has the potential to include co-creation and co-maintenance, but this potential is not realized. The possibility of facilitating all kinds of initiatives involving co-creation and co-maintenance – collective gardens or other collective spaces and attributes, like a band stand, an open-air auditorium or a puppet theater, with the exception of semi-commercial amenities like a tea garden or a kiosk – is not recognized or used as a productive force. The participation of different publics could have been moved from the usual input in the design phase to co-creation toward shared responsibility in the phases of realization, use and maintenance.

The approach chosen for Vienna's MuseumsQuartier is an example of user participation. As a result of the strategy to transform the complex into an attractive place, promoting public life by combining versatile seating elements with a varied program of activities, the MQ became a hotspot in Vienna's cultural scene. It became a livelier, yet still parochial space. It is doubtful whether the visitors, both to the real site and to the internet site where they could vote on the color scheme, all belong to the cultural scene. The area is likely to attract a large number of students and young professionals who live nearby, along with other residents and tourists as well as other groups, depending on the programming. It has the potential to do so, and if that has not been the case until now, it would be interesting to pursue new experiments.

We could compare the MuseumsQuartier with other cultural buildings that have an iconic quality, which attract a large and differentiated public, for example the roof of the new Oslo Opera House or the new MAS Museum in the northern docks of Antwerp. These buildings attract a large and differentiated public without using added elements, but by building a stage in public space. The difference, and the difficulty it should be added, is of course that the MuseumsQuartier is enclosed in a series of courtyards. That is probably the reason why the baroque stage set of the existing buildings needs complementary interventions to transform it into an urban stage. The monumental stage of the 'tragedy' needs the scenery of the 'satire' to develop another more informal and spontaneous life in it.

The Vienna project has to do with revitalizing failed public space and it is unclear whether we should see it as an experimental way of creating meaning and developing the place's potential so that, in time, it will no longer need that kind of help, or whether the conclusion should be that the place will never work on its own, without this kind of intervention. If the latter is the case, the place will serve as a permanent playground for creative interventions.

### 5. Permanent Strategies based on Temporary Uses

The 'This is not a vacant lot' strategy in Zaragoza can be classified among traditional social democratic strategies aimed at emancipating low-income social groups. The natural space for such a strategy was and is the collective space of the neighborhood in contrast with the public space of the city. The character of an emancipation strategy finds notification in the employment program that was the starting point and the collaboration with schools, educational and other social programs in the neighborhoods were the project is implemented. On the other hand, there is also a divergence from the traditional emancipative project: 'This is not a vacant lot' does not create a new collective domain against the city (as the traditional emancipative strategies did in the 1930s and the 1950s). It uses the gaps in space and time within the urban fabric to create new opportunities, both for (unemployed) people and empty (in a sense, also unemployed) places. The principle is based on temporary activation of inactive parts (and people, we could add) of the city. In time, it has an effect on the economic cycle, which is currently creating more empty plots and more unemployed people.

It is interesting that this strategy of temporary uses has developed into a permanent strategy that allows for experimenting with the development of plots in such a way that it can always correct failures (which are implicit in experiments) in a very short time. Moreover, it then has the potential to generate a more generalized strategy of correcting failures, which are inherent to cities and city planning, to be integrated into the normal practice of urban planning, design and maintenance.

At first sight, the urban gardens in Rotterdam appear to be very similar to the plots in Zaragoza. However, they lack the broader emancipative ambitions of the latter. The main aim is the promotion of social cohesion between residents of different groups based on co-creating urban gardens in temporarily unused lots. Therefore, they are characterized more as collective spaces than as public spaces. In this sense, they are neighborhood gardens more than urban gardens. Nevertheless, they have the potential and the possibility for developing into temporary public spaces of a new kind. There is at least one urban garden in Rotterdam (not created by 'creatief beheer', but that is unimportant) with a band stand that is used on summer weekends for a (very) small open-air music festival. On those occasions, it acts as a kind of neighborhood lounge, which also welcomes people from outside the area. In this way, this urban garden adds the notion of hospitality to that of social cohesion and creates an overlap between different parochial realms in the city. Sometimes, it even forges a connection between the local and the global. The idea of a city lounge has come up in different cities in recent years. The case of Sankt Gallen is an excellent example, not as part of a strategy involving temporary use, but as an approach based on re-urbanism.

### 6. Re-urbanism: Top-down or Bottom-up

The projects in Tirana are associated with some strange controversies. Activating the population by first removing all kinds of small illegal built pavilions, which often fulfilled public functions as small cafés or kiosks, to create urban public space seems like a contradiction. Was it a necessary correction of the capitalist economy that boomed after the fall of Communism? Was it aimed at the creation of a civil society next to a capitalist economy? Undoubtedly, both arguments played a role, but it is a contradictory way of intervening. The same can be said of the rather top-down way the grey housing blocks were painted, but you can understand that intervention as a kind of shock therapy. Certainly, it has had an enormous and positive effect in changing the atmosphere and the general attitude toward the residential environment. It broke up the existing lethargy and the feeling of deprivation. It changed the scenery in the common every-

Published by
**Actar Publishers**
**New York, 2014**

Authors
**Jesús Hernández Mayor**
**Helena Casanova García**

Edited by
**Ricardo Devesa**

Graphic Design and Production
**Núria Saban**

Illustrations
**casanova+hernandez architects**

Translation and proofreading
**Angela Kay Bunning**

Distributed by
**Actar D**
www.actar-d.com

**New York**
355 Lexington Avenue, 8th Floor
New York, NY 10017
T +1 212 966 2207
F +1 212 966 2214
salesnewyork@actar-d.com

**Barcelona**
Roca i Batlle 2
08023 Barcelona
salesbarcelona@actar-d.com
eurosales@actar-d.com

**ISBN 978-0-9893317-0-8**
A CIP catalogue record for this book is available from the Library of Congress, Washington D.C., USA.

© of the edition, Actar Publishers, 2014
© of the texts, their authors
© of the images, their authors
© of the Case Studies and Test Cases projects, their authors

All rights reserved. No part of this publication may be reproduced, stored in a retrieval system, or transmitted in any form or by any means, electronic, mechanical, photocopying, recording, or otherwise, without prior written consent of the publishers, except in the context of reviews.

The editors have made every effort to contact and acknowledge copyright owners. If there are instances where proper credit is not given, the publisher will make necessary changes in subsequent editions.